The HISTORY of BRITISH and AMERICAN AUTHOR-PUBLISHERS

Anna Faktorovich

ANAPHORA LITERARY PRESS

BROWNSVILLE, TEXAS

Anaphora Literary Press
1898 Athens Street
Brownsville, TX 78520
https://anaphoraliterary.com

Book design by Anna Faktorovich, Ph.D.

Copyright © 2017 by Anna Faktorovich

All rights reserved. No part of this book may be reproduced in any form or by any electronic or mechanical means, including information storage and retrieval systems, without permission in writing from Anna Faktorovich. Writers are welcome to quote brief passages in their critical studies, as American copyright law dictates.

Printed in the United States of America, United Kingdom and in Australia on acid-free paper.

Edited by: Mallory Cormack.

Published in 2017 by Anaphora Literary Press

The History of British and American Author-Publishers
Anna Faktorovich—1st edition.

Library of Congress Control Number: 2017950922

Library Cataloging Information
Faktorovich, Anna, 1981-, author.
　The history of British and American author-publishers / Anna Faktorovich
　Includes bibliography and index.
　368 p. ; 9 in.
　ISBN 978-1-68114-373-6 (softcover : alk. paper)
　ISBN 978-1-68114-374-3 (hardcover : alk. paper)
　ISBN 978-1-68114-375-0 (e-book)
1. Biography & Autobiography—Editors, Journalists, Publishers.
2. Language Arts & Disciplines—Publishing.
3. Business & Economics—Entrepreneurship.
PS126-138: American Literature: Biography, memoirs, letters
973: History of United States

THE HISTORY OF BRITISH AND AMERICAN AUTHOR-PUBLISHERS

Anna Faktorovich

CONTENTS

Part I: The Publisher and the Author
Introduction — 8
Chapter 1: A Brief History of Publishing from the First Printing Through the Twenty-First Century — 21
Chapter 2: Censorship, Radicalism and the Press — 55

Part II: British Author-Publishers
Chapter 3: Scottish Insurrections: Sir Walter Scott's *Waverley* and the Ballantyne Publishing Company — 105
Chapter 4: Anti-Monarchical Sentiments and Mysterious Deaths: Lord Byron's "The Vision of Judgment" and Percy Shelley's "Lines to a Critic" in *The Liberal* — 122
Chapter 5: A Bestselling Revolution: Charles Dickens' *A Tale of Two Cities* in *All the Year Round* — 164
Chapter 6: A Woman's Burden: Virginia Woolf's Hogarth Press — 183

Part III: American Author-Publishers
Chapter 7: Brief Stories of American Publishers — 217
Chapter 8: Benjamin Franklin and the Spread of Publishing through the Colonies — 239
Chapter 9: The Anti-Plagiarism Campaign and Another Mysterious Death: Edgar Allan Poe's "Voluminous History of the Little Longfellow War" in the *Broadway Journal* — 250
Chapter 10: The Catastrophic Bankruptcy of Mark Twain's Charles L. Webster and Co. Venture — 267
Chapter 11: Herman Melville and the Unpopularity of Highbrow American Literature: The Private Printing of Three Poetry Collections — 283
Chapter 12: Henry Luce and Briton Hadden: The Development of Media Moguls and Time Inc. — 294
Chapter 13: Dudley Randall and Black Power Poetry — 302
Chapter 14: A Quest for Inter-Racial Equality: Alice Walker's Wild Trees Press — 311
Conclusions — 341
Bibliography — 356
Index — 366

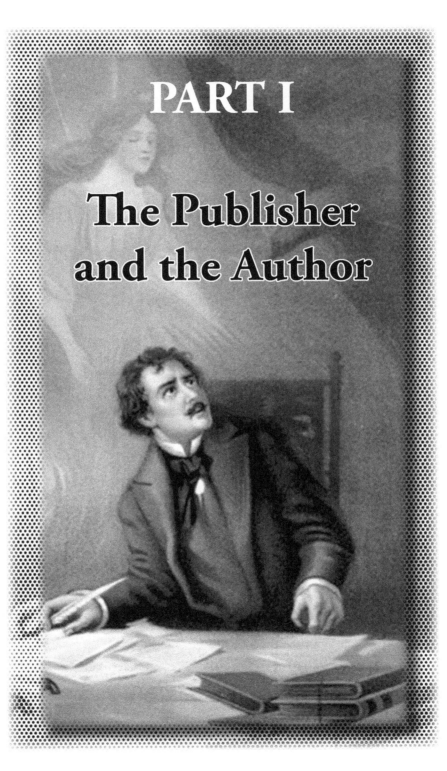

PART I

The Publisher and the Author

INTRODUCTION

The mainstream publishing industry has popularized the stereotype that "self-published" books are inferior to "traditional" ones because the author does not receive an advance and the services provided are less professional. The reality is that the Big Four publishers attained their enormous market share by at least initially relying on author subsidies. When advances were paid, they were typically loans that had to be repaid if a book failed to sell a volume of books that would cover the advance. The top classical American and British authors either founded their own publishing ventures, or occasionally subsidized their less "marketable" books. This is an extensive study into the top transatlantic author-publishers. What were the problems they faced with "traditional" publishers that made it necessary for them to start their own publishing companies and journals? Authors' greatest obstacle since the earliest books were released thousands of years ago has been censorship of radical, non-conformist, reformist, and otherwise contrary positions that stood in conflict with monarchs, presidents, corruption, and crime. Giant publishers use self-censorship to appease the demands of despots. It takes a radical self-publishing author to realize divergent ideas.

Without author-publishers: the sun would still revolve around the earth (Galileo) and book printing would lack exquisite artistic details (Rembrandt). And Americans would still be living in the colonies of the United Kingdom (Benjamin Franklin). It is harder to find an innovative scientist, politician or creative writer who did not self-publish than those who did.

Several initial research questions guided the study. What are the problems author-publishers encountered with "traditional" publishers that made it necessary for them to start their own presses or journals? Why haven't the publishing houses and journals founded by the world's best authors grown into the Big Four publishers, but rather were consumed by them? What stood in the way of these small publishing ventures' success and why did so many of them end in bankruptcy or a sale to a bigger competitor? Why did most successful author-publishers have to create their own companies to publish their radical work? How profitable has the publishing business been for independents over the centuries and is it becoming more or less so? Who funds the giant publishing companies? What is the relationship between their owners and governmental rulers and Big Business executives? How common is it for an author-publisher to be prosecuted and imprisoned for libel, blasphemy, sedition, treason and the other alleged offenses? Are censorship and treason laws designed to prevent independent attacks on the status quo? This study will address all of these concerns.

The Inquisition banned the *Dialogue of Galileo Galilei on the Great World Systems* because the idea that the earth revolved around the sun was contrary to the Bible. Meanwhile, the availability of bibles through the printing press made it possible for scholars like Galileo to quote scripture effectively during blasphemy trials. The printing press has been a tool for knowledge dissemination and empowerment of the masses. The few who govern these masses are more likely to win arguments and maintain power if their opponents cannot present this valuable knowledge. Since the introduction of the printing press could not be reversed, monarchs, emperors, businessmen, and presidents have been suppressing the radical media with censorship. "Chapter 3: Censorship, Radicalism and the Press" covers the history of the contentious relationship between the majority's need to express itself independently in the press and the leading minority's attempts to control this freedom through censorship laws.

Only by creating an independent journal, *All the Year Round,* was Charles Dickens able to publish a novel about the French Revolution, *A Tale of Two Cities,* a few years after the 1848 European Revolutions. The other publishers Dickens submitted this revolutionary work to self-censored or rejected it as too seditious. Meanwhile, Sir Walter Scott could only publish a series of novels about the Jacobite rebellions (a part of his Scottish nationalism campaign), *Waverley*, by anonymously founding the Ballantyne publishing business in Edinburgh. Lord Byron's "blasphemous" satire, "The Vision of Judgment," and Percy Shelley's objection to unfair reviewers, "Lines to a Critic," could only be published in their own journal, *The Liberal*. Most of Virginia Woolf's feminist and anti-formulaic novels, including *Monday or Tuesday*, would not have been published in the "mainstream" if her husband, Leonard, and she did not create Hogarth Press. Edgar Allan Poe's campaign was against plagiarism among popular authors and undue puffing in corrupted review publications. Poe's anti-publishing establishment views could only able expressed when he had temporary ownership of *Broadway Journal*, in articles such as, "Voluminous History of the Little Longfellow War." Herman Melville spent the modern equivalent of $29,571 to subsidize the printing of 350 copies of *Clarel*, his late epic poem about the Holy Land, with Harper because an inheritance allowed him to strive to create art instead of running after pop success as he did with his earlier releases. Even more outrageously, Mark Twain paid $1.3 million to J. R. Osgood, when adjusted for inflation, to subsidize the publication of *Old Times on the Mississippi*, before founding his own publishing company, Charles L. Webster and Co. Henry Luce and Briton Hadden spent a few disgruntled years as reporters before finding the funding to start the *Time* magazine, and later its offshoots under the Time Inc. umbrella. Dudley Randall used his savings from a college librarian career to found Broadside Press in part to release his own poetry collections like *Cities Burning*, and to propagate for the Black Power Movement through releasing works by other underrepresented black writers. Alice Walker imitated the Woolfs' example when she and her partner founded Wild Trees Press to publish works about the struggles of black people around the world, such as a book for which Walker wrote an introduction, *The Spirit Journey*. Few modern readers of the *Tale of Two Cities* realize that it was self-published. Changing readers' awareness of the role self-publishing played in the history of knowledge is critical to allow modern self-publishers to be heard.

These radical publishers lived dramatic, revolutionary lives that predominantly ended in violent deaths at sea, from poison, from malpractice, or from more blatant assassinations. Some of these deaths have been ruled as suspicious by biographers, while others have been dismissed as accidental or "natural." Since all of the reviewed author-publishers delivered a radical, anti-establishment message, it is only logical that the establishment has done its best to suppress them and their messages. In some cases, libel or treason prosecutions stopped the presses, but in others there was nothing illegal in the truthful and democratic messages, so no open retaliation was possible. The suspicious nature of these radicals' deaths is obvious because of their intersecting similarities. The subversive executioners of these radical authors have frequently been greedy physicians. Elite medicine as a whole in the eighteenth and nineteenth centuries was torturous. Sir Walter Scott died an excruciating death from bleedings, blisterings, drugging and other torments. The treatments either created the symptoms or worsened them. These symptoms included epileptic seizures or strokes, and partial paralysis. These same symptoms have been proven in Charles II's case to have resulted from inhaling high amounts of mercury, which causes internal bleeding in the brain. Seizures, confusion, fevers and other symptoms that reoccur frequently in the deaths of author-publishers in this study are closely associated with the four poisons most commonly used by physicians: mercury, arsenic, antimony and lead. The details of many of these deaths clearly indicates malpractice. A harder causality to prove is if the malpractice was motivated by the physicians' greed or if a specific monarch and his spies ordered an assassination because a legal censorship battle in the courts had been unsuccessful. For example, all biographies of Lord Byron's death describe similar symptoms and "treatments" to Scott's and repeat that there were "spies" in Byron's household as he was actively funding and leading a Greek revolution in his final months. Benjamin Franklin also actively assisted a revolution after running a successful publishing business, but either because his revolution succeeded or because an ocean separated him from his monarch, he lived to achieve great things in his later years. Not all of these author-publishers died horrifying deaths, but even one unproven assassination is worthy of examination.

Imagine a world without books. There would be no education. There would be no films without a coherent script. Humans would still be living in makeshift shelters, in caves, or in prehistoric huts without construction manuals to pass down knowledge in this trade. Perhaps humans would be scribbling characters or drawings on the walls of caves or on tree bark. But if these could not be carried away, a language that is understood by those outside of a local community could not develop. When a fish evolved into the first mammal this took hundreds of thousands, if not millions, of years, while people developed airplanes in a few generations simply by recording findings for future generations' development. There might have been a monkey out there that put a seed in the ground and watched a tree grow, but until that monkey passes this knowledge to the next generation in print, the monkey-kind will not make agriculture a part of their society. Therefore, having four publishing executives in charge of the majority of human communications is akin to allowing four emperors to rule the world and dictate which innovations are allowed and which are censored out of human knowledge. The freedom to publish both great scientific and literary innovations is more important than the freedom to vote. The number of independent publishers in a society reflects on its ability to evolve and grow, both fiscally and culturally.

The misconception that self-publishing is something only the worst writers do is contradicted by the experience of some of the best writers in western literature, who were all desperate enough to see their great works in print to start their own publishing ventures. Their lives offer lessons about publishing that are essential for growing publishers, authors, librarian, and researchers that want to understand the essence of how recorded ideas can die or bloom depending on the power of the author-publishers that yield them.

There have been few books written about the publishing industry. This is odd because the publishing industry makes books, so it is unusual that it has failed to reflect about itself. There have been some studies such as *British Book Publishing as a Business since 1960s*, but it is a selection of disjointed essays that fail to touch on the central problems in the publishing industry. The section on "Mergers and Acquisitions" gallops through a list of various mergers without explaining why these happened or what they meant for the industry. There are chapters designated to Penguin, Chatto, Collins and other giant publishers, but they summarize profits, types of titles released, shares' price changes, and major censorship or other legal controversies. Better books, such as *Early American Women Printers and Publishers, 1639-1820*, go through major rises and falls of numerous small publishers, but only lightly compare them or explain their experiences. There are even some fictionalized histories of publishers' experiences, such as, *With the Stroke of a Pen: A Story of Ambition, Greed, Infidelity, and the Murder of French Publisher Robert Denoel*, wherein the author, A. Louise Staman, explains in the introduction that evidence is missing on who killed Denoel (the subject of the book), so he has engineered a fictional plotline that fits with known facts and expands them into a mystery novel. I have frequently been tempted to speculate and reach conclusions about whodunit in this study, as reading publishing biographies is usually an exercise in speculation because the tragic ends are seldom explained in police reports. Another publishing study, John Maxwell Hamilton's *Casanova Was a Book Lover*, attempts to summarize the world's publishing history in non-chronological sub-sections that cover topics like: "Writing on the Bosses' Time," "The New Model

Is Marketing," "Books, giving as gifts," and "Lesson Number Three: Writing a book is like painting a large target on your chest to help your opponent sight in better." The latter section explains how people who publish great books and articles are never elected in the United States because they make enemies, and because they can be incriminating themselves when they put questionable actions in print; the conclusion in this section is that we live in a time like the Spanish Inquisition, during which a Jesuit priest commented that "one should think carefully before writing books."[1] We live in the Inquisition? If this is the case, this book runs over the details too rapidly. Hamilton claims that we live in a completely censored and retarded culture that prevents intellectuals from fixing problems. Surely, this is not a book that can explain the publishing industry's problems with detached logic and clarity. I reviewed many books on censorship, modern indie and self-publishing design and marketing, publishing histories of other countries, histories of individual publishers, propaganda, trial records, periodicals' archival materials, assassination true crime studies, and corporatocracy critiques. Amidst all this information, I discovered many relevant details, but no study that explains the reality of how and why the publishing industry has changed since the first printing press through the critical present moment, and the problems authors have had in this hostile and yet enriching environment. This is the niche this study attempts to fill as much as any single book can.

Each of the central authors in this study has been covered by a major biography, if not numerous biographies and some autobiographies too. Many of these biographies have tragic titles, such as Peter Ackroyd's *Poe: A Life Cut Short*. The tragic ends of most of these writers are idealized into romances or mysteries, with shady speculations about who might have done them in, or why they might have done it themselves. However, there are few comparative biographies that show the parallels between these lives, as this book attempts to do. Poe's end is very similar to Byron's end, so that the biographies almost read like formulaic novels, with repeating plot movements. The brief biographies here focus on segments related to self-publication. With their struggles with spouses and house decorations swept away, readers can better understand their writing and publishing.

---

1   John Maxwell Hamilton. *Casanova Was a Book Lover: And Other Naked Truths and Provocative Curiosities about the Writing, Selling, and Reading of Books.* (Baton Rouge: Louisiana State University Press, 2000), 215-8.

This study does not attempt to cover every author-publisher from the beginning of time because there have been hundreds of thousands of self-published releases just in the last few years. The focal author-publishers changed the publishing industry, created new genres, or have been canonized by the establishment.

I have been making a living from a cooperative publishing company, Anaphora Literary Press, for the last nine years, so my perspective on publishing is colored by my own daily struggles. It is easier to set type in Adobe InDesign on a computer screen today than it was for Woolf or Franklin to set each individual letter and then hand press the words onto the pages. With print-on-demand, there is no need to print thousands of copies and store them in your basement as Randall had to do half a century ago. Occasionally, authors ask me if I could print their book "traditionally," and I have to explain that the old way of printing and distributing books should be left in the past. Small, independent publishers cannot survive 50% or more in returns that "traditional" bookstores generate when they purchase more books than they could ever sell. This is not the bookstores' fault, as they are also struggling in the modern book marketplace. Buyers only had local bookstores to supply their reading needs just a couple decades ago, and now an infinite variety of books can be shipped from online stores. Leonard and Virginia Woolf had to sell their innovative titles to individual small bookstores, and they barely stayed afloat if the books were returned, but because there were few books competing in this market they remained profitable for decades. The expansion of the giant publishers has pushed such small ventures out of the equation. Bookstore buyers no longer have a personal connection with authors that would prohibit them from purchasing new books before old titles have sold. Thus, bookstores exploit returnable titles causing many small publishers to fail, or opt out of returnability thus mostly foregoing the physical bookstore marketplace. Meanwhile, as these publishers sink, they imagine that they failed to spend adequately on advertisements, catalog mailings or book editing. Given this climate, I had to invent a publishing model that would guarantee a profit from each released book, thus eliminating the risk of catastrophic failure. One of the reasons so many of the examined author-publishers eventually suffered bankruptcies or sold their companies is because they took on debt and risk in quixotic attempts to donate cheap books and give huge advances to writers. These efforts are admirable, but a closure creates many negative side-effects for investors, authors, bookstores, bankers, and others in this chain. Instead, the subsidized origins of the Big Four provided inspiration for my own publishing model. I ask authors to purchase 50 copies of their book at 25% off the cover price. Ideally, writers will be able to resell them to students or at readings at the full price for a profit. I have been working to increase sales of each title by mailing catalogs to libraries, improving metadata by including html tagging, sending emails with review copies to 10,000 librarians, reviewers and professors, and numerous other innovative approaches. This model helped me to expand by allowing me to take four years off from teaching college. This year, I taught full-time once again, while also running Anaphora, and the resulting profits might provide for sustained fiscal independence in the coming years. Recently, I have been working on applying to become a GSA contractor to provide publishing services to government agencies. Some giant publishers make a significant portion of their profits via such generous offers. I have also considered applying for the non-profit status. But, both government contracts and grants would be uncertain and fickle. Cooperative publishing funds from authors guarantee a steady stream of income.

Self-employment has allowed me to write over a dozen books, and a significant portion of the content for two of Anaphora's triannual periodicals, *Pennsylvania Literary Journal* and *Cinematic Codes Review*. This explains why Charles Dickens, Mark Twain and the other writers were particularly authorially productive when they were running publishing companies. Combining authorship with the publishing trade is the only way for a writer to become self-sufficient in terms of not being censored by other publishers, or relying on them or other forms of employment for sustenance. This study has helped me to understand this path, and hopefully it will similarly help the writers I publish.

This book is separated into three parts. The first part reviews the history of publishing and printing, with sections on censorship, radicalism, the Big Four, unapproachable reviewers, and subversive assassinations. The second part focuses on British author-publishers, with chapters on Sir Walter Scott, Lord Byron, Percy Shelley, Charles Dickens, and Virginia Woolf. The third part, on Americans, has a longer introduction that looks at several small American author-publishers, from the first in the colonies to some recent innovators. Then, individual chapters look at the major author-publishers: Benjamin Franklin, Edgar Allan Poe, Mark Twain, Herman Melville, Henry Luce, Briton

Hadden, Dudley Randall, and Alice Walker. The Conclusion explains the patterns that emerged in the previous chapters.

A few key terms need to be defined before jumping into this study. I have frequently been asked by confused writers querying Anaphora, what separates "self-publishing" from "traditional" publishing. Most dictionaries, encyclopedias, interviews with major publishers, and books use definitions that confuse rather than answer this simple question. The words combined to create **self-publisher** are "self" and "publisher." A **publisher** is a person, two or more partners, or a corporation that offers a set of publishing services that are necessary to publish a book, including some or all of the following: formatting, design, editing, proofreading, art (illustrations, photos, graphs) creation, editing, marketing, publicity, registration with book tracking agencies, setup of the title with a printer, order processing, royalty distribution, and various other tasks. If a service provider offers marketing, but none of the other services, hence being unable to independently release a book into the marketplace, it is not a publisher. Now for the word "self," which seems to be self-explanatory, but this is the word that leads to misperception. Obviously, the "self" in question is the author that wants to release a book. But, the myriad of publishing service combinations offered today complicate what constitutes being published by somebody else or publishing yourself.

One major service that even giant publishers hire out is book printing. A book printing machine costs millions today. Thus, all publishing service providers except for those that can keep this printer running around the clock cannot afford to print in-house. Using giant, industrial, automated printers subtracts the human labor that Virginia Woolf or Galileo had to put in when they used relatively cheap hand presses in their living rooms or studios to print their own books. A **press** or **printer** is a company that has a printer that can print books. Frequently, printers also package and ship these books to wholesalers, distributors, bookstores, libraries, or other buyers upon the publisher's request. If a printer not only processes orders, but also sends information about available books in print to buyers, it is also a **distributor**. But, to return to the "self." If CreateSpace offers book cover templates and allows for the upload of simple pdf interior files that can be generated on a home computer; then, it is allowing most writers, without special formatting or design skills, to create electronic book files needed to print and release them into distribution. According to conventional definitions, when somebody releases a book with CreateSpace, he or she is self-publishing because they design their own book and CreateSpace simply prints and distributes it. In contrast, when authors in the nineteenth century used to have their books **privately printed**, they would pay a printer to typeset and design the book, and possibly also edit it and perform other services for additional fees. Today, private printing is typically called subsidy publishing, but this is a misnomer. A **subsidy** is a grant, typically offered by the government or by an academic institution to sponsor a scholarly book, or a book that results from a creative fellowship. If a writer pays a company out-of-pocket for services and book printing, he or she is not offering a grant. Further still, it cannot be called "private printing," if the paid-for book is distributed through the regular mainstream distributors by the company being paid, as "**private**" implies that the book is for private consumption to the author's family and friends. In earlier centuries, the distinction of "private" printing was essential because it allowed a writer to avoid being **censored** by the Inquisition or a censorship board if the book was not intended for public consumption. As this study explains, most of the publishers that eventually became the Big Four at some point charged authors for returned books, for review copies mailings and offered paid-for private printing services. A publisher does not stop being a publisher simply because a company is charging authors for its services instead of offering an "advance." The Big Four popularized the notion that censored books, or those that pass their review process, must be better than books published by authors that choose to avoid censorship by publishing them with publishers that are open to all who can pay the applicable fees or who can setup their own books for free. Historically, the opposite has been the case. "Successful" publishers are typically defined as those that are the most profitable. To maintain their profitability, they create formulas based on the majority of the public's taste. These tastes have been steadily declining from the nineteenth century through to the present. So that today, most readers prefer to read at the first through fifth grade level, and this is the range used in most popular mystery and romance novels. Therefore, the best or the most linguistically and structurally complex books submitted to the Big Four must be rejected to attain the profit objective. The best, or the most linguistically and structurally complex and innovative books can only be printed independently by the authors themselves, or by independent publishers who are investing in art, the intellect, or a less risky profit scheme. Of course, the worst books, or those below a first-grade level, are also rejected by the Big Four; and there are many more of these awful books than there are brilliant rejected books that are too complex for the **"average" reader**. In the nineteenth century, the lower end of this range would not have had the money to privately print their book, so only the very intelligent or very wealthy writers released books through private or paid-for printing or publishing. CreateSpace has dropped the minimum required salary out of this equation by offering free setup and distribution for anybody that can afford a personal computer. On the other hand, the writers who are paying publishers for design, marketing and other publishing services still mostly belong to this upper class of writers for whom the expense is irrelevant and they are writing for other reasons than the profit motive. The Big Four are aware of this and have their own paid-for service imprints. Obviously, authors, including myself, who cannot afford to pay a publisher and who hope to make a living from writing highbrow books, are rightfully frustrated with this writing marketplace. If we release a book with CreateSpace or another free service, it is automatically disqualified from tenure calculation formulas, from major awards, and major reviewers. CreateSpace occasionally prints their books with Ingram, a top printer of books for academic and small press market, and other international printers, so its printing cannot be discounted as inferior to what "major" publishers offer. While the author enters information into CreateSpace's templates themselves, he or she would provide this information to one of the Big Four prior to publication as well. All authors also do basic formatting and typesetting for their books today in Word or other word processing programs that would have been the most time-consuming part of publishing a book before computers. In this sense, all authors, unless somebody else transcribes the book for them, publish themselves today. The boundaries between printer, distributor, publisher, and author are blurred, and legal definitions are needed to separate these roles, rather than theoretical ones. If an author performs any of the services that constitutes a publisher, including marketing or publicizing themselves, he or she is **self-publishing**. In fact, it would be very strange for anybody in the nineteenth century to hear this term as they would think it was a grammatical error. Consider these two sentences: "I published the book." "I self-published the book." The second sentence is technically a "fragment" according to Word, and it repeats a variation of the pronoun "I" twice. In other words, it is saying, "I, yes, truly myself, published the book." Thus, the correct term to describe free setup, distribution and printing of books is… **publishing**, without private or "self" added to it, as these books are publicly released, and an outside company other than yourself helps to print and distribute it. If a writer pays for publishing services, or profits from an advance is not a matter for reviewers to contemplate because the exchange of funds between an author and the publisher is a private transaction between two consenting contractual parties, and should not be the major factor in disqualifying a book from review and therefore access to readers.

***

…[I]t comes over me in a kind of rage every now and then, like * * * *, and then, if I don't write to empty my mind, I go mad. As to that regular, uninterrupted love of writing, which you describe in your friend, I do not understand it. I feel it as a torture, which I must get rid of, but never as a pleasure. On the contrary, I think composition a great pain.
—January 2, 1821, Byron to Moore[1]

…[Y]ou can only produce to order works which are no better than works of mere craftsmanship because of their lack of essential conditions of art… a true work of art is the revelation (by laws beyond our grasp) of a new conception of life arising in the artist's soul, which, when expressed, lights up the path along which humanity progresses.
—Leo Tolstoy, "On Art"[2]

If we project Leo Tolstoy conclusions onto the publishing industry, we can extrapolate that solicited submissions by major publishers from popular authors must be works of "mere craftsmanship" because they lack the three essential elements of art, "importance," "beauty," and "sincerity."[3] The "traditional" model forces writers to find publishers that will sign multi-book contracts with them or will commission future books based on the sales success of previous titles. Thus, authors are always forced into reproducing formulas from their own and other writers "successful" publications, which leave the modern publishing

---

1   Lord George Gordon Byron. *Byron's Letters and Journals, Volume I-XII.* Leslie A. Marchand, Ed. (Cambridge: Harvard University Press & Belknap Press, 1973-1982), January 2, 1821, Byron to Moore, Vol. VIII, 55.
2   Charles Neider, Ed. *Essays of the Masters.* (New York: First Cooper Square Press, 2000), Leo Tolstoi, "On Art," 1895-7; 379.
3   Ibid., 377.

climate under a pile of crafted reproductions that fail to progress neither the writing art nor humanity. In contrast, canonical writers that started their own publishing businesses have been able to write art that elevated the form and humanity because they wrote what their "soul" or their mind conceived and not what a corporation ordered to fit its business interests. A writer needs money to win the liberty to write from the soul rather than for the wallet, and this liberty comes with the added bonus of literary associations when the writer makes a living from publishing not only themselves but also other writers.

CHAPTER 1

A Brief History of Publishing from the First Printing Through the Twenty-First Century

The volume of books published in the last decade rivals all of the books published from the dawn of written history up until this point. Two centuries ago, the titles of all books that have ever been printed could have been squeezed into a single library volume. A modern reader is exposed to an avalanche of free books during primary and secondary education and at their local library. The classics can even be found in free online databases such as Gutenberg. Thus, before starting a discussion about author-publishers, it is important to step back and consider the alternatives. What shaped the publishing industry over the centuries? Publishing is unlike the clothing industry or the food industry because the written word has been utilized to free and enslave, to govern and to rebel. Dissemination of both radical and conformist propagandist pamphlets, leaflets, and books has shaped all other parts of human life, from laws to culture. Studying politics or literature without examining who published the works that motivated or described the changes that solidified history is akin to ignoring the "magician" behind the curtain in the *Wizard of Oz*.

The modern publishing industry is an extreme abnormality amidst the prior millenniums when words were scribbled on caves or parchment. Gradually words started to be imprinted onto paper in stages of technical, artistic, financial and editorial development. The first bible printed on a press gained a monopoly over the market because there were few presses available to rival the innovator who cornered that market. But, as soon as the hand press became available to middle and upper-class intellectuals around the world in the seventeenth century, only censorship prevented thinkers from distributing their self-printed ideas to the wider market, thus sparking the rapid technological and intellectual advances that brought about the Industrial Revolution, the Renaissance, and all the other progressions that humankind had not seen in the previous thousands of years of its animalistic existence. If these early, radical intellectuals had been convinced that self-publishing was inferior and they had to seek publication with the official branches of the Church and State, the greatest thinkers, from Galileo to Franklin, would have instead recycled Church doctrine and sang hymns to their monarch. Thus, the current dominance over the vast majority of the world's publishing market by four or five corporations that control the reviewers, the publicizing media outlets, and all other components that bring books to the attention of readers creates a world where Galileos and Franklins are forced to write pop fiction, or suffer being silenced in this overwhelming war against small, independent, intellectual and radical self-publishing voices.

The popularity of the Christian and Jewish bibles was in part due to the ability of their authors to reproduce and distribute them to the leaders of the movement two millennia ago. Woodblock printing began in 200, movable type in 1040, Johannes Gutenberg invented the printing press in 1440, and etching printing on paper began in 1515. The Renaissance owed its peak to the easy availability of information to the middle class through printed materials.

In the Renaissance, many artists printed their own etchings to supplement income from their major painting commissions. One example of an early artist-publisher is Rembrandt Harmenszoon van Rijn, a Dutch painter who upon his death was primarily known for the skill of his etchings or prints that circulated more widely in that era than his, now multi-million-dollar, paintings. He bought his own printing-press and operated it from his house between 1626 and 1660, when he was forced to sell it, together with his luxurious house and artistic possessions, to pay off the enormous debt he incurred up to that point. In the interim he etched and printed classics such as *Hundred Guilder Print*, which was still being re-printed over a century later. His competitors were so happy to see his printing studio closed that the Amsterdam painters' guild declared that no one that has filed for bankruptcy could trade as a painter, forbidding him from selling prints without repaying his debts first, but since his art was his only source of income, it was hardly intended to assist the repayment, but rather to keep him from returning to work. Art dealers had to set up a business through which they hired Rembrandt as an employee, and via this arrangement he was hired to create a painting for Amsterdam's City Hall. He created, *The*

Conspiracy of Claudius Civilis, a work about the Batavian rebellion of 69AD, wherein Claudius Civilis is pictured with a raised sword, organizing the rising. Upon seeing this enormous work, the government rejected it, and did not pay Rembrandt his promised commission. While critics have speculated that the work might have been inferior, it is obvious that Rembrandt created a subversive artistic statement to express comradery with rebellious martyrs of old because of the circumstances under which he was kept from operating his printing and painting business, and the authorities responded by hitting his rebellious spirit once again in the wallet. At the beginning of his career, Rembrandt added a printing press to his independent studio a year after he founded it with Jan Lievens. This was after Rembrandt spent years as an apprentice to painters, developing his skills. When his printing studio closed, so did most of his means of advertising his abilities and finding new clients in the final years of his life, at the end of which he died as a pauper. Rembrandt's biography is a lesson in the importance of ownership of self-publication technology without outstanding debt. Owning the means of production in the form of a printing press or a publishing house of one's own has been one of the only means for a radical, self-reliant artist or writer to make a name and an income for themselves from the first days of the printing press to the present.

This study focuses on the publishing industries of the United Kingdom and the United States because a great deal is known about the individual publishers from these centers and many of the innovations they derived were mimicked by printers and publishers in other countries. In addition, because the United States began as colonies of the United Kingdom, many of the first colonial printers were British in origin, and so these countries are easily tied together by their transatlantic interrelations. In contrast, some other early printing cultures around the world had very different publishing developments with few parallels with Western publishing history.

China was among the earliest reading and book buying cultures in the world. As early as 206 BCE, Chinese scholars were studying books and cataloging books in print. "By the Song period (960-1279) at the latest, literacy and education, measured by a civil service examination system, were the gateways to social status, wealth, and political authority."[4] One of the central differences between European and Chi-

---

4   Cynthia J. Brokaw and Kai-wing Chow, eds. *Printing and Book Culture in Late Imperial China*. (Berkley: University of California Press, 2005), 3.

nese printing developments was technological. "Before the twentieth century, Chinese printing was dominated by xylography, printing by making impressions on paper from a carved wooden block."[5] In contrast, Western early etchings were made on metal, and on the printing press in the interim leading up to the twentieth century. Xylography needed less complex machinery and a publisher could easily set up shop anywhere as long as he had access to hardwood, paper, and printer's ink; thus, most European and American ventures were concentrated in the main cities, but Chinese printers popped up wherever there was a patron, religious order or another party interested in printing texts.[6] China saw peaks of censorship under the Kangxi (1661-1722), Youngzheng (1723-35), and Qianlong emperors. Because Chinese printers used xylography, and the Chinese landmass was enormous, with printers interspersed through the typography, there was little pre-publication censorship, unlike in Europe. Instead, works were banned after publication if they were discovered to be problematic for government officials. Censored texts included "unauthorized calendars and almanacs, prognostication texts, subversive or secret government documents, and 'licentious'" and "immoral popular novels."[7] Geography kept China from taking advantage of the European printing press up through the twentieth century, and the lack of an easy flow of textual information between China and Europe made its printing culture vastly different. Advances, royalties, pre-publication censorship laws, as well as the religious and moral rules that governed publishing in the United States and the United Kingdom were nearly identical up through the end of the States' colonization. Meanwhile, the study of publishing in countries like China introduce an entirely new vocabulary to describe the relationship between authors, publishers and readers. This divergence is the reason for the transatlantic focus herein, rather than attempting to describe the international publishing history.

Another example of the range of cultural variations in international publishing is Japan. While woodblock prints were also the primary printing method in Japan, the art of printing was more fine-tuned and limited to a few major publishers, such as Tsutaya Juzaburo and Nishimuraya Yohachi, who owned the "woodblocks and copyrights" that "controlled the production as well as the sales of many thousands

---

5   Ibid., 8.
6   Ibid., 10.
7   Ibid., 18-9.

of prints." In contrast with China, there were also guilds or *nakama* in Japan starting in the eighteenth century that protected against copyrights infringement, and some publishers served as self-censors (though this attempt failed). There was also a central Nihonbashi district, which was similar to London, where many publishers were based. In Japan, wild cherry wood was popular for printing blocks, combined with mulberry bark paper. Prints first started to become popularly distributed in Japan in the seventeenth century, and from this point through the early twentieth century, Japanese prints had a very identifiable style, just like the formulaic style of modern Japanese anime art that carries some of the contrasting bold and delicate lines that it inherited from its print predecessors.[8] One of Japan's earliest popular print publishers was Urokogataya Magobei, which operated between 1687 and 1811, and was "the most active publisher of actor prints in the first half of the eighteenth century." Urokogataya started by primarily publishing books and maps, before gradually focusing on the more profitable portraits of actors, and beatific, wealthy patrons.[9] As the Chinese, the Japanese people frequently viewed prints as beautiful decorations that added respectability via the smell of books to a home, rather than utilizing them purely for practical, educational purposes. Thus, China and Japan cannot even be grouped together in a study of publishing in Asia, as the ocean between their cultures sprung vast differences even well into the nineteenth century that did not exist between the geographically more distant United States and British Isles.

The Big Five Corporatocracy

Calling the Big Five (or Four, depending on size requirements) "publishers" is a misnomer because in 2011 they really controlled 90% of all media Americans see, and this percentage is only climbing. Hachette Livre, News Corporation, Holtzbrinck, Bertelsmann, and National Amusements control not only the bulk of bestselling books, but also most blockbuster film releases, news networks like CNN, and the most recognizable and "respectable" newspapers, such as the *Wall Street Journal*. This means that there are only five CEOs in charge of monitoring the media, and even if they consume dozens of energy drinks daily, it is

---

8   Andreas Marks. *Japanese Woodblock Prints: Artists, Publishers and Masterworks, 1680-1900*. (Tokyo: Tuttle Publishing, 2010), 180-1.
9   Ibid., 182.

unlikely that they can screen out content based on quality. Perhaps this lack of direct oversight has brought about the abysmall, illiterate state of the things Americans are offered to read, view, and listen to.

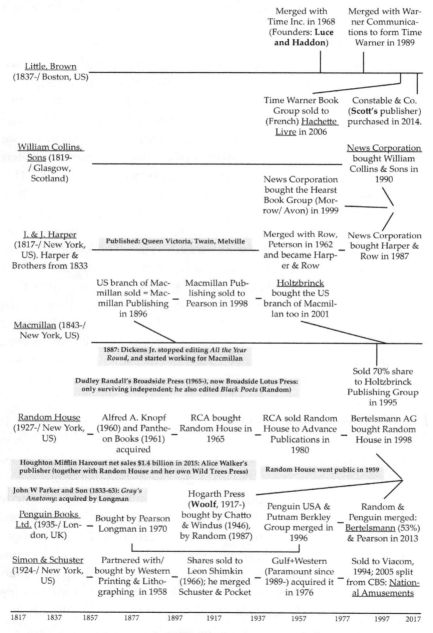

Fig. 1. Diagram of the History of the Formation of the Big Five

Control over book publishing by these five multi-media corporations has intensified the problems that have plagued publishing from the outset. Among the independent author-publishers reviewed in this study, the only publishing house that still exists and has not been bought by one of the Big Five is the late Dudley Randall's Broadside Press, now called, Broadside Lotus Press. It has been kept afloat by wealthy African Americans who felt that it was the only means of publication for radical black voices, and by charitable organizations in its Detroit community (a city that filed for Chapter 9 bankruptcy in 2013 and many call a ghost town because of massive out-migration). Sir Walter Scott's press went bankrupt during his lifetime, and his affiliate press, Constable, was recently purchased by Hachette Livre. Lord Byron and Percy Shelley's journal went under shortly after Shelley's mysterious death. Charles Dickens transferred ownership of his journal, *All the Year Round*, to his son, Charley Dickens Jr., and he kept it going until he found employment with Macmillan in 1887. Virginia Woolf committed suicide in part because she was forced to sell her share of Hogarth Press to keep it afloat. Despite this sacrifice, shortly after her death, her husband, Leonard, sold the press to a large company, which was itself later sold, and is now a fragment of Bertelsmann. Benjamin Franklin's press sizzled out across his lifetime, in part because he retired from it. Franklin's publishing ventures made an enormous impact on American publishing, but his press has failed to remain as an entity for posterity. Edgar Allan Poe was forced by necessity to sell his share of the *Broadway Journal* and never managed to find funding to establish his own *Penn* journal. The bankruptcy of Mark Twain's Charles L. Webster and Co. nearly took Twain to the poor house, so that he had to sell his publishing rights to Harper and Brothers, currently owned by News Corporation. Herman Melville paid to privately print his literary and experimental poetry as well as other passion-projects, never really owning the means of their production. Despite the fact that Henry Luce worked himself to death creating what became the enormous Time Inc. corporation, even this company was sold to the Big Five, or to Hachette Livre. Alice Walker closed her Wild Trees Press when she started seeing enormous profits from her publications with Random House and Houghton Mifflin Harcourt. Harcourt is a billion-dollar annual revenue generator, which is not one of the Big Five because it only specializes in books. In essence, the Big Five have led to the bankruptcy, acquisition or abandonment of all but one of the publishing houses established by the central authors in this study. Thus, to understand what led to these catastrophes, it is necessary to examine, in brief, the history of the Big Five with a focus on their book publishing operations. In articles about the publishing industry, the Big Five are not called, Hachette Livre, News Corporation, Holtzbrinck, Bertelsmann, and National Amusements, but rather by the names of the book publishing sub-companies: Hachette, HarperCollins, Macmillan, Penguin Random House, and Simon & Schuster. Calling them by these names, makes it seem as if they have a connection with the independent, trustworthy author-publishing companies that started them one or two hundred years ago, but this relationship is only an illusion.

Hachette

Little, Brown and Company was established in 1837 in Boston. It merged with Time Inc. in 1968, and then with Warner Communications to form Time Warner in 1989. Time Warner Book Group was sold to the French publisher, Hachette Livre in 2006. This conglomerate ate Constable when it was purchased by Little, Brown Book Group in 2014. The section on Scott will describe Constable's history, including how Constable managed to rescue the business out of a £250,000 bankruptcy in 1826, so that it managed to survive under other owners independently up until the 2014 sale. The consumption of Time Inc. is another sad tale for those who admire the American Dream and the spirit of independent publishing, as it is devastating that with all the resources at Time Inc.'s disposal, its owners still felt that a single cash-out purchase was better than continuing the fight through the hard times. Then again, Henry Luce and Briton Hadden raised $86,000 to start the company in 1922. Perhaps, this initially high profits-to-debt ratio of indebtedness set them up to eventually fail. Scott's publishing ventures, Constable and Ballantyne, had the same problem, taking on more debt than they could ever pay off without leveraging the company and risking a takeover. Another publishing personality who was instrumental in Hachette was Sir Harold Evans, a newspaperman like Luce and Hadden. Evans ended up working as the publisher of Hachette in the 90's, having to work on stressful ghosted biographies with resisting celebrities such as Marlon Brando. France's Hachette has been consuming iconic American and British independent publishing ventures for decades, with some of these entities consuming their neighbors ahead of this larger engulfment. The risks involved in smaller scale independent publishing is particularly apparent in the stories of the consumed publishers. Taking on significant debt typically pushes publishers into public awareness, but a banking crisis, or a few slow sales seasons frequently sway these ventures into disasters. Even if a publisher suffers a catastrophic bankruptcy, it retains value for giant corporations if before it fizzled out it released works that have canonical significance. Having Scott or Luce and Hadden on the roster translates into a symbolic, emotional appeal for a brand that otherwise avoids publishing new literary exercises as they are fiscally "irresponsible" due to the small scale of the highbrow literary marketplace.

HarperCollins

William Collins, Sons was a little print shop that was established in Glasgow, Scotland in 1819. A couple of years earlier, in 1817, J. & J. Harper was established on the other side of the ocean, in New York. James and John saved up $500 to buy their little hand printer and nearly failed before they finished surveying most of the booksellers in New York. At the last moment, they found one bookseller who ordered a couple thousand copies of *Seneca's Morals*. Harper changed its name to Harper & Brothers in 1833 when more brothers joined the business, and then merged with Row, Peterson & Company in 1962, becoming Harper & Row. News Corporation bought Harper & Row in 1987. At around the same time, in 1990, as if their natural, independent lifespans had come to an end at the same time, the News Corporation also bought William Collins & Sons to form HarperCollins. News Corporation was eating other publishers across this period, also buying the Hearst Book Group, which included William Morrow and Avon, in 1999.

Each of these subsidiaries still uses their culturally familiar names in marketing materials and on their covers, so consumers imagine that Avon's romance line is still a separate entity from the more literary William Morrow's title list. Many books, newspaper articles and other media coverage have been invested in building up the public image or brand of publishers like Avon and William Morrow. The power of these brands' messages is what giant media conglomerates are after when they purchase them. A corporation in Germany or France that is primarily concerned about its investors' profits does not translate into a returning, loyal reading and buying base; buyers are more easily swayed by the illusion of continued publishing independence of content.

The Harper & Brothers appears more frequently in this study than other publishers. One example, of Harper's significance is the early, 1868 publication Queen Victoria's memoir, *Leaves from the Journal of Our Life in the Highlands*. Towards the end of Harper's independent run, Virginia Woolf was rejected by *Harper's Bazaar* in 1941, and this played a role in depressing her in the years leading up to her suicide, as the rejection only reinforced the ideas Leonard was planting: that she was an inferior writer (to himself), and that her talent was starting to wane. Another dramatic publishing story that Harper was entangled in was from 1845, a few years before Edgar Allan Poe's mysterious death. Harper refused to sponsor his proposed *Penn* magazine, replying that they had received "complaints" about him from unnamed sources. Even when Harper accepted great writers' work, they frequently retained a sour taste from the experience. Mark Twain's first magazine story, "Forty-three Days in an Open Boat," appeared in *Harper's Monthly* in 1866 with his name misspelled, but this glitch was not as horrid as the problems he was having with other publishers. Thus, in 1898, Twain sold exclusive rights to all of his work to Harper. The canonical writers that had initial fiscal success from publishing with Harper frequently later lost money trying to keep up a winning streak. Herman Melville released most of his popular early novels with Harper, including *Omoo* (1847). Like many of the other writers that worked with Harper, Melville published the British editions with John Murray in London. While, profits from these formulaic popular books were pretty high, Harper still made Melville pay for an enormous quantity of review copy mailings, advertisements and various other costs out of these profits until the advances were mostly cancelled out. And later, Harper made Melville pay thousands of dollars in subsidies to publish an epic poem about the Holy Land, and other literary ventures, which were in stark contrast with his earlier pop successes. Harper was so successful in branding itself as the place where writers could profit and reach a wide marketplace that an enormous quantity of now canonical author-publishers reached out to them at some point. The abuses of these writers under Harper's profiteering model and the rejections of stronger literary accomplishments forced many great authors into self-publishing. Even Luce had submitted his essay for publication in *Harper's* before giving up on making a living as a writer for other publications, and founding his own venture.

A majority of the authors examined that started their own publishing ventures had negative clashes with Harper that contributed to their need to create a new publishing structure that would allow them to publish their own unique work without the negativity they experienced with this exponentially growing publishing giant. Therefore, it is particularly interesting to read a book about the Harper brothers written by a long-standing Harper employee, who started with the company after the family lost control of it and it became a corporate elephant, Eugene Exman. He frankly introduces the brothers in his Foreword: "None of the brothers wrote memoirs or kept diaries and only one instance is known of their writing for publication; that was a letter that Fletcher Harper wrote in 1862 to the editor of the *Athenaeum* (London) in response to a criticism of Mr. Anthony Trollope. This letter is the proverbial exception to a rule, their policy being not to acknowledge or reply to public criticism."[10] Thus, the Harpers represent the pure-business model of publishing that I have skipped over in this study, focusing instead on the author-publisher alternative of writers beginning a publishing venture primarily to publish their own radical works, which they failed to place within the profits-driven publishing business model. But, to understand what Dickens, Scott, Poe and others were rebelling against, it is necessary to understand publishers like the Harpers, who managed to succeed in publishing having only published one letter between the four of them across their lives. Exman begins the quadruple biography by relating that in 1810, James Harper was inspired by the story of Benjamin Franklin's publishing efforts when he decided on apprenticing with a friend's family, Paul & Thomas printing business in New York, instead of staying on to help on his large family farm in Newtown, Long Island.[11] The second oldest Harper brother, Joseph, followed James to New York in 1812, apprenticing with Pray & Bowen printers, and then in 1816, when Wesley, the next son, decided to follow the same path, the rest of the family rented their farm and moved to the City, enrolling their youngest son, Fletcher, in

---

10   Eugene Exman. *The Brothers Harper: A unique publishing partnership and its impact upon the cultural life of America from 1817 to 1853.* (New York: Harper & Row, Publishers, 1965), x.

11   Ibid., 1.

school there. Over these six years, James had worked up to journeyman printer for Jonathan Seymour and John was in the final year of his apprenticeship. The job of the apprentice to a printer was primarily operating a hand press by applying ink to the type, putting sheets in place, and then pulling the machine to make an impression, a job that earned around $14 per week.[12] A year later, James and John had saved $500 towards starting their own printing business, J. & J. Harper, Printers. James led this venture, as he had an ambition for independence, and convinced their father to invest another few hundred by mortgaging his farm. On this money, they bought "two old Ramage hand presses and… found a place they could rent."[13] They had to make the rounds to the bulk of New York's booksellers and publishers, who all rejected them for four months before they finally received their first order in July of 1817 for 2,000 copies of an English translation of *Seneca's Morals*, ordered by Evert Duyckinck. Then, in December, he ordered 2,500 copies of Mair's *Introduction to Latin*. Meanwhile, they also printed three books for Kirk & Mercein. One of their biggest, eighteen-months-long, early projects was the *Prayer Book of the Protestant Episcopal Church*. When they found out they'd lose money if they didn't create stereotypes themselves for this larger order, they started making stereotypes in-house, and this investment gave them greater control over the production process and allowed them to set lower prices than their competitors. After this, they started reprinting British popular novels, and these saw steady sales with the major booksellers in New York, which started regularly working with the Harpers. This reprinting of British pop fiction was a violation of the Brits' rights as they did not pay them royalties, avoiding prosecution because of the non-existence of international copyrights protections. Some American publishers had started attempting to secure legal reprint rights, and their interests clashed with publishers like the Harpers who attempted to cut out these costs. One of their early contested piracies was *Guy Mannering* by Sir Walter Scott in 1820. Harpers' major rival, Carey & Lea in Philadelphia, staked a claim for this novel as their "proprietary American interest." Carey & Lea later contracted with Scott's publisher, Constable, to "purchase proof sheets at £25 per volume" in order to attempt to receive new books ahead of the Harpers, and to have a chance to win the race over releasing Scott's novels first in America to booksellers that

12   Ibid., 3-4.
13   Ibid., 4.

only cared about timeliness of delivery.[14] While there were no international copyrights at this point, some printers could claim authors or works as their own, blocking other printers from pirating the work. Carey's deal with Constable failed to give them a significant advantage, so similar contracts that paid British publishers for rights or proofs were uncommon in America. Meanwhile, the Harpers had to move offices twice when their previous quarters went up in flames. The fires might have been set by overworked employees, and perhaps by one of the Harpers themselves, as the youngest Harper, Fletcher, reported once spending three days without leaving the "composing room," and having his meals brought in, and getting "snatches of sleep under the 'stone' on a rug" as the firm was speeding to release a new Waverley novel.[15] Wesley was bought into his older brothers' printing partnership in 1822 with fiscal help from his father, after spending some time working for a different printer because he expressed that the volume and type of labor he did for the Harpers was injurious to his health. In 1825, the brothers bought a number of buildings for printing, and a mansion to house their families. This was also the year they welcomed Fletcher to join them as a partner for $500. Their four-way partnership from this point until 1861 meant that "each partner could draw from the cash drawer whatever money he needed for his living expenses." By 1825, they were the "largest printing establishment in New York" and they kept up this momentum in the following decades, always striving to expand and expedite their printing process.[16] This was also the year when they started thinking of themselves as publishers as well as printers; this meant that they started advertising their forthcoming books in publications such as *The United States Literary Gazette*, and sending their books for review. Exman explains that when they released the Waverley novels in the preceding years, they were only partially publishing them because they failed to "solicit trade orders in advance." They had only solicited such orders by showing early copies to booksellers.[17] This seems to be a strange distinction as their first official publications were reprints of pirated British books. How they sold pirated books to buyers is hardly a significant enough distinction to mark 1825 as the year when they became full-fledged publishers. Another step that

---

14   Ibid., 9.
15   Ibid., 10.
16   Ibid., 13.
17   Ibid., 13-4.

might have defined them as publishers was that Harpers started putting the name of the publishing house on the title pages of their books. Then again, the definition used today to separate publishers from printers, presses, booksellers, and other categories is equally vague and misclassified. The Harpers' first reviews were about as negative as the first reviews of Byron and Shelley's journal, with *The Port Folio* warning that they should stick to pirating British works like their *Granby* by Lister, and should not venture into domestic literature as it was "*the consumer of waste paper.*"[18] In 1826, Harpers started a new experiment with their first monthly periodical, *National Preacher*, which delivered sermons, and was sold by what became an army of two hundred sales agents by 1831. This sales force created the foundation for their later extremely successful Harper periodicals. They also stayed up-to-date by investing in horse-drawn and steam presses, and then released the first "bound in muslin" or cloth bound book ever printed in America.[19] All this contributed to the Harpers becoming "the largest book-printing establishment in America" by 1829.[20] By this point, James was heading printing. Fletcher was heading publishing. John was the accountant. Wesley was the only brother that enjoyed reading, and wrote all of the company's letters, and prefaces to Harper editions of English reprints. In 1831, they reached their goal of issuing a new title every week, releasing fifty-two that year. Around this time, they hired readers, and started soliciting original work by American authors on a half-profits basis, which, at least at first, was nowhere as successful as their continuing piracies of British classics and bestsellers.

Exman mentions Herman Melville several times in the first half of the book, referring to the Harper books that Melville read that inspired him when he taught a small class at eighteen, moving him to journey out to have adventures on the high seas. Exman describes the first submission Melville made to publish a book with Harper, writing that Melville submitted *Typee: A Peep at Polynesian Life* in 1845, and, after some discussion within Harper, the book was rejected because the "tale could be true and it was therefore without real value." He was advised to publish it in England first. Against the odds, Melville succeeded in this regard, releasing it from Murray, and then having it picked up by

---

18 Ibid., 15.
19 Ibid., 17.
20 Ibid., 19.

Wiley & Putnam in their new *Library of American Books* series.[21] Melville then received a $150 advance for a reprint of *Typee* in 1846 with Harper. *Typee* was not enthusiastically published by Wiley because it included criticism of missionaries and Melville's second novel, *Omoo* included even stricter criticism of this group, so that Wiley had to pass on it, and it wound up back at Harper. Saunders, the reader who initially recommended publishing *Typee* with Harper, before he was overruled by the brothers, now recommended *Omoo* to Fletcher Harper, just as Fletcher was departing for Europe. Without reading it, Fletcher immediately agreed. Melville was offered a $400 advance, half share of profits and he retained British rights.[22] Exman offers a precise account of how authors such as Melville became indebted to the Harpers: "For any six-month period they credited income from sales and charged the total cost to date of manufacturing books, including copies for review. Thus, the first statement on *Omoo*, issued July 31, 1847, gave $1,499.40 as the total cost of manufacturing the 4,000-copy first edition. This amount was a charge against $2,936.90, the income from sales (1,841 paper and 1,766 cloth) less 5 percent deducted for guaranty, leaving a net profit of $1,437.58 to be divided." And yet, without noting any other costs than the purchase of a few Harper books by Melville for his research on a new book on the South Seas, he was paid under $250 in royalties that month. This amount does not match the $715 that should have resulted if the "net profit" was divided in half, though potentially Exman did not mention that Melville's advance was subtracted out of his share.[23] But, how high were the losses of the majority of Harper's authors who failed to attract the wide readership that Melville succeeded in reaching with his extraordinary stories. If the Harper brothers could avoid risk by allowing authors to pay for their losses, while pocketing the bulk of the profits, they could really benefit from working with current American authors, a partnership that was much more time-consuming than mere piracy of pre-edited and pre-marketed British books. In other words, if 4,000 copies were printed and none of them sold, Melville would have been (and was with later books) charged for the printing cost of $1,499 and for review copies and other expenses, without any profits to cancel out these losses. This becomes an enormous amount when we consider that Melville's father-

---

21   Ibid., 242-3.
22   Ibid., 285.
23   Ibid., 286-7.

in-law gave him $2,000 for the purchase of a new house shortly after his marriage, and Melville ended up only using half of this money for the purchase, saving the rest to later pay off charges to Harper. In other words, a house in New York cost less than the printing cost for 4,000 copies.[24] Harper offered Melville a $500 advance for *Mardi* on November 15, 1848, in the midst of the European revolutions of 1848. The contract allowed for a delay so that the London edition could come out first with Murray. These initial British printings helped to secure pedigrees of high British society respectability and top, esteemed London reviews. But, Melville's exploration of a revolutionary topic in the middle of a string of revolutions finally made his literature unpalatable to the British monarchy. Murray started seeing difficulties with *Mardi* from the outset, as he was informed by Sir Walter Farquhar that Melville's earlier two novels were "offensive to morals" and "good taste," causing Murray to question if while *Mardi* promised "to teach the vanity of human craving," instead "its metaphysical presuppositions were anything but Christian;" therefore, Murray took the book to Bentley, who accepted it on March 3, 1849. As Murray predicted, the reviews "were almost unanimously unfavorable." This is a great example of how mainstream reviewers are sponsored by business and political rulers and reject books that threaten their power monopoly. A few years later, Dickens succeeded with a similar account of revolutionary activities with *A Tale of Two Cities*, gathering positive replies from the same reviewers, but France had been Britain's long-time rival, and accounts glorifying the overthrow of France's aristocracy found political backers among British aristocrats. Additionally, Dickens had the unique power of printing the *Tale* in his own popularly consumed periodical, so that he did not need positive reviews for it to sell, and negative reviews in rival magazines would have been blatantly biased. Well aware of the contentious review climate, Harper utilized a trick to sell *Mardi*; they asked the son of the New York bookseller who was first to buy their printed books, Evert Augustus Duyckinck, to post a gossip column advertising *Mardi* in the *Literary World*, which was happy to run it because it had been paid for an advertisement of the book, and later ran an advance excerpt from the book to further garner interest. Despite this scheme, it did not sell, and outside reviews remained scathing. They charged Melville for the ads and review copies that they mailed

---

24   Ibid., 287.

regardless of the results.[25]

Some of the personages that have been introduced in this narrative require an explanation of their inter-associations. One of these is Evert Augustus Duyckinck who had a privileged upbringing in New York with the help of his father's bookselling profits. He graduated from Columbia, was admitted to the bar in 1837, traveled abroad, and associated with America's top literati. He reviewed books for top publications and ran his own publishing company. He helped Edgar Allan Poe print the *Tales* short stories collection in 1845. Then, he served as a joint editor with his brother George for *The Literary World* between 1847 and 1853, when the publication folded. His duties included weekly reviews of books with his brother George Long Duyckinck's help. He was also an author-publisher as he started and ran the *Arcturus* monthly magazine between 1840 and 1842 in partnership with Cornelius Mathews. Evert published a few books, including: *Wit and Wisdom of Sydney Smith* (1856), *History of the War for the Union* (1861-5) and *Poems relating to the American Revolution, with Memoirs of the Authors* (1865).

Another telling intersection is that while Evert Augustus Duyckinck was editing and reviewing for the *Literary World*, a friend of Melville's, Charles Fenno Hoffman, was also working there as an editor since 1847. At the same time when Hoffman was puffing Melville's novels in *Literary World*, in early 1849, Hoffman happened to undergo a nervous breakdown after his servant tossed a book he had long been composing into the fire, supposedly because the servant mistook it for unneeded scraps, a madness from which Hoffman never really recovered, dying in a mental hospital in 1884. Hoffman is not only relevant because his madness affected Melville's state of mind, but also because he was an author-publisher himself. After being admitted to the bar and an Ivy League education, Hoffman first established a student magazine, *The Knickerbocker*, in 1833, and later gained fame with a successful novel, *Greyslaer* (1840) and a poetry collection, *The Vigil of Fait* (1842). His last successful publication was in 1844, followed by a writing dry spell across the years when he was primarily employed as an editor before "madness" descended in 1849. As you read this study, Hoffman's "madness" should start to sound more like a conspiracy to drive him mad by attacking his passion-project, and less like an accident of a clueless employee. Additionally, this is a great example of how there is something eerie about the intricate intersections between

---

25   Ibid., 288-9.

the lives and self-promotions of many of these great author-publishers.

Back at Harper, Melville sold a new manuscript to the brothers without them seeing a word of it, calling it, *My First Voyage to Redburn*, and promising it "in two or three months or less," then delivering it promptly for a $300 advance and a release in July of 1849, with the "only change made" being to the title, into, *His First Voyage*, to be printed in London with Bentley. "Bentley's payment turned out to be less than the amount of Melville's debt to the Harpers…" Because of this shortage, Melville immediately started a new novel as *Redburn* was going through production, *White-Jacket*, "writing at least three thousand words a day," and finishing it by mid-August, so that these two novels were released at the same time. Both must have been edited by Melville's wife because they were immediately typeset and printed upon receipt, without any added editing.[26] Melville described these books to Judge Shaw as his "two *jobs*, which I have done for money… it is my earnest desire to write those sort of books which are said to 'fail'—pardon this egotism."[27] With his debt to Harper at $1,332.29 at this time, Melville sailed with the proofs for *White-Jacket* to England, hoping to agree on better terms with London publishers than they had been offering him up to that point.[28] Bentley offered him poorer terms than he had offered when Melville was querying him via Harpers from New York, giving £100 in advance for *Redburn* and £200 for *White-Jacket*. Melville thought the latter was too low and tried four other publishers who rejected the book because they were "unwilling to risk" releasing it "without copyright protection," so that Melville had to accept Bentley's initial offer, and apparently Bentley ended up losing £100 on that publication.[29] For the March 21, 1850 American release of *White-Jacket*, Harpers once again had Duyckinck run an excerpt in the March 9 issue, a two-page review on March 16, and a back-page advertisement on March 23 (which also included at least one other title from Harper) with quotes from a publication the ad was also running in the *Literary World*. Reviews from other publications were mixed because the book was critical towards the Navy. Self-reviewing and self-advertising apparently worked, and the first two editions sold. Something about the trip to London disgusted Melville with commercial speed writing, and

---

26   Ibid., 290.
27   Ibid., 291.
28   Ibid., 291-2.
29   Ibid., 292.

when he returned in February, he started, *The Whale*, which he claimed was completed on June 27, 1850,[30] though it was not really finished until long after the resulting contract with Bentley, so that he had to ask for an advance from Harpers in April, 1851, which was rejected because at that point Melville owed $700 to Harpers. Therein, Harpers refused to give him any advance for *The Whale*.[31] Meanwhile, Melville wrote a review for the *Literary World*, which is familiar to his modern critics, "Hawthorne and his Old Mosses," about the strength of American literature in contrast with English literature. Melville had given it to Duyckinck on his way out from a launch party where a heated discussion on this matter broke out.[32] The book was finally proofed, excerpt and published on November 14, 1851, taking Melville longer to write than any of his previous speedy productions. Perhaps because the Harpers did not purchase an ad, Evert and George Duyckinck wrote a scathing review of the book in the *Literary World*, suddenly complaining that *Moby-Dick* challenged "the most sacred associations of life" and objecting that the whaling details were "tedious."[33] 1,535 copies sold, but Melville was still $422.82 in debt to Harper. Thus, all of the work he had put into writing a set of novels for the brothers was coming out at a net loss, instead of earning him an income as an author. Melville cancelled his long-standing subscription to the *Literary World* on February 14, 1852, as he was completing *Pierre*. When explaining why Bentley finally had to reject *Pierre*, Exman tellingly calls Melville "insane" and accuses him of delivering a product different from the traditional pop novel he had promised, claiming that Bentley's rejection was a necessary outcome considering Melville's poor selling history up to that point. Exman glorifies the Harpers for their willingness to continue working with Melville despite his shortcomings and explains that when they offered a contract for *Pierre*, Melville was nearly clear of his debt, owing only $150, so that they now offered a new loan to him for $500 for *Pierre* (August 6, 1852), also offering to release it with their London agent, Sampson Low, due to Bentley's rejection. Once again, the Harpers failed to advertise in the *Literary World*, and Duyckinck was still bitterer in his review, writing that *Pierre* "completely befogged nature and truth... The most immoral moral of the story, if it has

---

30   Ibid., 293.
31   Ibid., 295.
32   Ibid., 294-5.
33   Ibid., 297-8.

any moral at all, seems to be the impracticability of virtue; a leering demoniacal spectre of an idea which seems to be peering at us through the dim obscure of this dark book, and mocking us with this dismal falsehood." To support the notion that Duyckinck's opinion was shared by other reviewers, Exman quotes from some other "critic" who called Melville "daft." Exman reports that Melville's indebtedness in 1853 was back up at $298.71.[34] The articles Melville published to make a living in 1853 were primarily for magazines that Harper (*Harper's*) and Bentley (*Miscellany*) owned. Exman introduces a very different reason for the termination of the publishing relations between Melville and Harper than the one offered in his biographies, explaining that Melville was given a $300 advance for a new book he was writing in November of 1853, *Tortoises and Tortoise-Hunting*, but instead of delivering the book as-contracted by January, 1854, he sent it for publication in *Putman's*, under the title "The Encantadas," because he had assumed that due to a yet another new fire at Harper, the brothers would be unable to release his book as-scheduled. Exman chides Melville for betraying the brothers in their hour of need and crossing over to a competing periodical. He portrays the brothers as having "stoically absorbing losses" on Melville's books, damages that justified their termination of further publishing relations with him for twelve years, before they finally released Melville's self-sponsored collection of poetry.[35] Exman claims that the poetry release was yet another loss for the brothers because "Melville's days as a productive author were over." Exman deliberately refrains from explaining that Melville had paid for these books to be printed and paid for other production-related costs out-of-pocket and that the Harpers had long been paid back by Melville by this point, and remained ahead after this new successful attempt to profit from Melville's authorial obsession. After Melville's death, the Harpers further injured Melville's memory by sending "severally melted" plates to Mrs. Melville, upon her 1891 request for them, so the book could not be reprinted with the United States Book Company. They only sent the plates because the copyrights finally expired in 1890, a point when Harpers had to take Melville's books out of their catalogs.[36]

    Harpers' relationship with Poe was also turbulent. One of their conflicts occurred when the new Mayor of New York, James Harper,

---

34   Ibid., 299-300.
35   Ibid., 301.
36   Ibid., 302.

passed an ordinance in 1844 closing saloons on Sundays, and Poe protested in the *Spy*, arguing that if saloons were immoral, they should be closed all week.[37] To reiterate, Evert Augustus Duyckinck helped Poe print his *Tales* collection in 1845, but it should be added that Poe first submitted this collection to Harper in June of 1836, where it was rejected upon advice from one of its readers. When Poe asked for a reason, Wesley replied on Harper's behalf that the short stories in it had already "appeared in print," were "detached… pieces," and were "too learned and mystical. They would be understood and relished only by a very few—not by the multitude. The number of readers in this country capable of appreciating and enjoying such writings as those you submitted to us is very small indeed."[38] Identical reasons are given to-this-day in reply to similar submissions, so perhaps the American reading public has only regressed in its comprehension. These early ponderings became templates that have been used to measure all incoming manuscripts. The continuation of this Americans-are-barely-literate strategy can be seen in the extremely low reading level of most popular fiction published today. But, while these are deep reflections indeed, Wesley went on to add something that was surely the real reason for the rejection. Wesley stresses that a "first failure" can be catastrophic to an author's reputation if a book is too learned and fails to sell to the common readers, before digressing into expressing how "pleased" he was with Poe's criticism in the *Messenger* of Harpers' books, though "we do not always agree with you," continuing to say that they plan on sending books for his review that they hope he will like. The obvious implication is not, as Exman concludes, that Wesley was attempting to soften the blow of the rejection, but rather that this is an obvious invitation for Poe to puff his future reviews of Harpers' books, so that he might have more success in having his own work accepted at Harper, *quid pro quo*.[39] This exchange occurred after Poe's 1835 explosion in a *Southern Literary Messenger* review of a Harper novel, *Norman Leslie* by Theodore Sedgwick Fay, where he called it "bepuffed, beplastered… for the sake of everything puffed, puffing, and puffable, let us take a look at its contents…"[40] Therefore, Poe took Harper's suggestion that he puff instead of huffing for what it was, and it enraged him, so that

---

37 Ibid., 196.
38 Ibid., 80.
39 Ibid., 80-1.
40 Ibid., 75.

his criticism became more negative and he increased his insistence that pop fiction is plagiarized and corrupt, as this letter, and other evidence suggests. A year after Harper's rejection, in 1837, Poe followed their advice and submitted his first and only novel to them, *The Narrative of Arthur Gordon Pym*. Curiously, this work seems to be a precursor to the whaling and sea adventuring themes in most of Melville's popular Harper novels. In turn, Poe mimicked ideas from Benjamin Morrell and J. N. Reynolds in this novel, copying the formulas that Harper previously accepted. Like many pop publishers since, Harper was soliciting authors interested in publication to purchase their earlier releases, so that they could study selling formulas in order to replicate them. The Harpers could not think of a reason to reject Poe's unified, pop novel, and so they accepted it, but deliberately delayed it by a year because "Poe's stinging review of Fay's *Norman Leslie* was still remembered by his rivals among the New York critics," but really by Harper.[41] Poe was so embarrassed by this attempt at selling-out that the book was released anonymously. At the same time, it had one of the "poorest" sales statistics amidst those released from Harper that year. Amidst the usual anti-literary avalanche of negative reviews, the *New York Review* actually revealed Poe as a likely contributor, complaining that there was too much violence in it and no ending. Why would the *New York Review* have guessed Poe's authorship if he had never written another novel? It seems likely that Harper leaked his identity to them, potentially as an additional retaliation for Poe's honest reviews. *Pym* was successful in the United Kingdom with a different publisher, in part because of Dickens' positive review of it, following Poe and Dickens' meeting during Dickens' first American tour. No statistics for exact sales of Harper's *Pym* are offered other than that they managed to sell 100 copies in London, so they probably left Poe with the bill just as they did with Melville. Unlike Melville, Poe was too poor to attempt publishing another pop novel with Harper under such unscrupulous terms.[42] Years went by and when Poe hit bottom in 1844, perhaps in a drunk stupor, he once again attempted to sell a new book to Harper, and five months later, the Harpers informed Poe through an intermediary, Professor Anthon, that they had "complaints" against Poe, implying that he was still raging against their pop fiction, as he was presumed to have published a "gibe" against *The Knickerbocker*

---

41   Ibid., 96.
42   Ibid., 114.

in *The New World* under the pseudonym L. Exman suggests that the reason Poe was rejected by several publishers was because of his manners and drunkenness, and not because of his frank, highbrow literary opinions. Meanwhile, Poe was also attempting to find funding for a literary magazine, *The Stylus*, from Harper and other publishers, who all firmly blocked this idea for the same old reason. The only echo Poe could find in these literati circles was in Duyckinck, who had also just been rejected in his plans to found *The Home-Critic* magazine with Mathews. Two author-publishers collided and Duyckinck took on the challenge of helping Poe in his ambitious struggles. Duyckinck helped Poe place *The Raven and Other Poems* with Wiley & Putnam in 1845, the same year when he helped him to privately print *Tales* with Harper (a printing he otherwise wouldn't have afforded).[43]

James Harper died in 1869, having been elected as mayor of New York back on April 9, 1844 without taking an "active part in the campaign,"[44] explaining to a visitor, during his time in office in 1853, that his job in the Harper partnership was to "entertain the bores."[45] Fletcher Harper died in 1877, after the final poetry collection they released for Melville, but before the final transfer of Melville's copyrights after Melville's death. The business remained in the Harper family, passing down to male descendants who became co-partners up until 1896. After this point, they became members in a firm, when Harper & Brothers became a stock company. The fourth and final generation of Harpers joined from the late 1870s to the late 1890s. The four original Harpers had remained a quadruple partnership up until 1869, when James died and one of his sons and a few of his brothers' sons joined to help fill the void he left. Exman ends his book in the spring of 1855, upon the printing of the brothers' first catalog of over a thousand titles, after a grand fire of 1853, which once again took out their buildings and forced them to relocate their press, this time finally to a set of fireproof new buildings that managed to last for seventy years, in contrast with the temporary abodes that preceded them. Exman explains that the last fire was started when a plumber tried to extinguish a burning paper he used to light a lamp in a highly combustible pan of camphene (used for printing), which he thought was water.[46] In total,

---

43   Ibid., 202-3.
44   Ibid., 187.
45   Ibid., 346.
46   Ibid., 353.

the Harpers lost $1,115,000 in property damages in this conflagration, only saving $450,000-worth from the flames. While the flames were still hot, they began planning how they would print the forthcoming books.[47] Exman mentions, in passing, that Harpers' first fire in the little office that housed James' first hand press might have been set by rival printers, which hoped to delay Harpers' production with the flames, and to profit by their losses. If this was the case, perhaps the Harpers were pressured to offer terms that were unflattering to authors, such as Melville, because they were constantly suffering from the cost of rebuilding due to vandalisms. These expenses would have been continually eating up the profits they managed to muster from printing and selling books at their top capacity. If this story was a modern pop film, Harpers would have been cast as insurance fraudsters, but Exman definitely did not mention details about insurance payouts. Concrete proof of what caused the fires, and how much their authors paid them to subsidize the cost of the destruction is also missing. It is certainly telling that Melville's version of events has unique gaps, and Harpers' version of events inserts insults and accusations against Melville. Somewhere between these two stories, there are informative lessons for current publishers that want to understand how great literary giants were made in earlier days, and why similarly outstanding authors fail to win publishers today.

Macmillan

Macmillan was founded in 1843 in New York. After a century of family ownership, in 1995, Macmillan sold a 70% share to the German media company, Holtzbrinck Publishing Group, and the remainder of the shares to the same in 1999. One of the family's chairs was the former Prime Minister of the United Kingdom, Harold Macmillan, who controlled the company from 1964 to 1986, after working for it in interims between other projects. The US branch of Macmillan was sold before the rest of it, thus creating Macmillan Publishing in 1896, which was then sold to Pearson in 1998. And then Holtzbrinck bought the US branch of Macmillan too in 2001. Charley Dickens Jr. went to work with Macmillan's London office at around the time the US office was sold. Dickens Jr. surrendered his independence because of a

---

47   Ibid., 356.

slump in sales of *All the Year Round*, and the reliability of a yearly salary. Charles Dickens had worked for newspapers and other publishers when he was younger, but his experiences were always so negative that when he suddenly had savings, he invested it in his own journal. His hope was that his son would not have to work for anybody else. Dickens and the publishers that came before him went through indentured service at the start of their publishing careers, so employment in a trade was always an inferior social position. Only by offering salaries that rivaled independent profits could Macmillan and other growing publishers attract a new generation that had these independent options. The brain-drain into giant publishers depleted independents when the social norms shifted to glorify steady ladder-climbing in a publishing career, rather than risky independent business ventures. Macmillan is an example of this and other radical shifts that occurred in the last two decades. Macmillan remained a family owned company up through 1995, happily passing leadership roles to the next generations. This shift can be attributed to the hundred-year expiration date most independent publishers suffer as knowledge, a passion for publishing, or other ingredients fail to reach the fourth or fifth generations, so that they feel detached enough from the company to be able to sell it for a profit, rather than wanting to preserve the legacy, or an enjoyment of the publishing work. Dickens Jr.'s surrender of Dickens Sr.'s journal is also indicative of the trend that pushed smaller journals and publishers out of business as the book buyers migrated to primarily purchasing books from the biggest publishers with the biggest marketing budgets.

Penguin Random House

Random House was founded in 1927 in New York City with a general publishing agenda. Penguin was founded in 1935 in London, United Kingdom. There is a similar parallel between Collins' and Harper's founding a couple of years apart, and Penguin Books' founding a few years after Random House (both on diverging sides of the ocean). Random House went public in 1959.

In the 50s, making a public offering of shares was very unusual in publishing, where most publishing houses were owned by a sole proprietor, two partners or a handful of partners that contributed some capital to enter the business and typically worked in key positions to grow the business they were invested in. Public offering became more common after this point, and they meant that companies were taking on debt to the shareholders, who were not also actively working for as little as nothing (if a company wasn't profitable), or for a small base salary (on top of profit sharing if any materialized) to recuperate their investments. Debt to investors has contributed to the high failure rate of both big and small indebted publishers from this point to the present, thus making vulnerable, bankrupt or near-bankrupt companies available for acquisition by the giants. However, even a giant can fail if it consumes too many companies and takes on their debt. Then, in turn, the giant is also forced to sell itself to still bigger competitors. This is how the domino effect of acquisitions has led to the current five (or four) surviving international media companies.

In this buying frenzy, Alfred A. Knopf (1960) and Pantheon Books (1961) were acquired by Random House. Then, RCA bought Random House in 1965, only to sell Random House to Advance Publications in 1980. This potato was too hot for Advance Publications as well, and they passed the company onto Bertelsmann AG in 1998. Meanwhile, during the same fallout, Penguin Books Ltd. was bought by Pearson Longman in 1970. Then, Penguin Books USA and Putnam Berkley Group merged in 1996 to form the Penguin Group. And, most recently, Random House and Penguin merged under the dual ownership by Bertelsmann (dominant partner with a 53% share) and Pearson Plc. in 2013.

Random House and Longman appear in this study a few times, particularly in discussions of copyrights acquisitions for canonical author-publishers. This raises the question if canons are formed by giant publishers' marketing campaigns or if they simply offer the most money for the rights to the top previously otherwise canonized authors. If only the Big Four have enough political and market power to feature their titles in course textbooks, sell them as top library acquisitions, and place them with the preferred review publications; then, only authors that sell out to these players are capable of reaching the consciousness of researchers and readers alike.

For example, Virginia Woolf sold her half of the partnership in Hogarth Press to their assistant, Lehmann, but then after her death, Lehmann could not continue working with the overbearing Leonard and he also issued a notice of intent to break the partnership. To survive the sale, Leonard Woolf approached Chatto & Windus for funding for buying back two-thirds of the Press' equity. Hogarth had been in active competition with Chatto, and it was certainly interested in taking its biggest competitor for top authors out of commission. In exchange for the funding, Leonard was demoted to the role of employee and became just one of Hogarth's directors. Deals like this one seem to have been negative investments for Chatto as well. Purchasing shares in struggling competitors like Hogarth made Chatto's portfolio unsound, forcing it to be sold in a string of mergers until it ended up under Random House.

One of the authors that Walker published with her Wild Trees Press, J. California Cooper, reprinted *A Piece of Mine* with Random House, after Wild Trees closed its doors. But then, Walker was publishing some books with Random House too. And John W. Parker and Son's (London) *Gray's Anatomy* kept them in business from 1833, until after Parker Jr.'s death, when it was sold to Messrs. Longman, which later merged to become part of Pearson Plc. Every human being dies at some point, but corporations can potentially be immortal, picking up the remains after the primary publisher is incapacitated or deceased.

Penguin survived the death of its founder in part due to their victory in an obscenity lawsuit, which resulted in the successful and unimpeded sale of millions of copies of D. H. Lawrence's *Lady Chatterley's Lover*. Penguin used this success to leverage their first public share offering, wherein they sold 750,000 shares that raised the issue price by 44%, making the sellers automatically wealthy, and infusing the company with riches that could be used to stomp out the competition.[48] However, these statistics are not as reliable as one would hope. Bellaigue fails to properly cite the thousands of figures he provides about the publishing business, making his study unreliable because the figures cannot be double-checked. Bellaigue overwhelms readers with statistics, but most of them are inaccurate, and while they seem to criticize the giant publishers, his conclusions always stress that these publishing entities are efficient and financially and artistically successful (i.e.: award-winning). For example, in the section on self-publishing, Bellaigue wraps up the topic in around two pages. He begins by explaining that Stephen King's experiment in 2000 with releasing *The Plant* online ended in failure because of "dishonor" via a lack of payment by

---

48   Eric de Bellaigue. *British Book Publishing as a Business since the 1960s: Selected Essays by Eric de Bellaigue*. The British Library Studies in the History of the Book. (London: The British Library, 2004), 30-1.

buyers of the chapters, so that he quit the experiment on Chapter 6. Online publishing was born shortly before 2000, and yet, Bellaigue does not look at the progress made in this field in the following four years before the completion of Bellaigue's study. He gives one example of a successful best-selling release of an over-priced $44.96 tome of 1197 pages by Stephen Wolfram, *A New Kind of Science*, which suggests that only these types of obscure works could succeed via self-published promotions. Then, without explaining where the figures come from, Bellaigue summarizes: "On average, the cost to an author is in the region of £7000 to £8000, a substantial outlay that in itself acts as an additional filter. Royalties are set at 30% of the cover price; should a second printing be justified, Book Guild assumes the financial risk and the royalty drops to 20%." The source, "Book Guild," is inserted far into the first sentence, so that a casual reader might assume that the average refers to all subsidy publishers, rather than to this specific company that is being singled out and stressed in most of the paragraphs in this section. The Book Guild is unfairly used to represent the entire self-publishing industry. As in many other biased studies about publishers that compete with the giants, the author stresses that the term "self-publishing" has "pejorative connotations," which are further "weakening" over time. This paragraph ends with: "Self-publication thereby becomes not simply an end in itself but a back-door entrance into mainstream publication for the rejected author."[49] One of the authors I published with Anaphora received a contract for $300,000 for film rights to a book he released with Anaphora, and because I offer non-exclusive contracts and do not retain film rights, he does not have to share a penny of these earnings with Anaphora. Does this sound like a "back-door" for a "rejected author," or a smart business decision that provided an entry into "mainstream" publishing? Because a majority of titles are self-published today, self-publishing is the mainstream, and only through propagandistic books like this one that divert attention from real statistics into engineered fictitious conclusions can the Big Four attempt to hold onto their market dominance against the tide of independent publishing.

---

49   Ibid., 207-9.

A Brief Story of an Acquired Author-Publisher: John W Parker and Son

John W Parker and Son published the standard anatomy textbook of the last two hundred years, *Gray's Anatomy*. In her study of how this textbook came to be published, *The Making of Mr. Gray's Anatomy: Bodies, Books, Fortune, Fame*, Ruth Richardson presents the history and biography of a few key figures in the book's publication. The focus is on *Gray's* author, Henry Gray, an anatomy specialist, Henry Vandyke Carter, the book's illustrator who also completed a medical degree shortly before starting this project, and happened to have a talent for drawing, and the book's publishers, John William Parker Sr. and his son John William Parker Jr. Sadly, the two Johns did not write books of their own, only their spouses and daughters dabbled in writing. John W Parker and Son's initial publishing projects, when they transitioned from merely printing books to also offering publishing services, included pamphlets created for the Society for Promoting Christian Knowledge, with a focus on nature and creationism. The Parkers established this business in 1833 at Charing Cross in London, in a building that also functioned as their home: 445 West Strand. In their first two decades, they primarily self-published. "There are two Parker authors on his early book lists: Anne and Elizabeth. Sometimes their works first appeared under initials, only later being attributed by name." These publications included EP's chapbook of *Popular Poems*, Anne Parker's *Fables and Moral Maxims*, illustrated "with 100 cuts" by the author-illustrator. "Both women may have helped with other works for the SPCK and for Parker himself which appeared anonymously." The Parkers then branched out into publishing books by outside authors, with a focus on radical abolitionist books such as Thomas Clarkson's *History of the Rise, Progress and Accomplishment of the Abolition of the African Slave Trade*, before they released *Gray's Anatomy* and became highly commercially profitable.[50] The early self-publications by the Parker women helped this publishing house display the diversity of their artistic, editorial, and content interests and attracted the outstanding writers who later helped them succeed as a publisher. The quality of these early books won Parker Sr. the management position over Cambridge University's Press. He was previously involved in mod-

50   Ibid., 63-5.

ernizing this press in the 1820s, when he was starting in printing in a different printing company. Parker Sr. stayed on as the manager of Cambridge Press from 1836 to 1852, meanwhile gradually building his own publishing company. He resigned from Cambridge after he became a widower and re-married a younger wife. Parker Sr.'s publications radicalized after his declaration of publishing independence, via separation from Cambridge, and he released *Words by a Working Man about Education, in a Letter to Lord John Russell,* as well as a pamphlet called, *The Opinions of Certain Authors on The Bookselling Question* that argued against the Booksellers' Association's monopoly on book prices. The *Bookselling Question* included letters written by Parker Sr. The collection also featured authors who wrote their complaints in the form of letters addressed to Parker Sr. because he solicited them with a letter that concluded in the following "Question":

> If a retail bookseller, of ascertained credit and respectability, applies to the publisher to purchase any book in which you may be directly or indirectly interested, on the terms at which those books are offered to the trade at large, but with the avowed intention of retailing his purchases at a smaller profit than that provided for between the wholesale rate and the selling price of a single copies, do you consider the intention to sell at a low rate of profit a good and sufficient reason why the publisher should refuse to sell the books, which such retailer is ready to purchase and to keep in stock at his own risk. John W. Parker, for self and son. West Strand, April 30th, 1852.[51]

The authors who replied to this call to commentary included Thomas Carlyle, Charles Darwin, Charles Dickens, and J. E. Gray F.R.S. The rhetoric Parker Sr. uses is very rousing, and it's easy to see how writers decided that he was on their side and wanted to work with him after this release. *Words by a Working Man about Education, in a Letter to Lord John Russell* was signed with "Working Man," but it is obviously written by Parker Sr. In this letter, Parker states, towards the end:

> 5. It is only in the responsibility attaching to administration created by, and amenable to, the law of the land, that the respect due to the laboring classes of our fellow citizens, in the education of their children, can be adequately expressed or realized. What must the better part of these fa-

---

[51] John W. Parker and Son. *The Opinions of Certain Authors on the Bookselling Question.* 2nd ed. (London, J.W. Parker and Son, 1852; Web), 11.

thers and mothers think of a state in which they are treated as if their only parental function was to stock a preserve for every spiritual Nimrod?[52]

Earlier in this work, Parker criticizes the focus on religion in education, and otherwise argues that a public education is necessary for the betterment of society at large. These radical publications attracted the attention of the best writers of the time who were also engaged in these movements, and that's how Gray learned of the enterprise and released *Gray's Anatomy* with the Parkers in 1858. By this point, Parker moved away from self-printing, and started hiring outside printers, while he focused on the tasks on the publishing side of the business. Parker Jr. was educated at King's College and socialized with intellectuals there. Parker Jr. later recruited them to the popular among intellectuals, due to its literary content, *Fraser's Magazine*, which was acquired in 1847 and edited by Parker Jr. until his early death at 40 in 1860. Parker Jr. was also one of a duo of editors for their *Politics for the People*, a Chartism weekly newspaper released for a short time in 1848 (during the 1848 Revolutions). Three years after Parker Jr.'s death, Parker Sr. sold the entire publishing business to Messrs. Longman, now known as Pearson PLC. Thus, the lack of an heir prevented another great publisher from continuing radical and outstanding independent publications.

Simon & Schuster

Simon & Schuster was founded in 1924 in New York City. When they started publishing, Simon & Schuster partnered with the Western Printing and Lithographing Company to print and finance their books. Because they already had a significant stake in the company, in terms of loans to Simon & Schuster, it was able to buy their interest in the company in 1958. This was the point when, like the other Big Four, the company's founders stepped aside and a corporation without the drive to strive for individual excellence took over the helm. Simon & Schuster had been sold before this point to the owner of the *Chicago Sun* newspaper and then sold back to the owners, who were motivated by profits from these sales rather than by ideals of leading the world with superior publishing. Then, shares were sold to Leon Shimkin in 1966 and he merged the parts of Simon & Schuster and Pocket Books

---

52 Ibid., 29.

back together, as Simon & Schuster had previously split these two imprints in their quest for funding. In 1976, Gulf+Western (which has been called Paramount Communications since 1989) acquired it. This was followed by Paramount's acquisition of Esquire Corporation (1984), Prentice Hall (1985), Silver Burdett (1986), Gousha (1987) and Charles E. Simon (1988), and other acquisitions too numerous to be relevant here. After all these hyper-expensive acquisitions, Paramount itself had taken on so much debt that it collapsed under its risk-burden, and was sold to Viacom (which is controlled by National Amusements) in 1994. Viacom split into the CBS Corporation (which kept Simon & Schuster) and Viacom, though both are still controlled with majority shares by National Amusements. This media elephant is primarily known for its theaters. In other words, one of the Big Five international publishers is now owned by a company that primarily sells seats in movie theaters rather than original artistic productions. In this climate, the quality of Simon & Schuster's releases has dived as it focuses on marketability and profitability.

The Impanetrable Reviewers

None of the four corporations that control the majority of the international book market specializes solely in books. They have interests in various other media platforms, such as film production and distribution, newspapers and broadcast networks. Thus, the major review publications are controlled by the same people who benefit from only advertising and publicizing books published within this interconnected media network. After the American Library Association conference, upon my request, one of the organizers of an ALA committee and the administrator of a library in a secondary school (who I will not identify, in case she wants to remain anonymous) emailed a list to me of the review publications among who she looks for three positive reviews before she can buy any book for her library. This list includes: *School Library Journal, Library Journal, Choice, Kirkus Review, Horn Book* [children/ YA], *Teacher Librarian* [K-12], *VOYA* [YA], *School Library Connection* [K-12], *Booklist, Book Links* [K-12 literature, related to *Booklist*], *New York Review of Books*, and also "major newspaper book review columns" and "professional teaching organization journals (i.e., *History Teacher Journal*, etc.)." The K-12 publications are not relevant to the majority of the titles I publish with Anaphora, and the smaller publications are too numerous to evaluate in terms of impact and affiliations. The remaining publications can be reviewed and their owners can be identified.

The *School Library Journal* and the *Library Journal* are currently under the control of RLJ Companies, a collection of companies owned by the first African American billionaire, Robert L. Johnson, who became a billionaire when he sold the BET network to Viacom in 2001, having founded it in 1979. If you check the diagram in the earlier section, Viacom is currently controlled by National Amusements, the same company that owns Simon & Schuster, one of the Big Four. Thus, Simon & Schuster is reviewing itself when reviews of its books are published in these journals.

Choice and *Booklist* are published by the American Library Association, which receives its funding from the federal and state governments in grants, and actively lobbies for funding for itself and other libraries from its Washington DC Office of Government Relations. While this seems like a neutral funding source, it really means that reviewing books that hold a critical position of the U.S. government can jeopardize the funding of the entire association.

After failing under Nielsen's leadership (media conglomerate), *Kirkus Reviews* was bought by Herbert Simon, a wealthy real estate broker, making it one of the least media-connected review publications, but Kirkus charges authors $425 for mostly negative, brief reviews, and few sales practically result for those who are thus reviewed (from my experience with submitting Anaphora's titles to *Kirkus*).

The June 23, 2016 online issue of the *New York Review of Books* has around thirty-four reviews. A few of these reviews are about pop and operatic music, and exhibitions, so on average no more than forty books are reviewed in the bi-monthly issues, an extremely small amount when one considers the volume of books released in the US monthly. This issue includes a review of Random House's, *Conquerors: How Portugal Forged the First Global Empire*, one of its own New York Review Books Classics releases, *Akenfield: Portrait of an English Village*, and a few titles by actual independent presses like Polity's *Farewell to the World: A History of Suicide*, and books by university presses such as Princeton University Press' *The Work of the Dead: A Cultural History of Mortal Remains*. Thus, out of the forty book reviews that month, there might be five by independent, non-affiliated, non-university presses against the avalanche of outstanding titles not finding mainstream reviews.

History Teacher Journal is controlled by the independent, grant-funded Society for History Education, but since it appears before an "etc." in the librarian's email, it seems as if it is not a key publication that would warrant spending over $10 to print and ship a book for their review. And, they concentrate on higher education teachers, so only a small number of published books would fit their review criteria.

In summary, the international book review market is as bleak as the publishing market. Librarians are taught to only consider reviews from review publications that are controlled by giant media conglomerates or government funding, or that charge for the reviews, or that review less than 0.16% of all the books published in the US in a given year. Buyers, authors and independent publishers should be aware of these facts to make educated buying and submission decisions.

CHAPTER 2

Censorship, Radicalism and the Press

Hamlet shocked all the Cromwellian Puritans, and shocks nobody today, and some of Aristophanes shocks everybody today and didn't galvanize the later Greeks at all apparently.
    —D. H. Lawrence, *Sex, Literature and Censorship*[53]

But even I would censor genuine pornography. It would not be very difficult. In the first place genuine pornography is almost always underworld, it doesn't come into the open. In the second place, you can recognize it by the insult it offers, invariably, to sex, and to the human spirit.
    —D. H. Lawrence, *Sex, Literature and Censorship*[54]

---

53   David Herbert Lawrence. *Sex, Literature and Censorship: Essays.* (London: William Heinemann, 1955; Google Books, Web), 69.
54   Ibid., 74.

A History of Publishing Censorship

Most of the author-publishers in this study endured some form of pre- or post-publication censorship, which occasionally led to their or their printer's or partner's imprisonment, banishment or fine payment. The cases look less isolated when they are compared. The topic of censorship is uncomplicated with help from case studies of major censorship trials, laws and prohibitions covered in this section.

British and other European countries' censorship laws are closely tied with the laws imposed by the Catholic Church in Rome because it governed the "blasphemy" laws that guided the Inquisition and other movements to suppress books based on their irreligiosity or immorality. So, this section will include a few cases from other countries across Europe that impacted this network of interrelated Catholic (and occasionally Puritan) countries.

Censorship in Britain went back to before the Inquisition. A change occurred when Charles I was forced to convene the Long Parliament in 1637 to raise funds, and he was forced to allow the Parliament to "abolish the former organ of censorship, the infamous Star Chamber." This opened doors to some scandalous printing, and in turn prompted a need for the 1643 "Order for the Regulating of Printing, and for suppressing the great late abuses and frequent disorders in Printing many false Scandalous, Seditious, Libelous, and unlicensed Pamphlets, to the great defamation of Religion and Government." This law meant that all books had to be "licensed" and entered into the Stationers' Register.[55] "Certain officers of the Company and of Parliament were empowered to make searches, apprehend delinquent authors, or printers, and to seize unlawful printing presses together with nut, spindle, and materials, and, in the event of opposition, to break open doors and locks." The licensing personnel were "lawyers, doctors, Members of Parliament, and a schoolmaster, and in the case of books of divinity, Presbyterian ministers." Even the King had to submit to censorship so that when "Charles moved his Court from London to Oxford, he was wise enough to take his own printer."[56]

George III was the first in the line of Hanoverian kings to lose the

---

[55] John McCormick and Mairi MacInnes, eds. *Versions of Censorship*. (Garden City (NY): Anchor Books, 1962), 4.
[56] Ibid., 5.

German accent of his ancestors. George was twenty-two when he started his reign, and despite his affairs and illegitimate children, the first thing he did was release a proclamation against immorality in 1760. In 1787, George III turned this general request into a law called the Royal Proclamation "For the Encouragement of Piety and Virtue, and for the Preventing and Punishing of Vice, Profaneness and Immorality," which had to be read quarterly in churches. It was edited and renamed for the first time in 1857 as the "Obscene Publications Act." George III was on the throne during both the French and the American Revolution, and it was his idea to install the Stamp Act (1765) that contributed to the American colonies declaration of independence. George III set a precedent of filing charges and handing out sentences for seditious writing instead of executing offenders at will. In part, legal proceedings became necessary because his main attacker was another author-publisher, John Wilkes (1725-1797), who became the first elected Member of Parliament in 1757, three years before George III became king. Wilkes' case is detailed later in this section.

The sedition and free speech laws in the United States diverged from Britain after the Revolutionary War, when the freedom of speech was written into an American amendment. This positive change was soon followed by the American Sedition Act of 1798, which was not utilized in great force until the prosecutions between 1917 and 1920 against various American writers and publishers that brushed on sensitive World War I-related subjects. An earlier American case that demonstrates how American censorship laws differed while also mimicking Britain's comes from the first half of the nineteenth century. The Attorney of the Commonwealth explained the laws concerning censorship for blasphemy during the trial of Abner Kneeland in the Municipal and Supreme Courts in Boston in 1834, arguing that "no man shall in a scurrilous indecent, scandalous, obscene manner blasphemy God or the Christian Religion..."[57] The Attorney won the argument by pointing out that "our feelings" were "hurt by offensive and disgusting obscenity" and that such an offense was not protected by the "liberty of free discussion" because it was not "fair" or "sincere." He also argued

---

57   Samuel Dunn Parker. "Corruption of the Poor and Unlearned by Certain Opinions." Excerpt from *Report of the arguments of the attorney of the Commonwealth, at the trials of Abner Kneeland, for blasphemy: in the Municipal and Supreme Courts, in Boston, January and May, 1834. Versions of Censorship*. John McCormick and Mairi MacInnes, eds. (Garden City (NY): Anchor Books, 1962; 167-70), 167.

that Kneeland was not protected by "liberty of the Press" because it did not extend to "murder or assassination, for mischief or malice on persons or reputation." He went on to call an atheist or the "undevout" "mad" and a "fool," insisting that: "If they choose to believe nothing themselves, let them not deprive others of their heavenly hopes, let them not sap the foundations of morality and law…"[58] Attorney Parker spoke for days in a similar manner, so the full collection of this trial's speeches take up a lengthy book. One might imagine that Parker is referring to a staunch atheist that was decrying that God did not exist, but he is actually criticizing an evangelist theologian, who simply held some radical religious views for his time: supporting rights of women to divorce and to perform birth control, as well as abolition of slavery, and other human rights. Kneeland published the more moderate of his opinions in his own publications, thus entering this study's lengthy list of author-publishers. He began his publishing career by editing a Universalist magazine in Philadelphia in the early 1820s. Then, he managed and edited *Olive Branch and Christian Enquirer* in New York City in 1828, and finally founded *The Investigator* in Boston in 1832, the latter leading to his prosecution two years later, as he published the objectionable content in its pages in 1833. The trial dragged on for years and he finally had to serve sixty days in prison in 1838. This is only one trial of a little-known "obscene" American publisher, and many more will be detailed in sub-sections that follow.

Brief History of Major Relevant British Monarchs

This book frequently mentions George III, George IV, Victoria, and a few other monarchs in passing, so for the sake of clarity, some facts about their lives and possible motivations for censorship or for loosening censorship laws are necessary here.

There were a couple of assassination attempts against George III, and a successful assassination of his prime minister, Spencer Perceval, in 1812, which might have contributed to his slide towards insanity in the later part of his reign. A part of his style of insanity was his affinity for farming, which got him dubbed the Farmer King. He published two letters on January 1, 1787 and March 5, 1787 on Duckett's Husbandry in Arthur Young's pamphlet, *Annals of Agriculture*, under the pseudonym of Ralph Robinson of Windsor. The name might have

---

58   Ibid., 168-9.

been a mockery of his son, George IV's affair at sixteen in 1779 with an actress, Mary "Perdita" Robinson, as the breakup cost George III a great deal in hush money. "Probably the monarch would have yet further indulged his taste for journalistic composition had it not been for the castigation he received from Jeremy Bentham, about two years later, in the Public Advertiser."[59] George III's greatest accomplishment was failing to suppress the tide of radical publications, presses, opinions and revolutions, while still managing to keep the British monarchy intact. George III's mysterious madness also has a lot of parallels with Byron's strange decline at the end of his life. It took a particularly odd turn in 1788 when the King tossed his son, the Prince of Wales, and later King George IV, into a wall during dinner. George IV used this violent outburst to medically torture and eventually permanently commit his father. Just as with Byron, George III was subjected to "bleeding, blistering, purging, and sedating," and he was additionally left in an unheated room in winter, which might have aggravated his ailments. Then, just as with Byron, a new doctor entered the scene and intensified the tortures. Dr. John Willis "put him in a straitjacket or had him tied to a chair and gagged" whenever he was not cooperative, in other words, when he refused to take a rainbow of drugs, bleedings and other nightmarish treatments being prescribed. George III was thus treated until 1789, all the while, his son, George IV, was attempting to declare him unfit to rule to take over the throne without waiting for George III's death. George IV wanted to take over primarily to be free of his father's nagging about his countless affairs, uncontrolled luxury spending and eating, and various other vices. One of the restrictions that particularly pained George IV was when George III created the Royal Marriages Act in 1772 that voided any marriage that George IV entered into before he turned twenty-five in 1787, leading to the voiding of George IV's first marriage in 1785 to Maria Fitzherbert, twice-widow, Catholic and commoner who he had threatened to kill himself over. It is hardly a coincidence that George III's madness started immediately after George IV came of age in 1787, and at a time when he was forcing him out of a marriage that he was passionate about. When the "madness" temporarily eased, George III forced George IV to marry a "proper" wife in 1795, Princess Caroline of Brunswick, but

---

59 "Literature: Catalogue of the Smithfield Club Cattle Show." *The Athenaeum*. (N. 1728. Saturday, December 8, 1800. London: British Periodical Limited, 1860; Web), 783.

she was so ugly, fat and smelly, that after she conceived their only child on their wedding night, the two separated and did not have further intercourse. Meanwhile, Mrs. Fitzherbert moved back in with George IV in 1800. Then in 1804, George IV lost custody of his only legitimate child, Charlotte, to George III. The custody battle must have pressured George IV to resume the attacks on his father's mental health. Two other treatment periods followed for George III in 1804 and 1810, the last one finally gave George IV the power of sovereignty in 1811, allowing him to permanently confine and restrain George III in Windsor Castle for the remainder of his blinded and deafened, torturous life. Meanwhile, George IV also attempted to incarcerate his legal wife, Caroline, in 1806 under the charges that she was the mother of one of the orphans under her care, a charge that was dismissed as unfounded. George IV tried to file charges against Caroline again in 1820 after becoming the monarch via the Bill of Pains and Penalties, when Caroline insisted on returning to Britain to rule by his side after years on a grand European tour, and a likely affair with an Italian; but she was again exonerated, before mysteriously dying a year later right after George IV's coronation, supposedly from an "inflammation of the bowels." Meanwhile, George III only started seeing hallucinations and talking with dead people during this latter period, when he was probably given a psychedelic cocktail of drugs that induced these delusions. Recent tests have proven that George III was suffering from extremely severe and prolonged lead and arsenic poisonings by the time he died. Researchers concluded that arsenic was present in the emetic tartar, the "medicine" that George III so violently resisted taking.[60] After thus maliciously gaining the crown, George IV focused on rebuilding London and his palaces, while his generals fought in the Napoleonic War. As George III probably feared, George IV's over-spending in a time of need led to a clash with the radical politicians, the press and that populace that was more violent than in the first decades of George III's reign. George IV responded to an appeal from manufacturers in 1816 with the Green-Bag inquiry in 1817, wherein "secret committees looked into a number of alleged cases of sedition." Then, *habeas corpus* was suspended. When an 1819 public meeting in Manchester was violently dispersed, leaving eleven dead, this catastrophe was used to officially outlaw all public assemblies. In response to this type of suppression, radicals un-

---

60   Ed Crews. "The Poisoning of King George III." *Colonial Williamsburg Journal*. (Spring 2010. Retrieved: 29 May 2016; Web).

dertook the Cato Street Conspiracy, an elaborate plot to assassinate the members of the Cabinet and to overthrow George IV just as he was officially named King in 1820.[61] In 1821, weeks after his wife's suspect death, George IV received an invitation to visit Scotland from Sir Walter Scott and went on his famous tour of that country and Ireland, becoming the first Hanoverian to risk entering those rebellious, Jacobite lands. The meeting with Scott might have created stereotypes that appear in popular culture to this day about Scotland, but it did not convince George IV to give way to reform (even if Scott and his Scottish nationalist friends were brave enough to ask for it). George IV did his best to stifle liberal progress across the following decade.

These disastrous reigns were followed by William IV (1830-1837), who gradually worked his way up the ranks of the Navy from the lowest able seaman, when he was fourteen, to Rear Admiral of HMS *Valiant* in 1788. He then became a duke, attended the House of the Lords, and then became the Admiral of the Fleet in 1811. William IV was George III's third son and only married after he got the surprise that George IV's daughter had died and that he was next in line to the throne. He was carrying on an affair with an actress for a couple of decades up through 1811. William IV is known for lobbying for the Reform Bill in 1832 and helping its passage after decades of failure. He also oversaw the Factory Act's abolition of child labor and the Abolition Act's emancipation of slaves in the British colonies. On the other hand, William IV also supervised the shipping of Tolpuddle Martyrs to Australia for holding a trade union meeting of agricultural workers in 1834. He also spent the bulk of his reign actively fighting against the growing Chartist unrest. Thus, Britain saw an odd mix of radical reforms and conservative suppressions under William IV.

Queen Victoria was the result of her father's, another of George III's sons, late marriage. These late nuptials also followed the news of Charlotte's death. The United Kingdom lost the Kingdom of Hanover, when Victoria took the throne because under Salic Law women could not rule in Hanover. Victoria was only eighteen at the start of her reign in 1837, and she was following on the heels of three tyrannical kings. Perhaps anticipating the worst from her, there were three assassination attempts in the first four years of her reign in 1840 and 1842. Victoria

---

61   Mike Ashley. *A Brief History of British Kings & Queens: British Royal History from Alfred the Great to the Present.* (New York: Carroll & Graf Publishers, 2002), 368-9.

appointed Melbourne as her Prime Minister. Curiously, Melbourne's wife, Lady Caroline Lamb, had the affair with Lord Byron decades earlier that might have caused Byron's break with the monarchy, and left Melbourne distraught after it became public knowledge. Meanwhile, Victoria proposed marriage to Albert in 1840 and the two had a happier marriage than her processors. Perhaps because of its length, Victoria's reign saw several reforms, such as the Education Act of 1870, public health acts, and the investment by the monarchy in technology via the Great Exhibition, or the first World Fair. Victoria was isolationist and pacifist and traveled across Europe to help negotiate peace deals. Albert died young of mysterious causes in 1861, after having a hand in the preceding reforms. Victoria's reign was one of colonial expansion, as she became Empress of India in 1876, just as her predecessor gained control over Australia. Victoria also successfully opposed in 1886 and 1893 the restoration of the Irish parliament that had been repealed in 1800 by the Act of Union. She had many legitimate children, grandchildren and grand-grandchildren that took thrones in Russia, Prussia, Romania and elsewhere before her death in 1901.

The details of these British monarchs' struggles with assassinations, rebellions and the power of the people and the press helps to explain many of the odd turns in the lives and businesses of author-publishers that worked under their reigns.

Galileo and Illegal Knowledge

One of the best-known and least understood censorship trials is Galileo's in Rome. Galileo endured decades of censorship by the Church from 1610 until a final judgment was issued in 1633 over his various radical publications about the planets, the tides, the moon and the relationship between the earth and the sun. The argument against Galileo, made by the Inquisition, shows the type of censorship scientists were facing in Italy that prevented them from advancing various fields across centuries of suppression. The book that the Inquisition finally banned because it was "contrary to divine Scripture" was *Dialogue of Galileo Galilei on the Great World Systems*, written and published by Galileo, which argued that the earth revolved around the sun and not the other way around.[62] He was accused of arguing for his theorem's

---

62   Inquisitors-General. "The Condemnation and Recantation of Galileo." (1633). *Versions of Censorship*. John McCormick and Mairi MacInnes, eds. (Garden

"probability" despite being advised that it was "heresy." The book was "prohibited by public edict," and he was sentenced to the prison of the Holy Office, and to repeat once a week for three years "the seven penitential Psalms."[63]

At twenty-five, after studying at the University of Pisa, Galileo became a professor of mathematics there in 1589. It was during these years when Galileo first started experimenting with throwing objects of different weights off heights, and started, but abandoned, writing *On Motion*. By the time his first three-year contract was about to expire in 1591, he barely enjoyed working for the school as the salary was low and further "reduced by fines for missing lectures and for failing to wear the required academic dress, the toga." To the latter he responded by writing a satirical poem, "Against the Wearing of the Gown," making an early, somewhat atheist statement that proposed that nudity was applauded in the Bible.[64] Galileo found a new teaching position for the University of Padua, and stayed there between 1592 and 1610. These years were noted by Galileo as some of his most productive in terms of scientific research, but he published near nothing across them, just a pamphlet, *The Starry Messenger* (illustrated observations through a telescope of the topography of the moon and stars), a privately printed instruction manual, and a few other minor pieces. His father died back in 1591, leaving him with a debt for his sister Virginia's dowry, for which he was sued by her husband's family in 1605, so that a great deal of his salary was going towards paying off this burden. He taught private lessons and took on boarders to "triple" his salary to stay afloat. In 1610, he moved for a better job, "the world's first research professorship," to Florence,[65] and there his financial problems stopped, and his leisurely radical publications began. 1610 was a turning year for Galileo because *The Starry Messenger* was an immediate success, selling the first edition of 550 copies within a week of the March 13 release, so that: "Galileo, who was supposed to get thirty free copies of the book, received only six because the book sold out so quickly: the printer could offer him only copies to which the illustrations had never been added, but these he rejected."[66] It was a sensation because it was the

City (NY): Anchor Books, 1962), 58.
63   Ibid., 59-61.
64   David Wootton. *Galileo: Watcher of the Skies*. (New Haven: Yale University Press, 2010), 46-8.
65   Ibid., 106.
66   Ibid., 105.

first book full of etchings based on observations through a telescope, and contained images and ideas that were entirely revolutionary in the scientific field. For this reason and because his drawings represented an imperfect moon that contradicted the Church's teachings on the perfect universe, Galileo's clash with the Church began at the same time as his fame spread. It was published in the Republic of Venice by Thomas Baglioni in New Latin. After his first publishing success, Galileo wrote a steady stream of books, but took a hiatus from these ventures between 1626 and 1629, only resuming work after a near-fatal illness. The new book, *Dialogue*, was finished by April 1630, when Galileo took a trip to Rome to "make arrangements for publication with Father Monster."[67] This trip was no tourist excursion, as Galileo had to endure great obstacles to receive permission to publish it, beyond his audience with the Pope. Wootton summarizes that: "There were three people Galileo had to convince in order to obtain permission to publish. First there was the cardinal nephew, Francesco Barberini…" Galileo explained to Barberini his "theory of the tides," which were caused by the movement of the earth, but Barberini asked if the earth's movement meant it was a star, so now Galileo had the arduous task of proving that the earth was not a star to keep the book from being branded as blasphemous. Galileo also had to convince Raffaello Visconti, with whom he had several conversations to offer evidence Visconti could take to the Pope, who was the final authority that had to be assured that the "theory of the tides" was not blasphemous.[68] All three eventually gave their agreement, but Galileo inserted a fourth voice, that of an anonymous commentator, likely Nicolaus Copernicus or Galileo himself, into the text that none of the censors screened, and this fourth voice offered the radical scientific argument that was used as evidence against Galileo at his later trial. When Prince Cesi died on August 1, 1630, Galileo was deprived of a patron who had agreed to supervise the publication of the book, and was advised to try publishing it in Florence, but he lacked confidence in the quality of Florentine printers. His inquiries about printing in Venice fell through because of a plague and a war, so he was stuck with Florence, and oddly enough the authorities in that city rushed through the approval process and "granted an imprimatur." While the book was being shabbily prepared for publica-

---

67   Ibid., 192.
68   Ibid., 196.

tion, he moved on to writing his next book.[69] Galileo even chose his own censor in Florence, Giacinto Stefani, who "wept" at the concessions Galileo had to make to appease the Church, but the Florentine inquisitor also had to receive letters of support from the grand duke and others before he finally gave consent on July 19, and the printer started the printing.[70] The publication was only completed on February 21, 1632, and due to measures taken against the plague, the first two copies only arrived in Rome in May, with six more coming in July. Thus, it was only in July when the authorities in Rome began research with the intent to turn the book over to the Inquisition. Because the Pope prevented the book's publication in Rome after giving the author some hope, he was adamant about now not simply banning the book, but also suing Galileo for heresy. Despite his age and infirmity, he was required to report to Rome for the trial. He departed Florence on January 20, 1633. He reported to the Inquisition on April 12 and was held there until April 30. Under the threat of torture, and seriously ill due to the poor living conditions, Galileo was insisting that the book had been legally approved by censors and was not heresy, but when pressed harder, he agreed to plead guilty and did so in court, after which he was released on April 30 to the Florentine ambassador, spending another couple of months in "limbo," awaiting a verdict in his case, while he continued to appear before the Congregation on May 10, and then before the Inquisition on June 21 for interrogations. At these, he had to deny his commitment to Copernicanism. His confession was clearly not complete, so he was held overnight, and appeared before the Inquisition again on the next day, when he was "declared guilty of having given grounds for vehement suspicion of having held Copernican doctrines and of thus being guilty of heresy." For this charge, he "was sentenced to the prisons of the Holy Office at the pleasure of the pope," but then on June 30, Galileo was allowed to travel to Siena to be put under house arrest "by his friend the archbishop." He arrived at the palace on July 9, and at this point, his situation eased as the archbishop fed him the best foods and wines, so that he put on some weight. Since reports reached Rome that the archbishop was openly defending Galileo, the Pope decided to end his confinement in that abode and allowed him to return to his own home in Florence, where he arrived on December 17, 1633, and remained in a more lenient home arrest,

---

69   Ibid., 197-200.
70   Ibid., 206-7.

wherein he could travel to Florence and Rome for consultations and the like. In 1636, Galileo arranged for the translation and publication of his complete works in Holland, with the exclusion of the *Dialogue*. Across this process and in his other communications he was very careful as to what he wrote because he was certain his letters were being intercepted by the Church.[71] While Galileo was on trial, work began on a Latin translation of the *Dialogue*, without his knowledge, and it was published in Strasbourg in 1635. So, when Galileo finally returned to completing and publishing a book he had started back in 1609, *Two New Sciences*, he discovered that Florentine, Venetian and other publishers he usually dealt with near Rome were all told they could not publish anything by Galileo. So, he turned to the Dutch firm of Elsevier that had sneakily released the unapproved version of *Dialogue*.[72] In most of his publications, Galileo acted as the publisher, creating illustrations, finding editors and government approval for his releases, rather than relying on the printers, who merely performed the technical work associated with the printing. There were hardly any publishers, in the sense this term is used today, at that early stage of printing, unless they were branches of the Church or the monarch. Any independent, radical or innovative ideas could only be self-published, and only with an enormous effort on the part of the author, and at the risk of imprisonment or execution.

Milton and the Illegality of Publishing in Support of Divorce

Just as Galileo's ordeal ended in Italy, John Milton's struggles were beginning in England. The first major objections to the 1643 "Order for the Regulating of Printing," which required licensing and entry of all books into the Stationers' Register, came from Milton. He wrote a work that is frequently quoted in philosophical discussions of censorship, *Areopagitica* (1644). Milton argued that Books may indeed have the power to "spring up armed men," but at the same time, "hee who destroyes a good Booke, kills reason it selfe" or "life beyond life," slaying "an immortality rather then a life…"[73] A notion of Milton's that has been repeated in many later censorships on the grounds of morality arguments is the distinction between material things that are

---

71 Ibid., 218-27.
72 Ibid., 229-30.
73 McCormick, *Versions*, 9.

factually bad for a person's health, and fictitious bad characters and ideas that can improve the reader's morality when they are described in a published book. "Bad meats will scarce breed good nourishment in the healthiest concoction; but herein the difference is of bad books, that they to a discreet and judicious Reader serve in many respects to discover, to confute, to forewarn, and to illustrate…"[74] Milton particularly objected that the process of banning books could not be random or based on individual preferences of poorly educated, overworked, unpublished, and otherwise unfit "readers" of the "huge volumes" of published books.[75] Milton further implored that a writer puts in an enormous effort "in the deep mines of knowledge" to create the best possible books, so it is "but weakness and cowardice in the wars of Truth" for the licensor to forbid the output to be published without even offering a strong argument against it.[76]

Milton was passionately anti-censorship by 1644 because a year earlier, on August 1, 1643, he published, *The Doctine and Discipline of Divorce: Restor'd to the Good of Both Sexes, From the bondage of Canon Law, and other mistakes, to Christian freedom, guided by the Rule of Charity, Wherein also many places of Scripture, have recover'd their long-lost meaning: seasonable to be now thought on in the Reformation intended*. It was one of a series of pamphlets Milton published on behalf of divorce, after leaving his own wife not long after their marriage. There were some threats of political retribution and some vigorous anti-divorce replies in print in response to this pamphlet. Perhaps because of the controversy, it was successful and saw four editions that were all promptly consumed, making it "easily the most successful in terms of readership of his early prose works."[77]

While most of Milton's early political pamphlets were privately printed and distributed to his political and literary friends, when Milton prepared his first major literary manuscript in 1645, he started working with publishers that could help him distribute his work to a wider audience. He toiled with Henry Lawes on printing, *A Maske Presented At Ludlow Castle, 1634*. He then worked with a bookseller, Humphrey Moseley, to distribute the collection he pulled together

---

74   Ibid., 11.
75   Ibid., 19.
76   Ibid., 31.
77   Gordon Campbell and Thomas N. Corns. *John Milton: Life, Work, and Thought*. (Oxford: Oxford University Press, 2008), 164.

himself, *Poems of Mr. John Milton, Both English and Latin, Compos'd at several times*. Moseley collaborated with Milton by approving the inclusion of an insult ("rotten artist"), which was directed at the anti-radical engraver of the front-piece, William Marshall. These words were engraved in Latin, so that he copied them without understanding their meaning. Moseley was growing into an established publisher by 1645, and specialized in royalist writers, publishing Fletcher, Jonson, Webster, and Davenant, so his willingness to publish a radical like Milton was due primarily to the quality of his poetry. Moseley solicited the poems that Milton had kept private for a decade. This prompting made Milton realize that he had to release a piece of "cultural history" if he was going to be perceived as more than a radical pamphleteer. Moseley later published Milton's sonnets in *Choice Psalmes Put into Musick*, a collection oddly prefaced with a portrait and dedication to the king.[78] Moseley died in 1661. Then, his wife ran his publishing business until 1664, with Milton printing with Mrs. Moseley intermittently until the end.[79]

After the purging of the Long Parliament and the trial and execution of Charles I, the new government nominated John Milton to serve as the Secretary of Foreign Tongues, a position he held between 1649 and 1653. He must have accepted the role expecting that the British monarchy would radicalize after the execution of a king, but instead the job forced him into an authoritarian role that he had opposed in his radical writings. The Bradshaw's Press Act was enacted in the year Milton took office, and it guaranteed that licensing books was "no longer required," but newspapers and political pamphlets still had to be submitted for licensing. One of Milton's duties was "searching for subversive papers." On October 24, 1649, "he was ordered (together with Edward Dendy) to seize the papers of the dissident pamphleteer Clement Walker and prepare a report for the Council," then on June 25, 1650, he "was issued with a search warrant and ordered to search the Lincoln's Inn rooms of William Prynne, who remained actively engaged in opposing the effects of Pride's Purge. He was an old adversary of Milton's, and had himself relished searching the papers of William Laud in preparation for the archbishop's trial…" On May 30, 1649, Milton examined "the papers of John Ley, who was arrested on suspicion of dealing with an enemy of the state," and then on June 11, he

---

[78] Ibid., 181-4.
[79] Ibid., 332.

did the same for William Small, "who was arrested for corresponding with an enemy of the state." Then he had to examine "the papers of Pragmaticus," or the *Mercurius Pragmaticus,* a royalist newspaper edited by Marchamont Nedham, with whom Milton later became friends. Under the pressure of examining all of these innocuous parties, John Milton licensed the English version of the radical, Polish manifesto, *Racovian Catechism*, in 1652. Parliament started an enquiry and the printer, Dugard, pointed the finger at Milton, who was then called to make a statement, wherein he "admitted licensing" it, and offered "the principles articulated" in his earlier treatise, *Areopagitica*, as a defense. While Milton's defense cleared him of criminal wrong-doing, he lost his licensing position because of the stand he took. Another contributing factor to his termination was his complete loss of eyesight by the end of this period.[80] Milton retained a minor civil service position and carried out his duties, even despite the 1653 coup, the imprisonment and trial of Sir Henry Vane in 1656, and through Cromwell's naming of a successor. In these later years, Milton barely complained about the turmoil or who was the ruler of the day. Milton was in part pleased with some of the unraveling changes, including the freedoms of the press that came with the Instrument law in 1653, wherein the government started to separate from the church, so that among other things, church attendance was no longer mandatory. More importantly, the new law meant that "the right to publish heterodox views… was taken completely outside the authority of the civil magistrate," thus allowing future writers hope that their radical opinions will not be censored.[81]

Milton's *Paradise Lost* came out of this blind period, when he finally had the time to write a poetic epic, as his political duties were diminished. The publication was a difficult undertaking because Moseley was dead by then. A disaster had also struck the publishing industry. Most booksellers and printers were in chaos after an enormous stockpile of printing materials was destroyed in a fire in St Faith's church, where they were kept, an estimated value of these was £150,000 to £200,000. "It made the press harder to control, since booksellers and printers could set up in improvised premises." Milton entered into a contract on April 27, 1667 with Samuel Simmons, one of the few surviving printers, who lived on Albersgate Street, nearby Milton's home. Samuel's father, Matthew Simmons, had printed Milton's early tracts

---

80   Ibid., 245-8.
81   Ibid., 254.

back in 1649. Their politics were a match for Milton as both father and son Simmons were Independent republicans. Campbell is careful to guess that it is likely that Matthew Simmons "was the printer of *Areopagitica, Of Education, Tetrachordon,* and *Colasterion,*" but this is not known with certainty because a printer typically did not confess his contribution to these types of radical, censorable tracts in this turbulent period. Upon Matthew's death in 1654, his widow, Mary, "continued the business, and was joined by their son, Samuel, whose name appears on the imprints from 1662 onwards." *Paradise Lost* was the first title Samuel "entered under his own name in the Stationers' Register." The contract between Samuel and Milton was for a £5 advance in exchange for Milton's "executors and assignees, the copy of his poem, 'now lately Licensed to be printed,' with all benefit accruing from it, with the right to all future editions," and if more than 1,300 copies sold, Milton would make another £5, this sum going up to £20 if many more copies sold. Samuel applied for copyrights and carried the manuscript through the censorship process for Milton. Censorship was ripe in this period, but temporarily deactivated after the fire, so that, surprisingly, Roger L'Estrange, the Surveyor of the Press, and his emissary, Thomas Tomkins, who had power to censor through the Licensing Act of 1662, cleared Milton's relatively radical, religious poem. While in the nineteenth century authors and publishers who were censored might have been temporarily imprisoned, during the 1660s, some of them were "executed" and "political activists mistrusted by the state were imprisoned or killed" without charges. Milton was allowed to make more radical, liberal and reformist statements in his creative writing than in his political essays that would have been more severally censored. With Samuel's help, and because there were fewer books in circulation at the major booksellers, *Paradise Lost* became a popular success, and established Milton as a major poetic voice.[82]

Milton's struggle is an example of how an author-publisher can maintain integrity of ideas while working from the inside the censorship operates. Milton gained a powerful political position with the help of his self-published pamphlets that established him as one of the top political philosophers and practitioners of his day. Much of modern western culture is built on top of Milton's pamphlets and poetry, so this foundation would have been lost if Milton was shamed out of sponsoring his own innovative publications.

---

82   Ibid., 332-7.

Spinoza's Censored Attack on Censorship

Another earlier defense of free expression was made by Benedict de Spinoza, a Jewish philosopher, in 1670 in the Netherlands, shortly before his death. Spinoza's banned *Tractatus Theologico-Politicus* was not immediately outlawed because it was published anonymously, with even the printer's name disguised and with Latin text on the front page to fool the censors. In it, Spinoza argued that "the real disrupters are those who condemn the writers of others, and seditiously incite the insolent mob against their authors, rather than the authors themselves, who generally write for the learned only, appealing to reason alone; and furthermore, that the real disturbers of peace are those who seek to abolish freedom of judgment in a free state, although it cannot be suppressed." He went on to develop a concept that writers like Scott and Dickens put into practice in their rebellion novels. Spinoza argued that when "good men" are punished, they become martyrs, and their suffering provokes the rest to rebel because they are moved to "pity, if not to vengeance." Dickens, Scott and other writers used this philosophical idea to powerful effects in their fiction. Dickens' *A Tale of Two Cities* and Scott's *Waverley* shows French Revolutionaries and Scottish Jacobites rebelling and suffering in martyrdom, thus prompting readers so sympathize with their causes. Spinoza summed up that the sovereign should be able to control "actions alone," and not what people "think" or "say."[83] Today this is a commonly accepted idea, but the freedom of thought and the written word was under threat when Spinoza made this declaration.

Wilkes and the Censorship of Radical Propaganda

A century after John Milton managed to publish numerous radical pamphlets without serving a day in jail, England regressed to much harsher censorships when it was faced with its first major democratically elected politician, John Wilkes. Alongside publicly supporting the American War of Independence and the protests that led to St. George's Fields Massacre, Wilkes started a radical weekly periodical, *The North*

---

83   Benedict de Spinoza. *Tractatus Theologico-Politicus*. (1670). *Versions of Censorship*. John McCormick and Mairi MacInnes, eds. (Garden City (NY): Anchor Books, 1962; 75-84), 82-4.

Briton, and used it to attack Whigs, the monarchy, aristocrats, and George III. As the only elected Member of Parliament, Wilkes could not get much done there without also soliciting public support for his campaigns through the press. Predictably, when Wilkes attacked George III's speech on behalf of the Paris Peace Treaty of 1764, he (together with forty-eight other people involved with the publication of his paper) were charged with seditious libel.

John Wilkes first made a leap out of his middle-class upbringing in the spring of 1757, when he ran for the House of Commons seat at Aylesbury. There were around four hundred eligible, landed voters in this district and Wilkes canvassed each of them. He discovered that the votes of the richest in the area counted more heavily than of those who rented smaller parcels of land from them because: "voting was not secret, and to vote against one's landlord was to risk one's livelihood." In addition, votes typically went to whoever could "pay the most," with the price range being £1-5. Wilkes explained in a letter to Dell, one of his supporters, that he was competing with the other candidate, Mr. Willes, and kept having to offer more, with the price of "lends… to the poor" or bribery possibly going up to £8 per head, before Willes withdrew from the race, and Wilkes won uncontested. He had already borrowed £500 to pay for early supporters, a sum that increased "fourfold" in the following twelve years.[84] Byron did not have to deal with this problem because he took his family's seat in the House of Lords. But, this is the sort of corruption that everybody that sought an election to the House of Commons had to face, even before they entered the chambers. Thus, what's unusual here is that once elected, Wilkes used this office for his radical agenda, rather than to recuperate the election losses by taking advantage of the post to bribe others for favors.

It was five years into holding a seat in the Commons, in 1762, when Wilkes realized that he could accomplish little without making himself heard in the press. "Both weeklies and dailies were thought to have a great impact upon politics, and some of them certainly did. So, politicians financed the papers that supported them and sometimes launched new ones."[85] Wilkes' politics were unlike those of his competitors in that he was against corruption and favoritism, spread by the bulk of politicians who were buying shares in the press. One of his

---

[84] Arthur H. Cash. *John Wilkes: The Scandalous Father of Civil Liberty*. (New Haven: Yale University Press, 2006), 45-6.
[85] Ibid., 67.

earliest political essays was the anonymous piece in the *Monitor*, in which he berated "favorites," proclaiming that they had an undue share of power by influencing the actions of the monarch, implying the tutorship of Lord Bute (or John Stuart, close relative of the pretender who still lived in Rome after his failed Jacobite Rebellion of 1745) over George III. Days after the essay appeared, Bute was promoted to "first minister as first lord of the treasury," and used his new power and wealth to found a new paper, the *Briton*. A month later, Bute used the first issue to poke fun at Wilkes' essay. Meanwhile, Wilkes released the first issue of his own paper, the *North Briton*, on the same day as the *Briton* was issued, June 5, 1762, certainly aware in advance that the *Briton* would satirize him, and intending to counteract this by fighting back not through a few *Monitor* articles, but with the breadth of a paper of his own, one of which he was the primary author and editor, despite leaving these credits out to avoid prosecution.[86] The first issue of the *North Briton* explained that its purpose was to fight for a free press, uncorrupted by "ministers." These types of bold statements meant that if he had put his name on the paper, "he would have been arrested after the second issue." Thus, he kept the secret long after his authorship was popularly known, only admitting, in the end, that he wrote three of the issues, rather than all of them.[87] The only difference between Wilkes' and Benjamin Franklin's journals, and similarity with Byron's, was that Wilkes worked through an outside publisher, George Kearsley, a bookseller with a shop in Ludgate Hill, printing the journal with William Richardson in his Salisbury Court print shop. Wilkes could not have entirely self-published his periodical not only because he would have had to put his name on the publication, but also because he did not have the money, experience or the time necessary to run a printing press. Wilkes was in debt, and could not independently finance the venture, so money came in from wealthy sponsors, such as Lord Temple, and the dukes of Devonshire, Newcastle and Portland. It was unlikely that the radical paper could recuperate costs from sales alone. The slow sales were due in part to the journal's primary buying audience being a few coffee shop proprietors and landowners, who passed it around to their visitors for free. Wilkes held a small share of the paper at the start, which he later sold to Churchill. The printer used a boy who pulled a lever to imprint an eight page, which was hand-

---

86 Ibid., 67-8.
87 Ibid., 69.

sewn together into a folio, with around a thousand copies per printing. Cash explains that in those early days, "libel" suits only had to prove authorship, while the falsehood component was not significant, as only the damages to the government (or its officials) had to be proven, and the government chose what was damaging to its public image, and therefore not "permissible" in print.[88] Wilkes later took on an editor, Churchill, who wrote "at least five" of the forty-six issues, and helped Wilkes deliver content so that he did not have to turn up at the publisher's office himself. Soon after the release of the first *North Briton*, Bute had enough funds to sponsor a second periodical, the *Auditor*, hiring Arthur Murphy to write and edit it. Both of Bute's papers were unpopular because they primarily defended his actions against Wilkes', as well as defending Bute from other accusations, selling around 250 copies each.[89] One of Wilkes rebukes was against clannish Scots who offered jobs and other favors to their countrymen. Wilkes argued that the Scots' corruption started when chiefs were paid after the 1712 and 1745 rebellions to stop their protestations. This sentiment won Wilkes a lot of hatred in Scotland.[90] In turn, because Wilkes was the best-known radical of the century, his stand on Scots might have contributed to the uncharacteristic anti-reformist position that Sir Walter Scott later took, while he was advocating rebellion and human rights in his novels. Wilkes' issue No. 5 suggested, with a story of Edward III, that Lord Bute was George III's mother's lover, leading Churchill to warn Wilkes that he might be "arrested" or "assassinated," though neither happened immediately thereafter.[91] The *Auditor* responded by publishing a story that Wilkes supposedly threatened Bute's son, saying that his father would have his "head cut off" numerous times until the boy ran off crying. Wilkes protested in response that no such incident ever occurred and attempted to meet with this boy to prove it.[92] Wilkes further fired back by submitting a letter to the *Auditor* signed, Viator, which described fictitious conditions of living in Florida, where "peat fires" are set to fight the cold. This story was printed as reliable fact by Murphy, who was then "roasted" by Bonnell Thornton in his *St. James's Chronicle*, wherein he objected that with Florida's unbearable heat-

---

88   Ibid., 70.
89   Ibid., 72.
90   Ibid., 73.
91   Ibid., 74.
92   Ibid., 76-7.

wave the need for "peat" fires was obviously erroneous. Apparently, discovering that the editor was so ignorant that he was printing obvious falsehoods lost a significant portion of the *Auditor's* already small subscription, and it closed two weeks later, followed days thereafter by the closure of the *Briton*.[93] The *North Briton* stayed active, publishing an exposé on "embezzlement in the army" (supported by letters and other documentary evidence leaked to Wilkes by insider sources) in issue No. 40, and various other attacks on Lord Bute. Meanwhile, it praised Mr. Pitt because he was the man Wilkes hoped would regain power, bringing him up the ranks as well.[94] Things started to take a dramatic turn when the first earl of Talbot was satirized for showing his "rump to the king" during a strenuous exercise on his horse in the coronation, in issue No. 12. Talbot demanded to know if Wilkes wrote the satire, and Wilkes refused to deny or confirm the accusation, so that Talbot suggested a duel, and one was fought on October 5, 1762, wherein both missed or fired into the air, and then got drunk together in a tavern.[95] Sadly, to convince Talbot to seize the fight, Wilkes had to admit his authorship, and this later led to a threat of prosecution by another satirized party, Lord Litchfield, who was now finally able to name Wilkes as the guilty party in a suit, but chose to drop it.[96] Then on November 6, Bute had Lord Halifax issue warrants for the arrest of Arthur Beardmore and John Entick, as authors of the rival *Monitor* paper, causing £2,000 in damages during the search of their printing house. It was a ploy to keep the *Monitor* out of commission while a peace treaty was discussed in Parliament. The ploy worked, as it did keep the *Monitor* closed for two weeks. When it resumed, since the authors were not indicted, and they managed to print a couple of issues before the debate was closed. Afterward, on Wilkes' solicitation, Entick filed a lawsuit against the illegality of "the search warrant" and an unfair search and seizure, winning in a settlement eight years later. While this should have set a precedent, other than Wilkes' later lawsuits, no similar countersuits were filed by other publishers or authors unfairly searched or arrested in this study. Meanwhile, the *Monitor's* and the *North Briton's* correspondences were opened and monitored with "King

---

93   Ibid., 77.
94   Ibid., 79-80.
95   Ibid., 81-4.
96   Ibid., 85.

George's specific approval."[97] On November 18, warrants were issued for the arrest of the "Authors, Printers, and Publishers" of the *North Briton*, against issues Nos. 1-26, but these were never executed and instead they were only shown to the vetting bookseller, William Johnston, and to the printer, William Richardson. The threat of being charged with libel made them both quit on the spot. Only the publisher, Kearsley, agreed to continue under Churchill's solicitation and because he was not directly threatened by the authorities. Wilkes immediately found a new printer in a friend of his, Dryden Leach, who was able to print issue No. 26 on time. "Then the king's messengers got to Leach's men," so that Leach was so frightened that he refused to print any more issues.[98] This time, Kearsley found a new printer in Richard Balfe, "a very poor printer who worked up two pairs of stairs in an alehouse in the Old Bailey," and it was he who kept printing the paper up until No. 45.[99] At this point, Bute decided to offer what Wilkes had initially wanted through his emissary, Henry Fox, the post of "the paymaster of the armed forces," or the governorship of Canada, but considering the number of lawsuits filed, a duel and the other obstacles Wilkes had overcome to keep his paper in print up to that point, Wilkes now refused to give into "bribes" and did not accept a post. Then the king and Bute made Fox the "cabinet councilor and his Majesty's minister in the House of Commons," and in this position, he set about bribing its members with "places in the government, commissions in the military, or chairs in the universities," or just "money," all to seal consent for the king's peace treaty. Despite suffering from the gout, Pitt made a four-hour speech to stop this crooked peace treaty, so that he had to be carried out in pain when he was done, but this "did not change a single vote," and the treaty passed 227 to 63. Fox then fired everybody who voted against the Peace of Paris treaty from their government posts. Unperturbed, Wilkes issued No. 38, after the Peace of Paris was signed on February 10, 1763. No. 38 included a satirical letter that was supposedly written by King James, the pretender, to congratulate his cousin on his success, and to suggest that the Jacobites would surely soon take the British throne. This upset King George so much that he was now ready to see Wilkes immediately arrested, but

---

97   Cash, *John*, 88.
98   "State of Facts: Wilkes against the Earl of Halifax." (Public Record Office, TS.II/1027/4317. ff, 4-25), 131.
99   Cash, *John*, 89.

Charles Yorke, the attorney general, interceded. On March 8, Wilkes received a new bribe offer from Lord Sandwich who proposed to secure a position for him as one of the directors of the East India Company, a post that was likely to lead to great riches, but Wilkes once again refused.[100] On April 11, Bute finally resigned, and the *North Briton* was put on hold since its chief purpose of seeing Bute's resignation was achieved, but then news reached Wilkes that Bute was staying behind the curtain in the King's office, and another corrupted official, George Grenville, was taking Bute's old job (instead of Pitt). So, No. 45 had to be released on April 23, 1763, and this was the issue that finally toppled the king's patience, though it was a natural progression from those that came before it. It simply had less sarcasm and stronger direct accusations against the king for relying too heavily on the flawed opinions of his ministers, and against the ministers for lacking the fortitude to stand up to the king. The bit that made the accusations more sinister was an extremist call to arms in rebellion: "when they are oppressed… that… *spirit of liberty* ought then to arise, and I am sure ever will, on proportion to the weight of the grievance they feel…"[101] Just as in Byron's case, the obstacle to arresting Wilkes for his radical writing with "political reasons" was "parliamentary privilege." As a member of parliament, Wilkes could express his political opinions in print with three exceptions being cases where he might have been guilty of "a felony, a breach of the peace (raising a riot), or treason." In the *North Briton* case, the latter was cited in the warrant issued for their arrest on April 26, which specified G. Kearsley as the printer, but left the names of the "Authors, Printers & Publishers" unfilled, leaving it for executors of the warrant to decide who they were.[102] The hired messengers "broke into Leach's house," though he was the old printer and not the current one, and arrested "all the journeymen printers and servants they could find… some twenty in number," and then kept them under guard in an alehouse for twelve hours. Then, they arrested George Kearsley, the publisher, with his servants, keeping him prisoner in one of the messenger's houses. These types of accommodations were the standard <u>temporary jails</u> in those days. Instead of fleeing the country, or hiding

100 Ibid., 90-5.
101 Earl Temple. *A Dissection of the North Briton, Number XLV. [by John Wilkes], paragraph by paragraph, inscribed to… Earl Temple. [The preface signed, Philanthropos.]*. (London: G. Burnet, 1764. Google Book. Retrieved 14 July 2016; Web), 38.
102 Cash, *John*, 99-101.

his identity, Wilkes immediately went to the house where Kearsley was being held to speak with him, and when he learned the contents of the warrant, he went to the Court of Common Pleas "to seek a writ of habeas corpus" for Kearsley's release, but it was closed for the day, and he had to return on the following morning. Meanwhile, Kearsley was violently interrogated and gave up Wilkes as the author. From the warrants, Wilkes knew the authorities did not know the identity of his printer, so he hurried issue No. 46 to Balfe's shop, and it began to be printed on April 29, when Balfe was finally arrested and the papers were seized. Balfe also gave Wilkes up, and a warrant was issued for Wilkes' arrest. This arrest was fumbled by the messengers who sympathized with him, so that he was free to get drunk, and then to retrieve a proof of the last issue from the set forms that the messengers failed to seize when they collected most of the issue from Balfe. Using this proof, Wilkes found a new printer for No. 46, so that it managed to appear a month later, on May 28, printed by E. Sumpter, a bookseller on Fleet Street. Because the messengers arrested forty-nine people when they were seeking only three, later lawsuits would outlaw "general warrants" without specified names. Later appeals also established radical precedents for privacy, against the seizure of all papers and machines, as well as against "false" arrests. The Court of Common Pleas promised to issue a habeas corpus because the warrant was illegal, but could not deliver this until Monday. Meanwhile, after several maneuvers on both sides, Wilkes gave himself up and was taken to the Tower of London, which was "not a tower at all, but a fortified village with heavily armed walls," in which Wilkes was confined "in one of the more modern houses." Meanwhile, Lord Temple, who would write the annotated version of No. 45 that was later issued, and other friends were lending Wilkes money and working to free him. To make his stay less comfortable, an order was issued to keep him "close" or to keep watch over him with a guard at all times. This angered Wilkes because such an order was illegal in all but "high treason" cases when a prisoner was extremely dangerous. He had to beg for paper and pen before they were finally granted, and he wrote a letter to Polly, his daughter, explaining that he had not done anything wrong to warrant the imprisonment. However, this letter did not reach Polly because it was confiscated as evidence. Then, Wilkes copied his arrest warrant and it was published together with an account of the arrest on May 4 as *Magna Charta, Cap. 29*. This account incited widespread support for Wilkes among lords and commoners alike. A parade was organized in his honor on Easter Sunday. The protests forced the prison keepers to lift the "close guard" and allow "open access" for visitors, and soon an overwhelming number of supporters flooded in to see Wilkes. A few days later, there was a trial, which Wilkes won because of "parliamentary privilege." When he returned to his house, he discovered his possessions had been robbed and ransacked, and he appealed this point in court on May 6. The appeal was denied, but there was no stopping Wilkes slew of appeals and complaints for radical causes from this point onward. The pursuit of justice and liberty took him into debt, and to escape from indebtedness he became a printer-publisher, a career that only sunk him further into debt, as it did many other speculating author-publishers in this study. His primary employment was that of an unpaid parliamentary politician, as he was repeatedly elected to public office in times when there were charges pending against him. Wilkes hardships were further exacerbated when the Court of the King's Bench brought additional charges against him and his printer and publisher.[103]

Wilkes imprisonment and trial were described in *Memoirs of the Reign of George III* by Horace Walpole, 4th Earl of Orford and the Member of Parliament for King's Lynn during the Wilkes Affair. Walpole had served in Parliament continuously from 1741 to 1768, retiring from politics after these incidents despite living for many years afterwards until 1797. Amazingly, Walpole was also an author-publisher, as his Strawberry Hill estate housed its own Strawberry Hill Press, founded in 1757, which released the first editions of many of Walpole's books, and also reprinted poetry, travelogues and memoirs by other writers. Walpole's best-known work was a trend-setting mystical tale, *The Castle of Otranto, a Gothic Story* (1764), which was initially released anonymously with an outside printer out of fear of being accused of portraying the supernatural. Previously, he anonymously printed pamphlet, *A Letter from Xo Ho, a Chinese Philosopher at London, to his Friend Lien Chi at Peking* in 1757, in which he wrote: "An Englishman loves or hates his King once or twice in a Winter, and that for no Reason, but because he loves or hates the Ministry in being. They do not oppose their King from Dislike of Royal Power, but to avail themselves of his Power; they try to level it till they can mount upon it… To have the Nation free!"[104]

---

103   Ibid., 102-20.
104   Horace Walpole. *A Letter from Xo Ho: A Chinese Philosopher at London,*

Walpole reports that Wilkes was imprisoned in the Tower, "a severity rarely, and never fit to be, practiced but in cases of most dangerous treason. This treatment served but to increase Wilkes's spirit and wit. He desired to be confined in the same room where Sir William Windham, Lord Egremont's father, had been kept on a charge of Jacobitism…"[105] Wilkes argued in court that his right to publish his opinions about the King were protected by parliamentary privilege of an MP, a law that was repealed shortly thereafter, before Lord Byron joined the House. In an environment where an accused, highly intelligent politician could rally support from the radical press and the populace when he was facing charges and could also defend himself knowledgably in court, it became difficult for British kings to execute radicals for sedition. However, Wilkes' ability to talk himself out of trouble expired when he and Thomas Potter wrote a pornographic, "most coarsely and disgustingly blasphemous" poem that satirized a courtier, "An Essay on Woman," which he printed on his newly bought home printing press, intending for it to be a twelve-copy, private, anonymous printing that would only get into the hands of those who would appreciate the joke.[106] Wilkes replied to the resulting new wave of prosecutions by filing a complaint with the House against the seizure of private papers from his house, which had not been returned. In counter-response, a more vigorous case on charges of libel and traitorous treason-exciting pamphlet writing was begun against him in a court that did not usually hear libel trials. "While the destruction of the character and fortune of Wilkes was thus prosecuted in one chamber of Parliament, a plot against his life was hatching in the other; his enemies not being satisfied with all the severities they could wring from the law to oppress him."[107] This passage shows that it is no stretch to assume that Byron's death or even King George III's madness were assassinations, which began as mere attempts at character assassination before turning into physical, though subversive, violence. In the passage, Walpole openly declares that the charges and attacks on Wilkes were offensive and premeditated rather than defensive replies to his treasonous publications. The House voted

to His Friend Lien Chi at Peking. (London: J. Graham, 1757; Internet Archive; Retrieved 5 June 2016; Web), 1.
105 Horace Walpole. "'The Wilkes Affair' from *Memoirs of the Reign of George III.*" *Versions of Censorship*. John McCormick and Mairi MacInnes, eds. (Garden City (NY): Anchor Books, 1962; 152-65), 155.
106 Ibid., 157-8.
107 Ibid., 160.

273 *for*, and 111 *against* and acting on Lord North's motion, Wilkes' paper was "burned by the hangman."[108] On the next day, Wilkes was "dangerously wounded" in the side by Martin in a duel, an outcome of Wilkes calling Martin "a low fellow, and dirty tool of power" in the *North Briton* a year earlier.[109] Walpole explained that Martin had delayed for so long to make the challenge because he spent the summer target-shooting to improve his aim. This slow plotting made Walpole conclude that this pointed to the duel being nothing less than "a plot against the life of Wilkes."[110] An attempt to burn the *North Briton* at the Royal Exchange followed on December 3, but the executioner was interrupted by a riot wherein constables were beaten and Sheriff Harley saw the glass of his coach broken and was wounded in the face by a lightened billet.[111] Meanwhile, Wilkes won his lawsuit for £1,000 in damages against Mr. Wood, the Under-Secretary of State on December 6. But, this wasn't the end of Wilkes censorship trials.

***

Slowing down a bit and going backwards, Wilkes had purchased "seventy-two reams of paper" from Leach shortly after his first release because Leach had refused to run a re-print of any of the past issues of the *North Briton* or to have anything else to do with publishing works by Wilkes. Because he already had the paper and content, Wilkes decided to set up his own print shop, intending to publish his own work by "subscription," "wherein people agreed in advance to buy the book." On May 21, 1763, Wilkes hired a press carpenter, John Yallowby and his son, to print the new editions of issues 1-44 in the front parlor of Wilkes' house. These printers were lent to Wilkes by Leach. The first printing was a pamphlet that described Wilkes' arrest. Then, they printed the suppressed No. 46, and then other works, including Wilkes' verses. Subsequently, they ran into a shortage of printing matter at a time when Wilkes was paying the printers he hired weekly regardless of if they were employed in printing or not, so he put them to work on his, "An Essay on Woman," with a front piece that displayed an erect penis, and content that satirized the clergy. Wilkes assumed that if he

---

108   Ibid., 160.
109   Ibid., 161.
110   Ibid., 162.
111   Ibid., 163-4.

printed only thirteen copies for private consumption by his men's club, it would not be considered a publication, and he did his best to keep it secret. Wilkes decided to rush the printing, but then stopped the printers on line 94 of the poem and asked them to first print the short poems at the end of the project that included, "The Dying Lover to His Prick." The printing of "An Essay on Woman" was never completed and stops abruptly in surviving versions on line 94. Four of the men working on this project were also among the large number of affiliated printers who were put on trial in the ensuing No. 45 lawsuit, which began in July. The first printer tried at the Court of Common Pleas was Huckell, who was defended by several lawyers sponsored by Lord Temple, and won based on the illegality of a general warrant, obtaining £300 for his troubles. The rest of the printers were tried on July 7 and all won £120 or more in damages. Forty other cases related to the arrest warrants over No. 45 followed in the next six years. Meanwhile, Wilkes finished printing volumes 1 and 2 of the *North Briton* (including No. 45), with annotations and some additional radical content by July 17, running 2,000 copies, when "he had only 120 subscribers, few of whom had actually paid," so to bind them, by August 2, Wilkes once again received funds from his chief sponsor, Lord Temple. In parallel, on July 8, one of Wilkes' printers took a portion of "An Essay on Woman" and delivered it to a party that transported it through dozens of hands before it ended up with the censors, wherein Philip Carteret Webb decided to convict Wilkes for it on the charges of "libel and blasphemy" for satirizing Bute's private parts. Wilkes traveled to France at this point. In France, he was accosted by a Scot called C. John Forbes, who said he was insulted by Wilkes' treatment of Scots and challenged him to a duel. Wilkes was willing, but Forbes failed to show up to some scheduled appointments for it, so that Wilkes said he was behaving more like an "assassin than a gentleman." In the end, Forbes received a military post abroad, and the duel never materialized. The government went so far as to use the stolen "Essay on Woman" to offer Wilkes a deal. They would halt their prosecution against his team if he stopped his counter-suits against their messengers, an offer Wilkes declined. The king then filed separate cases against Wilkes in the House of Commons for No. 45 and in the House of the Lords for "Woman," but these took a while to develop, so Wilkes had time to issue some other small propaganda pieces. Both of the cases were heard on the first day of Parliament's reopening on November 15 to Wilkes' complete surprise. The House of Commons had recently been bribed for the Treaty of Paris and they voted within party lines 273 to 111, condemning Wilkes of libel. In the middle of the ongoing motions of the trials, Wilkes was challenged to a duel by Samuel Martin to whom Wilkes wrote a letter objecting to his cowardice during the proceedings in the House, and they fought a duel. On the second shot, Wilkes was wounded in the abdomen. The bullet was roughly extracted, and the wound was infected, causing a handicap for a few months. Meanwhile, the Lords and the Commons voted against Wilkes, and a public burning was scheduled for No. 45, but was interrupted by a rioting mob. Another good news was that Judge Pratt ruled that Wilkes was not the author of No. 45 and awarded him £1,000 in damages for the illegality of the warrants, which meant he could not be once again accused of authorship by any other legal body. Then, Scotsman, Alexander Dun banged on Wilkes' door and threatened to kill him, but later submitted a proposal for a book on Wilkes for Wilkes to print, and Wilkes responded positively, sending some subscription money to Dun in prison's lunatic asylum (where the poor would-be assassin ended up). In February of 1764, Volume 3 of the *North Briton* was printed, and then Wilkes print shop was closed as he went into exile long before this point. Wilkes arrived in Paris on December 28, 1763 with an open wound, debt and unclosed trials pending. He was then expelled from the House of Commons, tried in absentia, found guilty and labeled an "outlaw." Meanwhile, Wilkes took a tour of Europe, but England kept calling him back and he stood for a City election, but was defeated. Then he was elected for Middlesex amidst a new string of riots, and in part due to this his status as an outlaw was reversed. When he attempted to take his seat, he was sentenced and imprisoned and served, all together, two years. He lost his seat again, faced additional libel charges, and was re-elected for Middlesex from prison. Well, the lawsuits, complaints, appeals, elections and various obstacles to serving an elected term kept plaguing Wilkes across his extremely long, for the times, political career. When the American Revolution took off, he, at the very least, sent money to sponsor it, and might have done significantly more to spark the flame for both the American and French revolutions, as the Founding Fathers were closely familiar with Wilkes' case and admired the principles he defended. Wilkes did not attempt to setup a new printing press, so for the purposes of this study the rest of his adventures are less significant.[112]

There are many precedents that were set with the Wilkes prosecution that later appear in other libel, sedition and blasphemy trials against authors, publishers and printers in this study. But neither the British nor American governments later attempted to arrest and prosecute forty-nine people at a time, with additional sets in new waves of the trial. The logistics of Wilkes case demonstrated how costly a trial like this could be in terms of damages and favors dealt out to all those judges, parliamentary members, and various other parties that each had to sign off on each new appeal. The subversive poisonings and assassinations of future author-publishers probably became less troublesome solutions rather than making martyrs out of them by bringing their "seditious" writings before a public that was always likely to side with them rather than with the king or ruling aristocrats. Wilkes survived a string of duels, and Byron avoided a few duels as well, so sending a duel challenge by an assassin was not likely to lead to a definitive outcome as surely as the prolonged poisoning that Byron endured in Italy.

When commenting on the Wilkes Affair, Horace Walpole argued:

> Of liberty a chief and material engine is the liberty of the Press; a privilege for ever sought to be stifled and annihilated by the Crown. The ministers of the Crown and its lawyers must misrepresent the liberty of the Press before they can presume to request the suppression of it. Every grievance set forth in print is misnamed a libel; and grave laws necessarily disapprove libels. If the Crown can arrive at precluding members of Parliament from complaining in print of grievances, no doubt the Crown could debar all other men, who are of less importance, and whose persons are regarded by no sacred privilege. Liberty of speech and liberty of writing are the two instruments by which Englishmen call on one another to defend their common rights.[113]

The Wilkes Affair is a debate about the right to opposition in general. What would be the purpose of being elected to congress, if one could not speak or write about the points on which one disagreed with the established rules? If a monarch and his predecessors have propagated for slavery for hundreds of years, the congressional members would have to voice their disagreement to make an attempt at its abolition. Similarly, the monarchy itself could be abolished if congressional members have

---

112   Ibid., 121-65.
113   Ibid., 162-3.

complete freedom of speech. As Britain and America democratized, many libel lawsuits like the Wilkes Affair were needed to establish the current balance between freedom of speech, and the rights of rulers to suppress opposition.

Shaw and the Necessary Immoral Play

There were some censorships of the British theater well into the twentieth century, after the point when pornographic and extremely violent content was legally allowed to appear in books. George Bernard Shaw summarized how morality and the progress of the theatrical art is frequently out of sync in the Preface, "The Necessity of Immoral Plays," to *The Shewing-Up of Blanco Posnet*: "An immoral act or doctrine is not necessarily a sinful one: on the contrary, every advance in thought and conduct is by definition immoral until it has converted the majority."[114] He goes on to explain that Jesus rebelled against the Jews' Moses concept when he said he was the son of God. Similar rebellions were taken on by Mohammed and Galileo. Thus, progress only happens when people take innovative actions or make innovative, artistic creations. Therefore, for the sake of human progress, these initially immoral changes cannot be censored. "It is immorality, not morality, that needs protection: it is morality, not immorality, that needs restraint; for morality, with all the dead weight of human inertia and superstition to hang on the back of the pioneer, and all the malice of vulgarity and prejudice to threaten him, is responsible for many persecutions and many martyrdoms."[115] *The Shewing-Up of Blanco Posnet* was rejected by Lord Chamberlain, who is addressed in this Preface. Despite the criticism, Shaw refused to take out the "blasphemous" statement regarding God and instead had the play performed in Dublin, Ireland, a location that was not covered under the censorship of the theater laws. James Joyce positively reviewed this 1909 performance, and it probably inspired some of his own immoral or anti-conformist literature.

---

114   George Bernard Shaw. "The Necessity of Immoral Plays." *The Shewing-Up of Blanco Posnet*. (1909). *Versions of Censorship*. John McCormick and Mairi MacInnes, eds. (Garden City (NY): Anchor Books, 1962), 335.
115   Ibid.

Orwell's Philosophy of Censorship by the Rich Against the Independent

In 1946, George Orwell published an essay titled, "The Prevention of Literature" in the *Polemic* in London, therein offering a unique perspective on censorship to the pornography debate that dominated the twentieth century. Orwell objected that professional writers of his age and country were not thwarted by "secret police" or the Church with "active persecution," but rather by "the general drift of society…" The enemy of free expression is the "concentration of the Press in the hands of a few rich men, the grip of monopoly on radio and the films, the unwillingness of the public to spend money on books, making it necessary for nearly every writer to earn part of his living by hackwork…" In this desperate economy, the writer simply works "on themes handed down from above… never telling what seems to him the whole of the truth." In contrast with radical liberals of previous centuries, the rebels of Orwell's time (and our own) are "rebelling against the idea of individual integrity" so that standing alone is "ideologically criminal" and writers' independence is "eaten away by vague economic forces…" In this tyrannical climate, "intellectual honesty is a form of anti-social selfishness." Orwell concludes that "the atmosphere of totalitarianism is deadly to any kid of prose writer" and that "it is probably that prose literature, of the kind that has existed during the past four hundred years must actually come to an end." Instead of being subjected to the Church's insistence on "faith" in God, the totalitarian state imposes schizophrenic fear of authority on writers because it "can never afford to become either tolerant or intellectually stable. It can never permit either the truthful recording of facts, or the emotional sincerity, that literary creation demands." Orwell further asserts that "serious prose… has to be composed in solitude." But in contrast to this preference, modern hack writers are writing "books by machinery." He explains that Disney films are created in a "factory process" where "teams of artists… subordinate their individual style" in a similar fashion as radio and magazines churn out repetitive content that follow the "ready-made plots." Other formulaic elements in the media include repeating "opening and closing sentences" or even an "algebraical formula," or "packs of cards marked with characters and situations, which are shuffled and dealt in order to produce ingenious stories automatically."

These formulas are said to be created by "literary schools." And since all literature is created like a Ford car in an "assembly line," "anything that was *not* rubbish would endanger the structure of the state" because it would stand out and thereby stress the repetitive nature of the rest. Thus, in a time when the freedom of the press has been guaranteed by federal court rulings, totalitarian rulers have found a way to suppress the spread of truthful knowledge because: "You can say or print almost anything so long as you are willing to do it in a hole-and-corner way."[116] Hack writers that conform to the formulaic plots and prescribed topics find fame and fiscal success, while anti-social liberals, who withdraw from the hubbub to write honest and intricately crafted literature by themselves in an imaginative and innovative way, cannot find a mainstream publisher willing to allow the light of recognition to shine on their intellectual prose. Since

Orwell is one of Britain's last canonical authors, so his theory on the decline of western literature is particularly helpful. Orwell is describing pre-publication censorships by publishers that prevent anti-formulaic and thus innovative writers from being published. The propaganda against small publishers as well as against "self-publishers" creates an environment where these radical and innovative works also fail to find reviewers and readers if they have to choose these alternative roads upon receiving rejections from the giant publishers.

The Ban on Miller's *Sexus*

Henry Miller argued in a letter to the Supreme Court of Norway that his book *Sexus* "is a dose of life which I administered to myself first, and which I not only survived but thrived on. Certainly, I would not recommend it to infants, but then neither would I offer a child a bottle of *aqua vite*. I can say one thing for it unblushingly—compared to the atom bomb, it is full of lifegiving qualities."[117] The Court requested a written reply from him after issuing condemning remarks with numerous, detailed infractions, which explain that he "makes sex pleasurable and innocent." In response, Miller confessed himself to be

---

116   McCormick, *Versions*, 286-98.
117   Henry Miller. "'Defense of the Freedom to Read,' a letter to the Supreme Court of Nortway in connection with the *Sexus* case." (1959). *Versions of Censorship*. John McCormick and Mairi MacInnes, eds. (Garden City (NY): Anchor Books, 1962. 223-30), 230.

"guilty" of this, but objected that there is far more violence in *Odyssey* and *The Iliad* as well as in "our detestable 'Comics'" than in his own comparatively mild work.[118] The Supreme Court sentenced booksellers to undergo a confiscation of the novel, and prohibited the novel in Norway. This was the first instance of a ban in that country's seventy-year history. When it was first published in Paris by Obelisk Press in 1949, it was soon banned in 1950, and the publisher was fined and given a prison sentence. Despite these problems, Miller followed *Sexus* with two other books in this series focused on his autobiographical first two marriages, *Plexus* (1953) and *Nexus* (1959). The US had initially banned this trilogy, but the reversal of the U.S. Supreme Court's decision against his *Tropic of Cancer* (1934) because it was proven to be "literature" or of artistic merit, and therefore unbannable, allowed for their releases (together with the newly unbanned *The World of Sex* and *Quiet Days in Clinchy*) in the US in 1965 to great commercial success.

This case is particularly interesting because it shows international censorship laws in action. It is also one of the only cases of intense obscenity in this study. Only Wilkes and Walker used similar, blatant sexual imagery in their writings and illustrations, both inserting penises and the like in odd places. There have surely been many other lawsuits about non-literary, sexual obscenity, but only these three cases have deeper implications for the freedom of expression.

Khrushchev's Take on Censorship: The Soviet Union Does Not Want to Eat Your Borscht

The Soviet Union is frequently used as an example of a state-controlled censorship apparatus of overwhelming proportions. So, an example from its heyday will help to exemplify this unique censorship style. One of the most curious, little-known arguments regarding censorship is from a *New York Times* transcript of an exchange that happened during Nikita Khrushchev's visit to the United States in 1959. Nikita attended a lengthy summit with Eisenhower in Washington, starting on September 15. He then spent a day in Los Angeles on September 19. During his tour of the Twentieth Century Fox Studios in Hollywood, Nikita was taken to the sound stage of the *Can-Can* movie, where he was accosted by the cast and crew, and the dancers in the film insisted on demonstrating a can-can dance to his mystified

---

118 Ibid., 224.

disgust. He did not object as they were showing him their rear ends, but it must have taken on more negative colors later that day when he was informed by the authorities that he was not allowed to visit Disneyland due to security concerns about what the crowd might do if he went. So that before the end of the day in Los Angeles' Town Hall, he threatened to build up more arms and possibly nuke the US for insinuating that he was afraid of a disease outbreak or some gang activities in Disneyland. Then, Khrushchev returned to DC and on September 22 had a new semi-violent clash where he used the can-can performance to describe his overall disgust with capitalist culture. Nikita later held a meeting with trade-union officials, who asked him why the USSR was preventing democratic elections in Germany on the issue of unification. One of the union leaders, Knight, also asked about the "harsh military suppression of the Hungarian Freedom Fighters by the Soviet military powers."[119] Khrushchev replied that he was proud of protecting Hungary from a "counter-revolution" carried out by "thugs and hooligans," just as Russia had to step in and fight against fascism.[120] Then, another union leader, Phillips, asked about radio jamming of Radio Free Europe and Voice of America, and Nikita replied that USSR's jamming of objectionable media was similar to his unique taste for borscht, while his American counterparts might like other dishes. Reuther countered: "But you prescribe and insist on borscht for all," explaining that if they were talking in metaphors insisting on only a limited number of government-approved programs meant force-feeding to the masses a single food the leader happened to enjoy. This enraged Nikita (who was probably inebriated by that point, it being 10:22PM), and he exclaimed that "as head of the working class," he had to "protect workers from capitalist propaganda," rather than support the "free flow of ideas" that Reuther questioned him about. Then, "Khrushchev, still on his feet, gave a burlesque demonstration of his idea of the can-can… He turned his back to the table, bent downward, flipped his coat up and gave an imitation of the can-can." He followed this presentation with a stern speech on the matter: "This is a dance in which girls pull up their skirts… This is what you call freedom—freedom for the girls to show their backsides. To us it's pornography. The culture of people who want pornography. It's capitalism that makes the girls that way… There should be a law prohibiting the girls from showing their backsides, a

---

119   McCormick, *Versions*, 123.
120   Ibid., 124.

moral law." Reuther then asked why *Pravda* and other Soviet media outlets did not report on his report on unemployment or his May Day speech in West Berlin. Nikita replied, "We only publish speeches that contribute to friendly relations between countries."[121]

This is the only pro-censorship argument in this collection. Perhaps because of my own Soviet and Hassidic upbringing Nikita's argument strikes a true note. For conservatives world-wide, displays of skin or sex in the media frequently crosses into the offensive. On top of this, Nikita was barred from doing the one thing he was excited about in the States, or going to Disneyland (in other words, he was censored from accessing this innocuous and wholesome activity, while the pornographic display was thrust upon him). Nikita's explanation that censorship is necessary in cases of obscenity and violent rebellion is similar to the arguments kings and presidents have made on both sides of the Atlantic for centuries. Would the can-can dance have harmed USSR's feminist, cultural values? Would articles in support of the Hungarian counter-revolution in USSR's media have inspired more violence? There are obvious problems as well as necessities in the censorship position, and Nikita's intoxicated explanations are stronger than most on the censorship side.

Expurgating as a Form of Censorship

While censoring a book out of publication was a threat to radical and morally progressive ideas across the history of book publishing, at the start of the nineteenth century the practice of expurgating books became popular on both sides of the Atlantic, and this subject is covered at length in Noel Perrin's *Dr. Bowdler's Legacy: A History of Expurgated Books in England and America*. Expurgation was the process of taking out passages that were unfit for youth because of their mature content or simply truncating books to a shorter size that was more digestible for less literate or younger readers. "Censorship is imposed by authority; bowdlerism is a voluntary act. Censorship is usually something done by governments for political reasons; bowdlerism is something done by private individuals, usually for moral reasons. Censorship usually precedes first publication; bowdlerism always comes after. But bowdlerism is also just one more mode of editing…" Dr. Bowdler did not simply truncate or annotate the texts he bowdlered, but rather

[121] Ibid., 124-6.

cut out components "'which may not with propriety be read aloud in a family,' meaning most overt sexual and religious allusions."[122]

Sir Walter Scott's efforts to reprint popular classical literature are frequently mentioned in scholarship, so it is telling that when he was offered to create editions of John Dryden's works for £750 in 1805, he did not expect that he would be asked to perform a bowdlerism, so that he wrote an outraged reply, refusing to "castrate" that Shakespearean author: "in making an edition of a man of genius's work for libraries and collections, and such I conceive a complete edition of Dryden to be, I must give my author as I find him, and will not tear out the page, even to get rid of the blot, little as I like it. Are not the pages of Swift, and even of Pope, loaded with indecency, and often of the most disgusting kind?"[123] However, as he inspected Dryden closer across the following two years, he recanted and proposed to "circumcise him a little, by leaving out some of the most obnoxious lines" to avoid "the Bishop of London and the whole corps of Methodists about" his "ears."[124] However, Ellis then insisted that Scott should preserve Dryden as a whole, and Scott agreed, releasing an unabridged version of his collected eighteen volumes by 1808, a year after Bowdler's *Family Shakespeare* and other similar expurgated texts became popularized.

Expurgation of radical or obscene sections out of the canon changes the political and cultural implications of these widely read books. A pro-revolutionary novel can become anti-revolutionary if the passages applauding the rebels are removed. Expurgation can also occur when editors take out radical passages before a publication. Galileo faced these types of requests to remove questionable sections of his works during the licensing process, and he ran into trouble when he ignored some of these prescriptions. Taking out parts of a work to change it to fit a nation's or the church's propagandistic platform is as objectionable as banning or burning a book.

Post Office's Refusal to Deliver as a Form of Censorship

Another contentious debate in the US was the rights of the Post

---

122   Noel Perrin. *Dr. Bowdler's Legacy: A History of Expurgated Books in England and America*. (New York: Atheneum, 1969), xi-ii.
123   Sir Walter Scott. *Letters of Sir Walter Scott, Volume I*. H. J. C. Grierson, Ed. (London: 1932-7), 264.
124   Ibid., 284.

Office to refuse delivery of "obscene" works by such authors as Ernest Hemingway, John Steinbeck, Alexander Dumas, Voltaire, De Maupassant, Zola and Tolstoy. The Post Office was banning books arbitrarily unlike the Customs Bureau that had "to bring an action in a federal district court to condemn the material."[125] Malin concludes that: "Part of that judicial art includes enabling the law to fit society's changing views of morality and decency, as reflected in legislation and tested by the courts for adherence to the basic Constitutional safeguards of our citizens in a free society with a democratic government."[126]

Customs in Middle Eastern countries refuse the transport in travel luggage, and their post office prevents shipments in packages of obscene materials such as vibrators, as well as pornographic films and books to this day. Thus, a discussion of the Post Office's bans is still relevant.

A 1959 case that looked at obscenity's bans by the Post Office was United States District Court, South District of New York's Grove Press, Inc. and Readers' Subscriptions, Inc. vs. Robert K. Christenberry, individually and as Postmaster of the City of New York, Civil 147-8. Herein, Judge Bryan wrote a lengthy opinion that clarified the matter. Judge Bryan explained that the book in question, D. H. Lawrence's *Lady Chatterley's Lover*, was not fit for banning because it was released by a "reputable publisher" that took care that "the format and composition of the volume, the advertising and promotional material and the whole approach to publication, treat the book as a serious work of literature. The book is distributed through leading bookstores throughout the country…"[127] He goes on to say that the preface was authored by a former Librarian of Congress, and there were many positive reviews of it in major critical publications, and that this universal approval raised it into the realm of literature. Bryan also cited an earlier case regarding James Joyce's *Ulysses*, wherein Justice Brennan stressed that sex alone was not enough to declare a work obscene. Bryan describes the plot and characters in the novel at length. Bryan explains that it is about Constance Chatterley's experience of being married to a baronet who

---

125 Patrick Murphy Malin. "Smut, Corruption, and the Law." *Versions of Censorship*. John McCormick and Mairi MacInnes, eds. (Garden City (NY): Anchor Books, 1962; 203-17), 210.
126 Ibid., 217.
127 Judge Frederick VanPelt Bryan. "Opinion by Judge Bryan on *Lady Chatterley's Lover*." (1959). *Versions of Censorship*. John McCormick and Mairi MacInnes, eds. (Garden City (NY): Anchor Books, 1962. 232-50), 240.

is paralyzed from the waist down from a war. The baronet advises her to become pregnant by another man. Then, the novel narrates how she has a passionate sexual affair with their gamekeeper, and by the end, decides to divorce the baronet, and marry the gamekeeper.

While the plot is absurd and humorous, this decision did a great deal for America's current free trade in pornographic materials via the Post Office. Without Lawrence's and Joyce's precedents, America might still have had the same strict anti-pornography laws as parts of the Middle East retained.

Poisoning and Malpractice as Subversive Assassination Techniques to Censor Independent Media

Deborah Blum begins her *Poisoner's Handbook* by explaining that prior to the "chemical revolution" of the early 1800s, poisonings were very "common," especially when an inheritance was involved. Only in the "late 1830s" was the "first test for isolating arsenic… developed," and it began to be applied in criminal prosecutions in 1840 in the trial of Marie Lafarge.[128] Thus, we must look at mysterious deaths of the author-publishers in this study prior to 1850 as more likely potential assassinations because there was no test or medical expert that could have confirmed or denied an accusation of poisoning. To this day, few of these cases have been examined by doctors or forensic experts. The clues might be in the recorded descriptions of their deaths, which might have been mysterious in pre-chemical days, but show textbook symptoms of specific poisonings or other unnatural causes to today's researchers. For example, in 1821 Napoleon Bonaparte is "suspected" of having died of arsenic poisoning, but no definitive findings have been made in this international case. When the new field of toxicology developed in the middle of the nineteenth century, with it came an explosion in newly developed, isolated with chemistry, poisons such as morphine, cocaine, palladium, and strychnine. The next turn in the war between chemists and poisoners came in New York City in 1918, when Charles Norris was hired as the first, trained medical examiner for the city's first toxicology laboratory, following "a series of scandals involving corrupt coroners and unsolved murders."[129] The bulk of Nor-

---

128   Deborah Blum. *The Poisoner's Handbook: Murder and the Birth of Forensic Medicine in Jazz Age New York*. (New York: Penguin Press, 2010), 1-2.
129   Ibid., 4.

ris' story ends in a breakthrough case in 1935. Before this point, the new field of systematic criminal toxicology was just being born. When Virginia Woolf died in 1941, this science was still too new to have ruled with certainty if her death was a suicide, or if she might have been drugged and dumped into the river. An indicator of just how undeveloped chemical awareness was even in Woolf's late period are the December 5-9, 1952 London Great Smog that led to the death of up to 12,000 people, and the 1959-1960s usage of thalidomide by pregnant women that caused birth defects in around 10,000 children; if these enormous-scale toxic poisonings could have taken place, victims clearly could be poisoned in this period without a solid "guilty" finding from a toxicologist.

John Emsley focuses on the poisons that most frequently appear in the medicines that author-publishers in this study were administered, and that contributed to their untimely demises in his Oxford University Press study, *Elements of Murder*. These common poisons are: mercury, arsenic, antimony and lead. They are common because they are frequently used in medicine and otherwise, with or without the prescribing physicians' knowledge of their toxicity. Emsley explains that mercury has been used as early as in 20,000-year-old cave paintings, and performed various other functions from that period to the present. Most recently, it has been widely applied in barometers and thermometers that take advantage of its unique heat-related powers.[130] Emsley gives the example of the madness of Isaac Newton, who was affected by mercury during his work as an alchemist, while he was a Professor of Mathematics at Trinity College. He was "heating mercury with various metals" in an attempt to produce gold out of the combination. These experiments caused the confusion that shows in Newton's 1693, *Praxis* [*Doings*], that includes "a combination of bizarre alchemical symbols and comments." Newton was also gray by this point, at a relatively young age, and was "suffering from poor digestion and insomnia," together with a "loss of appetite," and "delusions of persecution" and "loss of memory," all typical symptoms of mercury poisoning.[131] Emsley cites two 1979 articles that initially made an argument for mercury poisoning as the cause of Newton's death. These include P. E. Spargo and C. A. Pounds' essay in *Notes and Records of the Royal Society of London* that resulted from them testing samples of Newton's hair "by neu-

---

130   Ibid., 10-2.
131   Ibid., 13-4.

tron activation and atomic absorption analysis" and finding "high levels of toxic elements," which included not only high mercury (73ppm vs. the normal 5ppm) content, but also higher than normal lead (93 vs. 24), arsenic (3 vs. 0.7) and antimony (4 vs. 0.7) counts. He was experimenting with all of these substances in alchemy, and not only mercury. And some tests on other bits of Newton's hair have found mercury levels of 197 ppm, and it is presumed that these levels were higher when he was actually performing the experiments, rather than at the time of his death when most of the hair samples were extracted.[132] Newton survived even this extraordinary level of exposure in part because he was never diagnosed with insanity, and did not endure the bleedings and other procedures that Byron and others endured when on top of suffering from poisoning, they were subjected to harmful treatments to "cure" poisons' side effects.

Another example that Emsley offers is the suspicious death of King Charles II, who ran chemistry experiments, also with the hope of finding gold in mercury to solve his financial problems. Charles II started investing in these experiments when he established the office of Chemical Physician to the King, naming Dr Thomas Williams to the post in 1669. Decades into these experiments, in January of 1685, he started showing serious signs of mercury poisoning: faltered speech, paranoia, "apoplexy and convulsions," in response to which his physicians "blooded him," and "gave him a vomit [an emetic] and a glister [an enema]" that appeared to suppress the symptoms, but they returned days later with new "convulsions," for which he was given a "strong laxative" and "two doses of quinine." Charles II died shortly thereafter, as his epileptic seizures continued and caused partial paralysis from stroke-like symptoms that were really the results of inhaling a high amount of mercury that had made its way into his brain and caused internal bleeding in this fragile organ.[133]

Emsley also explains that arsenic is another chemical that has been used by humans for at least five thousand years. Early on, it was primarily created during the metal smelting process by smiths. The ancient Chinese knew of arsenic's toxicity and used it as a pesticide in rice fields, as described in the encyclopedia of Pen Ps'ao Kan-Mu.[134]

Antimony, a type of sulfide, was used for millennia too, includ-

---

132   Ibid., 14-5.
133   Ibid., 15-9.
134   Ibid., 19-20.

ing applications in medicine, mascara, Greek fire, printing type, and metal crafts. One of the earliest studies of antimony was by an author-publisher who did not put his name on the book as its author. *The Triumphal Chariot of Antimony* (1604) claims that it was written by a "mysterious monk," Basil Valentine, "who apparently lived in the 1400s, and belonged to the Order of St Benedict," but was really the work of Johann Tholde, "a pharmacist and part owner of a salt works at Frankenhausen in Thuringia." Because Tholde glorified antimony and mercury as having alchemist and medical benefits, they were used by physicians in the centuries that followed.[135] Emsley goes on to detail the various ways that these dangerous chemicals are still present in very high amounts all around us today (mercury in dental amalgam and fish from the sea, as well as arsenic in plants, wallpaper and drinking water). They are likely to be causing cancer, autism, seizures, and various other health problems to their unsuspecting victims.

"Antimony in a corpse persists indefinitely," so, even today, all of the potential murders with this weapon could be tested and adequately proven.[136] Physicians' prescription of high doses of antimony for a fever and a rash (that started on November 20, 1791 and lasted for fifteen days) led to Mozart's untimely death at thirty-five. Mozart had been taking antimony before this final illness because of his "hypochondria" that inspired his "predilection to taking patent medicines containing antimony" to cure various imagined illnesses.[137] Emsley clarifies that Mozart was exposed to relatively low doses of antimony, so that there are many other proposed causes for his death. In summary: "murder by antimony was so risky a venture that few attempted it, and those who did were generally medical men" such as Dr. Palmer in 1855 and Dr. Pritchard in 1865, who had to "control the doses of antimony potassium tartrate to simulate natural illness."[138] Dr. Palmer inspired the Palmer's Act that made it illegal to take out an insurance policy on somebody else's life (if they aren't related to you) because he attempted to cash in after poisoning a man to death slowly with antimony.[139]

Lead was used in the poisoning of a great composer, George Frederick Handel, in 1759, but it was indirect, as the lead was present in

---

135	Ibid., 21-4.
136	Ibid., 218.
137	Ibid., 220-2.
138	Ibid., 225.
139	Ibid., 225-6.

the tainted wine many Europeans consumed that caused serious cases of gout. Lead poisoning also caused Beethoven's deafness, "painful colic and constipation" and "damage to the nervous system," and later his untimely death.[140] Another lead poisoning is one that I closely inspected already in this study, the "madness" of George III. Emsley takes a closer look at one of the earlier episodes of illness that George III displayed back in 1788 because it was "clearly documented," and showed symptoms typical for lead poisoning: "severe constipation, colic, weakness in the limbs, difficulty in swallowing, sleeplessness, with progressive mental disturbances… progressing to delirium and coma." Emsley also points to the Prince Regent's motives for assassinating his father, namely his accumulation of over £630,000 in debts, the secret marriage to his mistress, and various other indiscretions that necessitated the acquisition of the throne. If it was not a direct assassination, Emsley suggests George III was exposed to lead in his favorite dietary components, "lemonade and sauerkraut," because they were "very acidic" and were likely to be "kept in a vessel with a lead glaze." This and other sources supposedly led to the King suffering from "mild lead poisoning for most of his life."[141] Of course, it cannot be a coincidence that the Prince Regent happened to be a beneficiary of his father's insanity or that Beethoven's musical competitors also stood to gain from his demise. The repetition of symptoms of poisoning among author-publishers surely points to the danger of subversive assassinations that threaten independent, radical publishing.

Because of the difficulties involved in proving causation post-mortem for lead poisonings, it is infrequent for death certificates to state "murder by lead poisoning." Only very blatant cases can be labeled with confidence. One such example is the murder of Pope Clement II in 1047 AD. His extremely high lead content was confirmed through a German test of his remains in 1959, which suggested that somebody in the Roman Catholic Church wanted to oust the Pope. "The… 1000s" were "noted for the corruption of the church in Rome." Pope Clement II was unpopular because he was a reformer: "He began by calling a Council of Rome which banned the sale of official positions which had been a lucrative business for some of the city's leading families." And these reforms were "brought to a sudden halt by his untimely death… Popular rumor was that Benedict's agents had poisoned him," though

---

140 Ibid., 295-6.
141 Ibid., 299-300.

Emsley still stresses that it is possible he was poisoned by an excess of wine rather than with deliberate lead insertions into his food by corrupted cooks.[142]

Considering the overwhelming evidence, it would be foolhardy to count any instances of physicians using lead, mercury, arsenic, or antimony as anything other than political assassinations of reformists or radicals for the sake of financial gain and career advancement.

The Seton and the Physicians that Prescribe It

While poison is particularly difficult to detect, deadly surgical malpractice has been used nearly as frequently in assassinations of radicals. The creation of a seton hurried and intensified the suffering involved in Sir Walter Scott's death. The seton was a relatively common device that physicians used to torture patients and quicken their death. A seton is a thread inserted through a fold of skin to create an opening through which (according to folklore) collecting, harm-causing fluid could drain out. Mary De Young defines a seton, also known as "haarseil, or, setaceum, or pus band" as: "A horsehair, silk or canvas thread, string of gauze, or a wire passed with a knife or needle through subcutaneous tissue usually at the nape of the neck or between the shoulders, and left there until it festered. The discharge of pus was believed at various times to either release the 'evil humours' or relieve the underlying brain inflammation that caused insanity."[143] It was used widely in the US and Europe "well into the nineteenth century." Another practitioner of seton applications was Dr Savage, who was Bethlem Hospital's superintendent. He was also instrumental in prescribing many of the harmful treatments that eventually led to Virginia Woolf's "suicide." Walter Abraham Haigh requested that Savage should apply the seton after editing Savage's book on the subject. Savage inserted a seton into Haigh's neck to supposedly cure his delusions, which never went away but kept Haigh from re-committing himself. Savage stresses the lack of re-commitment as a primary objective. By this measure the worst doctors have the best record of non-returns. Savage also expresses pride in the fact that Haigh went on to become a priest.[144] This suggests a con-

---

142   Ibid., 315-7.
143   Mary De Young. *Encyclopedia of Asylum Therapeutics, 1750-1950s*. (Jefferson: McFarland, 2015), 42.
144   Ibid., 41-22.

nection between the seton and self-flagellations that some Christians inflict on themselves to cure themselves of sin. The puss exiting is not so much the physical illness, but rather the spiritual evils. However, the harm that Savage and doctors like him inflicted on Woolf, Scott and others under the guise of ridding them of sin would be labeled as malpractice, or malicious infliction of "medical" injury today. Savage was also known for using and propagating the use of "artificial eruptions" or: "The raising of pustules, usually on the neck, shoulders, inside of the forearms or on the shaved head, by the vigorous frictional application of antimonial oils such as tartar emetic or croton oil... Erupting within hours after the application, the pustules produced a burning sensation and a purulent discharge of pus before scabbing."[145] Savage was supported by his subordinates at the Hospital, and there were other doctors that continued using tartar emetic "as a counterirritant in British asylums until the mid-twentieth century."[146] While this type of religiosity is not allowed in certified hospitals today, there are still plenty of deranged physicians out there that publishers should be aware of what can happen in malicious or incompetent hands.

The Role of Malpractice in the Death of US Presidents After Assassination Attempts

I received a review copy of Fred Rosen's *Murdering the President: Alexander Graham Bell and the Race to Save James Garfield* in the mail on July 15, 2016 from the University of Nebraska Press and reviewed it in the next issue of my *Pennsylvania Literary Journal*. It fits into this book as well. Rosen's study presents a curious lesson that the American public typically dismisses as conspiracy theory paranoia.

Rosen describes how Garfield was shot by Charles Guiteau, a rejected political office seeker, at point-blank range while they were shaking hands shortly after Garfield's election to the presidency on July 2, 1881 in Washington D.C. Garfield survived the bullet, and then Alexander Graham Bell invented the world's first metal detector just to locate the bullet trapped in Garfield's body to assure a safe operation. This heroic effort was undermined by Garfield's "friend," Dr. D. W. Bliss, who deliberately sabotaged the experiment and the operation and then tortured Garfield to death through September 19, 1881. In

---
145   Ibid., 29.
146   Ibid., 30.

one of these sabotages, Bell specifically asked Bliss to remove the steel wire underneath the horsehair mattress that was interfering with the "induction balance." Bliss refused to make this change and then publicized Bell's supposed failure, despite Garfield showing initial signs of improvement. Then Bliss suggested pumping "food up the president's anus" because he had a "poor appetite and needed his nourishment." Bliss used a similar technique to Dr. Savage's in Woolf's case, by referencing the "ancient Egyptians" who used "emetics and clysters… to preserve health." Bliss assumed that if it worked in ancient times, it must still work, despite medicine's progress since the leeches and purgatives of old. While this explanation suggests ignorance on Bliss' part, a look at medical history makes malpractice or ill intent more likely. Dr. William Beaumont had conducted experiments proving that the stomach was the only place that digests food, publishing this finding in 1833 in *Experiments and Observations on the Gastric Juice and the Physiology of Digestion*. Since half-a-century had passed since this medical breakthrough, Bliss' proposal of rectum feeding had to be a form of "torture."[147] Bliss wrote a book of his own on the rectum procedure, published in 1882, *Feeding Per Rectum: As Illustrated in the Case of the Late President Garfield, and Others*, describing that he used a similar procedure of forcing food up the "transverse colon" in a Senator's case (who also died), as well as "others" before perfecting it in his assassination of a president. "Bliss did this without anesthetic, tearing up the… lower intestine with his invasive tube." Then, he pushed defibrinated blood up the recently killed animal's tube that was used to deliver these toxins. Bliss later attempted shooting food, or more specifically, "a third of a pound of fresh beef…" with "14 ounces of cold soft water," "muriatic acid and… salt," and occasionally "yolk of an egg," mixed with a bit of "whiskey," "tincture of opium," "nerve stimulant," and "anodyne." All of these ingredients went up Garfield's rectum with the help of Surgeon General Barnes. The Surgeon General previously assisted with the assassination of Abraham Lincoln by putting a "Nelaton probe into Lincoln's brain…" after the attack. Bliss catapulted food up Garfield's rectum for at least a week, refusing to allow Garfield to eat anything by-mouth, thus starving the President. The bullet had not yet been found because the metal was preventing an accurate x-ray, so Bliss

---

147   Fred Rosen. *Murdering the President: Alexander Graham Bell and the Race to Save James Garfield*. (Lincoln: Potomac Books: University of Nebraska Press, 2016), 159-61.

then attempted a new surgery to locate it, and this operation was so injurious that it caused "blood poisoning" and after it Garfield "began a slow decline."[148] Bliss kept torturing the President for over two months before his death.

> The autopsy showed that Bliss had created a false wound track with his painful probing. He had taken a three-inch entry wound and, in probing for the bullet, made a pus-infected wound track, twenty-one inches long. Worse, it was a false wound track, leading away from the bullet. [And]... Garfiend was found to be suffering from extensive blood poisoning./... [T]he doctors had mentioned a four-by-six-inch abscess between the liver and the transverse colon that was filled with a "greenish yellow fluid...." It was Bliss's... probing... that had punctured Garfield's bladder...[149]

Rosen argues that Bliss deliberately misidentified the location of the bullet because his "practice" benefited "from his having treated a president, this time as a chief physician, no matter whether his president survived or died." He was billing by the hour, and a prolonged torture would make him more money than a quick recovery.[150] Bliss later appeared at the shooting assassin's trial in November to present evidence of the path the bullet took into Garfield. After hearing, Bliss' testimony, Guiteau argued *pro se* that Dr. Bliss "had shown depraved indifference to human life, the legal definition of second-degree murder," and so it was Dr. Bliss and not him that "should be tried for murder."[151] The jurors found Guiteau to be guilty, rejecting his plea of insanity, and sentenced him to hang, also ignoring his accusation against Bliss. Guiteau was hanged on June 30, 1882. It was only a month later when Bliss published his second and most gruesome article on his "treatment" of Garfield in the *Medical Record*, "Feeding per Rectum..."[152] Bliss was outraged when Congress put a cap on his earnings for "treating" the president for two months at $6,500, arguing that he had to "suspend" his regular practice to do it, and had thus lost "six months of earnings," which were "on average $1,500."[153] Bliss was hoping to make significantly more than all of his regular patients combined. If he had

---

148   Ibid., 162-6.
149   Ibid., 177.
150   Ibid.
151   Ibid., 183.
152   Ibid., 188-90.
153   Ibid., 191.

known in advance that Congress would refuse his appeal to go above $6,500, he probably would have left Garfield alone, and Garfield probably would have survived to serve the remainder of his term. Rosen then explains in the "Epilogue" that Bliss' horrific actions did not end with his own death in 1889, but continued to hurt numerous people indirectly after this point. For example, if Bell's X-ray machine had not been discredited by Bliss, it would have found the bullet in President McKinley after his assassination, sparing his life, but instead, doctors operated "without knowing where the bullet was" and McKinley died eight days later "from gangrene," with the bullet still inside of him on September 14, 1901.[154] The corruption of the medical profession has prevented progress in medicine for thousands of years because a "cure" is never as profitable" as continual "care." If malicious medicine is continuously applied, it usually leads to the patient's death. A fatality typically means there is nobody around to offer the evidence of malpractice with exactitude. Lincoln, McKinley and Garfield are just three deaths that were assisted by psychotic doctors. In 1981, after X-ray machines became common, Ronald Raegan and three of his men were shot. Raegan was shot in the chest. And yet all of them survived the shooting, showing that it had become much more difficult to kill a president on the operating table by the 80s. But, most of the author-publishers in this study died in the dark period of medical malpractice when doctors like Bliss got away with murder.

The Unusual Case of a Successful Malpractice Prosecution: Michael Jackson

Physicians have controlled the weapons in political assassinations for thousands of years. Over-prescription of harmful and conflicting drugs was recently brought to public consciousness in the lawsuit against Dr. Conrad Murray, who served two years on involuntary manslaughter charges for Michael Jackson's 2009 death. Jackson officially died of an overdose on an anesthetic, Propofol, while he was attempting to prepare for a grueling comeback tour. CNN reported that Jackson was also drinking Red Bull and playing loud music to help him sleep. Murray had given Jackson Propofol for sixty consecutive nights, and had just started attempting to wean him off. In his defense, Murray argued that he was not aware that Dr. Arnold Klein, a dermatolo-

[154] Ibid., 193-4.

gist, had injected Jackson with "6,500 milligrams of Demerol" across the previous three months, which is likely to have been the cause of Jackson's insomnia. As in the other cases in this study, malpractice is more likely when doctors assume that in the chaos of more than one attending physician administering different mixtures of harmful drugs, it will be impossible to pinpoint which poison in this cocktail actually caused the patient's death. Murray attempted to argue that like Marilyn Monroe and other celebrities who died of overdoses, Jackson self-injected the lethal dose because it was proven by the coroner that the drugs were not present in pill form in sufficient quantities in his stomach. In other words, it would have been more natural for Jackson to take extra sleep-inducing pills rather than inject himself, but no pills were found in the autopsy. Meanwhile, in the ten hours before his death, Murray was administering Valium, Lorazepam and Midazolam (sedatives) with pills and through an IV drip in the singer's leg, but since he was also on the Red Bulls and other uppers, he remained wide awake and became anxious. After lying awake for a while, Jackson asked for Propofol to help him sleep. As other physicians in this study, Murray acted on monetary motivations and disregarded the health of his patient, pushing 25 mg of Propofol into the singer, finally allowing him to go to sleep at around 11am. A sleep expert, Kamanger, has testified "that propofol has no therapeutic value in treating insomnia, and to use it is unethical and an extreme deviation from the standards of care. 'It is frankly disturbing.'" Knowing that Propofol had the power to stop Jackson's heart and to cause him to stop breathing, Murray did not call 911 for over an hour despite noticing signs that Jackson was not breathing.[155] While Murray's actions are grotesque, they are tamer than some of the less-known subversive murders by physicians, who have not been prosecuted.

---

155   Alan Duke. "'Perfect storm' of drugs killed Michael Jackson, sleep expert says." (14 October 2011. CNN. Retrieved: 19 July 2016. Web).

PART II
British Author-Publishers

CHAPTER 3

Scottish Insurrections:
Sir Walter Scott's Waverley *and the Ballantyne Publishing Company*

Sir Walter Scott started his career by apprenticing to his father, Walter Scott WS, who hired him during a series of bread riots, when it was difficult to find other helpers. Scott Jr. might have been otherwise weakened in his father's eyes by the lameness he developed in a childhood illness. Scott succeeded in this challenge and was then hired as a copying clerk for Scott Sr.'s Chalmers and Scott law firm in Edinburgh in 1786. This new job focused on speed copying court documents because he was paid "threepence a page," which if we believe the accounts that he occasionally copied 120 pages in a day, earning 30s, is a very high rate for a fifteen-year-old apprentice.[156] Scott was then offered a partnership in the firm in 1790, despite his father's criticism of his drinking, fiddling, and wandering around the countryside with shady friends. Scott refused the partnership because his father had stayed a Writer to

---

156   John Sutherland. *The Life of Walter Scott*. (Oxford: Blackwell Publishers Ltd., 1998), 28-31.

the Signet across the bulk of his career, never leaving the middle class as he did nothing other than running his law firm. Instead, the young Scott insisted on finishing his studies to become an advocate, a task that lasted between 1789 and 1792.[157] Scott qualified as an advocate in July of 1792. One of Scott's notable early cases was his defense of a delinquent clergyman, M'Naught, before the General Assembly of the Kirk in May 1793. The trial caused hilarity among Scott's youthful lawyer comrades because Scott stumbled on miniscule points, failing to make a convincing oration. At each glitch, his friends hollered. They were eventually thrown out from the proceedings because they were rolling with laughter at the fact that they were guilty of all of the crimes M'Naught was being accused of: "habitual drunkenness, singing of lewd and profane songs, dancing and toying at a pennywedding with a 'sweetie wife,'" as well as a crime they were not a party to, "promoting irregular marriages as a justice of the peace."[158] In his first three years of practicing law as an advocate, Scott made £23, £55, and £84, defending mostly petty criminals and one murderer. In these years, Scott seemingly took an anti-Jacobite stand, but he did it in a way that proved more rebellious than the mob he swore to squash. In one incident in April of 1794, Scott and his advocate friends "attended the Edinburgh Theatre armed with staves to ensure the singing of the National Anthem was not interrupted or mocked. A brawl broke out with some democratically inclined Irish medical students. Heads were broken (Scott boasted that he split three himself). Scott and his friends were arrested, and bound over to keep the peace."[159]

One of these patriotic friends was James Ballantyne, who founded his own printing press in Kelso, Scotland, where they were all residing, a couple of years after this incident, in 1796. Scott met James and John Ballantyne back in grammar school. Scott might have gone permanently unpublished if Ballantyne had not started this venture, thus making Scott feel as if he had a friend supporting his publications, rather than a censor who might reject or unjustly chop up his creations. Publishing with a friend is frequently similar to publishing with your own press in terms of the ease of access to acceptance. Scott's early publications were extensions of his academic pursuits, as he published translations from German, and a collection of Scottish ballads. Sometime later, he

---

157   Ibid., 41.
158   Ibid., 48.
159   Ibid., 50.

started publishing poetry with Ballantyne. It took James Ballantyne a decade to build up his publishing business enough for one of his Scott-releases to become a best-seller, *The Lay of the Last Minstrel*, in 1805. It was no spontaneous publishing success. The Ballantyne Publishing Company gave root to many writers and editors in the Ballantyne family. It predominantly published works edited or written by Sir Walter Scott, who financed a portion of the venture. One of the Ballantynes to spring out of this family was Robert Michael Ballantyne, who was born in the year when a UK-wide banking crisis left the Ballantyne printing business with £130,000 in debt, equivalent to $13,400,000 today. This enormous sum also shows the volume of business Ballantyne was doing before its collapse, and how potentially profitable the publishing ventures were, if only the investing environment had remained stable. The young R. M. Ballantyne went to Canada to work in fur-trading at sixteen, and only returned to Scotland in 1847, after his father's death. He released his first book in the following year, *Hudson's Bay: or, Life in the Wilds of North America*, probably sponsoring it with money from his inheritance. In his first years back in Scotland, he worked for Messrs Constable, a publisher in Edinburgh. R. M. Ballantyne went on to publish over a hundred young adult titles.

Back in 1799, Scott senior died, leaving the young Scott an estate to untangle. In the same year, Walter was appointed Sheriff-Depute of Selkirkshire with a salary of £250 annually. The appointment came with help from his mentor, Henry Dundas, who only assisted his rise because Scott had expressed the anti-Jacobite and anti-sedition views that seem so uncharacteristic for the ideas Scott expressed later in his career. Scott radicalized as he became secure in his legal post, and no longer needed to court favors from the conservative establishment. He held the same post of Sheriff of Roxburgh, Berwick and Selkirk from this point until his death, with the only change being a raise to £300, thus eliminating any need for further groveling and patronages. The bulk of the busy work was done by a Sheriff Substitute, similarly to modern American law clerks but with the authority to rule over sessions in the judge's absence in undefended cases (the vast majority). Scott only "dealt personally" with 112, mostly minor, law suits over his 33 years in office. This left Scott with plenty of time for his literary hobby, while he lived in Edinburgh and Abbotsford, mailing in his written judgements based on case materials he received from the

Substitute.[160] Scott served as the Principal Clerk of Session, administering the Supreme Courts of Scotland between 1806 and 1811, when David Hume, his old law school professor, took over the position. The Clerkship started paying £1,300 annually until the end of Scott's life in 1812, making his employment income £1,600 annually across his peak publishing years. Scott held this post in addition to his judgeship because he filed a special petition to maintain both jobs simultaneously despite their geographical disagreements. Another immediate challenge Scott faced upon his appointment to the clerkship was the fall of the Tory government, and the triumph of the Whigs in that election, which meant he had to defend his job to the other side. The fact that he managed this signifies that he had to be very close to the middle for the Whigs not to object to his appointment.[161]

During a period when Scott attempted to "rest," after the success of *Marmion*, in 1809, he was in a small group of investors who took over the patent of the Edinburgh Theater, paying out the previous owners, the Jackson family. Scott bought a share and became its trustee and legal representative. The Theater had early successes with Shakespearean productions, but Scott always had an ambition to bring new, innovative artistic masterpieces to its stage. He attempted to sell his own *The House of Aspen*, but failed to convince the other members of the board in the strength of his playwriting. Scott's search for a national Scottish theatrical masterpiece landed him on Joanna Baillie, a Scot who had spent her youth in London, and stayed with the Scotts when the idea for acquiring the Theater took root. He might have solicited a tale about a Highland feud from her, thus bringing about the nationalist, *The Family Legend*, a precursor to Scott's own hyper-Scottish-nationalist Waverley novels, which also glorified the Highlands, clan leadership, and the declining, "authentic" Scottish culture. Despite Scott's aggressive promotion of this play to the chieftains of the region's clans and other parties that the play propagated, it only played for fourteen nights in January of 1810. Scott put in a great deal of effort into the promotion of the Theater after this point, but never really saw a return on his artistic or financial investments, as it gradually declined, first under Henry Siddons, and after his death in 1815, under his widow's management until 1830, when it finally failed.[162]

---

160   Ibid., 71-2.
161   Ibid., 109.
162   Ibid., 132-4.

As Scott's books started to sell well with Ballantyne, he started publishing with a bigger Edinburgh publisher, Constable. He continued publishing with Archibald Constable until 1808 and then broke off this relationship and invested the bulk of the withdrawn money to bolster Ballantyne's volume of production. Scott went back to Constable in 1813, and in 1814, they published *Waverley* together to great popular success. Scott suffered fiscal losses as he tried to help both Ballantyne and Constable recover after the 1826 crash, and only Constable ended up coming out of the ashes. Constable reemerged only stronger for the great effort it took to survive the £250,000 in losses. Constable was partners with Robert Cadell in the publishing venture from 1809, but Cadell split from Constable after he filed for bankruptcy in 1826. Cadell took Scott's copyrights and rights to Scott's future publications, a prudent move on Scott's part as Constable died in the following year, 1827.

Constable & Co. was an independent publisher, operating under the name of the founder from 1795 until it was purchased by Little, Brown Book Group in 2014. The original founder of this entity was Archibald Constable. Constable was first to offer authors advances against royalties, and he was first to release three-decker novels, and mass-market editions. Archibald Constable started in publishing as an apprentice to a bookseller, then traded rare books, before buying the *Scots Magazine* in 1801, and then founding the *Farmer's Magazine* in 1801, followed by his founding of the popular *Edinburgh Review* in 1802.

Simultaneously with starting the Edinburgh Theater in 1809, Scott began plans for founding his own publishing company, John Ballantyne & Co., Booksellers to the Regent (later changed to Prince Regent, while initially it was intended to honor his wife, the Tory Princess Caroline, who had met Scott in 1806, and who the Whig Prince was bitterly attempting to divorce), under the leadership of a well-known Scottish printer, James Ballantyne, together with his brother John. Scott's need to start an independent publishing venture came after he felt his first primary publisher, Constable, "owned him" because he had received the bulk of a sizable advance prior to completing a massive book on Swift he was developing with Constable for six years (in contrast with the promised two years). Scott supplied the bulk of the funding, with the hope of recuperating the investment and seeing a profit. He also wanted to start a non-Whig venture, in opposition to Constable's political views. Scott's break with Constable really began in 1808, when he set up a Tory quarterly with Murray, *Quarterly Review*, to rival Constable & Co.'s Whig *Edinburgh Review*. Constable saw this startup "like a bomb," a treasonous disloyalty in proper publisher relations, but one that Constable let slide, keeping his contract with Scott intact, despite a few resulting disagreements. Scott served as a leading contributor to the *Quarterly Review* between 1809 and 1811, and continued in this role only with breaks between 1811-5 and 1818-24.[163] In at least one instance, Scott used his friend's William Erskine name in the *Quarterly* to review himself, writing a defense against Thomas McCrie D.D.'s attack in the *Edinburgh Christian Instructor* in 1817 that criticized Scott's near-blasphemous portrayal of Covenanters "as homicidal maniacs" in *Old Mortality*.[164]

Meanwhile, Scott opened doors to the new Ballantyne venture a few hundred yards away from Constable's, and began publishing "a Tory imitation of Constable's *Edinburgh Review*." In addition, Ballantyne's first journal was called *Edinburgh Annual Register*, the exact name and concept that Constable had proposed to Scott for editorship in 1807, but that had not yet materialized. Constable considered this particular betrayal to be a "literary theft." Constable forgave Scott's rebelliousness, but competition with Constable was not Scott's real problem when he set of on his own publishing enterprise, but rather "his choice of partner."

John Constable and his father failed in their neighboring clothier's businesses before joining James Ballantyne's Edinburgh printing works. John had held a £200 annual salary with his brother before Scott partnered with him, with a raise to £300 annually. At that point, other than in accounting, John had few usable skills in the publishing craft. While Ballantyne already had a running printing business and did not need the added investment, Scott voluntarily invested £9,000 into improving the business, an infusion that allowed it to become a leading publishing establishment between 1805 and 1810. After 1810, Scott invested still more money into Ballantyne, so that his investments overtook his profits from the books he released with this venture. Then Scott bought the lands and started building his estate at Abbotsford in 1811. This was such a huge purchase that Scott started borrowing from relatives and publishing contacts, beginning the trajectory that would

---

163   Ibid., 135-41.
164   Ibid., 200.

land Ballantyne and Scott's personal assets into bankruptcy. Sadly, John Ballantyne was not only ignorant about publishing, but also an alcoholic and womanizer, who apparently spent some of the money that came in on these passions, causing John Murray to refuse "to exchange bills with the firm" because he could "not be trusted." Like Mark Twain, Scott chose to keep his own name off the company's title to avoid being listed as both the author and the publisher of the books he released with the venture. At the start, Scott invested a half-share of the start-up capital, or £1,000, with the Ballantyne brothers jointly matching this amount. Thus, together, with his other investments in the firm, Scott gained a controlling share over what the company chose to release. Scott had been pitching his passion projects of "vast collected editions of dramas, transcriptions of historical documents, and reprinted tracks" to Constable and Murray, but they had rejected these schemes, with Murray "estimating, to his horror, that one of Scott's magna opera could cost over £20,000 in printing costs." Perhaps because he knew that he would need Ballantyne's printing apparatus, Scott also became the dominant partner in James' separate printing business. One of the reasons for the initial break actually also went back to a negative review of Scott's *Marmion* in Constable's *Edinburgh Review*. This scarring review made Scott end his subscription to this publication in 1808, while he was publicly claiming that his de-subscription was because of its Whig stand on the Peninsular War.

Between the *Quarterly Review* and the John Ballantyne publishing company, by 1810, Scott "could write his books, publish his books, print his books, sell his books and—if he were daring enough—review (or have friends review) his books in *his* journal. Each of his subsequent major poems was reviewed in the *Quarterly* by Ellis. A more friendly critic it would be harder to imagine… He had closed all gaps—or 'gateways'—across which literature habitually jumped or fell." The trouble was that even with the best reviews and complete freedom to publish any grand projects that Scott could imagine, the publishing business is a mercurial gamble that even the most experienced publishers usually lose in the end. One of the first books John Ballantyne released was Scott's epic poem, *The Lady of the Lake*, (£10,000 in resulting profits), which was his "first extended treatment of the 'aboriginal' Scots, the Gaels who were… displaced by civilized Saxons from the south and pushed progressively north to the barren highlands." High sales for this epic poem resulted from the seeds sowed by his sponsorship of Baillie's nationalist, *The Family Legend*. Immediately after covering all points of entry into publishing, Scott's first agenda was Scottish nationalism, and not the defense of the Tory position, as he publicly claimed.[165]

While Scott was a nationalist, Ballantyne was a profiteer. Starting in around 1810, John Ballantyne had been inflating their company's profits "by valuing up book stock,"[166] which could never sell since the extra stock of books was fictional. Meanwhile, Scott was also corrupted as he was borrowing money from the firm for his estate. And John was giving "credit to booksellers" that the company was unlikely to repay.[167] The Spring 1813 banking crisis brought about a collapse of trust and when Scott refused to out himself as a partner in Ballantyne to his bankers, Scott was forced to sell Ballantyne's "most sellable" stock to Constable at a reduced price to save Ballantyne from the brink of disaster. At the same time, Scott started asking for loans for Ballantyne using his own name, outing himself to dukes and publishers alike.[168] Then in July 1813, their banker, Sir William Forbes, refused to offer any more credit and Ballantyne failed to inform Scott of this until the due date of a crucial bill, when Scott had to send a horse over with his own money to avoid immediate bankruptcy.[169] In August, Constable stepped in to help and evaluated Ballantyne's inflated stock to be worth only £8,600 and not £18,000 as the books claimed, and it was calculated that the firm had to raise £4,000 immediately to avoid bankruptcy. Loans came in from Constable, Duke of Buccleuch, Morritt, and Scott's subordinate, Sheriff Deputy of Selkirk Charles Erskine. Debt was also written-off by James Ballantyne to avoid immediate collapse. Seeing how dangerous it was to trust his literary endeavors to unskilled hands, Scott returned to working with Constable as his primary publisher, and this newly formed alliance birthed the foundations of the historical novel.[170]

Scott continued to publish some of his poetry with Ballantine, releasing *Rokeby's* in 1813 to some success as nearly all of the first edition's 3,250 copies sold, but these sales were less than half of the *Lady's* profits. The best thing about this release was that the Prince Regent admired the poem "immensely" and informed Scott that "he might

165   Ibid., 135-41.
166   Ibid., 150.
167   Ibid., 151.
168   Ibid., 151.
169   Ibid., 152.
170   Ibid., 152-3.

use the royal library 'whenever he comes to town.'" Further still, when Henry Pye died in 1813, Scott was offered the Poet Laureateship, but on recommendation from the Duke of Buccleuch and out of concern that holding the title would make him a puppet of the Regent, he declined and recommended his friend, Southey,[171] who had previously been prosecuted for treasonous publications, but would later attack Byron in the incident that would be a leading controversy for Shelley and Byron's journal. Southey had to accept because he was too poor to hold on to his rebellious roots, and as the Duke of Buccleuch predicted, the post meant a blind allegiance to the sovereign, at the sacrifice of personal convictions. When Scott took a stand against such allegiances, he paved a road to become the authentic voice of the nationalist Scots.

It was a small literati world in the nineteenth century, so many of the key author-publishers reviewed intersected. Scott crossed paths with Byron during his London trip in the spring of 1815. They exchanged gifts, and had cordial relations, meeting at a couple of dinner parties. Despite these pleasantries, at their spring meeting, they clashed when Scott recited to Byron the unpublished poem by Samuel Taylor Coleridge,[172] *Christabel* (about a supernatural abduction). Coleridge had been gradually composing this poem since 1797, but due to opium addiction and doubts about his artistic abilities, he still had not completed it. The recitation meant something entirely different to Byron, who recognized that the poetic "Pindaric measure" of the poem was similar to his own, *The Seige of Corinth,* poem (about an Ottoman massacre of Venetians), which was nearing completion, but was also as yet unpublished. Aside from this similarity, Byron then felt compelled to mention another parallel. Byron believed he had given Scott proper credit for the technical elements he mimicked from Scott's 1805, *The Lay of the Last Minstrel* (about sixteenth-century Scottish Border feud), but now he had realized he might have failed to give proper credit to Coleridge. The idea that he might have committed a plagiarism ate away at Byron and he wrote to Coleridge explaining that Scott, and not he, had committed a plagiarism of Coleridge's poem. This angered Coleridge, but Byron softened the blow by convincing John Murray to publish Coleridge's still unfinished poem in a pamphlet in 1816, the same year when Byron's poem came out without alterations. Accusations of plagiarism solicited duels among other top authors in this pe-

171   Ibid., 163.
172   Ibid., 183-5.

riod, so this was a very tense situation. It is also telling that there were so many technical and thematic similarities between these three great poems. Scott developed a new historical novel genre with *Waverley*, and Byron also made numerous innovations because they were competing to progress the writerly craft, as mere master of formulas was beneath their aristocratic names. Scott and Byron also collided over the *English Bards* journal. Their repeating failures to find similarities (both were Scottish) might not have been accidental. Reviewing their history suggests that everybody from Murray to the Regent conspired to create a rift between them to avoid potential collusion that might have succeeded far better than Byron's affiliation for his journal with the Shelleys and the Hunts.

Scott has been called a conservative, a royalist, a moderate and a radical depending on the political leanings of his critics. One of the reasons his radicalism can be ignored is because he did not out himself as the author of the Jacobite Waverley novels until he stopped actively publishing them. He did his best to disguise his radical leanings by taking measures that made him appear as a committed royalist and unionist. During an insurrection in Scotland in the winter of 1819, which was in part inspired by Scott's Waverley novels, Scott proclaimed that as Laird of Abbotsford he was responsible for "beating" the attacking rebels down, and rallied his neighbors to petition to raise a "corps of Foresters." He must have anticipated that this offer would fail if he asked the government to finance it, and it did so by 1820.[173] While these actions can be seen as anti-radical, they were simply dramatic gestures that did not result in any real moves to suppress the insurrection.

Scott's posturing clearly worked because even the king trusted him, and stayed with Scott on a visit that Scott solicited. George IV's visit to Scotland in 1822 has had greater historical significance than his visit to Ireland in 1821. Given the previously described history of how George IV suppressed his own father George III, it should not come as a shock that his jaunt to Scotland aligns, in dates, to a string of suspicious deaths. On the surface, the visit was a dramatic success. Scott orchestrated a theatrical event, using knowledge he gained from running his Edinburgh Theater. He had convinced the Prince Regent that he was the last of the Stuarts, and therefore a Jacobite at a dinner party back in 1815. Now, Scott had to organize a massive public spectacle in a fortnight from July 22. Scott used this power-position to build on

---

[173] Ibid., 233-4.

the Stuart foundation he built in George IV's imagination. He issued an order that: "No gentleman is allowed to appear in anything but the ancient Highland costume." As Sutherland points out: "Thus an item of clothing for the wearing of which a Scotsman could face execution until 1782 became the uniform of Lowland gentlemen who before August 1822 would no more have thought [of] wearing a kilt than a suit of medieval amour." The King was informed of this policy and ordered a Royal Stewart tartan outfit from his Royal tailor for £1,354 18s. This was the first visit by a reigning monarch to Scotland since the 1630s, breaking a two-hundred-year tradition of keeping out of the troublesome, northern kingdom. Scott ran a nationalist campaign for Scottish cultural separation across this visit, inventing traditions for the sake of stressing the value of Highland clan rituals. The kilts, bagpipes, and various other elements that most modern media consumers assume to be signs of Scottishness were all props to show the grandeur and historical weight of the kingdom to its new monarch. This fiction took root internationally and served the function Scott intended.

Meanwhile, the two men at the center of it, Scott and King George IV were both too "fat" and "ailing" for the "heavy-drinking" that came with the randomly scheduled dinners, and all the walking, prancing, dancing, and yachting that were crammed in. At one point, Scott was so drunk that he hid the monarch's glass in his pocket and sat on it after forgetting it was there. But, was Scott merely drunk or was George IV more offended by being forced to wear a kilt than he let on? Why would Scott have put somebody else's glass into his pocket? Is it more likely that the King put the glass in his pocket, hoping Scott would injure himself when he sat on it?

As will be discussed in Byron's section of this book, George IV had dealt harshly with his Foreign Secretary, Lord Castlereagh, before his departure for Scotland. Castlereagh, presumably, cut his own throat at the same moment the monarch "set foot on his norther realm." The suicide is questionable because Castlereagh was drugged and otherwise mishandled by his physicians, and there were no credible witnesses who might have attested that it was he and not somebody else that slit Castlereagh's throat. If King George IV deliberately left for Scotland to allow his agents to assassinate Castlereagh when he was out of town, this might have explained why Scott was only given a fortnight to prepare the festivities, as the King's final rapture with Castlereagh happened very abruptly in a conversation that brushed among other things on the Secretary's homosexuality.

In parallel, William Erskine also supposedly committed suicide on the day of the King's arrival. William Erskine had been friends with Scott since they passed the bar together in 1790. Erskine was the friend who gave his name for a defense Scott penned in the *Quarterly* of his own novel. It was also William's relative, Charles Erskine, who had served as Scott's Deputy Sheriff and had offered a loan when Ballantyne was at bankruptcy's door. William Erskine, a widower, was accused of "adultery with an apothecary's wife," and this, supposedly, drove him into a "deep depression" that his "physicians" treated with "excessive bleeding." These treatments were so painful that William finally asked for his window to be opened, and, presumably, jumped out of it. Scott's leaves essential specifics out of his account of these events. The few details that are provided are nearly identical to both Castlereagh's mistreatment by physicians and Byron's, with the only difference being that most of Scott's letters on this subject were burned and there are no remaining detailed accounts of the physicians' treatments in Erskine's case.

Meanwhile, as if she was given drugs by somebody accompanying the King, Lady Scott started showing symptoms of extreme intoxication from opium addiction and possibly other pain-killers, an addiction that plagued the rest of her life. And Scott started suffering from a "prickly heat" that he summarized as "apoplexy," or internal bleeding (including strokes). These symptoms started with the visit and lasted for two months after it. Then, these symptoms returned in the form of strokes in 1826 and thereafter, and finally led to Scott's death.[174] Were Scott and his wife prescribed poisons (opium etc.), during this visit, by the King's physicians that led to their untimely declines? Scott's heat and convulsions certainly mimic the symptoms Byron was suffering in his final illness.

There were no other similar suspicious deaths in Scott's long legal or publishing careers, only this set that coincided with the King's visit. Was it an epidemic of mad physicianry that England suffered in the first years of King George IV's reign? Considering the Scottish Insurrection two years earlier in 1820, how could the King's visit have been something other than an attempt to suppress persistent Scottish rebelliousness? But then again, the King was rather unwell himself at the festivities, so was he the central player, or his spies and army of

[174] Ibid., 257-60.

politically opinionated physicians that had motives for assassination? One thing seems clear, there was a subversive campaign against radical politicians, lawyers, publishers and aristocrats after George IV took the throne and by inviting him into his circle, Scott might have unintentionally brought the massacre to dinner.

Having survived the King's visit, Scott carried on with the business of writing and publishing. His affairs started taking another turn for the worse when Constable began failing. Ballantyne was going under too, and Scott's personal debts continued to climb. The question of filing for bankruptcy became urgent on January 16, 1826, when Hurst & Robinson rejected one of Constable's bills, a pebble in a very large heap of fiscal problems. In total, £121,000 ($13,532,655.49 in 2016) in claims were levied against Scott simultaneously. Scott decided on filing for a trade bankruptcy (a path that Constable took at the same time with his incredible £250,000 indebtedness) because he was embarrassed by the idea of being labeled a "tradesman." The modern-day equivalent to the term "tradesman" is "self-published"; there were the same types of societal pressures against running a publishing business back then as the state and business elite always lose in proportion to independent publishers that embrace these types of terms. Thus, to avoid a prickly label, Scott set up a trust deed that guaranteed complete repayment of all of his debts at a later time. This bet required his concealment of a stroke he had a week earlier, which threatened his ability to live long enough to repay such extraordinary debts. The trust allowed Scott to remain in Abbotsford. It also allowed him to keep his £1,600 annual judgeship salary, and income from his writing. Meanwhile, it rid him of the tasks he detested, including management of his farms, and Ballantyne's printing works, which managed to stay in operation despite £90,000 in debts because James Ballantyne created a similar trust when it failed. Scott did have to sell his Edinburgh house for a mere £2,300. Scott also set a rigorous writing schedule to pay off not only his personal debts (£20,000), but also debts generated by Ballantyne and Co. (£12,615) and backed debts from Constable (£9,129). The remainder of the debt was to third parties for everything from expenses on his house to other accommodations. Unlike Melville and other unlucky author-publishers, Scott received £10,000 in advances for nine outstanding works by the point when Constable collapsed under the pressure of unrepaid investments in 1826. The problem that Ballantyne, Constable and Scott faced leading up to 1826 was that they took on extremely risky debt that was as easy to obtain as sub-prime mortgages in the modern age. These loans allowed them to bubble up into giant enterprises, the biggest publishing houses in Scotland. They also made Scott one of Scotland's most popularly known authors. But loans come with fees and this took out a chunk of their profits, one that was comparatively small to the loans at hand, but grew exponentially as they kept taking on new debt without catching up on old promises. Scott managed to retrieve most of his conveniences, including 4,000 wine bottles from his Edinburgh home before it was sold. In contrast, the Constables and the Ballantynes were ruined, and had to sell their luxurious homes and otherwise never recovered from the settlement. Constable died "apparently of dropsy" in 1827, and his son went "mad."[175]

Lockhart and other biographers of Scott depict Scott's eventual repayment of his and his publishers' debts as a heroic act, but as Sutherland stresses Scott used his legal knowledge and connections to maneuver an agreement that allowed him the luxury to keep writing at his leisure while he did not really help his sinking friends beyond the legal bare minimum. Then again, with all the crookery Scott had observed with cooked books and backhanded accounting from both Ballantyne and Constable, why would he have placed additional risk on his fortune to bail them out? It takes an extremely strong character to maneuver through both a founding and a collapse of a publishing venture, and people such as Mark Twain, Leonard Woolf, Mary Shelley, and Sir Walter Scott managed to survive it, while Virginia Woolf and Percy Shelley did not. Immediately after Constable's death, the court found that Scott's immensely successful, *The Life of Napoleon*, which Constable helped him outline and compose, was Scott's property rather than Constable's, and this repaid a third of Scott's debts. Shortly thereafter, on February 23, 1827 at a benefit dinner, Scott revealed his authorship of the Waverley novels.[176] The news seemed to be well received.

Meanwhile, perhaps because Constable was not around to fact-check Scott's speedy writing and tendency to insult, Scott slipped in his famous Napoleon study, and accused General Gourgaud of betraying Napoleon, a move that outraged Gourgaud so much that he objected against the misrepresentations, to which Scott denounced him as a "long moustachoed son of a French bitch" in the *Edinburgh Weekly*

---

175   Ibid., 292-8.
176   Ibid., 316-8.

Journal, leading Gourgaud to threaten to come to London to duel with Scott, an offer that Scott invited him to, though it never managed to take place.[177] By 1830, Scott made £50,000 for his creditors and £6,000 for himself to keep up with his expenses, not counting his regular wages from the law. He lived so comfortably that he retired from his Clerk of Court position that spring to focus on his more profitable writing, keeping a £864 annual pension.[178] Later that year, while keeping up a strenuous writing schedule despite partial handicap due to strokes, the trust turned over a gift of £10,000 in property to Scott's estate, allowing him to draft wills of inheritance to his family.[179]

Scott's decline accelerated for the same reason as most of the other radical authors from this period. On April 17, he was "bled and blistered" and put on a "diet" by doctors. He initially tried to resist having an "insertion of a seton in his neck, to drain off fluid," but his son, Walter, insisted, and the seton was inserted on May 18. Scott commented on April 27, "dying like an Indian under tortures is no joke."[180] The seton was inserted on General Election day, after an angry mob "spat at, abused and pelted" Scott "with stones." The mob's dissatisfaction with him made him feel dejected enough to agree to this new torture. Unlike other writers who typically took the doctor's advice and refrained from strenuous brain activity during purgative and similarly painful treatments, Scott worked steadily through it, completing the first volume of *Castle Dangerous* by July 3, and receiving a £1,200 advance for it from Cadell. It was printed by Ballantyne, but Scott for once did not consult Ballantyne during the writing process, supposedly because Ballantyne was too much of a pro-Reform Whig. He finished the manuscript by September with the help of dictation because he was too weak to write. Without Ballantyne's hand, Scott inserted more of his rebellious spirit and more pro-Scottish nationalist propaganda into this work.[181]

It might have been a subversive assassination attempt when the "admiralty" offered Scott "free passage to Malta in one of their warships, the Barham," an offer orchestrated by "Scott's political rivals,

---

177   Ibid., 319-20.
178   Ibid., 336-7.
179   Ibid., 341.
180   Edgar Johnson. *Sir Walter Scott: The Great Unknown, 2 vols.* (Boston: Little, Brown and Company, 1970), 1173.
181   Sutherland, *Life*, 346-7.

the party of Reform under Lord Grey."[182] It might have seemed like an olive branch when Scott accepted it to avoid a cold winter in Scotland, but from the beginning, Scott anticipated that the voyage would be as fatal to him as the "final journeys to the sun" were for "Smollett and Fielding," as they were for Byron and Poe from this study.[183] The trip was so exhausting that even Scott's relatively healthy daughter, Anne, died shortly after their return. The party arrived in London on September 28, 1831, in the midst of riots by pro-Reform agitators. While Scott was in London, he was seen by Dr Abercrombie, his regular Scottish physician, who "advised him against literary work." Scott ignored this lecture, and focused on his non-fiction editing duties, working on exhaustive revisions and annotations.[184] The military vessel Scott took to save money ended up costing him a great deal more than it saved because it was delayed for months at most ports, and they only reached Malta on November 22. When they landed at various stops, Scott acted out his duties as President of the Edinburgh Royal Society, and wrote detailed reports on what he was observing of a "volcanic landmass" and other oddities for his fellow scientists. After a great deal of touring, socializing, drinking and eating, they sailed to Naples on December 13.

At around this time Scott started writing a new novel about the region, *The Siege of Malta*, and completed it by the time he reached Rome on April 17. While Cadell offered an advance initially, he decided that it was unpublishable by the time he received the entire manuscript, partially because the last part seemed to be a "plagiarism from the Abbe Vertot's *Knights of Malta*" and other parts were disorganized and incoherent.[185]

On February 9, they made an expedition to Pompeii. Across all these luxurious stops, Scott was deluding himself that the new novels he was writing would finally rid him of debt. Meanwhile, Cadell was hiding the once again growing debt Scott was accumulating during this trip abroad.[186] Scott was optimistic that now that his debt was cleared, he could stop writing his silly novels, and return to poetry, which he said he abandoned because, "Byron *bet* [i.e. beat] me."[187] They kept

182	Ibid., 348.
183	Ibid., 348-9.
184	Ibid., 349.
185	Ibid., 351-2.
186	Ibid., 352-3.
187	Donald Sultana. *The Siege of Malta Rediscovered: An account of Sir Walter*

touring Florence, Bologna, Venice and other sights in May, then Germany in June (where Lockhart refused to meet with Scott, writing that he was busy with the Reform bill). Scott had a few strokes across these travels. An especially intense stroke hit on June 9 in Nijmegen, but he insisted on continuing the journey. Scott finally decided to head back to England because he saw the end coming and wanted to die in his own bed. They arrived back in England on June 11. "Scott recognized Lockhart and Jane, but he was clearly disturbed and wandering in mind." They arrived in London on June 13, where Dr Robert Ferguson attended him. Scott insisted on dying at Abbotsford and they all journeyed there on July 7 via steamboat, arriving in Edinburgh on July 9, then leaving in a carriage on July 11 for Abbotsford, finally arriving to Scott's infinite delight. Lockhart commented on the state Scott was in upon their arrival: "Recovery was no longer to be thought of: but there might be *Euthanasia*."[188] Despite this dire judgement, Scott was trying to write again in the three clear days he had after settling into his abode. In this span, doctors "were trying to help him" with the usual torturous bleedings, blisterings and the like, he objected with what the unsympathetic observers called "unintelligible but violent reproaches."[189] One of the things he was uttering was, "Burke Sir Walter," echoing the criticisms levied against him by the reformers that had attacked him. Scott was screaming this ceaselessly for twenty-six hours before he died after two months of extreme suffering.[190]

Scott's death happened before his time, and the circumstances surrounding it are tragic. Constable, Ballantyne and Scott's bankruptcies are also dark spots on the history of publishing. The best publishers have made the same mistakes since Scott's time, taking out unrepayable loans because of their ambition to create best-selling and critically applauded authors. Scott's insistence on writing even as he was dying shows the honorable and true dedication he had for the writing craft. Like so many ambitious author-publishers, his writing and his social obligations preceded his health, his family, his riches, his house, and life itself.

Scott's Mediterranean journey and his last novel. (Edinburgh: Scottish Academic Press, 1977), 77.
188   John Gibson Lockhart. *Memoirs of the Life of Sir Walter Scott,* 5 vols. (Boston: Houghton, Mifflin and Company, 1902), 5, 431.
189   Johnson, *Walter,* 1267.
190   Sutherland, *Life,* 354-5.

CHAPTER 4

Anti-Monarchical Sentiments and Mysterious Deaths: Lord Byron's "The Vision of Judgment" and Percy Shelley's "Lines to a Critic" in The Liberal

Within two years of starting *The Liberal* journal, Lord Byron had died of a fever in Greece and Percy Shelley had died in a boating "accident" in Italy. While there have been many speculations regarding these two mysterious deaths, no solid proof has yet to surface to prove that they were assassinations, and not simply the result of adventurous travels. Both writers were engaged in writing about the supernatural, about liberal unconventional love, and against the British monarchy. They were hoping that exiling themselves from England would allow them to publish radical works without fear of reprisal, but just as Putin is suspected of assassinating Russian dissidents in the US, it is hardly a stretch that King George IV, who ruled between 1820 and 1830, managed to reach out to assist their early deaths.

The Liberal was founded by the Shelleys, Byron and Leigh Hunt. It was published by Leigh's brother, John Hunt, who was a staunch radical and frequently published books and periodicals that earned him libel and sedition charges. Several critics have described the odd mix of radicals that formed this periodical:

> ...their strange and forced association in that famous short-lived journal *The Liberal: Verse and Prose from the South* (1822-1823 [July 30]). *The Liberal* was to be the product of the Snake and the Eagle and the Wren (Percy Bysshe Shelley and Lord Byron and Leigh Hunt), but it nearly foundered upon the death of Shelley on July 8, 1822. Nevertheless, Hunt (who contributed thirty-four articles) and Byron (who contributed nine, including his satire on Robert Southey, "The Vision of Judgment"), aided by other writers including Mary Shelley, were able to produce four issues of this journal, the first published on October 15, 1822.[191]

The story behind *The Liberal's* founding, publication and death includes many, complex layers. The players involved were leading both political and literary campaigns of which this periodical was the pinnacle. The intersections between their paths and the histories of their publishing ventures explain not only their struggles, but the tribulations of periodical and book publishing at large.

Byron's Self-Publications and Political Roots

The decisions Byron made surrounding founding and closing his own journal can be explained with a look back at his first publication. Thomas Moore reported that Byron first conceived the idea that he could print his own book at the Pigot house in July of 1806, when Miss Pigot was reading aloud one of Burns' poems and Byron said that "'he, too, was a poet sometimes, and would write down for her some verses of his own which he remembered. He then, with a pencil, wrote the lines beginning, 'In thee I fondly hope to clasp.'"[192] Soon after this conception, Byron's first published book was "privately printed" in 1806, at a time when he thought he gained an extra £30,000 by winning back control over his Rochdale estate at Lancaster Assizes. It says something about his ambition that the first thing he wanted to invest his new fortune in was in printing a few review copies that he distrib-

---

191 Charles E. Robinson. "Chapter Two: Hazlitt and Byron: With a New Look at *The Liberal.*" *Publishing, Editing, and Reception: Essays in Honor of Donald H. Reiman.* Michael Edson, Ed. (New York: Rowman & Littlefield, 2015), 26.
192 Moore, *Letters,* 75-90.

uted to educated people he admired with the hope of soliciting their reviews. The resulting reviews called Byron's poetry obscene and unfit for Ladies, and this forced him to withdraw the book, "burning all the copies he could. Only four survived, including the one belonging to the original complainant. The Reverend J. T. Becher doubtless believed that Byron's 'amorous lay' could not taint *his* 'spotless mind.'"[193] Byron started writing poetry to express amorous feelings, but he failed to align them to societal regulations, and ended up with a book that was not fit for traditional publishing, and had to be printed at his own risk and expense. In fact, to support his addiction to self-publishing, Byron took out loans that in part contributed to his later problems with creditors, and his need to leave England to escape them. In 1807, using loaned funds, Byron privately distributed a heavily edited and obscenity-cleansed version of the earlier book, now called, *Poems on Various Occasions*.[194]

Thus, it was really extraordinary that when Byron first queried Murray, some years later, Murray was willing to risk libel and sedition charges because of the literary merit of Byron's work. Still, to be on the safe side, Murray proposed that Byron should edit the manuscript prior to publication to make it a bit less offensive to the monarchy. Murray explained in a letter that there were "some expressions concerning Spain and Portugal which… do not harmonise with the now prevalent feeling" and "some religious sentiments which may deprive me of some customers amongst the Orthodox."[195] Byron's reply in a letter to Murray was negative:

> With regard to the political and metaphysical parts, I am afraid I can alter nothing; but I have high authority for my Errors in that point, for even the Aeneid was a *political* poem, and written for a *political* purpose; and as to my unlucky opinions on Subjects of more importance, I am too sincere in them for recantation… As for the "*Orthodox*," let us hope they will buy, on purpose to abuse—you will forgive the one, if they will do the other.[196]

Byron explained the nature of his unyielding anti-religious views in an

---

193 Gilmour, *Byron*, 154-5.
194 Ibid., 155.
195 Rowland E. Prothero. *The Works of Lord Byron, Letters and Journals*, 6 vols., 1898-1901. (London: John Murray, 1922), 1811, i, 208.
196 Ibid., 5 September 1811, ii, 25-6.

earlier letter to Hodgson:

> I will have nothing to do with your immortality; we are miserable enough in this life, without the absurdity of speculating upon another. If men are to live, why die at all? And if they die, why disturb the sweet and sound sleep that "knows no waking"?... As to revealed religion, Christ came to save men; but a good Pagan will go to heaven, and a bad Nazarene to hell... I hope I am sincere; I was so at least on a bed of sickness in a far-distant country... I looked to death as a relief from pain, without a wish for an after-life...[197]

These passages directly state the radical sentiments that Byron insisted on keeping in a subverted form in the epic poem that made him famous over-night with John Murray's brave help, *Childe Harold*. In fact, after reading Byron's brisk response, Murray decided to use this blatant radicalism to sell more copies of this radical work. Murray advertised *Childe Harold* deliberately after Byron's "speech in the House of Lords against the government bill to impose the death penalty on Luddite rioters convicted of destroying the new machinery that was causing unemployment."[198] Lord Byron took his hereditary peer seat in the House of Lords immediately upon coming of age at twenty in 1808, taking over the seat Lord Carlisle, his guardian, was holding for him. Before taking this seat, Byron was asked to prove his legitimacy by producing his grandfather, the Admiral's, marriage certificate to his grandmother, a task that his solicitor charged him £158 for at a time when Byron was in debt and had to borrow money from his mother to settle this and other claims.[199] As a result, when Byron arrived in the House of Lords, he was in a bad humor, and must have felt that the leadership of the House was hostile towards him or they would not have asked him to prove a matter of honor like his legitimacy, a topic that he had previously proved via less formal means. Byron was also not well received in the House because he immediately took seats with the opposition, criticized his fellow politicians in his writing, and otherwise showed his distaste, so much so that after taking the seat and attending eight meetings, he went on an extensive trip abroad.[200] Byron's passionate maiden speech in support of the Luddites was the first time in four

---

197   Ibid., 3 September 1811, ii, 18-22.
198   Elwin, *Byron*, 140.
199   Moore, *Letters*, 100-1.
200   Gilmour, *Byron*, 174-6.

years when he overcame his shyness to speak before the House. In this speech against making frame-breaking a capital offence, Byron argued on behalf of "these men, as I have seen them, meagre with famine, sullen with despair, careless of a life,—which your lordships are perhaps about to value at something less than the price of a stocking-frame…"[201] Lord Byron explained his opposition to the strict handling of the rioters more directly in a letter to the man he was trying to convince on the other side of the debate, the leader of the Moderate Whigs, Lord Holland: "My own motive for opposing the bill is founded on its palpable injustice, and its certain inefficacy. I have seen the state of these miserable men, and it is a disgrace to [a] civilized country. Their excesses may be condemned, but cannot be a subject of wonder. The effect of the present bill would be to drive them into actual rebellion… P.S.—I am a little apprehensive that your Lordship will think me too lenient towards these men, & *half a framebreaker myself.*"[202] Byron was faced with overwhelming opposition, and failed to protect the rioters, as twenty-seven of them were hanged.[203] Still, this is a great example of just how the future King George IV might have heard Byron's direct pro-rebel sentiments, and then oversaw Byron's financial success on the notoriety of this open attack. In addition, if the King was given rights to his crown by God, then an attack on organized religion was also an attack on the source of a monarch's power. Byron must have gone beyond even these radical statements in his autobiography to some height of sedition that even John Murray could not tolerate, which prompted him to collaborate with associates in the burning of Byron's memoirs, supposedly to protect his posthumous reputation.

Byron did not anticipate the cold shoulder he received from other Lords in response to his rhetoric. After a year of trying to make a difference with his House speeches, he became disgruntled, and on March 26, 1813 he wrote to Augusta Leigh, "…my parliamentary schemes are not much to my taste—I spoke twice last Session—& was told it was well enough—but I hate the thing altogether—& have no intention to 'strut another hour' on that stage."[204] Then, on November 14, 1813 he wrote in his *Journal* that he "declined presenting the Debtor's Peti-

---

201   Thomas Carson Hansard. *Parliamentary Debates from the Year 1803 to the Present Time*. (London: Hansard, 1824), XXI, 964-72.
202   Prothero, *Works*, 25 February 1812, ii, 103.
203   Gilmour, *Byron*, 328.
204   Byron, *Byron's*, Vol. 3, 32.

tion, being sick of parliamentary mummeries."[205] In the following year, his disgust intensified still farther into a pro-anarchy position, and he wrote on January 16, 1814 in his *Journal* that he has in "utter detestation of all existing governments."[206] By 1821, he became a revolutionary, writing in his *Ravenna Journal* on January 13: "The king-times are fast finishing. There will be blood shed like water, and tears like mist; but the people will conquer in the end."[207] This track of thought led him to focus on a "liberated" and "free Italy!!!" in particular.[208] Since he lived in Italy at the time, it was natural for him to fixate on this area in the last years of his life. He could not have made such revolutionary statements in the House, as they would've been seditious and punishable by death, so as he marched towards an anti-totalitarian position, he neared openly joining the peoples' revolutions.

Byron came in direct contact with the future King, and then Prince Regent George IV in June of that same year when he made his first pro-rebel speech in the House of Lords, 1812. Byron was presented to the Prince Regent at a party at Carlton House by either Lady Caroline Lamb, or, more likely according to Doris Langley Moore, Lady Oxford. Byron had a volatile relationship with Lady Lamb, after their passionate affair. The friction between them included Byron being rejected in a proposal of marriage to one of Lady Lamb's cousins. Byron wrote to James Wedderburn Webster from the Piccadilly Terrace on September 4, 1815 that "she is a villainous intriguante… mad & malignant—capable of all & every mischief… there is an indefatigable & active spirit of meanness & destruction about her… keep her from all that you value."[209] Meanwhile, Lady Oxford, the Countess, "was forty… but had retained her beauty and seductiveness" and had a "classical education" and Byron had a lengthy affair with her in 1812. "Lady Oxford was an intimate friend of Caroline of Brunswick, the Regent's discarded consort."[210] Returning to Byron's meeting with the King (regardless of which jealous Lady introduced them), during it, "the Prince had been so agreeable and so pleasing in his conversation that Byron decided to pay his respects at Court." Byron ordered an uncharacteristically expensive "green coat" and other components of

205 Ibid., Vol. 3, 206.
206 Ibid., Vol. 3, 242.
207 Ibid., Vol. 8, 26.
208 Ibid., Vol. 8, 47.
209 Byron, *Selected*, 112.
210 Moore, *Letters*, 199.

an outfit to match the latest fashions for £52, and for the first time had his hairdresser "powder his hair—still requisite for Court attendance." Just when Byron finished the strenuous and expensive task of getting in "full regalia," he received a notice that the levee was being put off till a later date. Instead of waiting to use this outfit at the next Court visitation, Byron realized how embarrassed he was by the idea that his liberal friends might discover that he was planning on paying homage at Court, and he never again attempted visiting the Prince Regent and later King George IV, and this slight must have contributed to the later tensions between George IV and Byron.[211]

Byron's Early Attempts to Start a Journal

Meanwhile, Byron was always among the first to be informed of new places to publish radical works in Britain, so he was excited when John Murray invited him to submit to a new journal he was contemplating starting, but knowing Murray he did not take the attempt seriously and wrote a poem to Murray about it from Venice on January 8, 1818:

> …For the Journal you hint of.
> As ready to print off;
> No doubt you do right to commend it
> But as yet I have writ off
> The devil a bit of
> Our "Beppo", when copied—I'll send it…[212]

Murray later ended up buying a half-share in William Blackwood's *Edinburgh Monthly Magazine* (founded in 1817) half a year later in August of 1818, only to sell it a year after that. Meanwhile, Byron did indeed send *Beppo* eleven days later and it was published in February as a standalone book. This exchange shows how both passionate and sarcastic Byron felt about starting a new journal venture years before he attempted it with the Shelleys and Hunts.

Byron was also discussing starting a new *newspaper* with Thomas

---

211   Ibid., 195.
212   Lord George Gordon Byron. *Lord Byron: Selected Letters and Journals: The liveliest and most revealing letters from the acclaimed 12-volume edition—together in one volume*. Leslie A. Marchand, Ed. (Cambridge: Harvard University Press & Belknap Press, 1982), 168.

Moore, suggesting on December 25, 1820 that it could be a general paper for all sorts of genres, but particularly aimed to "give the age some new lights upon policy, poesy, biography, criticism, morality, theology, and all other *ism*, *ality*, and *ology* whatsoever."[213] Byron reminded Moore of this idea with more certainty in a letter on August 2, 1821, but Moore did not share Byron's enthusiasm for creating a radical paper that would touch on the subjects most likely to be labeled as seditious, libelous or heretical. The speed with which shares in journals were bought and sold, and journals opened and closed in this period is also significant in explaining why as the first few issues of *The Liberal* did not sell well, Byron quickly decided to stop investing and cut his losses.

Percy Shelley's Self-Publications and Oratory Attempts

Percy Shelley had a similar early publishing history to Byron. By the time Percy started at Oxford University in 1810, he was already actively sending manuscripts to publishers, hoping to begin a career as a writer. From these earliest ventures, Percy's ideas were too radical and his funds too limited. In December of 1810, Percy's father received a letter from a London publisher, Mr. Stockdale, who had received Percy's "MS. of a novel, *St. Irvyne, or the Rosicrucian*, filled with the most subversive ideas, and the worthy tradesman could not see without misgiving the son of so estimable a gentleman as Mr. Shelley treading this dangerous path." Mr. Stockdale also informed Mr. Shelley that Percy should not be associating with a "false and dangerous... character" like his only friend at Oxford, Mr. Jefferson Hogg. Of course, the point of sending the letter was to solicit printing funds from Mr. Shelley due to the risky nature of the venture, to which Mr. Shelley replied "that he refused to pay one penny of the printing bill, which greatly increased the metaphysical and doctrinal anxieties of the publisher."[214] Thus, Percy had found out, the hard way, that publishers are not kindly investors looking for controversial political literature, but rather shrewd businessmen, willing to step over authors to get to their fathers' money in exchange for printing whatever dribble writers were churning out.

213   Lord George Gordon Byron. *The Works of Lord Byron: Letters and Journals.* Rowland E. Prothero, Ed. 6 Vol. (London: 1898-1901), V, 143.
214   Andre Maurois. *Ariel: The Life of Shelley.* (1924). (New York: Frederick Ungar Publishing Co., 1968), 24-5.

This discovery together with being rejected by his early love interest, Elizabeth, because of his radical theological opinions led Percy to place "a loaded pistol, and various poisons… by his side" one night with the intention of committing suicide, but he did not go through with it.[215]

To recover from the loss of a beloved and the failure of his traditional publication attempt, Percy escaped into writing poetry and philosophy. Percy's first amateur publication began as a prank letter writing campaign, which suddenly became a book when he persuaded Philadelphia Phillips, a fellow Oxford student, to print at Worthing the pamphlet on the metaphysics of the potential for the existence of a deity. It was co-authored by Shelley and his friend, Thomas Jefferson Hogg, and was advertised for sale in an Oxford paper under the title, *The Necessity of Atheism*.[216] In addition, Shelley "sent it to many of the heads of houses" at Oxford and "plastered Slatter and Munday's shop with it, telling the shopman to sell it for sixpence. The display lasted for less than an hour. A Fellow of New College, seeing it in the window, entered the shop, and having glanced at its contents 'advised the principals' to destroy all copies—which they did." The matter could have ended there, but then Shelley "sent a copy to Edward Copleston, the Professor of Poetry, later a bishop," who had recently warred with critics at the *Edinburgh Review*. Copleston filed an official complaint, which led to Shelley and Hogg's expulsion from Oxford in 1811.[217] Hogg went on to study law in London, became a barrister, and lived a long life with his family, never publishing such radical treatises again. As an early biographer of Shelley's life put it, Hogg "became a timorous, disillusioned old gentleman, reading Greek and Latin all day long to kill time and cheat his immense boredom."[218] On the other hand, for Shelley, a widely distributed and noticed publication was more important than completing a degree from the top college in the land. He did not choose atheism as his topic because this was a cause that he was willing to die to defend, but rather because it was a cause that he knew was so outrageous that it would not fail to attract the maximum attention from his teachers and peers.

With no classes to attend, Shelley went to work in London on writing new books. Shelley's more professional first poetry collection,

---

215   Ibid., 29.
216   Gilmour, *Byron*, 141.
217   Ibid., 142-3.
218   Maurois, *Ariel*, 334.

Original Poetry by Victor & Cazire, was privately printed, but on a budget, and so it was "waggishly" and "grotesquely printed," and received negative reviews from Shelley's correspondents for obscenity and the like. Unlike Byron, Shelley decided to correct these problems by printing with Henry Slatter a much more radical and, at 22 quarto pages, shorter book called, *Posthumous Fragments of Margaret Nicholson; Being Poems Found amongst the Papers of that Noted Female who Attempted the Life of the King in 1786*. With this work, Shelley "wanted to attack George III, and even under the pseudonym of Margaret Nicholson that could only be done with reasonable safety by attacking monarchy in general. The second of the two longer poems is an epithalamium of two people who, unlike Margaret Nicholson, had succeeded in their assassination attempts, Francis Ravaillac, who murdered Henry IV, and Charlotte Corday, who disposed of Marat."[219] The book was a commercial failure, according to the publisher, Henry Slatter, with only 250 copies printed. Simultaneously, Shelley's identity leaked out and was known in Christ Church at Oxford University only three months after this release.[220] Shelley's support for assassinations of kings through a pseudonymous book is likely to have contributed to making Shelley a priority target for King George III's successor.

Shelley made his maiden public speech in the same year as Byron, on February 28, 1812, in Dublin, addressing a public meeting. In preparation, Shelley wrote and "cheaply and shoddily," privately printed, the *Address to the Irish People*, which contained "22 pages of small print and some 12,000 words." It mimicked some of Thomas Paine's *Common Sense*, in that it also supported independence, in this case of Ireland from British rule via the Repeal of the Union Act, with rhetorically passionate language. Despite Shelley's attempt to find the cheapest available printer in Dublin, the cost of the pamphlet was still prohibitive to the Irish poor who attended the meeting, as Shelley found out when he received the books from the printer and began trying to distribute them. "Some of the remaining 1,100 copies were got rid of by Shelley and Harriet [Westbrook, his first wife,] giving them to passersby or by throwing them down from their balcony, which amused Harriet, particularly as 'Percy [looked] so grave' while doing so. Shelley was evidently surprised that no prosecution had been 'yet attempted',

---

219   Gilmour, *Byron*, 129
220   Ibid., 130.

but the authorities, like the poor, had probably not read his address."[221]

There is a clear parallel here between the angst both Byron and Shelley felt at their attempts to rouse the people or the House to radicalization. Theory and political philosophy taught them that people are logical and act in the interest of the public, but in reality, they clashed against corruption, illiteracy and other plagues that are still delaying positive political progress today. Their self-publications at least resulted in tangible books that they could show their critics, so they focused their lives on publishing rather than on actively rousing rebellions, that is up until *The Liberal's* failure.

Intersections Between Byron and Shelley's Rebellions and Families

The Shelleys and Byron were in close correspondence that inspired them to start a journal together in part because Byron had an "ill-starred affair" with Claire Clairmont, Mary Shelley's half-sister, who followed him around on his travels and became the mother of his daughter Allegra in 1817.[222] Claire initially contacted Byron when she was hoping to succeed as an actress and he was directing the Drury Lane Theatre. Byron was fresh out of a tumultuous courtship and a year-long marriage, between 1815 and 1816, to Annabella Milbanke. Byron had decided on marrying hoping to escape the slew of awful, crazed relationships he had, after his fame commenced in 1812, with the bulk of London's society. There were even a rumor of an affair between Byron and his half-sister. There were also plenty of gossip about Byron's bisexuality, which was groomed in his school years when it was socially acceptable, but became life-threatening in adulthood because "the number of executions for sodomy was growing. Astonishingly, between 1805 and 1832, executions for murder outnumbered by less than six to one executions for sodomy."[223] In his biography, Ian Gilmour examines several passages from Byron's letters, and his friends' accounts, and concludes that: "Whereas in Greece he had been predominantly homosexual, in England he became predominantly, if not

---
221 Ibid., 308.
222 Malcolm Elwin. *Lord Byron's Wife*. (New York: Harcourt, Brace & World, Inc., 1963), 470.
223 Ian Gilmour. *Byron & Shelley in Their Time: The Making of the Poets*. (New York: Carroll & Graf Publishers, 2003), 179.

wholly, heterosexual… Only when he returned to Greece at the end of his life were his homosexual inclinations fully revived…"[224] Claire Clairmont was a welcome change from this dangerous passion as she was educated and focused on developing her skills as a writer and actress. She also wooed him with romantic letters. But, soon after the sexual fling between Claire and Byron, he departed for a long trip to Europe. Undeterred by distance, Clare insisted that the Shelleys take her to meet Byron in Switzerland. When she arrived, Byron realized that she was pregnant with his child, and this tied him irrevocably to a friendship with the Shelleys, as they were now biologically connected. Allegra, the resulting daughter, had a very short life, dying at five, after being put in a convent by Byron, from typhus or malaria in April of 1822.

***

The length to which both Shelley and Byron went to distribute their writings at their own expense says a great deal about what it took for a radical author in the nineteenth century to become "famous" as if "overnight." This sudden fame happened for Byron in 1812 after one of his poetry collections finally became a commercial success after all those years of building an audience through these types of paid-for publicity campaigns. Shelley's speech and Address made a mild impression "on the two government spies who attended the meeting" and published a report where his name was briefly mentioned to King George IV.[225] While Shelley's antics got him noticed by critics, university administrators, spies and all sorts of other administrative censors, he never managed to gain fame, "respect and recognition during his lifetime."[226] Byron only attained fame after making a public speech to the House on a topic in parallel with his poetry book's release, shrewdly diverting those who were shocked by his radical politics to buy his books. Despite failing to make a similar marketing push during his life, Shelley's insistence on self-publication and self-promotion paid off in his literary afterlife, as he is now firmly in the forefront of the Romantic canon. Neither Byron nor Shelley could have found publishers for their later works if they did not establish a track-record of aggressively

---

224 Ibid., 260.
225 Ibid., 309.
226 Ibid., 332.

promoting themselves with privately printed experiments.

Unlike the film stars of the present day, Byron and Shelley did not want to gain fame for its own sake, but rather in order to become recognizable enough to make a difference with their writings and speeches in political affairs. Byron's speech in the House of Lords on behalf of Greek independence inspired the development of philhellenes in the general public as well as in his good friend, Percy Bysshe Shelley. Percy drowned "with a copy of Aeschylus in his pocket," soon after publishing his own revolutionary poem, "Choruses from Hellas."[227] Shelley and Byron shared a passion for Greek literature and politics, but Byron caught this passion first, and then spread it to Shelley. Byron had translated at the Harrow on December 1, 1804 Aeschylus' *Prometheus Bound*, which he called, "Fragments of School Exercises, From the Prometheus Victus of Aeschylus", and later in 1816 or so he wrote his interpretation of the Prometheus myth in "Prometheus." Byron's speech for Greek independence reverberated through the following decades, so that Edward VII, who was born after Byron died, in 1841, and served as Britain's king from 1901 to 1910, caused a scandal by welcoming Garibaldi, the Italian revolutionary, to England in 1864 during the Schleswig-Holstein dispute between Prussia and Denmark. Edward VII's move was particularly radical for a monarch because, like other members of his royal family, he suffered an assassination attempt related to the Boer War in South Africa in 1900, while he was travelling through Brussels on his way to Denmark.

Back during Shelley's visit to Pisa, Mary and Percy Shelley took lessons in Greek from Alexandros Mavrokordatos, the revolutionary president of the provisional government in western Greece, whom the Shelleys and Byron were supporting in his run for prime minister of Greece, but who lost this attempt soon after associating with this radical group. Byron held the title of commander-in-chief of Army of Western Greece during his involvement with the Greek revolution, so it was natural for him to affiliate with a politician such as Mavrokordatos. Mavrokordatos withdrew from politics after this defeat, only to return in 1825, and then he finally became the Prime Minister of Greece in 1833. He later regained this position at intervals in the following decades. It might have been their friendship with a revolutionary such as Alexandros and the Gamba family that attracted "police spies in the

---

227   Gary J. Bass. *Freedom's Battle: The Origins of Humanitarian Intervention*. (New York: Alfred A. Knopf, 2008), 58.

pay of the Austrian-dominated Government" to watch Byron's progress in Pisa very closely.[228] Byron wrote in his journal that when he met with the Gamba family on January 5, 1821, they immediately jumped into a discussion of warfare, wherein Byron advertised that he was a moderate "master of fence," and then, "Settled that the R[evolution]. will break out… One must not be particular, but take rebellion when it lies in the way."[229] Thus, a Revolution was put in Byron's way by the Gambas and other revolutionaries and he accepted the challenge to rebel against tyranny. Byron must have agreed to purchase weapons for the revolutionaries during the January meeting because he writes on February 16, 1821 that "Count P. G." sent "a bag full of bayonets, some muskets, and some hundreds of cartridges to my house" when the Government issued an order stating that anybody "having arms concealed… shall be liable." Byron had ordered these for Gamba. He felt betrayed when the arms were sent to him instead because the Gambas wanted to avoid being caught carrying them. Byron also stated that he did not trust his servants with keeping the secret if they had received this delivery, "except Tita and F[letcher] and Lega." This indicates that Byron had reason to suspect there were spies or counter-revolutionaries in his household, and also that he could not fully trust the Gambas, even as he was putting his money and freedom on the line for their cause.[230]

The Radicalization of the Hunt Brothers

John Hunt's other left-wing periodicals included *The Reflector, The News, Yellow Dwarf* and *The Examiner*. The latter was edited by Leigh Hunt and was more widely known than the short-lived *Liberal*. John Hunt remained in England and lived a comparatively long life despite being imprisoned, while Byron and Shelley both escaped imprisonment but met more subversive ends. John wrote little himself, but he certainly wrote some short pieces. It is unusual in the publishing business to find a publisher that does not publish him or herself. The clash between the Shelleys, Byron and the Hunts against affiliates of George IV might have started when he was the Prince Regent in 1813. Leigh Hunt had worked in the War Office up to 1808, where he gained first-

---

228   Moore, *Letters*, 283.
229   Byron, *Selected*, 240.
230   Ibid., 250.

hand knowledge of the political administration of Britain. Disgruntled with the monarchy, instead of seeking further political appointments, Leigh became the editor of his brother's new newspaper, *The Examiner*. They published a great many radical pieces and criticisms before, in 1813, Leigh edited and John published a direct attack on George IV, for which both were sentenced to two years at the Surrey County Gaol. Lord Byron and the Shelleys visited the brothers and were among the wealthy radical friends that made his stay in prison tolerable with their luxurious gifts. Byron must have sympathized with the Hunts because his own sexually liberated work was frequently the subject of "violent attack" even from independent papers, such as the one owned by John Murray, *Edinburgh Review*, in 1808.[231] Byron supported Leigh Hunt's literary efforts by connecting him with his own publisher, John Murray, a meeting that resulted in the printing of *Rimini* in 1816, in 500-750 printed copies and a profit for Hunt of around £45, a sum that was too small for Murray to work with him again.[232] In part because Byron and the Shelleys helped the Hunts pay their fines and contributed to making their life comfortable in prison back in 1813, the Hunts continued to publish radical works, and John Hunt was sentenced to a year imprisonment and heavy fines for libeling the House of Commons in the *Examiner* on July 23, 1820. Leigh Hunt withdrew from ownership of the *Examiner* to avoid sharing John's prison sentence this time around.[233]

Meanwhile, the Hunt brothers took a four-year hiatus before starting a new radical periodical in 1819, *The Indicator*, with contents leaning on satire, rather than on outright seditious criticisms of the monarchy. It was a year after *The Indicator*'s founding, when George IV was crowned. Soon thereafter, Leigh Hunt became so sick in 1821 that he wrote he, "almost died over the last numbers" and had to discontinue the publication. What was the nature of this yet another mysterious "illness"? Was it an assassination attempt? If so, the attempt was averted when the Shelleys and Byron sponsored Leigh's trip to Italy to join them and to mutually publish a new periodical, *The Liberal*. Their aim was to spread Liberal ideas from exile. Byron described his motiva-

---

231   Malcolm Elwin. *Lord Byron's Wife*. (New York: Harcourt, Brace & World, Inc., 1963), 131.
232   William H. Marshall. *Byron, Shelley, Hunt, and* The Liberal. (Philadelphia: University of Pennsylvania Press, 1960), 7.
233   Ibid., 19-20.

tions for helping to sponsor *The Liberal* in a letter to Mary Shelley on November 16, 1822: "I engaged in the Journal from good-will towards [Leigh Hunt]... and no less for his political courage, as well as regret for this present circumstances: I did this in the hope that he might... render himself independent."[234] Leigh Hunt's decision to join Shelley and Byron in *The Liberal* venture in Italy was hardly the fiscally conservative thing to do because at around the time he departed, he owed his brother, John, £1,868.6.5, with the trip from London to Pisa adding to this loan. Byron and Shelley only lent Leigh £550 as well as contributing furniture and traveling expenses between the time of his departure and shortly after his arrival.[235] Thus, Leigh was fiscally desperate when he started *The Liberal*, and this financial strain negatively affected his performance.

The Hunts' previous radical journals failed because George IV was funding the pro-monarchical publications, and thus made it difficult to compete with them in price and printing quality. Byron described this corrupt practice shortly before his death on February 10, 1824, to Colonel Stanhope. The conversation was recorded by William Parry. Byron attributes the liberal journals' failure to among other parties, "the King of France, who was said to expend large sums of money in bribing some English journals, which were consequently, the agents of *his* policy."[236] It was common in this age of sedition prosecutions for authors to blame foreign rulers or minor players instead of placing blame on the English King to avoid directly offending the crown.

Murray's Rival Journals

Murray was a business-minded publishing speculator more akin with Hearst than with Dickens, as he was born into a publishing fortune that he inherited from his father, who was also called John Murray (I). His father founded their publishing company in 1768. John II took full control of the business when he was twenty-five and immediately began to speculate on risky ventures including the 1807 joint publication with Archibald Constable of Sir Walter Scott's early effort, *Marmion*. Murray went on to control critical periodicals, such as the *Edinburgh Review* and the *Quarterly Review*, and publishing some of

---

234   Byron, *Selected*, 290.
235   Marshall, *Byron*, 33-5.
236   William Parry. *The Last Days of Lord Byron*. (London, 1825), 32-7.

Byron, Jane Austen and Thomas Moore's best-known works. While Murray's journal, *Edinburgh Review*, was critical of his fellow Scottish countryman, John Murray was impressed with his talent and published him after Lord Byron's *Childe Harold* was rejected "by Miller on account if its attack of Lord Elgin for removing the Marbles."[237] In a letter from Pisa on November 3, 1821, Byron expressed a concern to John Murray regarding Murray's request to be "anonyme," writing,

> You have played the Stepmother to D[on] J[uan]—throughout.—Either ashamed—or afraid—or negligent—to your own loss and nobody's credit.——Who ever heard before of a *publisher's not* putting *his* name?—The reasons for *my anonyme*—I stated—they were family ones entirely… you affect to wish to be considered as not having anything to do with that work—which by the way—is sad half and half dealing—for you will be a long time before you publish a better poem.——/ You seem hurt at the words "*the publisher*" *what! you*—who won't put your name on the title page—would have had me stick J. M. Esqre. On the blank leaf—no—Murray…[238]

Murray's suggestion that his name be kept off one of his books kept Byron angry until March 8, 1822, when he wrote to Thomas Moore that he was willing to reconcile and publish with Murray again as long as he agreed to publish his riding friend, John Taaffe's "Commentary on Dante," "against which there appears in the trade an unaccountable repugnance,"[239] and Murray agreed to this odd request, printing this book in Italy later that same year under the title, *A Comment on the Divine Comedy of Dante Alighieri, Vol. I* of XIII. It was reviewed pretty negatively in *The Monthly Review* in 1823 as "commentary on commentary"; in addition, the review forecast that while XIII volumes were promised, this was a "Herculean" labor that was unlikely to be fulfilled.[240] After Murray accepted the terms, Byron followed up on around May 26, 1822, or perhaps a couple of months later, by asking Murray to take care of the funeral and burial of his illegitimate daughter Allegra, who died at five in a convent because he was at Pisa and

---

237　Thomas Moore. *Letters and Journals of Lord Byron, With Notices of His Life*. (London, 1830), 75-90.
238　Byron, *Selected*, 281-2.
239　Ibid., 286.
240　Ralph Griffiths. *The Monthly Review, Or, Literary Journal, Volume LVI*. (London: R. Griffiths, 1823), 225.

Montenero and could not make the arrangements himself.[241] Murray failed to secure what Byron asked for because of opposition from the Church, in part due to Allegra's illegitimacy. Then, Murray wrote a letter in which he made comments that made Byron respond angrily that he was "brutally mistaken about Shelley who was without exception—the best and least selfish man I ever knew.—I never knew one who was not a beast in comparison.—"[242] This exchange shows how Byron's publishers were his bitterest enemies and most trusted friends.

Meanwhile, after his tirade to Murray on November 3rd, Byron stresses that Sir Walter Scott has not read any of his reviews for "*thirteen years.*" Therefore, Byron insisted that he no longer wanted to receive any reviews of his works from Murray to avoid being upset not so much by the reviews, but rather by how they made Murray want to take his name off Byron's book. Earlier that same year, on January 5, Byron wrote in his *Ravenna Journal* that he had read all of Scott's novels "at least fifty times" and that he longed "to get drunk with him." Thus, despite their clashes, Byron was Scott's fan and aware of Scott's publishing efforts, especially since they shared some publishers.[243] Byron understood why Scott bought a portion of his publisher when he was facing similar disinheriting remarks from disparaging publishers. Taking control of the artistic and business aspects of publishing one's own works deletes the censoring voice of an outside publisher. Some revolutionary content cannot find a publisher willing to put his or her name on the book, and in these cases the author has to put their own name as both the publisher and author, or put the book in a drawer and let it die without seeing the light of publication.

The John Murray publishing house was later picked up by John Murray III, who published a line of new outstanding authors, such as Charles Darwin and Herman Melville. Then, amazingly, Sir John Murray IV took over and published none other than Queen Victoria, as well as Sir Arthur Conan Doyle and others. Still more miraculously, this publishing house was then passed on to Sir John Murray V, John Murray VI and John Murray VII before it was taken over in 2002 by Hodder Headline and then was eaten by the Lagardere publishing conglomerate and merged with the Hachette UK brand. In other words, between 1768 and 2002, for two-hundred-and-thirty-four years or

---

241 Byron, *Selected*, 288.
242 Ibid., 289.
243 Ibid., 239.

nearly the entire span of British publishing history, a John Murray ran this business with great financial and cultural success, and then the promise of quick money squashed this legacy with the last John Murray still in great health.

But the narrative must return to John Murray II; he was hardly a radical, and he broke off his deal with Constable when he noted that Constable was deliberately pricing their books at extremely low levels to disseminate radical, anti-monarchical propaganda to the masses. Murray also broke off a budding publishing relationship with Byron by delaying the publication of the later cantos of *Don Juan* in 1821, perhaps suddenly finding content that he thought would bring sedition charges against him. Another reason for the break was that Byron started to abuse him in letters as early as 1816. Judith Noel describes Byron's abuses in a letter to Lady Byron, or Annabella Milbanke: "I find that Murray says the letter Byron wrote to him was as if he was writing to the greatest *Scoundrel* and *Blackguard*—but Murray passes it over for consideration of *insanity*…"[244]

To return to the founding of *The Liberal*, as John Murray II suspected, the satire about George III not exactly going to heaven was interpreted as seditious by George IV in 1822. Byron's name did not appear with the story, so George IV fined Leigh Hunt, the Editor, £100, assuming that he was the guilty author. A fine without a prison sentence signaled a new tactic of hitting Leigh's wallet, rather than making a martyr out of him with excessive imprisonments. After Percy Shelley's death, Leigh and John became financially depended on Byron. Leigh only left Italy after Byron's death in 1825. He struggled through a series of publishing failures, editing periodicals and writing books, before he received an annuity of £120 from Mary Shelley in 1844, which allowed him to write more serious books independently of trying to make a financial success via publishing to rival the popular appeal of *The Examiner* (which, due to this very popularity, had landed him in prison).

A Subversive Altercation with Pisa's Law Enforcement

The climax of Byron and Shelleys' stay at Pisa (before Shelley's death) occurred on March 24, 1822, when a large group of Byron's friends and servants was returning from "shooting practice," deep in conversa-

---

244 Prothero, *Works*, 24 January 1816, 206.

tion, when "another horseman, coming from behind, suddenly pushed between Taaffe and a ditch running beside the road, making Taaffe's horse rear up and plunge against Byron's and frightening those of the other riders."[245] Byron, Shelley and Trelawny followed the rider that just assaulted Byron and asked for an explanation, which did not come because the rider, a sergeant-major of dragoons, called Masi, appeared to be intoxicated. Thus, unsatisfied, Byron demanded a duel, assuming that Masi was a gentleman. Masi gave a rude reply. In retaliation, Pietro to struck him in the chest with a riding-whip, while calling him "*Ignorante*." Masi was late for roll call, so when he was struck, he yelled to the guards at the town's gate, "Arrest them! Arrest them!" Byron and the others tried to push past the guards to go after Masi, and at this point, the soldiers assaulted them. Shelley lost consciousness when he was knocked off his horse. Trelawny was beaten about the thighs with swords. Hay tried to stop Masi from striking at Shelley while he was down, and "received a stroke with the naked sword which… bruised his face, and severely cut his nose." With the next stroke, Masi slashed at Giuseppe Strauss, puncturing his lung, which later led to repeated hemorrhages.[246] At some point in this conflict, Byron's coachman, Vincenzo, "rushed at the soldier with a pitchfork under the impression that he had made an attack on Byron and was running away."[247] Because Byron was portrayed in the reports of Luigi Torelli, the informer or spy on his case, "as an assassin surrounded by a dangerous gang," the news of Masi's hospitalization and horsewhipping aroused the police to aggressively prosecute all involved in the incident.[248] A few of Byron's servants were arrested, but Masi recovered and this lightened their potential sentences. Torelli reported that "Byron paid bribes on all sides—Torelli estimated three thousand crowns—for the prisoners' freedom."[249] In contrast with this report, Doris Moore concluded that Byron could not have paid any such bribes because his account books do not show any large unnamed expenses. Moore explained, "had Byron spent thousands of crowns on getting the men released, he might assuredly have done a little better than stand helplessly by while they were deported, all innocent as he knew them to be."[250] Giuseppe, Tita

245   Moore, *Letters,* 280.
246   Ibid., 281.
247   Ibid., 289.
248   Ibid., 283.
249   Ibid., 286.
250   Ibid., 289.

and Antonio were all banished as part of this settlement, and they and a few other servants spent time in Pisa's prison. Byron kept his coachman, Vincenzo, safe from prosecution and nobody else from the party betrayed him to the authorities, even as they were suffering abuses in prison. Byron did spend a large sum on "fees to doctors and lawyers, express postage, payments to employees who could not perform their normal services, passports and journeys for those who were banished" up to a sum of around "five hundred crowns," according to Moore.[251] Is there really any doubt that this conflict was deliberate? There would be too many coincidences if Masi just happened to strike, of the dozens of people in the party, Byron, and then proceeded to insult and provoke the group as he sought protection from soldiers, who happened to be just ahead of the spot. If Masi was really as drunk as he tried to appear to be, could he have struck so many men with near-fatal blows? It took a great presence of mind and shrewd litigation skills for Byron to defend his friends against the onslaught of legal prosecution. Byron barely survived the attack. If Masi was a soldier in a plot against Byron and his army of rebels; then, the outcome proved that a direct physical or legal attack on Byron's life was likely to end in Byron's triumph. Regardless of if this was an accident or a deliberate assault, this conflict only served to radicalize Byron. The assaults that followed involved poison, drowning and other subversive or disguised techniques.

The Suspicious Deaths Around Leigh Hunt's Arrival (Including Shelley's), and the Literary Disasters That Befell *The Liberal*

Allegra's death oddly corresponds with the end of Leigh's journey to Italy. Leigh finally arrived after eight months' trip in July of 1822. The voyage was accompanied by not only the usual storms, but also by an unnamed sickness and misadventures that smell of sabotage. Eight months to travel between two countries in Europe near the end of the Industrial Revolution? Only weeks after Leigh's arrival in July, Percy Shelley also died, as if the assassins that had unsuccessfully tried to assassinate Leigh (traveling on the same boats with him) killed Percy instead once they hit the shore. Before Shelley's death, he wrote "Lines to a Critic" that appeared after he was dead in issue No. 3 of *The Liberal*,

---

251   Ibid., 290.

in 1823. It was ideas like the ones expressed in this poem that might have inspired antipathy towards Percy by the establishment and a potential assassination at sea. The poem is about critics that were derisive of his beloved liberalism. Percy is accusing them of hatred, misguided religiosity, greed and bigotry.

2.

>…Hate men who cant, and men who pray,
>And men who rail like thee;
>An equal passion to repay
>They are not coy like me.

3.

>Or seek some slave of power and gold
>To be thy dear heart's mate;
>Thy love will move that bigot cold
>Sooner than me, thy hate…[252]

Percy "drowned" in a schooner called *Don Juan* close to shore, and foul play has long been suspected. The *Don Juan* was sponsored by Byron and built at the same time as his own larger vessel, *Bolivar,* which was classified by Trelawny as a "small yacht."

In the weeks before Shelley's death, there were many violent outbursts among Byron's affiliates and staff. One of the central agitators was a coachman, Vincenzo, who nearly led to Byron and Shelley's imprisonment in Pisa. On June 29, 1822, the day of Leigh's arrival, Byron's "redoubtable but untrustworthy cook," Gaetano, had a fight with Vincenzo where "a knife was drawn" and Count Pietro was "slightly wounded in trying to separate the combatants." The police had to be called. Gaetano was only temporarily relieved of duties, staying on to spy for Count Pietro in his alimony dispute with Teresa. And Byron only made a showing of planning on firing Vincenzo Papi, but this crazed man remained with him till his death in Greece, and seems to be the likely trouble-making spy in this group of poets. The brawl broke out, oddly enough, on the day of Leigh Hunt's arrival with his

---

[252]   Percy Byssh Shelley. *The Complete Poetical Works of Percy Bysshe Shelley*. Volume I. Thomas Hutchinson, Ed. (Oxford Edition: 1914; Project Gutenberg; Retrieved: 27 July 2016; Web).

six children, and Byron sponsored putting them up in a hotel in the neighboring seaside city, Leghorn. Byron met Leigh in the summer of 1813 through Moore, and submitted to him "two Turkish tales" in November of that year.[253]

Shelley "came from his temporary summer residence near Lerici to" spend a couple of days with Hunt in Leghorn before they both traveled to Byron's palazzo in Pisa. Shortly thereafter, Shelley went back to Leghorn to meet with his sailing partner, William, and then they embarked for Lerici on July 8. They died, supposedly, during a storm in Shelley's small yacht despite having two sailors on board and traveling close-to-shore. Days later, Mary Shelley, Byron and his men set out to try to discover what happened with the missing yacht. Byron recorded the large sum of money he spent on the search for Percy Shelley in detail in his accounting books. They eventually found the disfigured remains on a beach and had to conclude that Percy must have died in a boat wreck during a storm.[254]

How could so many deaths around Hunt's arrival be coincidental, especially when a similar series of unfortunate deaths followed the arrival of George IV in Scotland? Knowing that in part as a result of befriending the Hunts in prison, the Shelleys and Byron started *The Liberal* with the Hunts in 1821 abroad must've infuriated George IV. *The Liberal's* early issues proved to contain several seditious, anti-monarchical criticisms, and who knows what impact it might have had on ending the British monarchy if Byron and Shelley survived beyond 1824.

After Allegra's death, and while Byron and Shelleys were waiting for Leigh Hunt to arrive from his lengthened trip to Italy (delayed by the family falling ill with tuberculosis, stormy weather, poorly crafted ships, insufficient travel funds, and a desire to tour foreign lands along the way), Byron started writing, "The Vision of Judgment." He finished it in a still darker mood after Percy's death in October, and this piece was published in *The Liberal's* October 15, 1822 issue after it was rejected by Byron's regular publisher, John Murray. Meanwhile, the Masi affair forced Byron to attempt to relocate to a house near Monte Nero for half a year, "but, not long after he moved into the house in May, Byron discovered that the water supply was impure, and he decided

---

253   Byron, *Selected*, 92.
254   Doris Langley Moore. *Lord Byron: Accounts Rendered*. (New York: Harper & Row, 1974), 337-9.

to return to his more permanent residence at the Palazzo Lanfranchi. In his attempts to break the lease, he became involved with litigation, which was to last until July 1823."[255] The next delay occurred when Byron could not resume publication after learning of the "illness" of his only legitimate child, Ada Lovelace. Byron only managed to get back to work on a new issue, working as the primary editor and author for the October 17, 1823 issue, more than a month after he learned that she was better, writing: "I know not why I resume it even now except that standing at the window of my apartment in this beautiful village—the calm though cool serenity of a beautiful and transparent Moonlight—showing the Islands—the Mountains—the Sea… have quieted me enough to be able to write…"[256] Byron had experienced more loss and tragedy in the less than two years of this journal's operation than across the rest of his life, and before long the tragedy was complete when he died as well. So many disasters hardly look natural or accidental.

One of the causes for *The Liberal's* premature failure, despite the great minds that folded over it, was the avalanche of negative reviews in the year before the first issue's release. Harsh criticism was printed in *The Edinburgh Review, Blackwood's Edinburgh Magazine, The New Monthly Magazine, The Imperial Magazine, The Gazette of Fashion, The European Magazine, London Review,* and pretty much all of their other competing periodicals. One exception was *The Examiner*, which obviously sided with its contributors and owner, John Hunt. One of the most telling of these appeared in a biography of Byron that John Watkins published in May of 1822. Watkins explained that Byron was conspiring with a "set of writers" that included "the proprietor and editor of the most seditious paper in England" to create an "academy of blasphemy" and a "poetical school of immorality and profaneness" that might end up "overturning religion" by the "combination of talents."[257] While the concern about morals and religion might be commendable, obviously, these rival magazines were troubled that a share of their profits would be diverted to this powerful trinity's flashy new publication, and they acted in unison to crush this literary rebellion.

The Liberal saw a myriad of problems before the first number was

---

255   Marshall, *Byron*, 38.
256   Byron, *Selected*, 300.
257   John Watkins. *Memoirs, Historical and Critical, of the Life and Writings of the Right Honourable Lord Byron, with Anecdotes of Some of His Contemporaries.* (London: 1822), 48-54.

released, not only because of the news of Shelley's death, but also because of the clashes on political and rhetorical matters between Hunt and Byron. There were also difficulties due to the distance between Byron and Leigh and their printers in London. Byron was particularly upset that John Murray did not send the "Preface" to "The Vision of Judgment" together with the rest, an act that Byron called borderline premeditated malice because it opened Byron up to litigation. Without the "Preface," it became easy for censors to misconstrue it as being directed at George III, and not at Robert Southey, the intended victim of the satire.[258]

The "Preface" to "Vision of Judgement" was directly addressed to one of Byron's harshest critics, who had accused him of running a "Satanic school." This critic was Robert Southey, who accused Byron in his eulogy to King George III, which had the same name as Byron's later satirical version: "Vision of Judgement" (1820). Byron's "Preface" to his "Vision of Judgement" begins by pointing out that only a few years earlier, before he became the Poet Laurate, Southey was himself on trial for sedition for the publication of his play about a medieval rebellion, *Wat Tyler*, a theme that was popular in the period of the French Revolution, when it was written, but became seditious because of its anti-monarchical sentiments by the time it was published in 1817. With that, Byron begins his long, satirical, "epic" poem with:

I

    Saint Peter sat by the celestial gate:
        His keys were rusty, and the lock was dull,
    So little trouble had been given of late;
        Not that the place by any means was full,
    But since the Gallic era "eighty-eight"
        The Devils had ta'en a longer, stronger pull,
    And "a pull altogether," as they say
    At sea—which drew most souls another way.

II

    The Angels all were singing out of tune,
        And hoarse with having little else to do,
    Excepting to wind up the sun and moon,

---

258   Marshall, *Byron*, 90.

> Or curb a runaway young star or two,
> Or wild colt of a comet, which too soon
>   Broke out of bounds o'er the ethereal blue,
> Splitting some planet with its playful tail,
> As boats are sometimes by a wanton whale.[259]

As Byron anticipated, a majority of the post-release critical attacks on *The Liberal* touched on the profanity and blasphemy of "The Vision of Judgment," using it to dismiss the quality and immorality of the periodical. The lack of the "Preface" caused just the type of censoring comments that Byron hoped to avoid. Most of the reviews plagiarized each other, claiming that the journal was hardly "liberal," and that it was "brutal" and immoral. Other reviews focused on ridiculing one of the collaborators as unfit to work with the other two, or pointed to Byron's Scottish roots by stressing the "bad grammar and Cockney English" (*John Bull*) in his deliberately linguistically derisive satire in "Judgement."[260] Following this avalanche of critical ridicule, a legal indictment from the Grand Jury in Middlesex was levied against John Hunt for the "Judgment," the content of which was reprinted by him in *The Examiner's* No. 789 on January 5, 1823 in England. The lawsuit complained that it suggested that George III was "a person of mean and avaricious disposition… an enemy to the liberties of his people and of other nations… a person of bad and vicious character."[261] A few pirated editions of the issue appeared, and John Hunt did not pursue litigation against these because of the pending threat of a libel lawsuit. Booksellers in Edinburgh suppressed *The Liberal* on the tail of this controversy. French Bourbons went much further as *The Examiner* reported in its No 782 on January 19, 1823: "The police have strict orders to prevent its introduction…" And London booksellers refrained from sending it in parcels with other books to France out of fear that the whole package might be seized because of it. Byron noted similar policies by the Austrian authorities in Italy, so that he advised John Hunt not to send copies of their periodical over to his foreign abode.[262] While the first issue only includes works by Leigh Hunt, Shelley and Byron, the

---

259 Lord George Gordon Byron. "The Vision of Judgment: By 'Quevedo Redivivus.'" Jack Lynch, Ed. (Newark: Rutgers University; Retrieved: 27 July 2016; Web).
260 Marshall, *Byron*, 104.
261 Ibid., 127.
262 Ibid., 134.

second issue includes pieces from Mary Shelley (who was paid £36), Hazlitt (£28) and Thomas Jefferson Hogg (£18.18.0). 7,000 copies were printed of the first issue for £400 (including stitching, advertising, paper and the like), and 6,000 copies were printed of the second issue for £560.2.0.[263] The second issue was also criticized on similar blasphemy, libel and general immorality and stupidity charges by rival periodicals. Meanwhile, by February 1823, 4,050 copies of the first edition had been sold at a revenue of £777.16.0, which left £377.16.0 in profits after costs were deducted, and of these Leigh Hunt's share was the largest at £291.15.0.[264] The second issue did not sail as well with only 2,700 sold, yielding £518.8.0 in sales, contrasted with the higher cost of printing, £560.2.0. The deficit increased to £58.14.0 by June of 1824.[265] Thus, starting with this second issue, there was pressure to close the periodical to avoid further losses. The periodical was in trouble even if its founders decided to avoid negative criticism from the media and potential imprisonment for libel. Discovering this fiscal failure, Byron started writing to the Hunts that perhaps he should withdraw from the venture as his London publishing "friends" were advising him since the start. Nine out of sixteen pieces in the third issues were by Leigh Hunt, in part because he was suddenly aware that his cushy funding from Byron would end with the journal. Many of the contributors to the second issue also returned for the third. 3,000 copies were probably printed of the third issue, though according to Marshall, the profits and expenses for this third and the following fourth issues are sketchy.[266] Yet again, periodicals such as *The Literary Register, The Literary Museum and The London Literary Gazette*, and *The Edinburgh Magazine* all offered the, now half-hearted, ridicule and derision about the third issue. All this animosity hit Byron harder than the other contributors and partners in *The Liberal*. They were intended to hurt Byron because Mary Shelley was already an outsider due to her gender, and the Hunts were outsiders with criminal records for sedition, and Percy Shelley was already in the grave, so the strongest link in this Liberal chain was Byron and the copious reviews did their conservative duty in developing in him "a disgust to Authorship—and he hurried to Greece to get a new name as a man of action—having

---

263   Ibid., 148-9.
264   Ibid., 160-1.
265   Ibid., 162.
266   Ibid., 178.

arrived at the highest praise as a poet," as Mary Shelley explained it in a letter to John Murray on June 8, 1832.[267] In other words, competing journals attacked Byron's writing and liberalism and forced him out of authorship, and into direct involvement in the Greek revolution, a step that precipitated his death. Byron gave Leigh another £30 for his move to Florence, before Byron moved to Greece.[268] By the time the fourth issue appeared on July 30, 1823, Byron was sailing to Leghorn and Mary Shelley was back in London, after a brisk parting without a "goodbye" between the collaborators in this venture. The final number had printer errors and typos that showed a speedy and cheap release by John Hunt. The same periodicals that had been waging attacks, gave a few final yelps of objection, this time around adding light humor as there was no longer a need "to tremble" now that they knew they had won and the periodical was dissolved.[269] Byron and Shelleys' donations to Leigh Hunt during his stay with Byron and his income from the journal were so small compared with his expenses that he owed his brother more than he did when he arrived in Italy, £1,790.19.10 in 1824. Instead of paying his brother back and living more frugally, Leigh now claimed ownership of *The Examiner*, despite surrendering ownership in 1821 to avoid prosecution, and attempted to get more money out of John.

Byron's *The Vision of Judgment* appeared in *The Liberal's* first issue, and immediately brought a "prosecution for sedition on Hunt's brother," John Hunt, the publisher who printed it back in the UK.[270] John's trial for publishing "The Vision of Judgment" finally began on January 15, 1824. He was found "Guilty" because the issue had the tendency to "disquiet the mind of the present King," despite the fact that George III was no longer living. The defense lawyer's argument for historical and artistic liberty was also disregarded.[271] On June 19, 1824, John was fined £100. "After learning of the conviction, Byron had expressed his intention to pay John Hunt's fine, but Byron had been dead for two months on the day that John received sentence" and the "executors" of Byron's estate did not "fulfil this intention."[272] The timing of Byron's death before he could fulfil this obligation adds one additional motive

267   Ibid., 186.
268   Ibid., 194.
269   Ibid., 202.
270   Moore, *Byron*, 352.
271   Marshall, *Byron*, 206.
272   Ibid., 209.

for his potential assassination, as his support for the Hunts had stirred up hundreds of reviews, even if negative, of Liberal ideas and probably inspired young liberals who later asserted their "blasphemous" and "treasonous" ideas in the social and revolutionary upheavals in Europe in the following decades.

Byron's Assassination via Malpractice

In the December before Byron's death, he gave a £4,000 loan to the commander stationed in Mesologgi, Mavrokordatos, and used additional funds to create a small troop of men to accompany him as he decided to enter direct fighting in the revolution upon nudging from the Greeks. Shortly after this, Byron was named Commander in Chief of Western Greece and was put "in charge of a raid against an Ottoman fortress at Lepanto (Nafpaktos)."[273] As he was starting his military duties, Byron's health took a sudden turn on February 15. As Dr. Julius Millingen describes, William Parry, Byron's private physician:

> prescribed some punch of his own composition, so agreeable to Lord Byron's palate, that he drank immoderate quantities of it. To remove the burning sensation his lordship, soon after, began to experience, he ordered a bottle of cider; and having drank a glass of it, he said it was "excessively cold and pleasant." Scarcely had he said these words when he fell upon the floor, agitated by violent spasmodic movements of all his limbs. He foamed at the mouth, gnashed his teeth, and rolled his eyes like one in an epilepsy. After remaining about two minutes in this state his senses returned, and the first words he uttered were: "Is not this Sunday?"[274]

This description shows a direct correlation between the drugged drinks Parry gave for Byron's consumption and the fit that followed. Colonel Leicester Stanhope describes the same incident by focusing on the fact that Byron "complained of a weakness in one of his legs." Byron attempted to stand up, but was unable to walk and "called for assistance" and only then fell into a violent nervous convulsion."[275] These symptoms point to the likelihood of a muscle relaxant and an opiate or some other mental activity suppresser being given in the drink, and

---
273 Bass, *Freedom's*, 105-8.
274 Julius Millingen. *Memoirs of the Affairs of Greece.* (London, 1831), 114-5.
275 Leicester F. C. Stanhope. *Greece in 1823 and 1824, to which are added, Reminiscences of Lord Byron.* (London: Sherwood, Gilbert and Piper, 1825), 115-6.

more likely a fatal combination of two counter-acting medical poisons. William Parry himself describes the incident in positive terms, saying that after these events, Byron told him "to consider" himself "as at home in his apartment." This might have been a financial incentive for Parry to increase the frequency of the drugging to remain in Byron's residence. When Byron asked for a diagnosis, Parry recorded that "it arose from... his not taking sufficient food and stimulant drinks," but instead of prescribing a heartier diet, Parry prescribed various purgatives and laxatives, together with bleedings, and various other things that all worked together to drain Byron's vitality. He suffered "a strong shock of a Convulsive description," for which he was "bled profusely" "with eight leeches... applied to his temples..."[276] The latter description comes out of William Parry's account of the incident. Parry goes on to blame the other doctors for their incompetence, writing: "but when the leeches were removed, the doctors were so unskillful that they could not stop the blood. It continued to flow on, and Lord Byron fainted and lancets, or two-edged surgical knives at his wrists." Parry writes that he helped to save Byron on this occasion by tearing off his own clothing and burning bits of it under Byron's nose, as well as rubbing brandy on his face to revive him out of the faint. Parry concludes: "Had he turned them [the doctors] out of doors, and returned to the habits of an English gentleman, as to his diet, he would, probably, have survived many years."[277]

"Blisters" were applied with caustic agents, such as mustard plaster, and then these were drained. Byron was simultaneously given "strong purgatives and repeated doses of antimony." The latter was called the everlasting pill because it was frequently re-used by different patients after it "helped" them to purge the bowels. Byron was really given at least three different purgatives in combination, as he was also prescribed castor oil. There is evidence that he was definitely prescribed at least one hallucinogenic in the form of henbane, which can cause restless sleep and death if eaten.[278] Peter Macinnis uses "castor oil" as an example of a painful punishment for misbehavior: "Punishment by purging or worse has long been part of a certain political style. Mussolini's thugs would force political opponents to consume castor oil to cure their waywardness. Sometimes they would administer as much as

---

276   Bass, *Freedom's*, 109.
277   Parry, *Last*, 44-6.
278   Moore, *Letters*, 415-6.

a liter of the oil, enough to cause severe purging, but not death…"[279] By Mussolini's time, the dangerous properties of castor oil were better known than in Byron's, but the quantity, duration and the combination of purgatives used suggests that they were employed in a similar punishing manner towards Byron, and it is likely he interpreted it in this sense, allowing himself to be flogged by his instructing physicians. He wrote that he could not tell if the shock was a sign of "epilepsy—catalepsy—cachexy—apoplexy—or what other *exy*—or *opsy*."[280] The drugs clouded his mind, so that he had a sense that the physicians were misdiagnosing him, but he could not focus on a medical book long enough to even distinguish between the different -opsy's.

The three-hundred-strong Albanian Suliote troops he hired were simultaneously demanding a raise through means that Byron called "extortion," despite Byron already paying them "a dollar per man more each month—than they could receive from the G[ree]k Gov[ernmen]t."[281] They were in part angered because they were sick with food poisoning from bad bread. Byron suspected that the bread spoilage was a subversive Lepanto attack. In response to the Suliotes demand for additional funding, Byron wrote: "I will have nothing more to do with the Suliotes—they may go to the Turks or—the devil."[282] If a modern, wealthy aristocrat traveled alone to a dangerous, impoverished warzone and started handing out a year's salary in a matter of days to a troop of let's say, African warriors for protection, it would not surprise anybody in the western world if they poisoned and robbed him of his chests of gold. Thus, it is likely that spies from the opposing camp (if not Byron's troops themselves) were tempted to contaminate the food supply. As the main funder of the Greeks' revolution, Byron made himself into a primary target for a subversive attack.

Byron seemed to recover from the first bout of illness, and was named as "one of three commissioners who would oversee the London Greek Committee's long-awaited loan." The smooth administration of this loan was interrupted when the artillery corps mutinied again because of the bad bread. Meanwhile, Byron intervened personally to

---

279   Peter Macinnis. *Poisons: From Hemlock to Botox and the Killer Bean of Calabar*. (New York: Arcade Publishing, 2005), 151.
280   Leslie A. Marchand, Ed. *Selected Poetry of Lord Byron, Vol. II*. (New York: Modern Library, 2001), 112-3.
281   Byron, *Selected*, 297.
282   Marchand, *Selected*, 112-3, 122-3, 141, 145, February 15 to March 30, 1824.

prevent the "flogging of a man caught stealing, and stopped a duel between some officers."[283] While Byron was taking steps that might have been honorable amidst liberals in Britain, it is possible that his strong-handedness and monarchic over-reaching into the affairs of his officers and commanders inspired hostility.

On April 1, Byron learned that the Greek Capitano Caraiscachi had kidnapped two Missolonghi primates and took possession of the island of Vasiladi, thus starting a counter-rebellion that threatened to throw Greece into civil war. Byron was still disturbed by this news, and trying to figure out if the rebels should be punished with extreme severity, when he received news that Augusta had suffered a mysterious illness at the same time as his own convulsions. Perhaps because this news distressed him, Byron went out riding with Count Pietro Gamba later that day, on April 9, despite the gathering clouds. "Three miles from town we were overtaken by a heavy rain, and we return[ed] to the town walls wet through, and in a violent perspiration," Gamba writes, and adds that they then spent half-an-hour in a boat, as was their custom. Then, "two hours after his return home" Byron "was seized with a shuddering: he complained of fever and rheumatic pains," but they went riding again at ten o'clock on April 11.[284] Moore stresses that it was on the 11th when Byron suffered from "alternate cold and hot shiverings, with a pain that wandered over his body," and he had a "torturing thirst."[285] At this point, Gamba refocuses on the fact that on that evening of April 11, Byron was informed by the police "that a Turkish spy had taken refuge in his house. He was a relation of the mater of the house. Byron himself gave orders for his arrest."[286] Between Caraiscachi and the discovery of the Turkish spy in his household, it is hardly questionable that there must have been at least one more undiscovered spy who was unhappy with the arrest of his comrades, and who must have contributed to the strange illness that exploded after this point. Meanwhile, a review of Gamba's description of Byron's symptoms above explains the root of Byron's illness. Because Byron was given three purgatives, he was dangerously dehydrated after weeks of this treatment. According to modern insights on purgation, the dehy-

---

283   Bass, *Freedom's*, 109.
284   Count Pietro Gamba. *A Narrative of Lord Byron's Last Journey to Greece.* (London, 1825), 247-9.
285   Moore, *Letters*, 415-6.
286   Gamba, *Narrative*, 247-9.

dration alone could have killed him. The doctors kept insisting that he should be bled, and because he kept refusing, they gave him calomel (or mercury, a toxic purgative) and colocynth (used as an anti-diabetic today, but back then it was a super-purgative that induced violent vomiting tinted with blood).[287] All this while, the doctors were telling Byron that he was suffering from a "common cold," an illness that Byron told William Fletcher he had "a thousand times," to which Fletcher objected that he was certain that Byron never had a cold before "of so serious a nature," and Byron agreed. Here Byron both downplayed the seriousness of his illness, and questioned the doctor's ability to diagnose him properly.[288] These doubts might have led the doctors to prescribe a stronger hallucinogenic or another mind-altering drug to keep him from being able to coherently object to the poisonings because Byron's thoughts disintegrate in the following days. Dr. Julius Millingen reported that on April 15, Byron was asking for a "very old and ugly witch" to repel the "evil eye" that he thought somebody had cast on him, and he was recalling a Scotch fortune-teller that foretold that Byron would die at thirty-seven.[289] These irrational fears suggest that he was under the influence of a hallucinogenic, opium or some other mixture of psychedelic drugs that left him without the ability to rationally determine the cause of his unnatural affliction. Finally, Byron gave in and allowed himself to be bled again on April 16, after Dr. Julius Millingen told him that if he refused bleeding, "the disease might… operate such disorganization in his cerebral and nervous system as entirely to deprive him of his reason," to which Byron exclaimed in an "angry tone": "Come; you are, I see, a damned set of butchers. Take away as much blood as you will; but have done with it."[290] Byron kept saying that his lack of sleep was likely to drive him mad if it continued beyond the previous weeks, so Millingen was echoing this fear when he threatened that Byron would lose his mind if he did not follow his much more dangerous advice. The doctors immediately pumped pounds of blood out of Byron, and kept up the letting across the days that followed. "He was bled three times more the next day, which caused the debilitated poet to go into fainting fits…"[291] He was

287 Bass, *Freedom's*, 109-10.
288 Lord Broughton John Cam Hobhouse. "Lord Byron in Greece." *Westminster Review*, II ((July 1824); 225-62), 254.
289 Millingen, *Memoirs*, 138-40.
290 Ibid., 132.
291 Bass, *Freedom's*, 109-10.

able to walk a bit on the afternoon of the 18th. But then, he agreed to allow two new doctors to inspect him. These did not even tell Byron their prognosis, applying prescriptions without a consultation with the patient. These new doctors were Doctor Treiber, "a German of the Artillery Brigade," and Dr. Luca Vaya of Missolonghi, "a Greek who had attended Ali Pasha," and who was at that moment also serving as Mavrocordato's physician. Treibert and Vaya suggested stopping the bleedings, but they were rebuffed by Bruno. Bruno did agree to add a few new drugs to Byron's list of medicinal poisons: draught of cream of tartar (purgative that contains arsenic, which led to the "madness" and death of George III) and boracic (insecticide known to cause death in humans), as well as bark (in which, the quinine serves as a muscle relaxant), and "two drams of extract of tamarind" (fruit laxative), and finally "laudanum" (a version of opium that acts as a narcotic purgative) and "ether" (painkiller). These additives finally produced "fitful sleep," which slowly progressed into the final sleep.[292]

Peter Macinnis explains that aristocratic Italians were a bit more skilled in poisoning than their British counterparts, and it is possible Byron's death reflects this Italian style, while the other deaths in this study were less obvious. The Borgias were known for using a white powder, *La Cantarella*, which included arsenic, phosphorus, or lead acetate, or a combination of the three. "The family kept a staff of Italian astrologer-chemists who worked with mercury, arsenic, phosphorus, hemlock, monkshood, henbane, yew, and poppy."[293] While the Borgias operated a couple of centuries before Byron's time, Byron had the aristocratic Gambas in his household and he was leading a revolution against the region's established government. Thus, the comparison between the Borgias and Byron's household is a fitting one. Byron's Italian physicians were also likely to be the descendants of these poisoners of old.

In the brief interim between the application of this concoction of new drugs and his final rest, Byron became aware of the severity of his illness, and was able to have a disjointed talk with William Fletcher, who proposed sending for Dr. Thomas, the English and more experienced doctor. Byron agreed to Fletcher's proposal, but asked Fletcher to keep this order from Parry and the other doctors already in his house because "they would not like to see other doctors here." Fletcher im-

---

292 Moore, *Letters*, 417.
293 Macinnis, *Poisons*, 158.

mediately disobeyed this order and informed the other doctors of his intention to call Dr. Thomas, to which they feigned agreement.[294] If one of them was intentionally administering a combination of poisons, this poisoner might have briskly given Byron a fatal doze at this point to avoid allowing Dr. Thomas to inspect the poisoning in progress. Meanwhile, increasingly incoherent, shouting for his daughter and other relatives, Byron tried to give last instructions to a servant. He seemed to be suffocating, and made a rattling noise in his throat," and shortly after this, he said, "I must sleep now," and remained unconscious from this point. It was April 20.[295]

Doris Langley Moore points out that there were "many features in common" between Byron's death "of a fever" and his daughter, Allegra's, as:

> both were subjected to repeated blood-letting which reduced their chances of survival, and both were posthumously victims of large claims by medical attendants. (Even the Greek doctor, Vaya, sent the executors a bill for putting in an appearance at Byron's deathbed.) Both too were rejected where a resting place had been sought. Westminster Abbey refused interment to Byron and Allegra was not allowed beyond the porch of Harrow Church.[296]

Instead of a burial, they were embalmed, and only Allegra received the benefit of having an "altar of roses and oil of lavender" though this doubled the "pharmacist's bill" for the service, which was sent to Byron.[297] The descriptions of Byron's mysterious illness come from untrustworthy sources because the doctors who surrounded him could all be implicated in malpractice. Meanwhile, his one non-medical friend, Parry, "was not encouraged to be present." The doctors claimed that Byron "increased the quantity of spirits he drank" and was eating too much meat, despite his personal physician Bruno's advice. These claims of malnutrition are contradicted by Lega and others, who were astonished by Byron's strict diet of chicken broth and overall an "extreme sparsity in his regimen." Bruno also complained that Byron was not following his hot Epsom salt bathing schedule. This claim is also disputed by accounting records recorded by Lega, which indicate that

294   Hobhouse, "Lord," 255-7.
295   Bass, *Freedom's*, 109-10.
296   Moore, *Lord*, 331.
297   Ibid.

Byron regularly paid for and utilized the Epsom salt baths.

On October 6, 1821, before the tragic events that led to his death, Byron wrote to Moore that he does not like to drink very much because they fail to "exhilarate," and instead make him "savage and suspicious, and even quarrelsome." He then added: "Laudanum has a similar effect; but I can take much of *it* without any effect at all. The thing that gives me the highest spirits (it seems absurd, but true) is a dose of *salts*—I mean in the afternoon, after their effect. But one can't take *them* like champagne."[298] This is a telling passage because this partially explains why Byron agreed to take such a heavy mix of various stimulants on his deathbed, as he was used to taking large quantities of laudanum, which he views as less impactful than his salt baths. A more likely explanation than poor nutrition or too few baths for the catastrophe, is as Moore points out, that Byron probably caught sepsis from dirty bleeding instruments and unsanitary procedures across this long illness.

Poisonous Mushrooms and the Suspicious Suicide of the British Foreign Secretary

Even if all of the recorded poisons that Byron was administered could not have been the cause of his early death, it is possible that additional poisons were added, without being put on the books. One common poison from this period was poisonous mushrooms. Charles VI, Holy Roman Emperor was poisoned by a meal of death cap mushrooms in 1740. The same fate befell Johann Schobert, together with his wife, children, servants and guests, who all died from eating poisonous mushrooms that looked edible for dinner in 1767. There is one particular strand of mushrooms that contain the fungal genus Gyromitrin, also known as the false morel mushroom, which comes closest to reproducing Byron's described symptoms as it can lead to convulsions, dizziness, lethargy, vertigo, tremor, fever, headaches, delirium, seizures, shortness of breath, respiratory arrest, coma, and death within around a week. "Gyromitra species fruit in the spring, and most poisonings occur during spring or early summer." This definition parallels with Byron's springtime illness. Further still, "gyromitrin-containing mushrooms have been associated with significant mortality in Eastern

---

298   Byron, *Byron's*, Vol. 8, 236.

Europe."[299] No natural illness, other than sepsis, has been suggested because cholera, malaria and other common disease from this geographic area and time period do not match all of the complicating symptoms Byron exhibited. Byron would have had to be given relatively small amounts of this species of mushrooms for a prolonged period of time for him to have suffered from convulsions months earlier, before his health finally collapsed in April.

Giving hallucinogenic or poisonous mushrooms or other intoxicants together with a bleeding was attempted with the direct prompting of King George IV in the suspicious suicide of Lord Castlereagh, or Robert Stewart. He was the British Foreign Secretary in the critical decade from 1812 until August 12, 1822, the date on which he died, a month after Shelley's July boating "accident." Byron was hardly impressed with Castlereagh while he was in office, writing to Rogers on July 29, 1816, "…we have had lately such stupid mists—fogs—rains—and perpetual density—that one would think Castlereagh had the foreign affairs of the kingdom of Heaven also—upon his hands."[300] Byron also criticized Castlereagh in the Dedication to *Don Juan*, but took the line that called him an "intellectual eunuch" out because, as he wrote to Scrope Berdmore Davies from Venice on January 26, 1819, "I am not now near enough to give him an exchange of shots."[301] And Byron even published "Epigrams on Lord Castlereagh" in the first issue of *The Liberal*, though it was initially sent to John Hunt with the hope of publishing it in *The Examiner*. It was a quatrain and two couplets rejoicing at Castlereagh's suicide. The negative image Byron had of Castlereagh must have been an outcome of the King's campaign to darken his name, so that Byron probably did not recognize a fellow rebel in Castlereagh when he expressed these harsh criticisms. Among the various interests Byron had income with Castlereagh was that both had homosexual predilections, so their circles of "friends" must have intertwined.

Lord Castlereagh began his political career by serving as Chief Secretary of Ireland. In this role, he was pivotal in suppressing the Irish Rebellion of 1798, and in securing the Irish Act of Union of 1800, which united Ireland to England. He was instrumental during the Na-

---

299   Reed Brozen. "Gyromitra Mushroom Toxicity." MedScape: WebMD Health Professional network. (14 April 2015; Web).
300   Byron, *Byron's*, Vol. 5, 86.
301   Byron, *Selected*, 187.

poleonic War as he stepped into the role of Secretary of State for War. However, he had a breakdown when he was drawn into a relatively minor argument about the Walcheren Expedition with Foreign Secretary George Canning, and ended up shooting Canning in the thigh in the resulting duel in 1809. He resigned after this incident and only returned to politics in 1812 to take the Foreign Secretary position, in which he oversaw the Treaty of Chaumont that unified British interests with those of Austria, Russia and Prussia in 1814. He spent the following years juggling peace negotiations, and it was only in 1822, in parallel with the time of Castlereagh's death, when this peace agreement started to fall apart. King George IV was vocal about his opposition to Greek liberation because he was hoping to play the other parties against each other to the imperial advantage of Britain. In August, just before his death, Lord Castlereagh said that he wanted to "soften, as far as possible, the rigour of war between the Turks and Greeks."[302] But, he had a more personal worry on his mind when he met with King George IV on August 9. "Castlereagh worried that the next personal attack," after the outbursts against him in the House over the 1822 Massacre of Scio, "would be a charge of homosexuality" a predilection he shared with both Shelley and Byron.[303] Castlereagh was confronted by a sudden shift in public opinion after the Massacre of Scio, "by which the most flourishing community of the Greek archipelago was wiped out of existence." The massacre began to inspire men, such as Byron, to intervene to prevent similar slaughters of Greeks by the invading Ottomans.[304] While Castlereagh angered those who were protesting against the Ottoman Empire in the House by giving examples of atrocities on both sides, he had written a letter to the Ottoman government denouncing "the atrocity of their execution" that "inflicted a sensible wound on the King's mind and filled the British Nation with horror and disgust."[305] While this was a noble sentiment, it contradicted the King's actual opinions. Castlereagh was treading against the King's will

---

302 Duke of Wellington Arthur Wellesley. "Castlereagh to Wellington, 14 September 1822." (delivered posthumously). *Despatches, Correspondence, and Memoranda of Field Marshal Arthur, Duke of Wellington, Vol. I.* (London: John Murray, 1867), 285-6.
303 Bass, *Freedom's*, 73-4.
304 John Emerich, Ed. *The Cambridge Modern History, Volume 10.* (New York: University Press, 1907), 185.
305 Philip P. Argenti, Ed. *The Massacres of Chios Described in Contemporary Diplomatic Reports.* "9 July 1822." (London: Bodley Head, 1932), 25-6.

in this official correspondence to the Ottoman leadership on the King's behalf. Castlereagh was being swayed by Byron and Shelley's poetics and poetic speeches into becoming a supporter of the Greeks, and this was a dangerous political move from King George IV's perspective. To return to Castlereagh and the King's meeting on August 9th, wherein the King advised Castlereagh to reign in his "blue devils" and Castlereagh in return confessed that he was indeed homosexual. Of course, it was unthinkable for Castlereagh to use the term "homosexual" or "blue devil" (as the King dared to call him), instead exclaiming that he was "mad," a term that carried the same meaning. Then, "the shocked king" promised to keep this secret, and kindly suggested that Castlereagh be bled. In response, Castlereagh proposed saying "good-bye to Europe." In other words, Castlereagh proposed banishing himself to avoid embarrassing the King with his sexuality. The King did not insist on banishment, so Castlereagh simply traveled to his country house in Kent to cry hysterically. Meanwhile, both the King and Wellington were running around trying to get a doctor to bleed Castlereagh, until he finally consented, out of fear that the King would execute him for sodomy. His own

> doctor drugged and bled him. This induced delirium. Castlereagh asked his wife for his pistol. This was not forthcoming. The next morning, he took an alarming interest in a shave, and she locked away his razors and ordered her maid to check his dressing room for anything sharp. But on August 12, Castlereagh was left alone in his dressing room for a few moments. Britain's foreign secretary enterprisingly found a little penknife in a drawer in his washstand. He slashed his neck, cutting deep into his carotid artery. His doctor entered the room an instant later. Castlereagh, fifty-three years old, spoke his last words: "Bankhead, let me fall upon your arm; 'tis all over." Blood gushed from his neck. He died almost instantly.[306]

This is a scene worthy of a Shakespearean tragedy. Curiously, it means that Castlereagh was alone with the doctor at the time of the death. Thus, blood might have spilled onto the doctor not from a friendly embrace, but rather from a violent struggle. The doctor might have entered the room with the blade, which Castlereagh's wife was careful to remove from the room, and cut Castlereagh's throat on the King's order. The drugs and weakness induced a psychotic state on Castlereagh,

---

306   Bass, *Freedom's*, 74.

under which a murder could easily have been disguised as a suicide. In contrast, Byron was too accustomed to both bleedings and intoxication, and it took over a month for him to die from what appears to be a series of poisonings. Even if Castlereagh slit his own throat, the drugging and bleeding was ordered by the King, and "successfully" led to Castlereagh's death at a politically convenient moment for King George IV.

The Beneficiaries of Byron's Death

One direct group of beneficiaries of Byron's untimely death was the London Greek Committee, which "became mired in questionable accounting" immediately afterwards, so that the "Greeks only got £300,000 out of the £800,000 total of the loan Byron was to administer" and the "lenders would never receive anything back from their ill-managed investment."[307] The £800,000 "arrived at Zante six days after [Byron's] death, in the ship that was to carry his corpse to England."[308] £500,000 converted via modern inflation rates and into USD equals approximately $76,910,040 in 2016 (using Stephen Morley's "Historical UK Inflation" calculator and the Google currency conversion calculator).

For perspective, Byron's loan to fund his Greek troop for £4,000 is worth around $615,280 today. Byron formed his Suliote guard after an incident on January 16, 1824. Byron was spending the evening with Mavrocordato, probably discussing Mavrocordato's attempts to "electrify the troops" with his presence, as Byron described it in a letter to John Cam Hobhouse on October 27, 1823.[309] They were interrupted by "two sailors, belonging to the privateer which had taken the Turk, came into the room, demanding in an insolent tone that their prisoner should be delivered up to them." Lord Byron insisted that the sailors must leave. They refused. So, he drew his pistol at them, and only at this did they finally withdraw from his room. Disturbed that his life could be so easily threatened by sailors, Byron told Mavrocordato: "If your government cannot protect me in my own house, I will find means to protect myself." He then immediately hired the guard for this

---

307 Ibid., 112.
308 Moore, *Letters,* 414.
309 Byron, *Selected,* 310.

purpose.[310]

The guard turned out to be troublesome as they "rioted in the town" of Seraglio on January 17, 1824, and in response to this Byron threatened to discharge them.[311] The riot was due in part to the guard's dissatisfaction with the sum Byron was paying them, as well as the notorious bread spoilage. Considering these hardships, any of these men could've been tempted by the promise of enormous riches in exchange for ousting the one man who was proclaiming that he was "suspicious of Greek corruption."[312] On the day of Byron's death, a letter reached his servants that the Sultan of Turkey had "formally proclaimed Lord Byron an enemy of the Sublime Porte."[313] Europe and Russia have been referred to as "enemies" of the Sublime Porte in the midst of wars, so it was a stronger term of animosity than an Islamic *fatwa* is today. Since Byron was single-handedly sponsoring the Greek rebellion, he was seen as the leader of this uprising, and surely this is cause to see his death as a subversive political assassination. Such executions of leading rebels are frequently used as deterrent from further rebellion. It was an added benefit that Byron's death also allowed for the diversion of the funds he was controlling towards corrupt ends.

***

Byron and Shelley's tragic deaths had a powerful impact on world and literary history. They became martyrs, and most of the causes they championed eventually became victorious. But the wins came much later. The monarchy and the censorship machine in Britain attempted to defame Byron and Shelley by prosecuting their surviving publishers even beyond their deaths. In 1841, one of Shelley's publishers, Edward Moxon, was charged with blasphemy for publishing Shelley's *Queen Mab*. Moxon was found guilty, and was forced to expunge the "offensive" passages. This trial came at a time when Shelley was finding fame for the first time from beyond the grave, so finding blasphemy in his work was a counter-strike.

The birth and death of *The Liberal* has many parallels with recent suppressions of the freedom of speech and of the press. As long as there

---

310   Gamba, *Narrative*, 109-10, 115-6.
311   Stanhope, *Greece*, 103, 109.
312   Bass, *Freedom's*, 112.
313   Moore, *Letters*, 418.

are forces interested in stealing millions out of government programs, or suppressing rumors about behaviors shunned by religion, liberal reporting on these corruptions will be their strongest enemy. Martyrs that fall for the freedom of expression inspire future anti-censorship rebellions.

CHAPTER 5

A Bestselling Revolution:
Charles Dickens' *A Tale of Two Cities* in *All the Year Round*

The popular story of Charles Dickens' childhood relates how he worked at a factory that belonged to James Lamert's cousin, George, at Hungerford Stairs between the Strand and the river bank, "where boot and shoe blacking was manufactured and put into pots to be sold,"[314] while his father, John Dickens, was in a debtor's prison under the Insolvent Debtors' Act. He had previously served as an otherwise respectable clerk in the Navy Pay Office. Charles' mother attempted to run a school at 444 Gower Street North, but failed and could think of no other way to make money than to send Charles to the factory, while she and the rest of the children soon moved into the prison with John Dickens. His father's imprisonment terrified Charles, while his father's journalistic career starting in 1826, as the parliamentary correspondent for *The British Press,* inspired him. John's mother's inheritance and a retirement pension from the Navy assisted with John's liberation. John Dickens career was lifted when his brother-in-law, John Barrow, started a newspaper in 1828, *Mirror of Parliament*, for which John became the parliamentary reporter. This was the very publication that employed Charles Dickens in an identical position in 1831; both of them wrote about the House of Commons. Dickens had spent some time in 1827 as a law clerk, but there was a long gap between 1828 and 1831 when Charles worked as an apprentice to another relative, Thomas Charlton, a freelance shorthand reporter in the Consistory Court of Doctors' Commons. To obtain a shorthand gig, both of them spent most of their time waiting for a proctor to hire them for a case. Charles spent his "free time" during this four-year

---

314   Claire Tomalin. *Charles Dickens: A Life.* (New York: The Penguin Press, 2011), 23.

period on a reader's ticket at the British Museum's Reading Room, devouring classics. This independent study concluded his education, which otherwise had to be cut short due to his family's financial problems. Only with the help of his relation was Dickens able to make a leap from scattered writing attempts to serious full-time work in journalism. Charles was first employed by the *Mirror of Parliament* "as a supernumerary of some sort," then on March 5, 1832 when the first issue of Barrow's new publication, *True Sun,* appeared, Charles became an official on-staff reporter.[315] Dickens' writing productivity in these years and his fear of going bankrupt like his father, can be seen in a letter he wrote to Thomas Beard from Bentinck Street on Saturday evening, November 29, 1834, in which he mentions the need to speak in person with Beard about "a very distressing subject," referring to the new arrest of his father for debt. He begins this letter with, "I arrived from Birmingham at 7 this morning and remained at the office until 10, correcting the proofs of the *whack* for a second edition. I am rather fagged as you may suppose, having perpetrated four columns in as many hours before I left the town of dirt, iron-works, radicals, and hardware."[316] Dickens is speeding through his work more diligently than usual after receiving the news about his father, with the threat of financial ruin hanging over his head.

Shortly thereafter, Dickens started reporting for the *Morning Chronicle* and traveled to cover election campaigns. This paper launched an evening edition in 1835, calling it the *Evening Chronicle,* under the editorship of its music critic, George Hogarth, and it was to this paper that Dickens contributed *Street Sketches*. At first, Dickens was contributing for free, but then he asked to be paid and his salary went up to seven guineas per week. Hogarth was an Edinburgh lawyer, and an associate of Sir Walter Scott's. Since Scott was Dickens' idol, he transferred this adoration onto Hogarth, and insisted on going to a lot of his dinners. Impressed by the family's intellectual attainments and connections, Dickens married Hogarth's oldest daughter, then nineteen, Catherine Thomson Hogarth, and they had ten children together.[317]

After Dickens saw the profits that came from his first short stories collection, *Sketches by Boz* (1836), he started rebelling against the unfair conditions he was laboring under for the newspapers, which had

---

315   Johnson, *Walter,* 61.
316   Dickens, *Selected,* 10.
317   Tomalin, *Charles,* 55-6.

been his primary employers up until that point. He began this rebellion with the newspaper that had published most of his Boz sketches. In a letter to Sir John Easthope, a "liberal politician and chief proprietor of the *Morning Chronicle*," on November 18, 1836, Dickens wrote that he was outraged that his absence due to ill health and family duties had resulted in Easthope demanding a refund for the latest sketch, which according to Easthope, Dickens was late in delivering. Charles agreed to the refund, adding, "I wish I could return at the same time every additional six pence… that I have received from the Establishment, although I have rendered in return for it, the money's worth." Dickens goes on to complain that the "abrupt terms" in Sir Easthope's letter are the sort of thing common "between master and servant," but unfit for a writer such as himself, who has "at a sacrifice of health, rest, and personal comfort," taken on "harassing duty… traveling at a few hours' notice hundreds of miles in the depth of winter—leaving hot and crowded rooms to write, the night through, in a close damp chaise—tearing along, and writing the most important speeches, under every possible circumstance of disadvantage ad difficulty…"[318] This letter shows just how strenuous and "harassing" the work of a professional writer was in this period, and the disrespect that it was met with from the proprietors. All this compiled to make Dickens wish that he could be his own master, and not a servant to the "Establishment."

In 1836, Dickens became the editor of *Bentley's Miscellany* and served in this position for three years, falling out with Bentley, the owner, after a series of squabbles. For example, Dickens attempted to resign as the editor as early as on September 16, 1837, when he sent a letter to Richard Bentley in which he stated that when he left town he "placed a number of accepted articles in the Printer's hands," with directions to prepare them for publication, but when he returned he was handed "proofs of articles which I never saw in Manuscript" or accepted, with an insistence from the Printer that these additional articles be included in the upcoming issue. Dickens stated that this insistence was "in direct violation of my agreement with you, and a gross insult to me." He then attempted to resign, writing, "I therefore beg to inform you that henceforth I decline conducting the Miscellany or contributing to it in any way…"[319] Bentley must have agreed to take

---

318   Jenny Hartley, Ed. *The Selected Letters of Charles Dickens*. (Oxford: Oxford University Press, 2012), 23-4.
319   Ibid., 37-8.

the unwanted articles out because Dickens stayed on as the Editor at this juncture. This interaction is a great example of the uncomfortable dependence on somebody else to publish a high-brow author's work or employ him or her as an editor that exists in all types of publishing other than self-publishing. By 1839, Bentley was competing with Chapman for Dickens' books, with Chapman constantly paying more than Bentley. So, in January, Dickens "decided he wanted to give up the editorship of the *Miscellany*, and to postpone the delivery of the promised next novel, *Barnaby Rudge*."[320] He sent a written complaint to John Forster on January 21, 1839 from London, in which he stated:

> The consciousness that my books are enriching everybody connected with them but myself, and that I, with such a popularity as I have acquired, am struggling in old toils, and wasting my energies in the very height and freshness of my fame, and the best part of my life, to fill the pockets of others, while for those who are nearest and dearest to me I can realize little more than a genteel subsistence: all this puts me out of heart and spirits… This net that has been wound about me, so chafes me, so exasperates and irritates my mind, that to break it at whatever cost… is my constant impulse… six months from the conclusion of *Oliver* in the *Miscellany*—I wash my hands of any fresh accumulation of labour…[321]

Bentley responded that Dickens had to put aside his ongoing Chapman serialization of *Nickleby* for six months to finish his obligations to Bentley's *Miscellany*. Dickens gathered that Bentley was trying to create a conflict between him and Chapman by freezing a publication in the middle of serialization, so he responded that this was "offensive impertinence." He retaliated by convincing Ainsworth to take over the editorship of *Miscellany*, so that he could exit without stopping work on *Nickleby*. Before quitting Bentley, Dickens received a bonus for the completed *Oliver Twist*, and committed to finishing *Barnaby* for Bentley by January 1, 1840. Richard Bentley, years later, signed over his rights in *Oliver Twist* back to Dickens. Meanwhile, Dickens went on with the work on *Barnaby Rudge*. On September 18, 1841, he wrote about his progress with finishing Chapters 65 and 66 to John Forster: "I have let all the prisoners out of Newgate, burnt down Lord Mansfield's and played the very devil. Another number will finish the fires, and help us on towards the end. I feel quite smoky when I am at work.

320   Tomalin, *Charles*, 100.
321   Dickens, *Selected*, 22.

I want elbow-room terribly."[322] The quarrel with his publisher added a fire to his sentiment, which he used in the novel, adding graphic violence and writing about the rebellion with heart, as he sympathized with the need to rebel to defend his own rights.

Back in 1836, as Dickens started releasing novels regularly, he began a friendship with William Harrison Ainsworth, who ran a bachelor salon in Harrow Road, where Benjamin Disraeli and other politically-minded men of letters met. Ainsworth liked the Boz sketches and deliberately worked to discover Dickens' identity, as he wrote under a pseudonym, to propose that Dickens should publish a collection of the sketches with his own publisher, John Macrone, and have it illustrated by another one of his friends, George Cruikshank. In October, Dickens negotiated with Macrone over "Scotch Whiskey and Cigars." Dickens then wrote "A Visit to Newgate" in anticipation of the publication that soon became *Sketches by 'Boz', Illustrative of Every-day Life, and Every-day People*, which was scheduled for publication on February 8, 1836.[323] John Macrone had "cut a few corners by borrowing money from an old woman, enough to set himself up in an office in St James's Square, and ditched her to marry another woman, an American." His romantic manipulations thus helped him start the publishing business that released Dickens' first major book.[324] Dickens became embarrassed by his association with Macrone a year later and was desperate to stop Macrone's reprinting of *Boz* in time to take advantage of Dickens' sales of *Pickwick*. Macrone had bought *Boz* for £100, but was now asking £2,000 to return the copyrights, and to Dickens' surprise, Chapman & Hall paid this large sum in exchange for releasing *Boz* themselves. Then, before *Boz* started to appear from Chapman, "Macrone fell ill and died. He was only twenty-eight, and his business had failed. Characteristically, Dickens forgot his rage against him and at once started a scheme to raise money for his widow and children."[325] This is a great example of how fragile London publishers were in this period. Within a year of major, successful publications of Dickens, Victor Hugo and other greats, Macrone died in poverty at this extremely young age. Dickens was associated with so many printers and publishers that they almost make up a survey of the success and failure rate of some of the

---

322   Hartley, *Selected*, 89.
323   Tomalin, *Charles*, 60.
324   Ibid., 62.
325   Ibid., 85.

top publishers in Britain, and these odds are against them.

After *Boz'* release, Chapman & Hall proposed new projects to Dickens, resulting in works such as *The Pickwick Papers*. Dickens published with Chapman between 1840 and 1844, and then from 1858 to 1870. At the start of Dickens' collaboration with Chapman, on November 1, 1836, Dickens wrote from the Furnivals Inn on Tuesday evening to Chapman & Hall that he was "exceedingly gratified" by "*Pickwick's* success," but that he had to entreat them to allow him some leeway on the submission deadlines because he had "many other occupations." He also complained that his "spirits" were "not to be forced" into writing *Pickwick*, as he frequently sat "down to begin a number," but felt "unequal to the task," and needed to "get up, and wait till" he was.[326] This was sandwiched between many congratulatory remarks, but the publishers certainly noticed that their young, first-time author was attempting to force their hand towards a looser schedule, instead of quietly working to fit with their demands. In 1868, Anthony Trollope, one of their authors, bought a third of the company for his son, Henry Merivale Trollope. Anthony Trollope had become closer with Dickens after he gave a Christmas ball in 1865, where Fanny and Nelly Ternan were among the guests, and then crossed paths with him during Dickens' tour of America in 1868.[327] After many mergers, Chapman is called CRS Press today, and primarily publishes "science, technology, and medical resources," according to their website, which does not mention Charles Dickens, though they were a major publisher of his work in the twentieth century.

Soon after he signed contracts with Chapman and Macrone for the first time, Dickens also agreed to release a children's book with Thomas Tegg for £100 in August 1836. And since he was being pursued by yet another publisher, Bentley, he signed up with him as well for £500. Dickens also published an opera in a pamphlet, and took over the editorship of the monthly *Bentley's Miscellany* magazine. By working with four different publishers, Dickens was able to find enough writing work to do it for a living and to first take a leave from writing for the *Chronicle* and then to stop reporting all together.

Chapman & Hall printed their books with a printer that later, in 1841, also became a publisher, when it bought the *Punch* magazine, Bradbury & Evans. Dickens left Chapman for Bradbury and worked

---

326   Hartley, *Selected*, 29-30.
327   Tomalin, *Charles*, 348, 370.

with them between 1844 and 1859. As with all of his publishers, Dickens was unhappy with their services from the start. On January 30, 1846, he wrote a letter "To Messrs Bradbury & Evans," regarding his brief editorship of their *Daily News*, writing that he agreed with them that the "Paper" had to be "made perfect," and that to achieve this they had to hire the Sub Editor that he had recommended, Mr. Powell, and had to reveal the "nameless authority" that had said that Mr. Powell is "quite unfit for the place he holds!" He threatened to leave immediately if the critic's name is not revealed and that it was "extremely probably I shall leave it when you have done so" because he felt their rejection was "disrespectful, and quite unendurable," so that he was "thoroughly disgusted."[328] In this case, Bradbury & Evans must have stuck to their decision and Dickens did quit this editorship. After the final break that happened over a decade later, they continued publishing *Household Words* (1850-1859) without Dickens as the editor. In 1850, half of *Household Words* was owned by Dickens, a quarter by Bradbury & Evans and an eighth by Forster. Dickens was paying himself £40 a month for the numerous pieces he contributed over the years on various social issues.[329] In February of 1850, as the periodical was picking up steam, all contributions were anonymous, including a significant portion of works from Mrs Gaskell, who contributed her novels, *Mary Barton* and *North and South*, along with many other canonical works. One of the reasons Dickens broke with Bradbury & Evans was because they refused to publish the infamous "Personal" statement, where he attempted to stop the rumors about his extramarital affair with a younger actress, Mrs Ellen Lawless Ternan, or Nelly, in *Punch*. He did manage to release it in *The Times* and in *Household Words*. In response, Dickens forbade his children from continuing their friendships with the Lemon and Evans children.[330] It is possible that Charles Jr. took this edict as a challenge when he married Evans' daughter two years after Dickens broke all ties with his long-time publisher, Bradbury & Evans. In response, Charles Dickens Sr. "tried to stop friends from attending the wedding, or entering the Evans house." This contributed to creating bad roots for the "paper-making company" partnership that Charley Jr. was working on entering with Evans' son, Frederick in 1861. Charles Sr. warned against it, but Charley Jr. "chose to ignore" this

---

328 Hartley, *Selected*, 161-2.
329 Tomalin, *Charles*, 229.
330 Ibid., 298.

edict.[331] Frederick and Charley Jr's printing business failed in 1868, leaving Charley Jr. "bankrupt and with personal debts of £1,000 and five children to support."[332] All Charles Sr. could do by that point was offer Charley Jr. a job at his *All the Year Round* to lighten his financial burden.

Back in 1857, the news of Dickens' affair with Ternan (the actress) caused him to sever the relationship with shareholders of the *Household Words*. For Dickens, this meant stopping its publication and replacing it with his own, now fully independent and self-owned periodical, *All the Year Round*. The separation from Catherine (his ex-wife, and Hogarth's daughter) made Dickens see his busy social world in a new light. He stopped holding theatricals, and family holidays. He even ceased all charitable work for Miss Coutts and for the Home at Shepherd's Bush, so that no more young vulnerable women were taken into this shelter within a few years' time.[333] At the moment when he suddenly saw that his friends might be malicious and his family might just want his money, the most drastic change he was compelled to make was starting his own periodical, as this was a symbolic and a practical realization of his need for independence and freedom from painful social and literary interactions.

It is unclear if Charles Dickens became depressed in 1841, or if he was simply enamored with a young woman, Eleanor Picken, the fiancé of his solicitor. Eleanor wrote that they had been dancing, and playing games, including gambling with small sums while cheating openly for fun, when Eleanor, Milly, Dickens and his brother Fred all walked over to the end of the pier to watch the sunset and the tide. "Dickens seemed suddenly to be possessed with the demon of mischief; he threw his arm around me and ran me down the inclined plane to the end of the jetty till we reached a tall post. He put his other arm round this, and exclaimed in theatrical tones that he intended to hold me there till 'the sad sea waves' should submerge us…" Eleanor started screaming that her best and only dress was about to be ruined as the water climbed to her knees and the entire party came to her assistance, but Dickens' mother's scolding did not stop him, and Eleanor finally had to break herself free, thus ending whatever flirtation might have happened between them on a sour note for her, and making the observers

---

331   Ibid., 321.
332   Ibid., 371.
333   Ibid., 289.

think that he was suicidal.[334] Eleanor went to one of Dickens' readings from *A Christmas Carol* on November 1858, and when she got to the front afterwards, "he had already left, through the window. Evidently he was not always happy to meet his public."[335] Since Dickens kept giving these readings even after he had a stroke, it is surprising that he disliked them so much that he snuck out through a window. This scene also stresses that Eleanor did not really feel threatened by Dickens when he dragged her into the sea, as, if this was the case, she would not have gone out of her way to see him.

One of the reasons Dickens might have acted irrationally when he dragged Eleanor out there was because he was developing plans for a weekly magazine in 1839, *Master Humphrey's Clock*, which "he was proposing to edit for Chapman & Hall; they would publish this anonymously, because he could not be seen to be breaking his agreement with Bentley to publish no other books with rival publishers. So, the tangle of his dealings with the rival publishers grew worse." The American publishers offered a down payment of £100 for both *Master Humphrey's Clock* and *Barnaby Rudge*, a very low offer, yet he still put off this magazine's release until after he discussed this matter with the Americans. Meanwhile, Dickens reached a decision to confront the American publishers that were reprinting his work on their own soil. They were ripping him off because "there was no legislation of any kind covering the rights of foreign authors," so they did not feel obliged to pay Dickens any royalties. For example, Carey, Lea & Blanchard released *Sketches by Boz* "under several different titles in 1837," as well as a part of *Oliver Twist* without compensating or notifying him. Dickens was trying to create contracts with these publishers, but they were paying him a tiny share of the enormous profits they were reaping. Their only payments were made to obtain advance proofs to get an edge on their similarly pirating competition.[336] Dickens was fighting with the Americans for a couple of years, until in 1839, it became obvious that he had to go over to America to confront them, or he would never see a fair share from these dealings. Amidst this turmoil, in 1840, Dickens finally reached an agreement with Chapman & Hall for the *Master Humphrey's Clock*, wherein they would "pay him £50 per issue,

---

334   Elanor Emma Picken. "Reminiscences of Charles Dickens from a Young Lady's Diary." (London: *Englishwoman's Domestic Magazine*, 10 (1871)), 336-44.
335   Tomalin, *Charles*, 302.
336   Ibid., 105-6.

plus half the profits," with copies distributed in Germany and America. This magazine started strong at 70,000 copies sold for the first number in April of 1840, but then sales slumped as it "failed to appeal to readers."[337] As part of a "drastic" attempt to find buyers, Dickens started writing the oddly popular *The Old Curiosity Shop,* and then released his novel about the Gordon Riots, which was in development since 1839, but only started to appear in *Master Humphrey's Clock* in 1841.[338] As if he started the magazine solely for the purpose of releasing *Barnaby Rudge,* Dickens proposed closing the periodical with the last portion of this serialized novel, despite its popular success.[339] *Barnaby Rudge* was a radical work that was written on a similar rebellion theme to Sir Walter Scott's *Waverley* with its focus on the Jacobite rebellions. Thus, it is likely that Dickens was re-reading a good deal of Scott during his marriage to Catherine Hogarth. *Barnaby Rudge* might not have been accepted for publication if Dickens had to submit it to a journal other than his own because of its pro-labor sentiments. Scott had written *Waverley* in a partial Scottish dialect, released it in Edinburgh, and hid many of the rebellious bits subversively. In contrast, Dickens used plain English and released his novel in the heart of London.

One of the main issues that Dickens was concerned about since he started commercial publishing was seeing a fair share of profits. Because he frequently had negative experiences with publishers, he always expected problems. So, when he learned that publishers in the United States were reprinting his popular novels in hundreds of thousands, if not millions, without giving him a penny in royalties, he decided to at least take advantage of his popularity there with a lecture tour, while also attempting to negotiate contracts that would give him more than zero. During his first visit to the US, he complained in speeches about American publishers reprinting his work without permission and breaking his copyrights. International copyrights is still a contested issue because there are only loose, international laws governing publishers' use of materials published in other countries. In a letter to Jonathan Chapman, the Whig Mayor of Boston who escorted Dickens around town, on February 22, 1842, Dickens wrote from Carlton House in New York that he was "shocked and disgusted," and "sick and sore at heart" at being so mistreated regarding the International Copyrights

---

337   Ibid., 111.
338   Ibid., 121.
339   Ibid., 125.

question, and that he felt like "the greatest loser by the existing Law, alive."[340] Dickens did manage to make some arrangements with American publishers, so that they would start paying him royalties. But, the bulk of his work still continued to be illegally printed without any recourse to prevent this piracy.

Dickens was overwhelmed with the quantity of work he had to do to keep himself and his brood of dependents alive on his literary efforts from his earliest publications to his final novel. He soldiered on despite these misgivings, occasionally quitting publishers or periodicals, hoping to find friendly waters elsewhere, but only meeting with the same problems. In a letter to Lord George Howard, Viscount Morpeth, later 7th Earl of Carlisle, a Whig politician who visited America simultaneously with Dickens, on June 20, 1846, Dickens asked Lord Morpeth for any "Commissionership, or Inspectorship, or the like." He offered an extremely long list of various public service and educational positions that he might be interested in undertaking, stressing that he had always wanted to become a "Police Magistrate." Dickens explains that he "entertains the wish, common to most Literary Men, of having some permanent dependence besides Literature. But I have no though of abandoning that pursuit, which is a great happiness to me: and only seek this new avocation as its not unnatural offspring and companion." Dickens kept writing at break-neck speeds because he was always afraid that some calamity or drop in sales would leave him bankrupt or in debtor's prison. Hartley explains that Forester reported that Lord Morpeth replied that Police magistrates "had to be barristers for seven years' standing," making Dickens ineligible.[341] If Dickens had picked some more fitting dream to pursue aside from Literature at this juncture, we might have missed the bulk of his mature literary masterpieces. This attempt helps to explain why Dickens founded his periodicals. He hoped that they would provide a stable, long-term self-employment that would assure some safety net if his dealings with other publishers, regardless of their interest, disinterest, bankruptcy, or success. And by starting *All the Year Round*, Dickens succeeded in finding a revenue stream that meant he did not have to write as many novels in his last decade. The periodical also created a self-perpetuating inheritance for Charley Jr.

After all those years editing for other publishers, Dickens finally

340 Hartley, *Selected*, 96.
341 Ibid., 167-8.

had the funds and energy to start his own periodical in 1858. Dickens wanted to call his own independent magazine, *Household Harmony,* a name that closely resembled the periodical he was giving up, *Household Words*, but "Forster suggested the words might raise a few eyebrows in view of the recent events in the Dickens household," so Dickens called it *All the Year Round*, and became its "publisher, proprietor and editor."[342] The first number, at the end of April 1859, serialized *A Tale of Two Cities*, which by 1868 was Dickens' best-selling novel. It started selling extremely well immediately upon its release, though at that time, "Forster was almost alone in praising" it.[343] *A Tale of Two Cities* has many parallels with *Barnaby Rudge*. The primary difference being that the *Tale* is more radicalized and violent, as it focuses on the French Revolution. Dickens' research for it was guided by Thomas Carlyle, who previously released the 1837 historical study, *The French Revolution: A History*, on this upheaval. Dickens received a reproachful and critical letter on this novel from Sir Edward Bulwer-Lytton, who was an inactive member of the House of Lords, as well as a light, formulaic best-selling author who coined the term "pursuit of the almighty dollar" in his 1871 novel, *The Coming Race*. Sir Bulwer objected to certain components of the *Tale*, and Dickens replied from Gad's Hill on Tuesday, June 5, 1860: "I do not quite agree with you on two points, but that is no deduction from my pleasure [at receiving your letter]." Dickens then writes a technical report on the *Tale's* realism, offering research-based proof for the elements Sir Bulwer contests. Meanwhile, he explains the real reason for Sir Bulwer's displeasure: "…as to the condition of the peasant in France generally at that day, I take it that if anything be certain on earth it is certain that it was intolerable… The tax-taker was the authority for the wretched creature's impoverishment…"[344] In other words, Dickens' novel had too much realism rather than too little for Bulwer's taste, as it depicted the deplorable conditions of the poor in France that forced them into a revolution.

The success of at least one of his offspring was always a top goal for Dickens, as most of his relatives were in a state of constant struggle that frequently ended in catastrophic failure. Dickens was particularly proud of his oldest son, Charley Dickens Jr., who was born in 1837 as Charles Sr.'s career was just taking off. Dickens Jr. was educated at

---

342   Tomalin, *Charles,* 304.
343   Ibid., 308.
344   Dickens, *Selected,* 256-7.

King's College, London and Eton College, but having failed at banking, he became a traveling tea merchant, and then married his father's publisher's, Frederick Mullett Evans' daughter, Bessie Evans. This association inspired Jr. to start a printing business of his own. This print shop went bankrupt in 1868, despite Dickens Jr.'s connections and financial support from at least two extraordinary publishers. In the same year as this failure, 1868, Charles Dickens Sr. hired Charley Jr. to work for *All the Year Round*, firing his long-time subeditor, Henry Morley, who had worked with him since he was on the staff of *Household Words* in 1851. In making this switch, Dickens also passed by his long-time associate, William Henry Wills, who suffered a concussion that disabled him in 1868, to make Charley the editor of *All the Year Round* instead, after Sr.'s death in April of 1870. Wills had been Charles' subeditor since 1846 under *The Daily News*, and owned a significant share in *Household Words,* and later a quarter share in *All the Year Round*. Charley Jr. was only a subeditor for a short period before Wills' disability and his father's death. *The Daily News* was a newspaper that Bradbury & Evans founded under Dickens' editorship, for which Dickens was paid £2,000 annually. For this paper, Charles Sr. hired his uncle, John Barrow, to go to India to report on the Sikhs' war against Britain, repaying him for his employment of both his father, John, and himself when they were starting out.[345] Dickens also employed his father at *Daily News*, and at sixty, his old man suddenly became a "popular and respected figure in Fleet Street," becoming a useful asset for his son, while also recovering his solvency. Tomalin exclaims about John's work ethic at the paper, "Boz's father had found his niche at last."[346]

Charley Jr. inherited *All the Year Round* at his father's death and became the editor in 1870. He is best-known for the popular dictionaries he published, which banked, in their titles, on the similarity of his name with his father's. In 1887, Charley Jr. "gave up editing *All the Year Round*, went to work for the publishing house of Macmillan and served them well, writing biographical introductions to new editions of his father's works. In 1893, he closed down *All the Year Round*, which had run for thirty-five years…"[347] The majority of this journal's life was under Charley Jr., as Dickens was only alive for its first decade, and this is a great example of how the publishing ventures that survive for

345   Tomalin, *Charles,* 172.
346   Ibid., 176.
347   Ibid., 408.

decades or centuries typically have to be picked up by relatives. On the other hand, nepotism might also weaken publications. If Dickens left the journal with Henry Morley, the stronger editor, perhaps Morley would have expanded it, so that it would still be around today.

On the last day of his life, June 9, 1870, Dickens cashed a check, came back home to rest and smoke a cigar. Then, he went back to work on *Drood* at his cottage, and then came back home to write letters. Georgina, his sister-in-law, and some have suggested that she was also his lover, "was the only person known to have seen him" after he cashed the check. Georgina Hogarth (the 12-years younger sister) had lived in Dickens' household since Dickens and Catherine's trip to America in 1842. Georgina sided with Dickens during their tumultuous divorce. Her residence was not unusual for this large family, as Catherine's sister, Mary (who died young tragically in 1837), and Dickens Sr.'s brother, Frederick, also lived with them. Was Georgina benevolently housekeeping for Dickens' family or did she harbor darker motives? The likelihood of mischief is strengthened by the different versions of events that Georgina described. The plot becomes less "natural" when the primary suspect is forgetful or untruthful in its telling. Supposedly, he had a stroke after eating Georgina's dinner. Similarly to Byron's case, Dickens happened to become incoherent and she could not understand what he said until his last words, which were, "On the ground," in response to Georgina's request that he "lie down..."[348] Curiously, also in parallel with Byron's destroyed autobiography, it was Georgina who edited Dickens' letters and final manuscripts and did so with a very heavy hand, deleting and changing the positioning of many key letters, thus allowing her to control the narrative so that she came out as a savior rather than as a potential villain or incestuous woman that slept with her sister's husband and contributed to their separation. Georgina's version of Dickens' last words is almost too fictionalized, as it dramatically stresses his fighting nature. Sadly, nobody has as of yet come forward to object that Georgina could have poisoned Dickens with the dinner she served him after he had a perfectly healthy day running errands and working. If one looks at only the "Index" of Claire Tomalin's Dickens biography, he suffered from the following illnesses across his life: spasms in his side, stress, colds, operation for fistula, muscular twitches, complains of "spectres," near-breakdown in

---

348   Arthur A. Adrian. *Georgina Hogarth and the Dickens Circle*. (Oxford: Oxford University Press, 1957), 136-7.

Switzerland, depression, gouty and swollen foot, rheumatism and neuralgia, suspected gonorrhea, sunstroke in Paris, heart trouble, catarrh in US, and stroke. In response to the latter, doctors forbade "further reading," similarly to Virginia Woolf's prescription from Dr Savage to avoid mind work. Considering that the majority of his enormous family died at relatively young ages from various poverty-related diseases, like bacterial and fungal infections, it is really an achievement that he was able to live as long as he did. Thus, it is especially strange to imagine that with all of his health problems, somebody had to poison him. But, if this is not the case, it is odd that Georgina was acting as if she had something to hide after his death.

Then again, as one reads more of Dickens' biography, it's hard to imagine who among the people he knew did not want to kill him. For example, Dickens met with Queen Victoria on March 9, 1870. She said she regretted not hearing him read, but he objected that the "readings were over." Yet, he was not done with reading. He happened to give a memorial speech a month later for Maclise at the Royal Academy dinner on April 30. Later in their chat, the Queen complained that it was difficult "to find good servants in England, and he suggested the educational system might be unhelpful." In response to this comment: "She talked of the rising price of food," perhaps suggesting that if servants were more educated, they would want higher wages, thus raising the price on the food that both Dickens and her enjoyed eating. Then, she gave him a copy of her book, *Leaves from the Journal of Our Life in the Highlands*, which Dickens had previously objected to Wills publishing in his magazine, but thankfully Dickens did not express this sentiment directly to the Queen. The book sold well when it was published in America, in New York and Chicago in 1868 with Harper and Brothers Publishers. The "Preface" to this book explains that the Queen suggested that some portions of her Scotland trip be printed privately, so that she could share the copies with her family and friends, but the publisher then proposed a traditional publication.[349] Thus, the Queen actively solicited a self-publication before she found a publisher in the less morally stringent American book market. The Queen's jour-

---

349   Queen Victoria and A. Helps. *Leaves from the Journal of Our Life in the Highlands, from 1848 to 1861. To Which Are Prefixed and Added Extracts from the Same Journal Giving an Account of Earlier Visits to Scotland, and Tours in England and Ireland, and Yachting Excursions*. (New York: Harper & Brothers Publishers, 1868), v.

nals focus not only on her travels through the scenic highlands and to meetings with the region's aristocracy, but also describe her contribution to the region via overseeing the building and opening ceremonies of the cairn on Craig Gowan, the Balmoral Castle, the new bridge over the Linn, the Prince's statue at Balmoral, the statue of the Prince Consort at Edinburgh, and the Queen's statue at Balmoral. In other words, she used these trips to Scotland as state visits for the purpose of building the monarchy's infrastructure in this rebellious region in need of a stronger national bond. The *Highland Journals* quote extensively from Sir Walter Scott and describe a tour of Scott's Abbotsford home in great detail, so it's clear that she read voraciously and must have been a fan of not only Scott, but also of Dickens.[350] Her passion for great British writers must have contributed to her willingness to invest financially in a self-publication to enter the honorable ranks of great Victorian authors. If the Queen was told that Dickens disliked the *Journals'* reprint in his periodical, she might have had a strong reaction… At the same time, the Queen was probably used to writers bringing signed copies of their books, but in Dickens case, she had to beg him to give her a copy of some of his work before he finally said he would mail a set of his books to her.[351]

Dickens sent a follow-up note to Arthur Helps, the editor of the Queen's books, confidential advisor to the Queen, and the Clerk to the Privy Council, on March 26, 1870, reporting that the "binder" told him that it would be "'another fortnight' for the completion of the set of my books which I have entrusted to him to bind for the Queen." Since the books were forthcoming, meanwhile, he sent an unpublished, "new story," and offered to send additional pre-publication chapters as he wrote them for the Queen's perusal.[352] This timeline suggests that the Queen probably received *A Tale of Two Cities*, *Barnaby Rudge* and other major books of Dickens' on around April 15, less than two months before his death. Then again, there is no letter I know of that records the Queen actually receiving these books as-promised, so there is a chance Dickens forgot or ignored this order, as he had forgot to submit a due sketch to the *Morning Chronicle* decades earlier, a mistake that led to his termination from the paper. This letter is very cordial, but it is also odd that he addressed it to the Queen's editor,

---

350   Ibid., 132.
351   Tomalin, *Charles*, 386.
352   Hartley, *Selected*, 434.

instead of directly to the Queen. There is certainly something here that is out of the norm.

One explanation for Dickens' coldness toward the Queen is that back in 1840, he wrote a satirical and mocking love letter about Queen Victoria shortly after her marriage because he had heard of "various madmen" entering Buckingham Palace and Windsor Castle to attempt to meet her in person. The letter was addressed to Daniel Maclise and dated February 13, 1840, wherein he writes: "What if I murder Chapman and Hall…. If I did this she would hear of me…" He then proposes murdering himself to get into the morgue where she might see him. Then, he suggests that the Chartists might "serve" their purpose because: "They have no doubt in contemplation attacks upon the palace, and being plain men would very likely resign her to us with great cheerfulness."[353] Thus, Dickens is jokingly suggesting murdering his publishers, and assisting in a *coup d'état* to gain access to and rape Queen Victoria. This might be the only surviving letter of this type, but perhaps he sent others of this sort to his friends. Thus, it might have been awkward for him to go back on this negative sentiment to pay homage to the queen in his later years. In 1840, Queen Victoria was twenty-one and pregnant with her first of nine children, when she suffered an assassination attempt at the hand of Edward Oxford, so if Dickens' joking assassination satire was forwarded to her in 1840, she might have had him imprisoned immediately. While in 1868, as a widow, she was flattered at being called an author of equal standing with Benjamin Disraeli, a great realist novelist, who was briefly the Prime Minister. Then, 1870 was another traumatic year for her, as there were calls for her removal from the republicans' camp, and this might have contributed to her negative interpretation of Dickens' coldness. Dickens had a meeting with the Queen prior to the 1870 encounter, which he recorded in a letter to Daniel Maclise, on July 8, 1857. He wrote that Queen Victoria "was undoubtedly wonderfully taken" by his private performance of *The Frozen Deep* a few days earlier on July 4. "I had a letter on Sunday, of the most unofficial and uncourtly character. She sent for me after the Play, but I beg[ged] to be excused from presenting myself in any dress but my own."[354] The casual manner of the Queen's letter probably contributed to the casual manners Dickens had when they did end up meeting over a decade later. And his reticence about

353   Ibid., 62.
354   Ibid., 318.

attending is similar to Lord Byron's objection, wherein he had to pay a lot of money to buy an outfit that met the stringent dress code at the court before his appointed meeting was canceled. Dickens might have been making a living from writing by 1857, but he did not have the funds to buy an outfit for a single presentation at court. So, he took this opportunity to make a social statement and protest, insisting that the rules of court dress should be changed, starting with his own attire.

Dickens must have known that the Queen would want signed copies of his books and that this was the proper decorum for authors approaching aristocrats because back on February 8, 1836, he sent *Sketches by Boz*, to which he refers as, "the first I ever published," with a humble note that reminded Lord Edward Stanley, later the 14th Earl of Derby, of their earlier meeting when Dickens was a reporter for the *Mirror of Parliament*, and reproduced a portion of Stanley's speech "on moving the second reading of the Irish Disturbances Bill." Dickens explains that he is sending the Volumes because, "The wish of Authors to place their works in the hands of those, the eminence of whose public station is only to be exceeded by the lustre of their individual talents..."[355] Sir Stanley was the Chief Secretary for Ireland between 1830 and 1833 (decades after Lord Castlereagh served in this same role, before meeting a suspicious end). The speech Dickens is referring to was on the 1833 "Bill for Suppressing Disturbances in Ireland." Stanley served as the Prime Minister of the United Kingdom in 1852, between 1858 and 1859, and between 1866 and 1868, after a long political career going back to 1827. Dickens first met him when he was still young. Stanley wrote this letter to Dickens when he was between his two terms as the Secretary of State for War and the Colonies. Dickens was probably especially thankful to Stanley because in 1833 when Stanley was gracious enough to help him with his story, "there was still a formal prohibition against the publication of debates, and the Duke of Wellington was only one of many members of Parliament who denied that the English people had any right to know what was said in either House."[356] The speech took place when Dickens was recognized as the top Parliamentary reporter, and he transcribed the beginning and end of Stanley's very long speech flawlessly, while the other reporters that worked in shifts through the center of the speech left numerous errors. Stanley "wished copies of the speech to be circulated in Ireland," so he

---

355   Dickens, *Selected*, 13-4.
356   Johnson, *Walter*, 62.

asked for Dickens, or the reporter who transcribed the flawless section, to come by his residence to take the rest of the transcription, a request that Charles Dickens warmly accepted and took the transcription in the style that was typical at the House of Commons "on his knees." After this positive exchange, Lord Stanley wrote to Barrow to compliment him on the work of his "able" reporter.[357] Thus, naturally, when Dickens saw his first major publication in print, he was compelled to send a note of thanks and the volumes to Sir Stanley. Given these types of courteous exchanges, it is a puzzle as to what happened in the interim that made Dickens so cold and critical during his visit with Queen Victoria. It was a major conscious rebellion for Dickens to have objected to the Queen's comments and to have failed to bring his books for her perusal.

The facts surrounding Dickens' final days raise many questions, but few obvious conclusions. There is no mention of "spies" in his friends' accounts of this period, nor are there any revolutions Dickens was directly supporting. The idea that Dickens' distaste for Queen Victoria's book led to his assassination is a far-fetched one. Dickens is more likely to have died from over-working and failing to take care of his health. Thus, the more important story to take away from this section is about Dickens' self-publishing successes, and the difficulties even the best writers have with outside publishers.

---

357   Ibid., 66.

CHAPTER 6

A Woman's Burden: Virginia Woolf's Hogarth Press

[It] must surely be a fantasy for a writer—being one's own publisher, subject to no control, no judgment but one's own, with the great power of producing and distributing oneself what one has written. The connection may be no more than accidental, but it is certainly true that her first completely distinctive and original works were the first works that she and Leonard published themselves...
—Phyllis Rose, *Thrown to the Woolfs*[358]

First Writing Successes

Virginia Woolf's early successes in writing began in 1905, when she was approached by Bruce Richmond, the editor who previously worked with her father, Sir Leslie, when *The Times Literary Supplement* was founded in 1902. Richmond invited Virginia to contribute articles, and she kept contributing these until the end of her life, making this her longest professional connection. Between 1908 and 1909, *The Times Literary Supplement* was Virginia's "chief employer," while she was also writing longer reviews for *The Cornhill* and working on rewriting *The Voyage Out*.[359] Soon after she started writing articles, Virginia was invited to teach at the Morley College by Miss Sheepshanks, a daughter of the Bishop of Norwich and Principal of the school. Virginia was invited to instruct the evening institute for "working men and women" with a combination of "amusement and instruc-

---

358 John Lehmann. *Thrown to the Woolfs*. (London: Weidenfield and Nicolson, 1978), xi.
359 Quentin Bell. *Virginia Woolf: A Biography*. (New York: Houghton Mifflin Harcourt, 1972), Vol. I, 153.

tion… about books and pictures."[360] Other Stephens siblings already taught there: "Venessa… Drawing, Thoby (and Clive Bell) Latin, and Adrian Green; but unlike Virginia, they soon lost interest."[361] Virginia taught at Morley for three years, though she became disgruntled with the "useless tasks" that the school's "authorities" were forcing her to teach, and the "half-educated" and passive condition of her "Underworld" students.[362]

Leonard's Background and the Founding of Hogarth

Leonard Woolf describes his courtship of Virginia, their marriage and the founding of Hogarth Press in the third volume of his autobiography, *Beginning Again: An Autobiography of the Years 1911 to 1918*. He explains that in 1911, he returned from Civil Service abroad and spent half a year staying with different friends and traveling across western and eastern Europe in a state of ecstatic joy about everything he encountered after the dark seven years he spent in the volatile service. He explains that the "Bloomsbury" group was intellectually and socially inviting and helped him to feel welcomed back in society. It also made him want to focus on his writing instead of returning to service at the end of his leave. When he was not taking Virginia out to the Russian ballet or otherwise engaging with the artistic world and with society, he was writing a novel called, *The Village in the Jungle*, about the Sinhalese jungle villages in Ceylon. During his service to the colonizing government, he started to become "obsess[ed]" about the villagers' plight. With *The Village*, he "tried somehow or other vicariously to live their lives. It was also, in some curious way, the symbol of the anti-imperialism which had been growing upon me more and more in my last years in Ceylon." Leonard's radical political statements here are crucial to explaining why he had to start his own press shortly thereafter. The propaganda of the day insisted that civil servants like him fight to control Ceylon with imperialist vigor. Thus, a novel from an official, which rebelled against the occupation was certainly unwelcomed, and did not find a home with another publisher that it might have deserved. Leon-

---

360   Virginia Woolf. *A Writer's Diary: Being Extracts from the Diary of Virginia Woolf*. Leonard Woolf, Ed. (London: Berg Collection, 1953), Virginia Woolf to Violet Dickinson, 3 January 1905.
361   Ibid., Vol. I, 104-5.
362   Ibid., Vol. I, 107.

ard goes on to elaborate on this point:

> The Sinhalese way of life, in those entrancing Kandyan hills or the rice fields and coconut plantations of the low country, and above all those strange jungle villages, was what engrossed me in Ceylon; the prospect of the sophisticated, Europeanized life of Colombo, the control of the wheels of the intricate machinery of central administration, with the dreary pomp and circumstance of imperial government, filled me with misgiving and disgust. And I knew that if I went back to Ceylon it was almost certain that I would be returning, not to the village in the jungle, but to the seats of power in Colombo. The more I wrote *The Village in the Jungle*, the more distasteful became the prospect of success in Colombo.[363]

Anybody that has ever tried to describe warfare and suppression of indigent people with artistic detail knows that it is only natural to sympathize with poor villagers. Early in the narrative, Leonard described how the "Bloomsbury" group helped its members by instilling common moral and political values, in addition to inspiring a passion for crafting brilliant literature. Because Leonard found this inspiration to write as a member of the group, it is easy to see how he felt more capable of starting an independent press with Virginia, as opposed to on his own.

His newly shaped anti-imperialist position complicated his return. In addition, he had asked Virginia for her hand in marriage and she asked him for time to consider it. But, the Secretary of State for the Colonies refused to extend his leave. Therefore, he resigned from the Ceylon Civil Service effective May 1912. He was making £22 a month up to this point in salary, and suddenly was left "without a job and means of subsistence" other than the £600 he had saved.[364]

This was a difficult time for Leonard, but he was not yet at the lowest point of desperation when starting your own publishing house is essential to survival. His savings stretched all the way down to 1917, when they got down to £41. 15s. 3d., and this was the sum he used to found the Press. According to the Woolfs' friend and biographer, Quentin Bell, they conceived the idea of buying a press on Virginia's birthday, January 25, 1915. They also made plans to buy a bulldog,

---
363   Leonard Woolf. *Beginning Again: An Autobiography of the Years 1911 to 1918*. (New York: Harcourt, Brace & World, Inc., 1964), 47-8.
364   Ibid., 53-4.

but Virginia was more "excited" about the press.[365] Leonard makes a detailed account of the expenses that went into finally making this idea a reality in 1917: "This sum was made up of £38. 8s. 3d., which was spent on small printing machine and type, and £3. 7s. 0d., which was the total cost of production of the first book which we printed and published. We made a profit of £6. 7s. 0d in the first year on the first publication and that 'went back into the business', so that at the end of 1917 the total capital which we had put into the Hogarth Press was £35. After that the business financed itself out of profits and we never had to 'find capital' for it."[366] This description is particularly interesting because it explains how truly independent of all outside investors and influences this press was. It allowed the Woolfs to have a sense that they could write and publish whatever they wanted because there were no censors between their pen and the sold copy of the book.

After a long description of Virginia's manic-depression and their half-a-year long honeymoon, Leonard reports that they both returned to the work of writing. Virginia succeeded in selling *The Voyage Out* to Gerald Duckworth, her half-brother who owned the publishing firm of Duckworth & Co. on Henrietta Street. Virginia accused both Gerald and George, her half-brothers of molesting her and her sister Venessa, at a time when their mother and later their father were dying. Gerald had founded the publishing company in 1898. Today, Gerald Duckworth and Company Ltd is the oldest general trade publisher according to their website, now owned by a previous Penguin CEO, Peter Mayer. Because of their strained relationship, Gerald's publication decision must have been assisted by a positive review from a mutual friend and the company's reader, Edward Garnett. Gerald also published Virginia's second novel before she started publishing her novels primarily with her own Hogarth Press. Virginia's stream-of-consciousness style was rejected by other publishers because its unconventionality made it seem uncommercial. Gerald also published his step-father, Leslie Stephen's cultural studies book, *English Literature and Society in the Eighteenth Century*, in the first year of operation of Duckworth. One of the reasons Virginia felt she had to start her own press was because she "hated submitting her novels to Gerald Duckworth—he had what she called 'a clubman's view of literature,'" so she started to imagine that it would

---

365   Bell, *Virginia*, Vol. II, 23.
366   Woolf, *Beginning*, 54.

be a "comfort" to self-publish.[367] Leonard records the exact terms of the contract Duckworth offered. The author, Virginia, would be paid "on the published price of twelve out of thirteen copies sold the following royalties: 15% on the first 5,000 copies sold, 20% on all sales above 5,000." The rest of Leonard's description of his and Virginia's early publishing failures and successes is essential, so here it is in full:

> There was to be no advance payment on account of royalties. The book was not actually published until 1915. It was held up for the two years because of Virginia's breakdown. They printed 2,000 copies, and 14 years later, when in 1929 the Hogarth Press acquired the rights from Duckworth, there were still a few copies unsold. In the ten years before the Hogarth Press took the book over, 1919-1929, Duckworth sold 479 copies for which Virginia received in royalties £26.2s.10d. The fate of *The Voyage Out* in its first 15 years after publication shows what a long time it takes for a writer like Virginia to get any sale for her books or to make any money out of them. *The Voyage Out* had an extraordinarily good press; the reviewers were nearly all complimentary and she was recognized from the first as an important novelist. Soon, she had published *To the Lighthouse* and *Orlando* and had established herself as a highly successful writer. 4,000 copies of *To the Lighthouse* were sold in the first year of publication and *Orlando* sold 4,000 copies in its first month. But it took 15 years to sell 2,000 copies of *The Voyage Out*, as I said, and the earnings of the author from it in those 15 years were less than £120. However as soon as an author really establishes himself, all his books sell. That is why when we in the Hogarth Press reprinted *The Voyage Out* in 1929, we sold 781 in the first year, though it had sold fewer than 500 copies in the previous ten years.
>
> Meanwhile in 1913 Edward Arnold published my novel *The Village in the Jungle*. The book was not unsuccessful in its way. It had very good reviews. The first edition sold out at once and it was reprinted twice before the end of 1913 and again in 1925. Four editions of one's first book in 12 years sounds pretty good, but in fact the sound was a good deal better than the material reality. Arnold did not take a rosy view of the selling prospects of the book, and when the first edition sold out, he printed only a few hundred copies. Rather to his dismay, I think, he sold these immediately and had to reprint for the second time. By 1929 the book had sold 2,148 copies. My agreement with Arnold was less favorable for the author than Virginia's with Duckworth. I got 10% royalty on the first 1,000 sold and 15% thereafter, and, as the price of *The Village in the Jungle* was 5s. while *The Voyage Out* was 6s., by 1929, though my book

---

367 Bell, *Virginia*, Vol. II, 74.

had sold a few more copies than hers, I had earned £63.3s.0d. against her £110 to £120. As a publisher myself today, I am amused to find that in 1913 when I bought one of my own books (published price 5s.) from Arnold, he charged me 4s. and also 4d. for sending it to me in Brunswick Square. He was therefore charging the author 4s.4d. for a book for which he would get from a London bookseller either 3s.9d. or 3s.4d.

Leonard goes on to detail their books' sales over their first decade together. He explains that Virginia had £9,000 in "stocks and shares" and was making £400 from this in interests annually, but that they needed £845 or more annually to live on.[368] They were attempting to reach the difference with their writing and later publishing, but were usually dipping into Virginia's savings instead. Leonard also took on odd jobs, such as working as the secretary (clerk and art authority) for the second Post-Impressionist Exhibition, organized by Roger Fry in the Grafton Galleries in 1912, where Cezanne, Matisse and Picasso were featured. Leonard describes that the majority of the visitors "either roared with laughter at the pictures or were enraged by them."[369] It's interesting that a century later, the rage and laughter is suppressed, and artists dedicate their lives to trying to reproduce this post-impressionist style, as if hoping to mimic this supposed success.

In a later section, Leonard spends many pages on explaining why Asham Desmond MacCarthy could never write the brilliant novel he imagined he would write in his youth, before he started his journalistic career. Leonard projects his own insecurities into MacCarthy's choices when he proclaims: "Journalism is the opiate of the artist; eventually it poisons his mind and his art."[370] Leonard explains how working as an editor and journalist across the years created an internal, cyclic focus, so that he was constantly concerned with the news of the week only to forget them later, and was writing poorly crafted stories for the masses. All of these reflections seem like expressions of the reservations Leonard felt later in life about failing to write novels of equal literary value to his wife's. Creating the Hogarth Press helped him to regain faith in his own literary and scholarly writing and to tell himself as he instructs all writers to do, "I don't care what they say about it and me; I shall publish and be damned to them."[371] The key term here is "publish"

---

368 Woolf, *Beginning*, 88-90.
369 Ibid., 94.
370 Ibid., 139.
371 Ibid.

rather than "write," as a kindergartener can "write" a book, but only a publisher or a highly acclaimed writer can publish it, even despite his or her informed reservations about its value.

The more Leonard engaged with society, the more political he became, and his radicalism gained a new boost of inspiration after the 1917 Russian revolution. He writes: "I was born a little Liberal and also—though I did not realize it for some time—a little revolutionary. I am on the side of Pericles and Tom Paine; I am instinctively against all authoritarians, aristocrats, or oligarchs from Xerxes and Lycurgus to Edmund Burke…"[372] In response to this new-found sense of exhilaration about revolutions, Leonard accepted an invitation to attend the "Great Labour, Socialist *and* Democratic Convention *to hail the* Russian Revolution *and* to Organise *the* British Democracy *To follow Russia*," arranged by the United Socialist Council. He served as a delegate either of the Labour Party or the Fabian Society (which specifically, he does not recall) on June 3, 1917.[373] Unlike earlier British writers such as Charles Dickens, who described revolutionary violence without openly condoning it, leading some critics to conclude that they opposed it, Leonard directly declares his pro-revolutionary violence position across this moment in history and through his later years when he was writing his autobiography. "Like the French revolution, [the Russian revolution] destroyed an ancient, malignant growth in European society, and this was essential for the future of European civilization." He tempers this statement by adding: "The intelligent revolutionary knows, however, what all revolutions must disappoint him." But after thinking through the drawbacks of violence, Leonard returns to his initial conclusion: "Nevertheless the destruction of the ancient regime in France and of the Tsarist regime in Russia was essential—and indeed inevitable…" It is of little surprise, to me at least, that in the next paragraph Leonard proclaims that this was the year when Virginia and he "started the Hogarth Press."[374] The Press flowed naturally out of his need to express these hyper-revolutionary statements in a period when Russia's monarch was just assassinated, and Britain was starting to look like it would become the last surviving monarchy on the planet, if some radical altercation failed to materialize with help from radical publishers. Leonard mentions founding the 1917 Club just before describing how

---

372   Ibid., 208.
373   Ibid., 210.
374   Ibid., 215.

he founded Hogarth Press. Actually, this Club came about a significant amount of time before the Press. The Club was a political catalyst that necessitated an independent press. The Club's membership was dominated by politically-minded Labour Party members. One of his chief collaborators and rivals in the Club was Ramsay Macdonald, who got close to Leonard only to sabotage his plans in favor of his own. Leonard was being encouraged to start a radical labor periodical, but the leaders suddenly withdrew their financial support from the Labour Party for the review publication, when Ramsay objected. Ramsay opposed Leonard's plan because he was editing the *Socialist Review* with the same bundle of funding from the Club, and did not want to lose the money. Instead, Leonard was offered an editorship of the *International Review*, which was general in its topics, and did not have any radical funding.[375]

Leonard digresses into a variety of topics before finally returning to the founding of Hogarth Press. He explains that he learned from his nurse that "all work and no play did irreparable harm to all humanity" and thus he decided that it would do Virginia's mental health good to put her hands to a "manual" occupation like printing. They decided to learn the "art of printing" in 1916, but their dreams of going to school to learn the craft were shattered when they learned that they had to join a union to attend classes. In March of 1917, they finally discovered a solution when they came across the Excelsior Printing Supply Co., where the supervisor sold all of the implements they'd need, "printing machine, type, chases, cases" and a "16-page pamphlet" that could teach them how to print on their dining-room table at home for £19.5s.5d.[376] After a month of experimentation, they created their first 32-page, stitched on paper-cover pamphlet, with a short fiction story from both Virginia (*The Mark on the Wall*) and Leonard Woolf (*Three Jews*), which was released on May 3 in 150 copies. Leonard states that Hogarth was the first publisher to create "beautiful, uncommon, and sometimes cheerful paper" covers to bind their books. Leonard believes this stylistic element became fashionable with other publishers as a result of their success.[377] The Woolfs' biographers, George Spater and Ian Parsons described the process of creating the first pamphlet as taking "two months, working nearly every afternoon… The type purchased

---

375	Ibid., 225.
376	Ibid., 234.
377	Ibid., 236.

with the press was only sufficient to set up two small pages. After these had been inked and run off on the press, one sheet at a time, the forms had to be broken up so that the type could be used for the succeeding two pages…"[378] They advertised the books by stating that the two of them printed books entirely on their own. They further claimed that they printed works that had "little or no chance of being published by ordinary publishers." They sold the first edition of their little pamphlet predominantly to their "friends and acquaintances," and on this alone made this project profitable.[379] Thus, all of the work they put into socializing and making friends all over Europe in intellectual circles paid off through this sales strategy. The friends who bought this work mostly became subscribers, and bought many of the subsequent books and, at least at first, were willing to buy the books at the "full published price" instead of the cut-in-half price bookstores or other distributors would've offered if they could not sell these themselves. They only switched to selling to bookstores in 1923, six years into the press's life. Spater and Parsons concluded that the first two years of Hogarth Press' operations resulted in "a small paper profit," but simultaneously "involved the expenditure of hundreds of hours of unpaid work…" The Woolfs were only paid out of the small profits that remained after the authors were paid 25% royalties, the assistant received 50% or a salary, and publishing costs were paid. In exchange for these profits, Virginia was setting type, stitching bindings, pasting labels, filling orders, wrapping parcels, assisting with translation from Russian (without a credit, unlike Leonard), reviewing submitted manuscripts, and soliciting new writers. Meanwhile, Leonard operated the machines, kept accounts, and screamed at the employees when they were a couple of minutes late or failed to account for a few coins. All this frustration and effort went into hand-printing 400 copies, as well as supervising the printing of larger editions with outside printers that were always at risk of failing to sell. The unequal balance between the volume of work and the meager profits continued to be a problem across the thirty years of the Woolfs' marriage.[380] The Woolfs were fortunate in the authors they published and in the reviews their books received in major publications, which

---

378   George Spater and Ian Parsons. *A Marriage of True Minds: An Intimate Portrait of Leonard and Virginia Woolf.* (New York: Harcourt Brace Jovanovich, 1977), 100.
379   Woolf, *Beginning*, 236.
380   Ibid., 102, 108-9.

helped them go from releasing 1 book in 1917 to 40 books in 1927, for a total of more than 400 books across its operation. They kept making hand-set and hand-printed books, though they purchased a larger "Minerva platen press—second hand and worked by a treadle" to help them manage this labor, meanwhile they spent much of their free time on hand printing until they ceased this method in 1932.[381]

This arduous printing method the Woolfs used invites questions regarding how the Woolfs' technique fit into the history of printing. Would they have been more or less successful if they were starting a publishing company today, and were able to print-on-demand, without creating print runs in advance? They had to format each of the pages by setting the letters and inking them. If they only printed a book when the demand came up for it, they would not have taken on a printing like the 68-page long short story by Katherine Mansfield that they printed a year into Hogarth's existence. The Woolfs were using the letterpress printing method in 1917, nearly identical in process to how it was done in the fifteenth century. It did not even have an attached typewriter that would have made it easier for them to enter the text, a process popularized a few decades later. The laser printer was invented in 1938. By 1956, researchers at MIT, like Joe Thompson, were experimenting with direct keyboard input into computers, a step essential to modern book publishing. In 1960, the DEC PDP-1 was introduced and allowed for a graphic display and printing. Book publishers were using mechanical printers until the last few decades, when they finally switched to printing via computers and automated machines that imprint, fold, ink, and cover books. These printers cost millions and have made home-printing with something like the Woolfs' method incredibly fruitless by comparison. The print runs were necessary before computerized printing because printing one book at a time was unprofitable. While this made sense a century ago, it is amazing that the publishing industry is still clinging to this print-run "offset" printing model, when today it is as outdated as the first Ford model. Wouldn't it be strange if Ford kept selling that first model today and saying that all of the new, computer-designed models were inferior to their brilliant original? And yet today, the Big Four publishers advertise their enormous print runs of 20,000-100,000 copies per title, as if this is an achievement, instead of a potentially enormous loss. Print-run gambling has led to the failure and merging of so many publishers that

---

[381] Spater, *Marriage*, 106.

the Big Four dominate the marketplace.

But, to return to Virginia and Leonard's efforts, to create 300 copies of Mansfield's *Prelude*, they "printed only in the afternoon and even so not every afternoon" for what was probably an extended number of afternoons. If I had to spend each of my afternoons printing the new titles my press was releasing, and then had to package and ship them individually to my personal contacts; then, I would have failed to overcome these barriers to entry into the publishing business. All of these tasks fell on the publisher in 1917 because the cost of outsourcing printing and shipping was prohibitive. It is amazing that the Woolfs managed to do this strenuous work for so many decades. Virginia had thousands in the bank, and while Hogarth started to see some profits, the number of hours she spent doing this manual labor surely must have been depressing, though she probably did not show it to Leonard who thought he was giving his wife an entertaining treat.

The burden of self-printing was partially lightened when Leonard gave up in the middle of printing the *Prelude* at home on their "handpress." Leonard prefaced this surrender by expressing that their printing abilities had finally risen to meet the challenge by that point. When the Woolfs gave up on printing the Prelude themselves, Leonard "machined it on a large platen machine which printed four crown octavo pages at a time and which belonged to a jobbing printer called McDermott."[382] Leonard goes on to say that he discovered that McDermott's giant new printer was a "white elephant" because "it was too large to be economical for the size of his business." Leonard frequently found McDermott struggling with a mechanical problem with the printer he was ill-equipped to solve with his non-mechanical background. Watching McDermott's troublesome huge printer purchase probably saved Woolf from going bankrupt by investing in a larger printer for Hogarth. He describes a nightmarish attempt by McDermott and him at printing 1,000 copies of Virginia's short stories collection, *Monday and Tuesday*. The ink and paper gave them so much trouble between the color woodcuts and the thin paper that they collapsed and drank beer on the floor when this ordeal was over.[383] One of the reasons Hogarth survived despite these enormous challenges is because there was starting to be a demand for Virginia's own books and because the "Bloomsbury" group and other associations meant that when they published friends, they

---

382   Woolf, *Beginning*, 237.
383   Ibid., 240.

ended up publishing T. S. Eliot and E. M. Forster, releasing works that received positive reviews in *The Times Literary Supplement,* when they started sending a single review copy there.[384] The Woolfs also interacted with other small, independent, radical publishers and helped these competitors get started. Leonard describes how in 1918, Miss Harriet Weaver came by their house seeking advice on if it would be appropriate for her publish James Joyce's obscene and absurd novel, *Ulysses*. Virginia's description of Weaver in her diary is telling: "…how did she ever come in contact with Joyce and the rest? Why does their filth seek exit from her mouth? Heaven knows. She is incompetent from the business point of view and was uncertain what arrangements to make. We both looked at the MS. Which seems an attempt to push the bounds of expression further on, but still all in the same direction. And so she went."[385] Despite this criticism, the Woolfs decided to try and publish Joyce's book, but none of the printers they queried were willing to put their name on the publication. Weaver eventually found another printing method herself, as the Woolfs kept the book in their drawer until 1919. It took the Woolfs a decade to turn Hogarth Press into a "successful commercial publishing business," but because it remained their "half-time occupation," they did not "become a bigger, fatter, and richer business." Leonard goes on to state, "it would be quite impossible today to do what we did in 1917 to 1927, i.e. build up a successful publishing business from zero with no capital. Costs of production have increased to such an extent and publishing is so geared to large scale, best seller industry that today there is no place for the kind of books with which we began and which floated The Hogarth Press into prosperity." He goes on to argue that he believes it would be possible to replicate this success even in 1963, if a publisher follows the following guidelines: "First" he or she would need "to know or find a few writers, unknown but potentially of the first class. Secondly, one would have to start it, as we did, as a very part-time occupation, making one's living for the first years in other ways. Thirdly, one would have to refuse absolutely, as we did for many years, to publish anything unless we thought it worth publishing or the author worth publishing. I think that 'thirdly' is the most important of the three conditions of success."[386] Today, cooperative and subsidy publishing allows some

---

384   Spater, *Marriage,* 241-2.
385   Ibid., 245-246.
386   Ibid., 254-5.

publishers to succeed even if the writers they release are not as brilliant as Eliot and Virginia. But, otherwise these lessons still hold true. Leonard goes on to give another important lesson that still applies to the publishing business: "Most small publishers perish by trying to become too big too quickly. One reason why the Press survived was because for many years our object was, not to expand, but to keep it small. In business the road to bankruptcy is paved with what the accountant calls 'overheads' and too many publishers allow their 'overheads' to dictate to them the size of their business and the kind of books they publish. My theory was that the main object of a publisher, as business man, should be to keep his overheads as near to zero as possible, and, if he did that, he could forget about them and publish only what he wanted to publish."[387] It is easy to see how Leonard and Virginia's publishing program was enriched by their skills as writers and editors. If they were entering this venture purely as business people or skilled printers, as most printers at the time were, they would not have had the editorial wisdom to spot, for example, that T. S. Eliot's *The Waste Land* (1922) was an outstanding book that would eventually bring them scholarly acclaim and fitting riches. Because they had failed to find printers for their own radical and non-conformist works, they sympathized with similarly radical writers and wanted to help them release their authorial ambitions even if profits were unpredictable.

Virginia's Tortures

The regular problems with running a publishing company were intensified by personal and social struggles that interfered with Virginia's ability to excel. Her sex was almost a disability through most of her life, as physicians told her that she should avoid "brain" work if she wanted to keep her sanity. "Brain" work is certainly essential in a publisher, as it is for a writer.

Virginia Woolf's *A Room of One's Own* is essential reading for any woman in publishing because it forces readers to consider the philosophical necessity of money for the survival of a writing or publishing career. Art is a beautiful dream, but sexism has crushed this dream for most women who have attempted it. Woolf wrote this speech, and then turned it into a creative non-fiction essay in 1929, a decade after

---

387   Ibid., 255.

founding her own publishing company. She mentions publishing only a few times in this book, despite the fact that this subject seems naturally linked to women and writing. The central character Woolf alludes to across this essay is William Shakespeare's sister, arguing that she could not have succeeded as William did solely because of her gender and the legal and cultural restrictions on it, even if she had an equivalent talent. Woolf begins chapter "Four" by referring to the impoverished conditions mothers in Shakespeare's class were in and adds: "What one would expect to find would be that rather later perhaps some great lady would take advantage of her comparative freedom and comfort to publish something with her name to it and risk being thought a monster."[388] Woolf goes on to say that even if such a woman overcame the pressures on her to refrain from writing, reading, thinking and enquiring, "she has to encourage herself to write by supposing that what she writes will never be published."[389] While Woolf had been published before she started Hogarth, she was still constantly afraid that one of her laborious books would fail to find a publisher, and she needed the security of owning some place that would always accept her. She might never have written her prominent, modernist books if she did not feel that even if others rejected them, she could always bring them into the world herself.

It is impossible to understand Virginia's triumphs and tribulations as a publisher and as an author without examining the accusation that is most frequently levied against her, or that she was "insane." The bulk of Woolf biographers insert "insane," or its synonyms, in the brief summary of Virginia Woolf's life, as if this is a defining characteristic. As can be seen from Byron's and even Scott's ordeal in the last days of their lives, the "insanity" charge was historically used to torture creative men and women with bleeding, blistering and other concoctions meant to appear to be medicinal, while they are aimed to squash the spirit of rebellion. Was it accidental that Byron attempted to publish details about his homosexual affairs in a memoir right before his tragic end? Did Virginia threaten her husband's ego when she crossed the established gender lines to become his equal, as a successful businesswoman, author and publisher? Her "madness" was used against her by all around her to excuse their sexual, physical and psychological abuse. Meanwhile, they were projecting their own guilt onto her mind

---

388   Woolf, *Beginning*, 62.
389   Ibid., 64.

and accusing her of a flaw, when they were its cause and cultivators. Only a few studies question the insanity premise, including a recent critical biography, *Who's Afraid of Leonard Woolf: A Case for the Sanity of Virginia Woolf*, by Irene Coates. This study argues that Leonard Woolf drove his wife insane because he was "difficult to work for" and "live with," and was frequently "bullying and humiliating" the people around him, and battering Virginia with "sudden words" that devastated her. Coates claims that: "On one occasion it took her over a year to recover. Such episodes would have left some permanent damage as, painstakingly, she had to restore the tranquility she needed in order to write."[390] Leonard driving his wife to suicide would fit a lot better with the theme of assassinations and psychosis that befell many other radical author-publishers, as they simultaneously worked to perfect their art and their businesses.

Sources that claim that Virginia Woolf was insane are basing these presumptions on the findings of the psychiatrists that examined her and diagnosed her with neurasthenia. Woolf endured electrotherapy as well as "tooth extraction" as part of Sir George Savage's "treatment." Sir George Savage, knighted in 1912, was first called in to observe Virginia by the Stephen family in 1904. "Savage saw heredity as a primary cause: James Stephen, Virginia's paternal grandfather, had suffered from bouts of madness similar to hers; there was Laura; there was J. K. Stephen, the cousin, also suicidal. Savage had recommended force-feeding, rest, forbade reading: Virginia was to replace her book with a spade… Savage thought that education and exercise of the intellect was bad for women (and for working men)."[391] In a memoir entry in *A Sketch of the Past* on July 19, 1939, Virginia Woolf mentions that her grandfather, Jim Stephen, was diagnosed as mad by George Savage before Savage was knighted, and when Virginia's father was still alive and was the one responsible for dealing with his madness. Savage was "an old friend of the Stephen family." She writes:

> …Let me then, like a child advancing with bare feet into a cold river, descend again into that stream…/ Jim Stephen was in love with Stella. He was mad then. He was in the exalted stage of his madness. He would dash

[390] Irene Coates. *Who's Afraid of Leonard Woolf: A Case for the Sanity of Virginia Woolf?* (New York: Soho Press Inc., 2000), 19.
[391] Nicole Ward Jouve. "Virginia Woolf and Psychoanalysis." *The Cambridge Companion to Virginia Woolf*. Sue Roe and Susan Sellers, eds. (Cambridge: Cambridge University Press, 2000), 250-1.

up in a hansom; leave my father to pay it. The hansom had been driving him about London all day. The man wanted perhaps a sovereign It was paid. For 'dear Jim' was a great favourite. Once, as I say, he dashed up to the nursery and speared the bread. Another time, off we went to his room in De Vere Gardens and he painted me on a small bit of wood. He was a great painter for a time. I suppose madness made him believe he was all powerful. Once he came in at breakfast, "Savage has just told me I'm in danger of dying or going mad", he laughed. And soon he ran naked through Cambridge; was taken to an asylum; and died… This great mad figure… would recite poetry to us…[392]

All of the people that went mad in that family were likely to have been treated by Dr. Savage over the decades. He might have prescribed the same poisonous drugs that gradually withered their minds, so that they progressed from taking too many rides around London to running around naked, when they were threatened with institutionalization by Savage. A key point in this description is that Jim was an artist and a scholar and ended up dying after he was taken to an asylum. The horrific treatments and lack of upkeep in asylums killed many other well-off and educated people that were officially certified as insane by the government with the help of Savage and physicians like him. Thus, when Virginia is considering suicide or stepping into the cold river, she might view this as preferential to going mad and being sent to an asylum as Jim was. Virginia directly discusses suicide in the next entry she made on June 8, 1940: "If we are beaten then—however we solve that problem, and one solution is apparently suicide (so it was decided three nights ago in London among us)—book writing becomes doubtful."[393]

Dr. Savage's treatment is discussed in several other sources, though in Eilat Negev and Yehuda Koren's *The First Lady of Fleet Street*, it seems that Virginia tried to kill herself after Dr. Savage treated her rather than before. "She had suffered a nervous breakdown after losing her father, whom she'd been nursing six months."[394] Virginia's father was Sir Leslie Stephen, a reformist historian who married twice, and thus created an enormous combined brood of children; he died in 1904. Virginia

---

392   Virginia Woolf. *Moments of Being: Unpublished Autobiographical Writings*. Jeanne Schulkind, Ed. (New York: Harcourt Brace Jovanovich, 1976), 98-9.
393   Ibid., 100.
394   Eilat Negev and Yehuda Koren. *The First Lady of Fleet Street: The Life of Rachel Beer: Crusading Heiress and Newspaper Pioneer*. (New York: Random House Publishing Group, 2012), 260.

was molested by her two, new, older step-brothers, one of whom was George, who was born in 1868, so he was fourteen years older than Virginia. At least one of the later molestation occurred in 1904, when her father was on his deathbed, and she was twenty-two. In 1921 in a memoir essay called, "Old Bloomsbury," made for the Memoir Club, Virginia describes that she was reading in bed past midnight: "There would be a tap at the door; the light would be turned out and George would fling himself on my bed, cuddling and kissing and otherwise embracing me in order, as he told Dr Savage later, to comfort me for the fatal illness of my father—who was dying three or four storeys lower down of cancer.[395] Dr Savage did not name George as one of the mad members of the Woolf family, but rather blamed Virginia for being the mad object of her brother's "comforts." While many sources claim that taking care of her father drove Virginia mad at this juncture, it seems the continuing molestations were a more likely culprit. Sir George Duckworth later served as the private secretary to Austen Chamberlain before dying in 1934, after years when Virginia was out of contact with him.

Across these molestations, Dr. Savage was never on her side, and was forced on her by the dominant members of her family, who pressured her to obey his prescriptions under the threat of the asylum. She had previously suffered a collapse after her mother's death in 1895. But, she only started hearing voices "telling me to do all kinds of wild things" in 1904.[396] Bell explained that "she believed that they came from overeating and that she must starve herself." This was when she tried to commit suicide for the first time by jumping out of a window, which was not high enough to do her harm.[397]

Savage's theories were based on the "principles of the rest cure" originated by Silas Weir Mitchell, a neurologist who argued that "any brain work of more than two hours a day was harmful for women, causing nervous disorder." This treatment included isolating patients from everybody they knew, and forcing them to "remain in bed, in a darkened room, for up to two months. The only action allowed was cleaning the teeth; even sitting was forbidden. The treatment included overfeeding, massage and electrical stimulation of the muscles."[398]

395	Woolf, *Moments,* 160.	
396	Negev, *First,* 260.	
397	Bell, *Virginia,* Vol. I, 89-90.	
398	Negev, *First,* 260.	

Leonard assumed that Virginia was mad when she spent months resting without any activity in her room, but this was not a symptom, this was the cure that Dr. Savage prescribed. If she heard similar prescriptions from other doctors, being forced to perform intense physical labor and more than two hours of "brain work" daily by Leonard for the press must have been torturous because she was conditioned to think that this "brain work" was likely to lead her to insanity. At the same time, she was passionate about writing, and tried to avoid overloading her brain with this "brain work" by rushing to write as many words as she could in the two hours limit, and this pressure created her unique stream of consciousness style.

Savage's treatments continued for a decade. In the middle of it, in 1913, Virginia started saying that everybody was laughing at her, and this led Leonard to consult Dr. Henry Head at Gordon Square about her case, and he concurred with Dr. Savage's opinion that Virginia was indeed ill with a "cold or typhoid fever" as well as with the mental disturbances. Leonard had been campaigning with different specialists to find support for his diagnosis that they should avoid having children. Dr. Head agreed that she should enter a nursing home.[399] Virginia had been taking Veronal, a barbiturate for her insomnia, under Leonard's supervision and it, together with the contraceptives she had been taking since her marriage started, because Leonard had insisted that she could not have children, were the likely causes of her amenorrhea, or a lack of menstrual cycles, from which she suffered for a decade, with Leonard recording every occurrence when she did menstruate. For example, he noted that she did not have any periods between August and November of 1913. Virginia also smoked regularly, and nicotine might have interacted with the other drugs she was prescribed. On that tragic day, after the meeting with Dr. Head, Leonard left Virginia alone to "rest" as he went over to meet with Dr. Savage to tell him that he had consulted Dr. Head without his permission. While he was away, Virginia took too much Veronal, and nearly died. It is possible that after so many years of taking Veronal, Virginia's regular dose was much higher than normal, and Veronal is known to cause over-doses even if normal quantities are taken by somebody with a dependency. Sources repeat that Virginia took "100 grains" of Veronal, but it is highly unlikely that Virginia counted out 100 grains in the middle of a suicidal episode.

399   Viviane Forrester. *Virginia Woolf: A Portrait*. (New York: Columbia University Press, 2015), 145.

If the number was 96, it might have sounded much more realistic, as only a new and unused prescription was likely to have such a round number. The number most likely originates from Leonard's diary entry from September 9, 1913, which he wrote in a code he created immediately after the suicide attempt, "using Sinhalese and Tamilese symbols for the English alphabet." In translation, Leonard's entry reads, "6.30. Ka telephoned V. had fallen asleep. Returned at once by taxi. V. seemed unconscious. Telephoned Van to bring doctor. She brought Head. Found V. had taken 100 grains Veronal…"[400] Coates and a few other, recent critics probably justly interpret Leonard's need to concoct a code, as well as to hide or destroy documents, and other sketchy moves as suspicious behavior that points to an obvious desire to hide something. On the other hand, it seems that this letter was decoded by George Spater, and various other sources that popularized the 100 grains theory, so perhaps this was a code that was meant to be broken. Either way, Leonard was clearly much more paranoid when he wrote this diary entry than anything we can discover in Virginia's constantly clear-minded entries. As a side note, George Duckworth, her molesting, older half-brother, was present during this incident as he was during all of the previous major breakdowns of Virginia's, and it was he who "offered them Dalingridge Place, his large and well-appointed house near East Grinstead in Sussex."[401] Why would any doctors there have approved a plan to send Virginia to recover at the house of her molester, and why would Leonard have agreed to this plan unless he was maliciously hoping Virginia would attempt suicide again?

Leonard looked into nursing homes when Virginia was still in the hospital recovering, but her doctors advised him that caring for her with nurses at his home was a sounder solution. Leonard blamed Virginia's 1913 suicide attempt and her successful suicide in 1941 on her anxiety after she had completed books she had been toiling on for years before these moments. In a letter housed in the Berg Collection, Jean Thomas wrote to Violet Dickinson on September 14, 1913 with a similar sentiment, "It is the novel which has broken her up. She finished it and got the proof back for correction… couldn't sleep & thought everyone would jeer at her. Then they did…" Leonard accused Jean of feeling a "violent homosexual passion for Virginia," and this jealousy might have been one of the motivations for his potential homicidal

---

400   Spater, *Marriage*, 73.
401   Bell, *Virginia*, Vol. II, 16.

hatred of her at this stage of their marriage.[402] This might have been an accidental versus an intentional overdose. Shirley Panken stated in *Virginia Woolf and the Lust of Creation: A Psychoanalytic Exploration* that Leonard was "forbidding babies and sex,"[403] and this suggests that her menstrual cycles might have stopped more from the sleeping pills and weight loss than from contraceptive use. Leonard reports that Virginia was 119 pounds when she tried to commit suicide on September 30, 1913, and under his supervision, she gained sixty pounds in two years to reach around 179 pounds by 1915.[404] An average model weighs 107 pounds today, so her low weight would have been seen as appealing if she was a celebrity in today's media world, but a hundred years ago thinness was a sign of insanity. In March of 1914, after watching Virginia's weight since her break down, Leonard started complaining of "bad headaches" that were "violent and disabling," so that he had to ask for a "ten days' holiday," which he used to go to Wiltshire to stay in a cottage with Lytton, "who read him his *Cardinal Manning* and argued about Ulster—a strange cure, but it seems to have worked." Bell added the latter comment based on his own observations of Leonard's condition.[405] Leonard's need to get away from supervising Virginia says something about his intolerance and aversion to her ravings.

Three of Virginia's teeth were pulled in June of 1922, a year after Savage's death in 1921, and after Virginia was running a fever for a while. After this, Virginia had to wear false teeth. At the beginning of the escalation of her mental instability, in the final months of her life, she complained: "Sore jaw. Cant bite…"[406]

***

Dr. Savage had risen quickly in the medical establishment after the publication of his sole major scholarly book, *Insanity and Allied Neuroses: Practical and Clinical*, in which he mentions the word "wife" dozens of times when referring to the insane. For example he writes: "I myself have seen several patients whose temper and dispositions have

---

402   Ibid., Vol. II, 15-7.
403   Shirley Panken. *Virginia Woolf and the Lust of Creation: A Psychoanalytic Exploration*. (Albany: SUNY Press, 1987), 69.
404   Spater, *Marriage*, 73.
405   Bell, *Virginia*, Vol. II, 19.
406   Virginia Woolf. *The Diary of Virginia Woolf*, 5 Vols. Ed. Anne Olivier Bell, Ass. Andrew McNeillie. (New York: Penguin Books, 1977-84), 29 September 1940.

been markedly affected by an acute illness such as rheumatic fever, so that a patient who had been previously of quiet, industrious and domesticated habits, and a good wife, became after recovery, a selfish, indolent, home-neglecting person."[407] Savage was called when Virginia was suffering from a fever and was probably neglecting her household duties, or otherwise failing to conform to feminine behavior "norms." Women who wanted or dared to actually step outside the domestic sphere were thus punished by the likes of Dr Savage. New laws had allowed them the freedom to own property, to divorce and other liberties, but they were still suppressed and kept in domesticity by these psychiatric theories of male superiority and female mental fragility. Savage further explains that a sane man is "sober and moral," while after an attack of insanity he can become "intemperate and vicious." He does admit that he has seen cases where a wife changed after an attack of insanity, becoming "more amiable and self-sacrificing than she was before…"[408] A century earlier the accusation would have been that the wife was a witch, or possessed by the devil, while in this period in Britain, psychiatrists substituted "evil" with "insane" and just like previously witches were burned or drowned to test their wickedness, so at this time, psychiatrists like Savage tortured their patients with sensory deprivation, electric shock and various other poisons and insanity-generating concoctions. One of the signs of insanity Dr. Savage repeats is that patients typically think that they are being poisoned or believe their spouses are plotting against them. Thus, it is possible that Woolf's repeated statements in her suicide letters and final diary entries that she only knew that Leonard was "good" and that he did not mean her any harm were either attempts to prove that she was sane, or ironic statements that clearly contradicted the reality of how badly he was treating her. Here is the text of Virginia Woolf's March 18th suicide note: "You have given me the greatest possible happiness… I know that I am spoiling your life that without me you could work. And you will I know… Everything has gone from me but the certainty of your goodness…"[409]

Virginia's Surrender of Hogarth's Shares and Suicide (or Homicide)

---

407   George H. Savage. Sir. *Insanity and Allied Neuroses: Practical and Clinical.* (Philadelphia: Henry C. Lea's Son & Co., 1884), 13.
408   Ibid., 270-1.
409   Woolf, *Letters*, No. 3702.

Irene Coates' account of Woolf's last year before her suicide in 1941 in *Who's Afraid of Leonard Woolf* betrays a personal sympathy Coates has with Virginia. The study is emotional rather than being a straightforward psychiatric evaluation. Coates explains that Woolf was not merely distressed in that tragic period because she had finished a book she felt was poorly written, but more importantly, because Leonard was blocking its publication after pushing her to sign a contract to sell her half of the Hogarth Press to John Lehmann for £3,000 in April of 1938, "ending Virginia's joint partnership in the firm. At the same time, Leonard got her to sign an agreement that effectively locked her in to the Press with no possibility of having her work published elsewhere."[410]

John Lehmann first came into contact with the Woolfs when he queried them about a poetry collection at the end of 1930, and they accepted it for their Living Poets series, subsidized by Lady Gerald, or Duchess of Wellington, who was also the "editor" of the series, though she happened to be a "passive editor" and primarily only paid to have it produced and occasionally over-ruled the Woolfs on the authors they wanted to publish. Lehman wrote to his friend, Julian Bell, on January 12, 1931, that he had to pay for a share to become a probationary partner for two years with the Woolfs: "It may be a little difficult to find all the money, but I hope all will be well if L. doesn't suddenly put up the price!"[411] Lehmann described the squalid conditions of the house in which the press was in when he started, writing that the Woolfs lived upstairs, rented rooms to solicitors, and housed the press in the sub-basement, where proofs served as toilet paper, and Lehmann once bloodied his hand when he made a strong attempt to open the stuck window in his little office.[412] When Leonard and Virginia left for Greece for a month and the front office secretary was mostly absent, Lehmann was in charge of most of the press' operations and was especially happy in this period because there was no pressure from Leonard and the others.[413] Immediately after the Woolfs returned, Lehmann took a vacation of his own and returned eager to resume his own writing, while Leonard was anxiously over-supervising his every move, mak-

---

410 Coates, *Who's*, 323.
411 Lehmann, *Thrown*, 6.
412 Ibid., 10-1.
413 Ibid., 31.

ing him unduly anxious as a result.[414] Lehmann was very busy across his time at Hogarth with picking blurbs, communicating with authors and especially with the tedious task of traveling to bookstores all across the region to convince them to buy Hogarth's forthcoming titles. The next blow came when Lehmann clashed with Hogarth over his friend Louis MacNeice's poetry collection that Dorothy Wellesley refused to subsidize, and Leonard told him he should attempt to re-submit in the following season when "Dottie might be willing to subsidize further volumes," but the next submission was also met with a request to send later on.[415] Due to these troubles, Leonard offered a salary advance and an additional 10% of profits beyond the £200 annual payment, but he did not offer the partnership that he promised two years earlier. This convinced Lehmann that he could spend his time better in leisurely travels and writing rather than working. He weighed the idea of switching to part-time employment at the Press, but decided that this would not be to his liking. Therefore, Leonard departed abruptly on the last day of the initial 2-year contract, without giving any notice, and this enraged Leonard so that a reconciliation was difficult for many years afterwards.[416] Lehmann was the Press' assistant employee between 1931 and 1932, before becoming a partner in 1938 and maintaining this partnership position until 1946. Afterwards, Lehmann started his own rather successful publishing business, John Lehmann Limited (1946-53) and two magazines, *New Writing* (1936-40) and *The London Magazine* (1954-61). His editorship ended in 1961 at *The London Magazine* and he semi-retired. All these publishing ventures to which Lehmann also contributed his writing, make him a successful author-publisher. His publishing company and magazines ran works by authors with names that are as recognizable as some of Hogarth's writers, including George Orwell, and Sartre. But Lehmann had a special affinity towards first-time, working class writers (and this was one of the topics he clashed with Leonard about), so his publishing list includes many less-known authors in contrast with the Woolfs' glittering recognizable names. Lehmann's chief disagreement with Leonard stemmed in his choices of writers; for example, in 1944, Lehmann supported publishing the future Nobel Prize winner, Saul Bellow's *Dangling Man* with Hogarth, while Leonard insisted against it. So, eighteen months

---

414   Ibid., 33.
415   Ibid., 35.
416   Ibid., 36-8.

later, when Lehmann was running his own press, and Bellow was still looking for a British publisher, Lehmann released his book.[417] Lehmann also considered and was forced to reject Sartre at Hogarth, before accepting him in his own venture.

***

Leonard trusted Lehmann because he was their first long-term assistant. They started trying to find a good assistant back in 1917, when they bought their first press. This was a young woman called Alix Sargant-Florence, who started and quit the job on October 16, after the Woolfs showed her how to operate the machine and left her alone as they went for a walk, and when they returned she said that "the work" was "totally without interest" and that she "saw no point in continuing."[418] In November of the first year, they did manage to find a protégé who admired Virginia's work, and thus stuck around. Later, they did manage to have an assistant of some sort over the years, so that it's unclear why accounts report that they spent months doing nothing but operating the press, if they were employing somebody for this task. After going through a few female assistants who were pliable and did not mind Leonard yelling at them, but failed to help as much as Leonard hoped they would, Leonard decided to hire an "intelligent young man to whom an apprenticeship" might lead "to an eventual partnership in the Hogarth Press."[419] Thus, it is likely that starting in 1920 they recruited male assistants by promising them an eventual partnership and failed to deliver this advancement until Virginia agreed to sell her shares in 1938. Meanwhile, one of their most contentious and helpful early assistants was Ralph Partridge, who in March of 1923 threatened to establish a rival Tidmarsh Press, and at the same time a proposal came to the table for the Woolfs to sell the press to Constable as "Heinemann made a most tempting takeover offer." The Woolfs decided on "freedom from commercial publishers, freedom from Ralph…" perhaps because they had just successfully released Virginia's *Jacob's Room*, their first full-length book, and Virginia was starting to see fame and higher profits from her writing, so selling

---

417   Ibid., 138.
418   Bell, *Virginia*, Vol. II, 49.
419   Ibid., Vol. II, 75.

their independence could be avoided.[420] While this was a marvelous notion, in reality, Leonard's constant clashes with assistants meant that they had to do a great deal of work when they were between assistants and to pick up on tasks assistants refused to do. Bell reports that on October 27, 1930, Leonard and Virginia "decided to make an end of the Hogarth Press" because it deprived them of "liberty and imposed altogether too much labour" and in fact Bell writes that it was Virginia who found the work of reading manuscripts, "onerous and dispiriting." At this juncture Leonard "could not destroy the remarkable edifice which he had built," so he propose hiring John Lehmann, whose poetry manuscript they had just accepted.[421] This measure, kept Virginia happy for seven years, but in 1937, Bell states that she was the one who did not want to spend time in the busy London reviewing manuscripts, and instead wanted to live in the country writing her books, so Virginia wrote that Leonard proposed "making the young Brainies take the Press as a co-operative company (John [Lehmann]: Isherwood: Auden: Stephen [Spender]… Would like L[ehmann] to manage it… Couldn't we sell and creep out?"[422]

Five years earlier, in 1932, Virginia wrote a section in *The Common Reader, Second Series*, on "How Should One Read a Book?" She describes her passion for reading, and calls it a heavenly reward, but mentions that reviewers are pressured to review enormous quantities of manuscripts, so that,

> books pass in review like the procession of animals in a shooting gallery, and the critic has only one second in which to load and aim and shoot and may well be pardoned if he mistakes rabbits for tigers, eagles for barndoor fowls, or misses altogether and wastes his shot upon some peaceful cow grazing in a further field. If behind the erratic gunfire of the press the author felt there was another kind of criticism, the opinion of people reading for the love of reading, slowly and unprofessionally, and judging with great sympathy and yet with great severity, might this not improve the quality of his work?[423]

Virginia argues that such reading would make books "stronger, rich-

---

420   Ibid., Vol. II, 88.
421   Ibid., Vol. II, 158.
422   Woolf, *Writer's*, 22 October 1937.
423   Neider, *Essays*, 437-8.

er and more varied."[424] In this passage, the term "press" means that Virginia is referring to her own review of submitted manuscripts to Hogarth Press. But she certainly must have also had reviewers of her books in mind, including Leonard, who frequently missed the essence of her meaning because of their speedy review process. Either way, Virginia became frustrated with reviewing incoming books when she started feeling the pressure to execute the job with this kind of rapid fire, instead of leisurely reading interesting books for pleasure, as she might have done when they had fewer submissions. Her dissatisfaction persisted despite the high caliber of the books coming in and being selected.

When Virginia was finally overcome by the pressure, she expressed her desire to surrender her share, and Leonard queried all of their affiliates. Only Lehmann was interested in making an investment and could only afford a 50% share.[425] Despite publishing an enormous volume of books by some of the best writers in literary history, the Woolfs felt that entering a cooperative agreement was the only way to profit from their press. The flaw in this plan, which they partially anticipated, but ignored, was that buying back this fifty percent portion, if Lehmann chose to separate, or watching it sold to a hostile third party was likely to cripple their business. This worst-case-scenario happened in January of 1946, when Lehmann gave notice of his intention to break the partnership agreement and Leonard bought back "two-thirds of the Press's equity" with the help of Chatto & Windus, a major London publishing company that had published some of the same authors as Hogarth. Chatto & Windus took over the operation of Hogarth at this point, when Leonard stepped away from a publishing company the loss of which might have cost Virginia her will to live. Leonard became one of Chatto's directors when Chatto created a board of directors for Hogarth. In his autobiography, Lehmann expressed his "regret" that Hogarth, "so admirable in its independence for nearly thirty years, became in effect part of a larger (though artistically first-class) business."[426] Chatto & Windus underwent a string of mergers after this acquisition, so that it is currently under the Random House umbrella.

Back in 1946, the sale to Leonard left Lehmann with a profit of more than 100% on the "money he and his family had invested in the

---

424   Ibid., 438.
425   Bell, *Virginia*, Vol. II, 201.
426   Lehmann, *Thrown*, 149.

Press," making this "one of the most profitable ventures in Lehmann's long career as a publisher." But, after this break, he experienced "bitter losses" that he described in his appropriately biting autobiography.[427] Lehmann objected to the line about Hogarth being his most profitable venture by writing that "it might easily have been my last venture, especially as the Paper Control refused point-band to allow me even an ounce of paper to start up again on my own," so that he felt cheated and apprehensive when Leonard basically forced him out of the partnership.[428] The publishing business is based on extreme risk, and he might have misinterpreted the isolated peak of success he saw in his years at Hogarth as a normal occurrence in publishing, only to be disappointed with the stark reality of the vast majority of publishing ventures. In this volatile autobiography, Lehmann concludes about his acquisition of the partnership: "Of course it was a complete fantasy to imagine that, as soon as she had my 3,000 pounds (theoretically) in her pocket, Virginia would run off and set up as a publisher on her own…"[429] Other than her gender and lack of confidence, it is difficult to imagine what aspect of the publishing business Virginia would have fared worse at than Leonard. And yet, she did not run off and start a new press without Leonard and Lehmann, perhaps because Leonard would not have allowed her an allowance for the venture.

If all the personal clashes and quarrels are put aside, Virginia was driven to suicide when Leonard forced her to give up the one thing in her life over which she had control and that made her happy, not only her writing, but more importantly, the publication of her writing and making it visible to the general public. Virginia had many hostile and mean-spirited people around her, from her sister Venessa who did not even come to her cremation, to her psychotic (i.e. easily angered) husband. So, she had to communicate with the world through the written word, a mode that allowed her to remain in the safety of her home, without needing to engage with the boring barbarians she met when she attempted to enter society to chat in person. It was not the physical labor of printing books on a hand press that made Virginia happy when she founded Hogarth with Leonard, but rather the knowledge that she could now write what she wanted without the fear of being censored by chauvinist publishers. The tragedy that broke her spirit oc-

---

427 Spater, *Marriage*, 110.
428 Lehmann, *Thrown*, 149.
429 Ibid., 145.

curred in 1940, when Leonard started rejecting her ideas and ordering her to write the articles that he thought would be commercial. Then, he altogether pushed her out of legal control over what was published with Hogarth, and even stopped her from publishing with any other publisher. Self-publishing was so important to Virginia, that its loss drove her to suicide. She stressed this point many times, and especially in letter No. 3678 to Dame Ethel Smyth from January 12, 1941, where Virginia tries to explain why she cannot even accept the car the Dame offered to hire for her to travel to London because she was being blocked by Leonard. She adds: "Oh yes, I can write: I mean I have a fizz of ideas. What I dread is bottling them to order. Didn't we start the Hogarth Press 25 years ago so as to be quit of editors and publishers? It's my nightmare, being in their clutches: but a nightmare, not a sane survey."[430] Virginia also wrote, "I'm the only woman in England free to write what I like. The others must be thinking of series and editions."[431] Coates explains that Leonard expounded on the fate of Virginia's newly completed novel, *Between the Acts*, at some point between March 14 and 18, when Virginia attempted suicide for the first time and failed, before succeeding a few days later. She wrote her first suicide letter on March 18. Leonard had told her not only that he would not publish *Between the Acts*, but also, "since she could not spend any money, she could not contribute to the cost" or she could not pay out-of-pocket for a publication with a publisher that would have needed such fiscal support to release a literary project of this sort.[432] Virginia left the suicide note for Leonard to find and ventured out, in pouring rain, for a walk in the "water-meadows." Leonard described that he found her on her way back, "soaking wet," and saying, "she had slipped and fallen into one of the dykes," but really having just failed at committing suicide.[433]

According to Coates, Leonard "began directly intruding on her published work" in 1939, when he ordered her to write an article on "Reviewing" for the Sixpenny Pamphlet Series that was released by Hogarth Press. Then, he added a five-page long "Dissenting Note" to her article that stated that some of Virginia's "conclusions seem to me

---

430   Woolf, *Letters*.
431   Woolf, *Diary*, Vol. 3.
432   Coates, *Who's*, 410
433   Leonard Woolf. *The Journey Not the Arrival Matters*. (London: The Hogarth Press Ltd., 1969), 90-2.

doubtful because the meaning of certain facts have been ignored or their weight under-estimated." This biting rebuke was an "intrusion" and made Virginia feel "as though her piece was being discredited."[434] Leonard was also extremely critical of the biography of Roger Fry, one of both Leonard and Virginia's close friends, and one of Virginia sister's lovers, who died in 1934. Virginia had completed the biography shortly after the "Reviewing" article. She wrote about Leonard's dissent in her diary, complaining that he "pecked very hard by a very hard strong beak."[435] Leonard and Virginia had friction in their marriage earlier on over Virginia's friendship with Fry. Back in 1938, Virginia guaranteed "an overdraft incurred by Helen Anrep, Roger Fry's companion at the end of his life," and Leonard responded to this by "insisting that she earn extra money to pay for this loan."[436]

On top of ridiculing her writing, Leonard was also playing practical jokes on her like the April Fools prank that Louise Everest, their part-time servant who lived in their cottage and answered to Leonard, played on Virginia. Everest had told her that she had a village woman waiting for her, and then Everest and Leonard laughed at her when Virginia discovered there was nobody waiting. Coates comments: "I see Leonard laughing louder than anyone, he no doubt put Louie up to it."[437] Another cruelty that Virginia suffered was when Leonard insisted that Virginia pay for "the expense of the removal" of Virginia's collected furniture from storage by "writing an article on Ellen Terry and a short story" ["The Legacy"] to be sent to Harper's "Bazaar in America," an act that Coates calls "bullying" and "enforced writing" that exhausted Virginia.[438] These pieces were rejected by *Harper's Bazaar*, and upon receiving the rejection letter, Leonard dictated a furious reply that demanded payment regardless of publication that Virginia signed. After the letter was shipped, Leonard accused Virginia of "no longer" being "able to earn money from her writing," and suggesting that he might not "be willing to publish any more of her work."[439] Leonard also kept dragging Virginia out with him on long excursions despite her revulsion from boring and emotionally painful interactions with the group of people Leonard associated with. At that difficult point in her life,

---

434 Coates, *Who's*, 367.
435 Woolf, *Diary*, March 20, 1940.
436 Coates, *Who's*, 324.
437 Ibid., 371-2.
438 Ibid., 385.
439 Ibid., 398-9.

Virginia was hardly able to enjoy the company of her own friends, and described the people she met along the way, in her *Diary* on February 26, 1941, as causing her "infernal boredom." Coates stresses that an especially difficult trip was their visit to Hogarth Press at Letchworth, supposedly for Leonard to spend a couple of hours doing something practical there, but to get to this location from their village, they had to taking a "long, cold train journey."[440]

Virginia caught the flu soon after April 1st, and she was only assisted through this difficult time by a housekeeper, Mabel Haskins. Perhaps seeing the positive impact Mabel was having or perhaps due to incurable cheapness, Leonard fired Mabel soon afterwards, and then forced Virginia to do the housework herself. She writes that she started to feel "harassed, damp," as she had to "scrub & polish & discard," while Louise and Leonard laughed at her and criticized her failures at housekeeping.[441] The dimensions of the cleaning problem were monumental, for example, Virginia writes in *Letters*, No. 3698, "water has come through the kitchen ceiling." And then she complains, "I'm in a dither of trying to contrive spring cleaning. Oh our carpets—I spent 2 hours carpet beating, and still the flakes of our bombed ceiling flock, and drown the books just dusted. I'd no notion, having always a servant, of the horror of dirt."[442] The only mention I found of Leonard helping with the housework is from Virginia's last diary entry which ends with, "L. is doing the rhododendrons…"[443] Coates explains that Leonard would have been removing the old flower heads from the rhododendrons at this time of the year. Regardless of the symbolism, this singular occurrence of Leonard helping her was significant enough for Virginia for her to end her life's work of writing on this note. In "A Sketch of the Past," Virginia referred to talking with Leonard, and the times when, "One… deals with things that have to be done; the broken vacuum cleaner; ordering dinner; writing orders to Mabel; washing; cooking dinner; bookbinding…" as "non-being" or moments that are "embedded in a kind of nondescript cotton wool" that she keeps forgetting as soon as they happen. In contrast, Virginia remembers what she is writing and reading and the walks she takes through nature in

---

440   Ibid., 404-5.
441   Woolf, *Diary*, 16 December 1940.
442   Woolf, *Letters*, No 3699.
443   Woolf, *Diary*, 24 March 1941.

great details and views these as truly "being."[444] Virginia had discovered that her mind was clouded, perhaps because of the drugs she was taking. This mental anguish was multiplied by Leonard taking steps to prevent her from publishing, meanwhile also extending her daily grind of "non-being" by assigning more strenuous household chores. All this compounded to make Virginia want to stop "non-being."

In another, much earlier incident, Leonard "tried to prevent her writing her diary on the grounds that she was wasting paper, and therefore money," but thankfully for her readers, she began a new Volume despite him, commenting in it, "I think I will be less verbose here perhaps—but what does it matter, writing too many pages. No printer to consider, no public."[445]

After she recovered from the flu, Virginia gave a speech at the Workers' Education Association in Brighton on April 27, 1940, in part to rival Leonard's speech at the same venue, as she focused her anger in the rhetoric on criticizing writers with "eleven years at school and college" of education that have separated them from the realities of the common human's daily life. She was aiming at Leonard's constant references to his own Ivy League education in contrast with her complete lack of a formal education.[446] Leonard retaliated to her speech by further stressing that they were destitute, and this depressed Virginia because she had been hoping that her success at selling her books would guarantee them a retirement, and instead she discovered that, "Yes, our old age is not going to be sunny orchard drowse."[447] Leonard's dramatization of their poverty was a misconception: "After her death, Leonard lived on the interest of Virginia's fortune and the money he made by publishing her work."[448] Another misconception is that Virginia wasn't eating in her final months, as this was supposedly one of the symptoms of her mental illness, but she records eating that fish she laboriously cooked herself, and stresses that she "decided to eat gluttonously. Turkey & Pancakes" on January 25, 1941, as she records in No. 3683 of her *Letters*.

Across all of these books, no critic or psychiatrist proposes that Leonard murdered Virginia. The furthest biographers have gone has

---

444 Woolf, *Moments*, 70.
445 Woolf, *Diary*, 1 January 1941.
446 Coates, *Who's*, 371-2.
447 Woolf, *Diary*, 24 December 1940.
448 Coates, *Who's*, 388.

been to assert that Leonard subversively drove Virginia to suicide. The popularly known story of how Virginia committed suicide was in part contrived by her "friend," Kingsley Martin, the editor of the *New Statesman & Nation*, who proposed the scenario that Virginia had "in her pocket, morphine provided by Adrian" for the proposed suicide pact that Leonard made with Virginia in case of a Nazis invasion following bombs falling close to their house, their alternative plan being sitting in their car and dying of carbon monoxide poisoning.[449] Leonard explained in his autobiography why he was considering suicide too, at this juncture, by saying that "Jews were hunted down, beaten up, and humiliated everywhere… I saw a photograph of a Jew being dragged by storm troopers out of a shop in one of the main streets in Berlin; the fly-buttons of the man's trousers had been torn open to show that he was circumcised and therefore a Jew…"[450] Leonard was afraid that if the Nazis reached them, they would not only be killed but also violated in this unthinkable fashion. This detail is missing from Coates' explanation of events, and naturally this justification makes it more plausible that Leonard was truly willing to commit suicide, rather than procuring morphine to assist his wife's "suicide." Why would Leonard dictate the three "suicide notes" that Virginia wrote in this state of mind, as Coates proposes? Irene Coates describes a scenario wherein Virginia travels to the River Ouse, takes morphine, puts stones into her pockets and then walks out and drowns herself. Has any similar suicide plan been recorded in any case that was not investigated as a potential homicide? Why not pick only one of these, the rocks or the morphine, and why jump in a river if the morphine itself would have been enough to kill her? On the other hand, how many proven homicides have there been where the murderer attempted to dispose of the body in a river? When doctors questioned Virginia about her mental illness, she frequently said that it was her fault. She also frequently refused medical assistance. The more probably theory might be that her apparent periods of insanity were the result of morphine abuse. Another possibility is that Leonard was a victim of Virginia's machinations and tortures, as her constant ennui, complaints, ravings and irrationality were distracting him from developing his own writing. Because so many alternatives are equally likely, this is a curious mystery to contemplate. If the

---

[449] Forrester, *Virginia*, 187: "I don't", October 2, 1940; "If Hitler": Virginia Wolf to ES, September 12, 1940.
[450] Leonard, *Journey*, 14.

parallels hold true with the other tragic deaths of author-publishers, the fault lies with the doctors and friends who prescribed or offered poisonous drugs that clouded and disturbed Virginia's brilliant mind. Coates concludes her study by offering a quote from Edgar Woolf's letter to Leonard in 1953, where he wrote: "As a boy you were mean and a bully… Having always been the lickspittle of greater intellects, you suffer from the deformity of the little man… Unfortunately with your mean nature you'll go the same way & delight in causing pain to all of us. But Virginia's diary shows you up for what you are better than any words of mine."[451] It is probable that Leonard was really as malicious and evil as his brother insists on him being. It is a fact that Virginia was constantly on sleeping pills, morphine, or suffering from toothaches and other ailments that kept her in a haze. If Leonard was a villain invading her room, she only had a few blissful hours of writing in a stream-of-consciousness as an escape from him. If we accept these ideas as facts, why did Virginia suffer through all those decades of living with a psycho without seeking a divorce? Her chief complaint in the last days of her life was that she was "perfectly happy until the last few weeks, when this horror began." The "horror" was that she suddenly could "hardly think clearly any more."[452] Such a drastic change in her mind had to have been drug-induced.

Many critics have used Virginia Woolf's mental failures as an excuse to dismiss the female sex as emotional and irrational. Woolf is frequently cited by chauvinist men as they are rejecting female writers, or refusing women promotions. The truth behind why and how Virginia Woolf died is a practical concern for all women and for all writers. Hopefully, this mystery will eventually be solved, but her body's incineration has made it nearly impossible.

If Virginia's personal life is put aside, the story of how she ran a successful publishing company and used it to become a canonical writer is still more important for current author-publishers, who are hoping to mimic her example.

---

451 Coates, *Who's*, 428.
452 Woolf, *Letters*, No. 3708.

PART III
American Author-Publishers

CHAPTER 7

Brief Stories of American Publishers

There might be far more author-publishers than non-self-publishers across the history of book publishing. But private printings are deliberately unavailable for public consumption, so many of the books in this category remain undiscovered. Author-publishers are typically more visible because they have the resources to launch campaigns to market themselves and their list of authors. Still, the history of these publishers' development is seldom examined. Thus, to understand them, we have to review the stories of the more obscure personalities and companies. Well-known printer-publishers like Benjamin Franklin, who is covered in the next chapter, can be better understood in contrast with these pioneering attempts.

Early American Printers and Publishers, 1639-1820

One book that tells the story of many, great, early and obscure American author-publishers is *Early American Women Printers and Publishers, 1639-1820* by Leona M. Hudak. She meticulously catalogs publishers that are difficult to find with online searches or in other books on publishing. While her focus is on female publishers, she frequently offers the biographies of their husbands, who ran the publishing businesses until they died or were incapacitated and their wives had to take over the ventures.

One of the early publishers that Hudak describes is a six-generation printing establishment, which operated from 1650 to 1825. It was founded by William Bradford in Leicester, England. William's son, William I, took over the press after apprenticing with an "unlicensed press" in London that "served as the mouthpiece of the Quakers," a radical sect for the time. William I then sailed to Pennsylvania with the founder of that commonwealth, William Penn, who was granted the territory in repayment of a £16,000 debt by King Charles II. William I returned to London in 1685 to purchase a printing press, which he brought back with him to Philadelphia and founded "the first typographic establishment in the Middle States."[453] Just as his father before him, William I ended up in hot waters within years of starting the establishment: "his imprints caused him difficulty of both a religious and a political nature. In 1692, he was arrested for printing some undesirable pamphlets which helped separate the Friends into two camps. His plant was seized." The press was returned to him in 1693, and rather than staying to fight another day, William I left for the "printless New York," where he was solicited to become the first "official printer" for the "state and city of New York," a post he held until 1742. In 1725, he established *The New York Gazette*, a paper created to issue propaganda pieces on behalf of the corrupt governorship of William Cosby. William I's son, Andrew, became partner in 1711, and then in 1712, established his own highly successful printing business in Philadelphia. Even before his father started his paper, Andrew started the third paper to be founded in the colonies, *The American Weekly Mercury* in 1719. Andrew became the official printer of Pennsylvania, mirroring his father. Andrew was also put on trial twice for printing "alleged seditious literature," and in his defense, he submitted humble apologies, which somehow managed to be more convincing that the verbose defenses his father and others had made (though he was still imprisoned for some duration). Because of his successful defense, Andrew is credited with the early press freedom that was allowed after 1730 in the radicalizing colonies. Andrew branched out into merchant, real estate and other businesses and made the bulk of his living of these rather than primarily from the press. In 1733, he accepted his nephew, William III, as an apprentice, and then made him partner in 1739. William II married his second wife shortly thereafter, Cornelia Smith, who attempted to arrange a marriage between her relation and William III. This union was so repellant to him that he withdrew from the business to avoid it, leaving Cornelia as the inheritor of William II's estate when he died in 1742.

A week after Andrew's death, Cornelia took over writing, editing and publishing *The Mercury* under her own name. Three months later,

---

453   Leona M. Hudak. *Early American Women Printers and Publishers, 1639-1820*. (Metuchen (NJ): The Scarecrow Press, Inc., 1978), 164

Cornelia took on a partner, Isaiah Warner, to help her edit the paper, and this partnership lasted through 1744. Cornelia followed the standard model of the time. She plagiarized content for her paper from other American and European papers, frequently re-printing stories published elsewhere verbatim. Also, like many other printers of her day, she ran a general store, for which she used her newspaper to advertise her wares. These are the roots for the current abundance of ads and re-printings in newspapers today. Cornelia closed the paper either in 1746, or as late as 1749, as some accounts propose. She then started printing almanacs, pamphlets and books. She died in 1755. Because she signed her will with an "X" and a "Bradford seal," Hudak proposes that it was likely that Cornelia was illiterate and this was the reason she made so many mistakes even when she simply re-printed materials from other papers. If this is the case, she certainly cannot be called an author-publisher, but the Bradfords who preceded her certainly were.[454]

John Peter Zenger apprenticed with William Bradford from 1711 to 1719, before becoming the printer of the Colony of Maryland in 1720, but this was not a very fruitful enterprise. So, in 1723, he rejoined William Bradford as a journeyman, and then in 1725, as a partner. He started his own printing business in 1726, and in 1733 used it to create an opposition paper to Bradford's conformist, *The New York Gazette*. Thus, Zenger's *The New-York Weekly Journal's* sole aim was criticizing William Cosby's corruption and bringing him to justice. "With it, a provocative and vitriolic spirit emerged in New York journalism." A year into its printing, Governor Cosby finally was so outraged by "doggerel rhymes" that he ordered Nos. 7, 47, 48, and 49 to be burned. "The Court of Quarter Sessions refused to enter the decree and have it executed. The task was at length accomplished by the sheriff's Negro slaves." A bit later, Zenger was arrested on "charges of seditious libel." Zenger continued to run his paper from prison for nine months, issuing some signed articles in this interim. The work was carried on by his wife, Anna Catharine Zenger. During the trial in August of 1735, two judges, who were in the governor's pocket, were disbarred for bias. Andrew Hamilton led a strong case, arguing that to charge Zenger with libel, the words he wrote had to be proven as false. Tailing at this, the jury returned a "not guilty" verdict. "The case represented the first significant breakthrough for American Colonial freedom of the press." He became the public printer of New York in 1737 and then of New

---
[454] Ibid., 164-78.

Jersey in 1738. When John died in 1746, Anna took over the press. She published some other pamphlets and books, but surrendered the paper to her son, John Zenger, Jr. in 1748, who ran it until his death in 1751, by which time Anna had retired to run a small book store in the countryside.[455]

John Bushell was the first official printer of Nova Scotia, Canada, between 1752 and 1761, a trade in which he was assisted by his daughter Elizabeth Bushell, who served as a compositor and presswoman to cut down on operating costs. John took on a partner in the business in 1760, Anthony Henry, who became the sole proprietor when he died in 1761. John had begun publishing *The Halifax Gazette* in 1752, thus joining the ranks of author-editor-publishers.[456]

William Goddard apprenticed with James Parker. Goddard was a printer and postmaster. He was also Benjamin Franklin's partner between 1755 and 1761 in New Haven, where one of their jobs was producing Yale College imprints. In 1762, Goddard started his own print shop in the printless Providence with the help of financing, £300, from his mother. He started *The Providence Gazette; and Country Journal* that same year. Goddard "vigorously… opposed the Stamp Act" in this newspaper, but the Act passed and because it was a "prohibitive expense," he had to close the paper in 1765. At this point, William left to partner with John Holt in New York, while his mother, Sarah Goddard, kept the Providence shop running, and her name as the printer appeared on the *New England Almanack* and *Answer to Pilate's Question* in 1765. Meanwhile, William was publishing his own books with the press as part of his Colonial fight against the Stamp Act. One of William's radical releases was *A Providence Gazette Extraordinary*, where he exclaimed: "*Sure none but Asses will stand still to be branded. However the said Jockies will not aver that the few Asses here will give much Trouble to the Branding Company.*" Back in New York (or New Jersey, where the plant was), he helped Parker print *The Constitutional Courant*, which had a motto that read ominously, "Join or die." This periodical struck a serious blow against the Stamp Act because it was sold in the thousands. It was also pirated by other Colonial printers that re-printed it for many more buyers. In part as a result of this bold printing, the Stamp Act was repealed on March 18, 1766. This allowed William to finally return to printing a paper, and he attempted to so-

---

455   Ibid., 191-201.
456   Ibid., 210-1.

licit eight hundred subscribers for *A Providence Gazette Extraordinary and Supplement* a few days before the repeal, as if he knew the repeal was coming. But, he failed to reach this goal. So, he left to try his luck in Philadelphia. Meanwhile, Sarah stayed behind and founded Sarah Goddard and Company, employing several apprentices to help her in this venture, for which she took up the publication of the paper that William had abandoned, *Providence Gazette*, and other books and pamphlets. Sarah later stumbled into a controversy when she released the *New England Almanack for 1767*, only to find out that the author, Benjamin West, had sold the same book to a Boston printer, so that while initial sales were strong, the competition made them trickle down. To solve this problem, she had to release the same book under a new title, *The New England Town and Country Almanack*, now authored under the pseudonym, Abraham Weaterwise. Meanwhile, William joined a partnership in Philadelphia with Joseph Galloway, a prominent attorney and leader of the Anti-Proprietary movement, and Thomas Wharton, a Quaker merchant, to found *The Pennsylvania Chronicle, and Universal Advertiser*. Wharton and Galloway were Stamp Act and Colonia government supporters, and the conservative articles they wanted to run in the paper soon left William in hot waters with his radical anti-Act friends. William attempted to appease his critics by supporting the publication of John Dickson's essay for American rights, *Letters from a Pennsylvania Farmer*, but Galloway and Wharton responded with "paroxysm of abuse," and started plotting "to ruin the gullible Goddard" and thus expel him from their partnership agreement. In 1768, they promised William a house and money for his mother to close their Providence shop and move to Philadelphia. William complied and sold his shop to John Carter for $550.82, but then his partners went back on their word and did not compensate the Goddards in any way for their troubles. The crooked partners were in collusion with Carter. They encouraged Carter not to pay up on the debt owed for the Providence shop. Attempting to collect this debt from Carter kept William out of Philadelphia for three months. During this wait, Galloway and Wharton claimed Goddard's mother had failed in her duties. As a result of this alleged failure, they were demanding that "he either buy out their shares or sell out his own." While William was feverishly trying to find the funds to buy his partners out in other locations, Sarah died in 1770, perhaps from the overwork involved in building up enough subscribers for their paper to become successful.

Thus, in a period where Colonial papers were finally free to publish revolutionary ideas, they faced fiscal battles from the wealthy merchants and lawyers, who were corruptly entangled with the Crown and worked to push forward anti-revolutionary ideals by crooked business practices that could blind honest publishers, such as the Goddards.[457]

However, William Goddard's fight did not end there. He eventually won back Towne's share, and then concentrated on outing Galloway by fighting to prevent his election to the Pennsylvania Assembly with the help of the self-printed pamphlet, *The Partnership*. This tract detailed the fiscal and character attacks Galloway had levied against him over the years of their partnership. After this battle, William flew off on another mission, that of establishing a new postal system outside of British control (which is known today as USPS). William left his press in the hands of Mary Katherine Goddard. William was not compensated for his efforts either with a position or monetary compensation for the expenses he took on to set up the system out-of-pocket, so that he was put in debtor's prison for lack of funds. Oddly enough, while William was dealing with these extraordinary difficulties, Mary was appointed the Colonial Postmistress of Baltimore, the first colonial woman to occupy the post, and since the Colonies were about to become States, she was also probably the last. Despite holding this Colonial post, Mary then managed to print the first official issue of the Declaration of Independence in 1777. And after leaving debtor's prison, William served as the Surveyor for the revolutionaries, a post that had a negligible salary and required a lot of travel, so he resigned in 1777 and re-joined his sister, Mary, at the press. Shortly after William's return, their paper ran two short essays regarding the British Ministry's willingness to discuss the terms of peace with the rebellious Colonies. One of these was ironic, advising the colonies to accept the proposed terms. The other was a revolutionary warning to colonists to "distrust the British tenders and to continue the struggle with all their strength." This was such a direct revolutionary outcry that the super-patriotic Baltimore Whig Club banished William for allowing these pieces to be published. The Lower House ruled against the Whig Club on the grounds that the banishment was unconstitutional, prompting William to write a pamphlet, printed by Mary, *The Prowess of the Whig Club, and the Manoeuvres of Legion*, which so enraged the Whig Club due to its immense popularity that they picked up sticks and stones and

---

457 Ibid., 231-52.

insisted on his banishment at the threat of death. Thus, he had to flee again to seek the protection of the Council of Safety, which renewed the protection of his life from these attacks. Then, in 1779, the Goddards published disgruntled, anti-colonial, rhetorical questions from the retired General Charles Lee, "Some Queries, Political, and Military, Humbly Offered to the Considerations of the Public." This pamphlet was so inflammatory that the Goddards' print shop was mobbed by the officers of the Continental Army, a clash that they and their journal managed to survive. General Lee rewarded the Goddards in his will for helping him clear his name, leaving them enough in 1782 for William to be able to pay off his long-standing debts. This was how William finally returned to being the active printer of their journal, and retook the full control of the press in 1784. Mary did not surrender control willingly. She even printed a rival almanac in 1785. She then filed five lawsuits in a day against William in the hope of recuperating what she felt she lost in the change of ownership of the press. Meanwhile, she remained the postmistress until 1789, frequently donating money to the troubled post office to keep it going near the end of the Revolution. When the Revolution ended, President Washington fired her from the job, despite popular support via a petition, stating that she was unfit for the necessary travel.[458]

Thus, the rebellious buildup towards the American Revolution assisted the spirit of freedom necessary for women to excel in publishing, but after it was over, women regressed and found it difficult to hold onto positions of power. The same phenomena happened after WWII, and happens with most wars, during which men are too busy fighting with weaponry to battle over civilian posts.

Jonas Green apprenticed to his relatives in their printing businesses before issuing the first release of his own, which happened to be the first Hebrew grammar book printed in America. After this, he worked for Benjamin Franklin, before becoming the public printer to Annapolis, Maryland in 1739. In 1745, he founded the second *Maryland Gazette*. Upon his death in 1767, his wife, Anne Catherine Green, took over the business with the assistance of her son, William, and successfully finished an order started by her husband of *Acts* and *Votes* for Annapolis' 1767 session. This led to the official approval from the government that Anne could take the post of City of Annapolis Printer, which was vacated by her husband. She then printed money and official city pa-

---

458   Ibid., 318-39.

pers, upon request. At first, Anne's name was the only one to appear on the *Gazette* as the printer, but then, in 1768, William's joined this by-line. But, he died in 1770, leaving her name by itself again. It was then changed to Anne Catherine Green and Son in 1772, when her other son, Frederick, joined the enterprise. Anne faced some difficulties in 1770. She expressed her frustration with the Revenue Act and with the restrictions on the importation of folio-sized paper from Great Britain, which made her cut the number of pages in an issue and add a two-page supplement to make up for it. Anne started a "Poet's Corner" section that included pseudonymously or anonymously written poems, which are likely to have been her own work, as the section was terminated at the end of her tenure. Anne died in 1774. The paper and the printing business were carried on by her sons, Frederick and Samuel, until 1811, and then by Samuel's son, Jonas, until 1839.[459]

William Rind partnered with Jonas Green between 1758 and 1766 in the publication of *The Maryland Gazette*, while Rind also operated a bookstore and library of his own. Rind was called out to Virginia in 1766 by Thomas Jefferson and other revolutionaries who offered to sponsor the founding of a new rival paper to the royalist, *Virginia Gazette*, resulting in the establishment of the *Rind Virginia Gazette*, which later was abbreviated to have the same name as its rival. Just like other major newspaper printers from this period, Rind also became a government printer. Rind died young in 1773, and his wife, Clementina Rind, took over the publishing business. After a ballot on the question, Clementina took over the government printing contract. Clementina upheld her husband's motto: "Open to ALL PARTIES but influenced by NONE," thus publishing articles that both supported the coming Revolution and Loyalists' arguments against it. She made an exception to this welcoming attitude in her first year, when she refused to publish a piece that she thought was libelous against a specific party. She wrote that it was best to leave the merits of the case to be ruled on by a court. Clementina published several books in addition to the paper, including the anonymous work by Thomas Jefferson, *A Summary View of the Rights of British America*. She died in September of 1774. The paper was sold to John Pinkney, who ran it into the ground within two years. One of Rind's children, William, later founded *The Virginia Federalist* in Richmond, and ran it between 1799 and 1800, before becoming the

---

459   Ibid., 265-77.

first printer of the District of Columbia.[460]

The tension over censorship in American publishing eased after the American Revolution because the new revolutionary government was unlikely to restrict the liberties of the press after using them to spark a successful overturn of the government. The British had attempted to suppress liberal opinion in the American press through prosecutions for libel, blasphemy and other anti-establishment claims. The transition to American independence meant that loyalists were now the suppressed party. Margaret Green Draper was forced to evacuate to Britain right before the end of the Revolution, abandoning nearly $100,000 worth of property, press materials, land and other valuables that were never recuperated, though she did file a petition to be compensated for her losses. Margaret had taken over *The Boston News-Letter*, which had the honor of being the "first newspaper printed on American soil." It was started in 1704 by John Campbell. Unlike the other publishers who left operations to their womenfolk, this paper was a staunch loyalist. It printed strictly pro-British ideas from its founding through its closure during the Revolution. Margaret only held the reins of the paper from 1774 to 1776, very dramatic and fast-moving years.[461]

The pro-revolutionary publishers had a different experience with the transition. Hannah Bunce Watson and her predecessor and husband, Ebenezer Watson, primarily took the revolutionary side. Their position meant that during the Revolution, they had difficulties with finding paper to print on, so that at times they used wrapping paper and other odd bits. Finally, they had to start their own paper mill in 1775, which burned down in a suspected arson sometime after Ebenezer's death in 1776. The town raised capital to rebuild the mill and Hannah managed to keep the enterprise going and published notices about the progress of the Revolution and revolutionary articles by the political and authorial leaders of the war. She even published Thomas Paine's *American Crisis, Addressed to General Sir William Howe* in 1778. The press became a joint venture when Hannah remarried to Barzil Hudson. The quality of the papers that Hannah and Barzil printed was closer to modern standards than their contemporary rivals'. These papers included illustrations, photographs, and clear type (as opposed to leaky ink). Their *Connecticut Courant* had been in print since 1764, and remained in their family until its dissolution in 1815. It was later

---

460 Ibid., 300-10.
461 Ibid., 397-411.

re-incarnated into what today is known as *The Hartford Courant*.[462]

While many printers had very negative apprenticeships before breaking out on their own, Charles Crouch was the only printer in this study who had a history of running away during his apprenticeship with Peter Timothy in Charleston, South Carolina. Timothy had to advertise "for his return" four times before he finally discharged him, writing to Benjamin Franklin, his partner, in 1754, that he had charged him for losses after three years when Charles was mostly engaged in "Drink, Play, and Scandalous Company." Charles managed to sober up by 1764, when he started a paper to compete with Timothy's in the same city, *The South Carolina Gazetteer; and Country Journal*. Soon after the founding, Charles immediately made a stand against the Stamp Act, "which had resulted in the suspension of Timothy's paper, *The South-Carolina Gazette* from October 31, 1765 to June 2, 1766." His radical position might have cost him ties with British paper suppliers. Thus, he had to make a trip to Philadelphia in 1775 to buy more paper during the paper-shortage that plagued most Colonial printers during the Revolution. He ended up drowning in a ship during this trip. His widow, Mary Crouch, took over the publication of the paper under the title, *The Charlestown Gazette*, in 1778, but only managed to keep it running until the siege of Charleston in 1780. At this critical point, Mary moved to Salem, Massachusetts. She had taken her press with her, allowing her to start *The Salem Gazette* in the new city. Later that year, she started the *General Advertiser*, but it only lasted for a year before it changed hands and went under the management of Samuel Hall. At that point, she retired from the printing business.[463]

John Holt learned the printing business from his public printer brother-in-law, William Hunter. His first venture was running a series of stores before becoming mayor of Williamsburg, Virginia in 1752 for a year. He held other public, official positions later on. He became a partner in the *Connecticut Gazette* with James Parker in 1755. They also operated the *New-York Gazette and Weekly Post-Boy*. When their partnership was terminated in 1762, Holt became the sole proprietor, and started publishing books, pamphlets and the like. Holt publicly opposed the Stamp Act. He was also actively involved in other revolutionary campaigns. The Sons of Liberty even helped pay his bail when he went into debtor's prison for owing £400. In part because of these

---

462   Ibid., 424-36.
463   Ibid., 451-66.

revolutionary activities, the British destroyed his printing materials when he evacuated New York City for the safety of New Haven in 1766. In 1775, Holt founded the John H. Holt & Company printing business in Norfolk, Virginia. It was left in the hands of his son, John Hunter Holt, and issued *The Virginia Gazette, or the Norfolk Intelligencer*. It got into trouble shortly thereafter by printing unfavorable remarks about the ancestry of Lord Dunmore, the Royal Governor of the state. Once again, the British came in and stole his printing press, but this time the fifteen royal soldiers were sent by Dunmore, on September 30, 1775, specifically to his establishment, rather than as part of an attacking army. The townspeople wrote a letter to the Governor asking him to return the printing materials, but he replied "that he had done them good service by depriving them of the means of poisoning their minds by rebellious doctrines." Holt escaped Virginia and moved to New York, where he became the public printer and re-started his newspaper. He only managed to run it for a few months before the British burned down his new domicile city, Kingston, New York, and once again destroyed a good deal of his printing materials. Unlike most other printers who usually allowed one arson to take them out of business, Holt kept at it, restarting the paper in 1778 in Poughkeepsie, New York and running it there with occasional stops and re-starts until 1783, when he renamed it as *The Independent New-York Gazette*. He then managed to run it non-stop until the end of his life in 1784, when his widow, Elizabeth Hunter, took over operations until 1788. During Elizabeth's tenure, she filed a claim against the state of New York for unpaid printing services carried out during the revolutionary years, 1777 to 1784, worth around $8,000. This claim was denied. In 1788, the executor of the Holt estate, her son-in-law, Eleazar Oswald, was denied on the same request. So, he submitted the case to the United States Supreme Court in 1792, and because New York refused to come to the trial, he won the case, and was awarded a default judgment, setting a precedent that meant future no-shows by the state would reach a similar fate.[464]

    The stories of the lives of printer-publishers in America after the Revolutionary War become repetitive and dull, and lack the spark and fervor of their predecessors. The same pattern is repeated. The publishers' careers begin with an apprenticeship, then they buy a press, then print a newspaper and some books and pamphlets on it, before dying

---

464   Ibid., 505-16.

and either leaving the press to their spouse or child, or letting it die with them. Since each of these printers, from the first printer in the Colonies through the early years of the independent United States, wrote at least some content for their paper, they were all author-publishers. Their budgets were extremely small and they were always on the brink of collapse, so if they could author some of their content or steal the content from competing papers to avoid paying authors, they certainly took these shortcuts to cut their human labor expenses. These printers were also frequently inter-related either through family ties or because a new printer frequently emerged after working for an established printer. In contrast, today, most editors and publishers remain as employees for a corporate publisher, without ever being compelled to attempt an independent experiment. Apprentices and journeyman were ambitious to run away from their contracts, or were awaiting the day when these obligations would run out. They all hoped for the freedom of owning a business and publishing themselves, without being at the mercy of a supervisor. There were so few printers in each of the colonies, and later the states that anybody with typographical and other essential skills and a press could strike up a successful, independent printing business. These printers were also closely connected with the governments that they served by printing state constitutions, revolutionary pamphlets, and regular minutes and laws that had to be put on paper to inform the public and lawyers of the law of the land. Anybody that believes there is something wrong with the modern corporatocracy with only four giant publishers in charge of world media should be inspired by these early experiments in independent self-publications.

The Travels and Publications of the Schiffrins

Andre Schiffrin's *The Business of Books: How International Conglomerates Took Over Publishing and Changed the Way We Read* helped me to identify one of the little-known stories in world publishing history. Andre eventually became an established publisher in his own right, and he is clearly an author if this book is an indication, but the story that essential for the purposes of this research project is how his father, Jacques Schiffrin, founded a few publishing ventures in an effort to publish his own translations, designs and other special projects that were the result of his creative efforts.

Jacques was born in Russia in 1892, then migrated to France, and then migrated to America via Casablanca in 1940. He had to pick up at least four languages across these forced migrations, which were necessary because of his Jewish heritage. He used this potential problem to his advantage by translating classics he loved in one language into other languages, in which they were still unavailable.

Back in France in 1831, Schiffrin started a publishing venture called *Editions de La Pleiade*, a series still being published regularly to this day. It has been working to make the world's classics available widely at cheap prices. "With very limited resources, he began publishing French classics and, with his new friend Andre Gide, he translated a number of Russian classics into French, editions of which are still in print."

Andre Gide is also a self-publisher because he was a major contributor and assisted the venture with finding a publishing home with the larger, *Editions Gallimard* in 1936. Gide had previously brought in a magazine for which he was one of the founders, *Nouvelle Revue Francaise*, so his word had a lot of weight in Schiffrin being welcomed at Gallimard. Gide worked with Schiffrin in the middle of his extremely long and productive writing history. While Gide was not Jewish, he sympathized with the plight of the underdog. He temporarily became a communist, and spent a great deal of time in the Soviet Union. However, this trip disillusioned Gide, and he became a critic of communism. Gide's journey toward literature and radicalism began after he served as the Mayor of La Roque-Baignard, a commune in Normandy in 1896. Then, there was nearly a decade when he was semi-retired before he helped found *Nouvelle Revue Francaise* in 1908. He was committed to the arts for the rest of his life.

Oddly enough, in the years when he was otherwise detached from publishing and politics, he wrote one of his best-known essays, "The Evolution of the Theater," which he delivered as a lecture at the Societe de la Libre Esthetique, in Brussels on March 25, 1904. He was probably reflecting on his own lethargy when he wrote: "Art aspires to freedom only in periods of illness, when it would prefer to live easily. Whenever it feel[s] vigorous, it seeks struggle and obstacle. It loves to burst out of its sheath, and for that reason it prefers a tight one... Art is born of constraint, lives by struggle, dies of freedom."[465] Gide continues by saying that books inspire readers "to kill themselves" or to

---

465   Neider, *Essays*, 93-4.

become heroes, and that the theater should "offer humanity new forms of heroism and new heroes," but only manages to provide examples of "resignation" and "acceptance" in the characters that modern theater depicts.[466] Gide was resigned to let others act heroically to fight against societal problems for a decade, but once this period of well-being and rest ended, he made sure to struggle for his art within the constraints of writing conventions. He created an extra challenge for himself when he helped found new publishing ventures that helped his associates become a bit freer in what they could put into print.

At around the same time when Gide was becoming critical of communism, a transition to mainstream publication meant that Schiffrin could suddenly be fired from a series that he helped to found. Schiffrin was let go as part of the occupying, German ambassador's mission to purge "from the French cultural scene" all Jews back in 1940.[467]

Soon after migrating to America, Jacques was back at work. "In 1942, with a small amount of capital from friends, he began a series of books under his own name, which brought the writings of the French Resistance to America for the first time."[468] The success of this series attracted the attention of Kurt Wolff, who had just started Pantheon Books, and Jacques was invited to join this venture as a partner. This business prospered by doing first translations of the Grimm fairy tales, along with other innovative projects. But, while they had some bestsellers, their success was still bolstered by subsidization from philanthropists such as Mary Mellon and her art-collector and wealthy husband, Paul Mellon, who worked directly with Jacques to create the Bollingen series, which focused on works connected to Jung, as well as other intellectual books that otherwise would not have found a major publisher. Jacques died not long after the peak of this successful career, in 1950, from emphysema, just before Pantheon's profits exploded. Meanwhile, the Wolffs moved to Europe to get away from conflicts with their American partners, and ended up breaking that connection and selling the publishing house to Random House in 1961 for $1 million. This purchase contributed to the acceleration of the growth of what is now one of the giant-four international publishers. Thus, a translator who was fired and could not find suitable work because of

---

466   Ibid., 99-100.
467   Andre Schiffrin. *The Business of Books: How International Conglomerates Took Over Publishing and Changed the Way We Read*. (London: Verso, 2000), 17.
468   Ibid., 19.

his Judaism had to found publishing ventures that became successful because of the passion and hard work he put into fighting to keep them intellectually enticing and profitable.

The Roots of the Hearst Media Empire

In *The Uncrowned King: The Sensational Rise of William Randolph Hearst*, Kenneth Whyte describes the rise not of only one publisher, but at least three. First, in the "Author's Note" he describes how he started researching William Hearst and Joseph Pulitzer's competition over the New York newspaper market when he founded his own "national newspaper in a relatively crowded Canadian market," called the *Maclean's* magazine, which now has a focus on current affairs. Whyte "read widely in the history of the North American press, paying particular attention to editors proficient in the almost forgotten arts of attracting readers and building circulation against established competition."[469] Before he engaged in his new publishing venture, he dismissed Hearst as a yellow journalist. According to *Encyclopedia Britannica*, yellow journalism is "the use of lurid features and sensationalized news in newspaper publishing to attract readers and increase circulation. The phrase was coined in the 1890s to describe the tactics employed in furious competition between two New York City newspapers," Joseph Pulitzer's *World* and William Randolph Hearst's *Journal*. Despite public agreement to the contrary, Whyte reversed his initial judgment of Hearst, reporting that when he returned to this study five years later, he suddenly found value in the yellow texts and positive account books, as he now understood the business from the inside, instead of merely as a journalist or a writer working for a publisher without being the one responsible for keeping the business of publishing profitable. Secondly, Whyte briefly reviews the road that William's father George Hearst took towards publishing success by quoting from William Hearst's biography by David Nasaw, *The Chief: The Life of William Randolph Hearst*, which reports that George was "uncouth, loud, and semi-literate" and to this Whyte adds that he was a "hick who drank too much, neglected his family, and bought his way into the Senate… a sociopathic tycoon who murdered his way to riches."[470] Whyte explains

---

469   Kenneth Whyte. *The Uncrowned King: The Sensational Rise of William Randolph Hearst*. (Berkeley: Counterpoint, Random House, 2009), 1.
470   Ibid., 10.

that the last bit is how the HBO drama *Deadwood* portrays him, rather than it being his own opinion. Then, Whyte describes George's climb. He come from the Missouri frontier from a slave-owning family, and attained a grade school education before graduating from the Franklin County Mining School. He then engaged in financial speculations and analytical advising on lead-mining, before gradually building up profits to purchase what, at the time, was just another one of his investments, *The San Francisco Examiner*. Thirdly, George's son, William, began his publishing career, after graduating from Harvard University, as a journalist at *The San Francisco Examiner*, making it significantly more profitable than it was when he joined it. William thus gained the experience he needed to start his newspaper empire in New York after his father's death in 1891. William's single newspaper, The *New York Journal*, ballooned into what we know today as the Hearst Corporation, which had $10 billion in revenue in 2014. Like his father, William was elected to public office, but to the US House of Representatives, rather than the Senate. The details of William's yellow climb to monopolistic dominance of American media that are covered in the rest of this heavy book are not relevant to this study, but these three curious starts say a lot about the vast majority of publishing founders in America. Whyte is a great example of an editor-writer who made a professional living from journalism, national political campaign writing and other practical ways a writer can make money before taking a loan on a magazine in a competitive market and struggling to keep it profitable. George Hearst is an example of somebody who invested a small portion of his vast capital into a newspaper just because it was cheap and he thought it would show a profit with some help from his corporation. And William is an example of somebody who is born into a fortune and inherits a newspaper and then has the opportunity to exit out of his father's investments in mining to focus on acquiring newspapers, magazines and other media across the US to gain control of markets in price-cutting and attention-grabbing competitions. Both William and Whyte did a good deal of writing themselves. Whyte wrote this book. William did a good portion of the yellow journalism that made his *New York Journal* famous himself. These three author-publishers still have more in common with George Hearst than with the major radical author-publishers discussed in the rest of this study. If they were engaged in a regular schedule of writing books across their careers, like Dickens or Scott, none of these three publishers would have followed a path towards commercial newspaper publishing. And the publisher who clearly did the heaviest writing of the three, Whyte, has not expanded his publishing business beyond his one Canadian magazine. Why? Perhaps, anybody that sits down to examine the modern world at length cannot think of rival publishers as competitors to bankrupt, or perhaps serious writing simply takes too much time away from the business of making money.

Gerrey and the First Feminist Press

Alta Gerrey founded the Shameless Hussy Press in 1969, near the time when Dudley Randall started his venture to support African American authors. Shameless Hussy is credited with being the first feminist press in the United States. Just as Randall responded to the disproportionately low quantity of published African Americans, Gerrey was reacting to the extremely low (6%) quantity of books published by women prior to that point. By the end of the sixties, after the assassinations of non-violent leaders like Martin Luther King and Mahatma Gandhi, it seems as if Randall and Gerrey realized that if they wanted to see positive statistical changes, they had to enter the capitalist system and compete in it, rather than simply marching with signs along its streets. Unlike Randall, who specifically only solicited works by African American writers, Gerrey allowed for the publication of a few men (6%). Gerrey was a member of the second wave of the feminism movement. And Randall was a member of the Black Power Movement. I learned about Gerrey, her press, and the movement from a documentary interview she did in *She's Beautiful When She's Angry*, directed by Mary Dore. Also like Randall, Alta began printing books in her garage. Like Alice Walker and Virginia Woolf, Gerrey was assisted in the business of running this press by her second husband. The other parallel with Randall was that she was a poet and published several of her collections with Shameless Hussy, including: *Letters to Women* (1970), *songs of the wife, song of the mistress* (1971), *No Visible Means of Support* (1971), *The Shameless Hussy* (1980) and *Deluge with Dudes* (1989).

Randall reported that after reviewing and editing so much bad poetry, he eventually could not write and publish any more of his own works. Gerrey closed this press in 1989, perhaps because other publishers started accepting works by a higher percentage of women by this year. One indication of a new acceptance of female writers is that Walker also closed her press shortly after this point, in 1992. Walker and the women who previously could only publish in feminist ventures like Gerrey's, suddenly had access to the giant presses and their advances. Censorship and lack of access for outstanding, radical writers has always allowed for the success of small, independent presses willing to risk offending the church and state. Outstanding writing and publishing frequently comes out of desperation and struggle. Thus, a review of important American author-publishers would not have been complete without a mention of Gerrey's feminist efforts.

A Fight for Independence from Inside the Establishment

One writer made it difficult for me to figure out if he was an author-publisher or if he did not fit in this qualification, and despite some research, I am still uncertain how to qualify his achievements. Sir Harold Evans added a Sir to his name when he was knighted a few years ago. He began his publishing career in the newspapers in 1944 in Manchester, England. He is still actively publishing and directing publications to this day, nearly a century later. It was difficult to determine his status because the summary of his autobiography, *My Paper Chase: True Stories of Vanished Times*, stated, "he would begin all over again as a book publisher, acquiring the memoirs of Colin Powell… Richard Nixon—and a then-unknown law school graduate by the name of Barack Obama…" The confusing phrase is "begin" followed by "book publisher," which typically suggests that someone has started a new publishing venture, but Evans was nominated to the role of publisher of Hachette Book Group (the publisher of the Evans' memoir). The bulk of the author-publishers I am focusing on founded their own periodical or book publishing ventures, so while Evans might have had fantastic writing, editing and publishing achievements, because he did not start a venture of his own, he was not fully in control of Hachette in the sense of owning the enterprise, but he was its publisher, so in that latter sense, he did self-publish his memoir. On the other hand, Evans served as the publisher of Hachette previously, from 1990 to 1997. In those years, he published two re-prints of his much earlier publications, including, *Pictures on a Page: Photo-Journalism, Graphics and Picture Editing* (1978; 1997). It was only after he left his position as the publisher of Hachette, when Random house and its imprints started releasing his non-fiction titles, including, *The American Century* (Knopf, 1998), named after the famous phrase from H. G. Wells that Luce also appropriated for his famous essay. Evans was successful from his teens through the present day, and there is hardly a glum cloud in his story. For example, he married very late in life and produced two children at an age when pretty much all of the other author-publishers in this study were dead.

Despite these faults, Evans did face a few battles with censorship like the other author-publishers. For example, On January 25, 1975, when he was serving as the editor of *The Sunday Times*, Evans sent to the press an uncensored "first serial" of Richard Crossman's memoir. Crossman was "a former Oxford don who was a member of the Labour cabinet from 1964 to 1970." Crossman had learned that he had months to live and he was hoping he could see his diaries released into print despite the standard rule that "ministers had to wait thirty years to publish a documented account of their experiences, and if they or anyone else wanted to publish sooner, they had to accept official censorship on pain of a criminal prosecution under the Official Secrets Act." The radical component in this memoir was Crossman's criticism of the "cabinet meetings," and his argument that civil servants were the ones with real power in Britain. While the conservative decision might have been to submit the work for censorship, Evans and his team held firm under pressure and published 100,000 uncensored words of Crossman's materials. Eventually, Evans reports: "We lost in the High Court but won in the Court of Appeal Soon afterward a committee of inquiry, to which I gave evidence, recommended that ministerial memoirs no longer be regulated by statute."[471]

Most of the censorship Evans was facing when he worked for Hachette was self-censorship, as the assignments he sent himself on made him question the appropriateness of the subject matter. Evans recounts how he had to court Marlon Brando at his Beverly Hills "hilltop retreat," saying that Brando had made previous "East Coast phonies" go down on their knees as they stretched out "open checkbooks," trying to secure rights to his autobiography. A *Library Journal* review shortly after the resulting release of *Songs My Mother Taught Me* stated that Evans paid Brando $5 million, so he was clearly one of these "phonies" with

---

471   Harold Evans. *My Paper Chase: True Stories of Vanished Times*. (New York: Little, Brown and Company: Hachette Book Group, 2009), 410-2.

checkbooks, and succeeded in having the biggest pockets out of the competitors. Evans reports that Brando told him a great deal of nonsense before he finally agreed to the contract, including accusing Evans of working for the CIA, and claiming that he could have "fucked the First Lady in the darkened kitchen," shortly before John F. Kennedy's assassination. Evans diligently double-checked the latter idea and verified that Brando did indeed dine in the White House shortly before the assassination, though naturally the lack of fucking could not be verified. Evans also stresses that Brando wrote his autobiography "with Robert Lindley," as opposed to with him personally. But, it is clear from this report that Brando was not in a state of mind where he could have done much writing. It is more likely that Lindley ghostwrote the bulk of this fiction project. Though Evans dodged the job of writing Brando's memoir, he had the bigger task of making it commercially successful after he paid $5 million. It turned out that "getting" Brando "to promote it was a nightmare and a farce. (He suggested that we make a film in which he would dress as a woman and I would interview him.) I winced as I watched the interview he finally organized himself with Larry King on CNN. King allowed him to go off on various wild riffs, ending with Brando kissing King on the lips. It was the kiss of death for my hopes, stopping the book dead in its tracks in its rise on the best seller list." Brando came out of retirement after writing this book with Evans for a supporting role in *Don Juan DeMarco* (1995), and co-authored a pirate adventure with his director "friend," Donald Cammel, called, *Fan-Tan*, which was released by Random House right after Brando's death in 2004. "Chapter 1: The Prison" of this potential ghosted project begins thus: "Under the black cloud, the prison. And within the prison, a bright rebel. The walls were extremely high, and although this was not possible, they appeared to lean inward yet also to bulge outward..."[472] This is a mesmerizing bit of fiction when it is compared with the style of Brando's autobiography. "Wes was in the terminal stages of tuberculosis. Pretty soon his back was a hump and he was carrying his elbows a little higher, so that when he walked they pointed back like arrows..."[473] It would be inspiring if an actor had such a passion for writing if it came to him before the final decade of

---

472   Marlon Brando and Donald Cammel. *Fan-Tan*. (New York: Vintage Books: Random House Inc., 2006), 3.
473   Marlon Brando and Robert Lindsey. *Brando: Songs My Mother Taught Me*. (New York: Random House Inc., 1994), 25.

his life, but these publications after his death, and when his mind was clearly afflicted are troubling… especially since the two styles clearly belong more to the co-authors than to Brando, if his frank interview kisses of Larry King and other irrational behaviors are indications.

After the Brando memoir publicity disaster, Evans was "smuggled into a Miami jailhouse" to interview and publish a book by General Manuel Noriega, "the deposed dictator of Panama and alleged torturer." Evans mentions that he faced a great deal of criticism from readers and the press about his willingness to publish a work by somebody like Noriega, but defended this choice by saying that to "publish" is "to make known," and atrocities is something that should be made known. Evans then asks: "were we censors? Bennett Cerf found Ayn Rand and Whittaker Chambers politically repugnant, but he published them." Evans blames the "thought police" for also criticizing his agreement to edit Richard Nixon's "foreign policy manifesto for America," for which he spent time transcribing Nixon's orations at his New Jersey home, thereby taking on the role he left to Robert Lindley in the Brando project. Evans reports that Richard Nixon finished writing the resulting book, *Beyond Peace,* in February 1994, and it was rushed to press immediately after his death, on April 22, for a release in June of that same year.[474] Between a crazed actor, a homicidal dictator, and a one of the most corrupt politicians in American history… is there any wonder why Evans stepped down from one of the most powerful positions in international publishing at Random House in 1997? Evans was driven to irrational decisions in his attempts to figure out how he could acquire and publicize books that would show a return on investments of millions in advances. He was not going out of his way to find subversive and radical politicians who were fighting against censorship in his role as Random House's publisher. But subversive texts found him, and he managed to mix profits with radicalism when he published top secret materials, and other questionable content. Crossman had an entertaining story to tell about British politics, and Evans must have hoped that Nixon would share something about his own resignation in his near-deathbed account. One thing is clear, if Evans owned Hachette, he would not have sat in a hot tub with Brando nor in a jail with Panamanian dictator; he would have assigned these groveling tasks to ambitious employees.

---

474   Evans, *My Paper,* 530-3.

Miniature, Recent, Indie Publishing Successes

Indie Publishing offers a few stories of authors who published themselves, and then grew these ventures into publishing companies that welcomed other authors. The publisher that released this book, Princeton Architectural Press, was founded by Kevin Lippert, a Princeton University architecture graduate student, when he wanted a reference book not easily available at the library, Paul Letarouilly's *Edifeces de Rome Moderne*, and decided to print it himself.[475] An author in this study who started with one of his own books is Edward Tufte, who was forced to self-publish his, *The Visual Display of Quantitative Information*, when he clashed with a potential publisher on critical design decisions. "He created his own company, Graphics Press, and took out a mortgage on his house to finance it. By publishing the book himself, he was able to keep the price accessible and maintain control over every aspect of the book's design and production."[476] While staking your house on the book of your dreams is extreme, Cary Tennis might have taken a more aggressive approach to self-publishing his *Since You Asked* anthology of "long, unfettered letters from readers about dark personal problems, followed by even longer responses from Tennis." A commercial publisher raised objections and the project "died." "Since he has an avid fan base [from being a popular advice columnist on Salon.com] (what's called a 'platform' in the publishing biz), he decided to produce the book himself and sell it online directly to his readers." Cary's wife designed the book and they printed 3,000 copies, and sold them out of their "garage and basement."[477] There are thousands of similar successes every year in the current marketplace because access for authors to publish themselves and others is thinner than ever before. Most of the successful marketing and publishing campaigns still tend to detail the whopping sums spent on design, printing and advertising, so wealthier authors still tend to reach larger audiences. Meanwhile, there are fewer breakout small presses for radical writers who are disinterested in sales, or perhaps there is just less awareness of their existence because they are failing to naturally find radical readers without the funds to attract them in an over-saturated marketplace.

---

475   Ellen Lupton, Ed. *Indie Publishing: How to Design and Produce Your Own Book.* (New York: Princeton Architectural Press, 2008), 13.
476   Ibid., 18.
477   Ibid., 24.

CHAPTER 8

Benjamin Franklin and the Spread of Publishing Through the Colonies

James Franklin was an early pioneer in independent colonial publishing through his founding of a radical newspaper, *The New England Courant,* on August 7, 1721, after working as an apprentice in England and bringing a hand press back with him to Boston. Benjamin Franklin joined his brother's business. Benjamin describes his apprenticeship in his *Autobiography*:

> This Bookish Inclination at length determin'd my Father to make me a Printer, tho' he had already one Son, (James) of that Profession. In 1717 my Brother James return'd from England with a Press & Letters to set up his Business in Boston. I lik'd it much better than that of my Father, but still had a Hankering for the Sea… I stood out some time, but at last was persuaded and signed the Indentures, when I was yet but 12 Years old.—I was to serve as an Apprentice till I was 21 Years of Age, only I was to be allow'd Journeyman's Wages during the last Year. In a little time I made great Proficiency in the Business, and became a useful Hand to my Brother. I now had Access to better Books… I now took a Fancy to Poetry, and made some little Pieces. My Brother, thinking it might turn to account encourag'd me, & put me on composing two occasional Ballads. One was called the *Light House Tragedy*, & contain'd an Acc^t of

the drowning of Capt. Worthilake with his Two Daughters; the other was a Sailor Song on the Taking of *Teach* or Blackbeard the Pirate. They were wretched Stuff, in the Grubstreat Ballad Stile, and when they were printed he sent me about the Town to sell them. The first sold wonderfully, the Event being recent, having made a great Noise. This flatter'd my Vanity. But my Father discourag'd me, by ridiculing my Performances, and telling me Verse-makers were generally Beggars; so I escap'd being a Poet, most probably a very bad one. But as Prose Writing has been a great Use to me in the Course of my Life, and was a principal Means of my Advancement...[478]

Franklin goes on to describe how he started writing prose in argumentative letters to friends, and then perfected his style by mimicking prose writing that he admired. This passage says a great deal about the parallel between access to a press and the ability of a person in this period to attain and disseminate ideas in print. When the brothers started printing in Boston (just as with the more widely known publishers that dared to publish independent, radical opinions), the two competing papers in the Boston market immediately began publishing attacks against the new arrival, *The New England Courant*. Cotton Mather was at the forefront of these attacks. Mather was also responsible for overseeing the infamous Salem witch trials of 1692 (shortly after he completed a degree from Harvard). The smallpox inoculations scandal was the second major controversy that Mather oversaw. Inoculations were practiced in India and elsewhere earlier, but they only entered England's domain in 1721, and Mather was one of the loudest voices decrying them as blasphemous. Thus, at the daybreak of his publishing venture, Franklin was taking on an enemy, who took down numerous innocent women at the start of his Puritan minister career. Mather was also a popular pamphleteer. Mather fired against *The New England Courant*'s support of "experiments with smallpox inoculation" and against "its almost atheistic views on religion." The attacks culminated in a brutal censorship: "An oblique reference in the June 11, 1722, issue to the Governor's dawdling about the pirates on the coast finally precipitated trouble. It cost James a month in jail, during which time Benjamin produced the paper and," braving the likely imprisonment, "'made bold to give our rulers some rubs in it.'" Mather wielded even more power in 1722 than back in 1692. When intimidating pamphlets failed to scare the

---

[478]   Benjamin Franklin. *Autobiography, Poor Richard, and Later Writings*. (New York: The Library of America, 1997), 577-8.

Franklins out of publishing arguments that the Puritan establishment opposed, he or those in his cluster of supporters must have lobbied to imprison James Franklin. Months later, the liberated James "alleged rude remarks about church members" on January 14, 1723, and "the city council and legislature forbade James 'to Print or Publish *The New England Courant*, or any other Pamphlet or Paper of the like Nature, except it be first supervised by the Secretary of the Province.'" What started as an obstruction, ended up creating the Benjamin Franklin all American children are familiar with to this day. Franklin was a minor in 1723, at only seventeen, but he was experienced enough that James decided to transfer the legal ownership of the *Courant* to Benjamin's name because the ruling only censored James, and did not mention the rest of his family, but the power got to Benjamin's head and be absconded from Boston when he could not find work with any of the other papers only months later on September 30, 1723, so that James had to find a new apprentice to write the business off to, and in the meantime taught the trade to his new wife, Ann Smith.[479] Benjamin's initial desire to flee is only natural, as anybody would want to escape a likely burning at the stake, which was likely to result if Benjamin continued his brother's habit of poking at the irrational rules of the Puritans in his paper.

Benjamin ran away from a brother who bestowed "blows" on him. Benjamin did so secretly on a sloop headed for New York. He later ended up in Philadelphia (population: 2,000).[480] Franklin started working for one of the smaller printers in town, Samuel Keimer. Benjamin socialized widely with people in the village, and pretty soon came to the attention of Pennsylvania's governor, Sir William Keith, who came to visit him at Keimer's print shop, and took him aside to offer to help him setup an independent print shop of his own. Sir Keith insisted that Benjamin should seek a letter of recommendation for the venture from his father, so he returned to Boston only a few months after running away, and did secure his father's blessing, but not his father's financial backing. Governor Keith promised to fund Franklin's trip to London to purchase the necessary equipment in 1724, but when Benjamin arrived there he discovered that the "flighty governor had supplied no letters of credit nor recommendation." Benjamin did find a job soon

---

479 Hudak, *Early*, 34-5.
480 Walter Isaacson. *Benjamin Franklin: An American Life*. (New York: Simon & Schuster, 2003), 34-5.

after arrival with the "famous printing house, Samuel Palmer's," where he worked for a year before finding "a better-paying job at a far larger printing house, John Watts's, moving up there from the pressroom to the composition room. Benjamin returned to Philadelphia in 1726 with help from Denham, who was planning to start a general store, and "offered to pay Franklin's passage if he would agree to sign on as his clerk at £50 a year." Benjamin agreed because merchants were more "exalted" than printers. Denham died shortly after they setup the shop. Benjamin returned to working for Keimer, this time as his manager. "Because there was no foundry in America for casting type, Franklin contrived" creating his own foundry "by using Keimer's letters to make lead molds. He thus became the first person in America to manufacture type."[481] Benjamin then entered into a partnership with Hugh Meredith with the help of Meredith's father, who supplied £200 for them to purchase the necessary equipment from London, which arrived in 1728. At this time, they setup a competing print shop to Keimer's. They became successful and took over some of Keimer's clients. One of their early projects was printing a portion of a Quaker group's history. Meredith then took to drink, so Benjamin's friends supplied funds to buy him out of the business. Thus, Benjamin finally became independent. Walter Isaacson stresses that Benjamin viewed printing as his primary "calling," showing as proof of this that Benjamin started his will with: "I, Benjamin Franklin of Philadelphia, printer," rather than inserting one of his other careers in this primary spot. Franklin's other occupations were "scientist, politician, statesman" and "diplomat."[482]

Meanwhile, tired of the constant clashes with Boston's clergy and officials, in 1727, James moved the press to the Colony of Rhode Island, starting the "first printing press" in its borders and issuing its first paper in 1732, *The Rhode Island Gazette*, which lasted for only eight months. James was an author-publisher because he wrote some of the stories he published in his newspapers. His wife, Ann, was a more serious author, perhaps because she had less busy-work to do up until the year of James' death in 1735, when she stepped up to run the business of the press, and became New England's first female printer. Ann surely wrote poetry collection that was anonymously labeled as written by "a Well-wisher to Truth," *A Brief Essay on the Number Seven* (1735). She also self-published and signed with her own name, *Copy of Some*

---

481   Isaacson, *Benjamin*, 36-52
482   Ibid., 53-5.

Queries Put to Mr. Auchmuty, Judge of the Admirality (1734), supporting Quakers' rights to hold office in Rhode Island. James had begun the *Rhode Island Almanack* back in 1727, and Ann revived it, because it was profitable, in 1736, writing some of the content under the pseudonym "Poor Robin" for the first year and then between 1739 and 1741. Since she wrote, edited, and printed this project, she is "America's first woman to pen an almanac."[483] In 1744, Ann got into trouble herself, even without James' radicalism, when she printed extra copies of *Acts and Laws of Rhode Island*, hoping to distribute them above the number the Colony ordered for their purposes. She was prohibited from selling these under the penalty of heavy fines. But later, when the Colony decided to print their minutes regularly in 1747, they inserted her right to profit from additional printings into the initial contract, showing their appreciation of her work.[484] Meanwhile, James' son, James Jr., finished his apprenticeship with Benjamin and became an equal partner with Ann in Rhode Island in 1748. James Jr. was not as efficient as his parents and lost some contracts during his years at the helm. James Jr. died early, in 1762, once again leaving his mother in control of the business. She had made an earlier attempt to revive her husband's *The Rhode Island Gazette*, but it was a false start. Now finally, in 1762, she managed to keep the paper her son founded, *The Newport Mercury, or The Weekly Advertiser*, running, while also keeping up with governmental and other printing orders. We can assume that the bulk of the paper was composed by Ann. She wrote articles about Benjamin Franklin's successes, gossip about international aristocrats, announcements, as well as various other news. Ann took on an apprentice, Samuel Hall, later in 1762, because the printer's work was getting to be a bit too strenuous for her age. She died in the following year, and Samuel took over the printing business.[485] Benjamin Franklin's achievements sprung out of Ann and James Sr.'s groundwork, so they deserve the credit for allowing Benjamin to grow beyond their limits.

To return to Benjamin's story, when he broke out on his own, he became the publisher of *The Pennsylvania Gazette*, a forum for political agitation and satire. Franklin was running a printing house in partnership with Hugh Meredith (1728 founding). Meredith later split off from Franklin to found new state papers, some of which were more

---

483 Hudak, *Early*, 35-6.
484 Ibid., 38.
485 Ibid., 47-8.

successful than others. Franklin worked with other partners, who later started their own publishing ventures. This interconnected series of partners, who eventually gained independence, became the first newspaper network in the colonies. These associates cooperated with Franklin's goals and ambitions and helped each other to grow in public access and power. In its early stage, the network resulted from the need to learn from an experienced printer before starting one's own shop, and out of inability to pay up front for the full cost of a press and other equipment. Thus, new printers had to solicit Franklin's investment in their press, which they eventually managed to buy back and own. Unlike the newspaper networks of today, Franklin setup this system to encourage printers to leave his network once they were profitable, rather than staying a part of the ever-growing corporation. He benefited indirectly from the comradery of seeing them eventually gain their independence. Franklin also printed six issues of *The General Magazine, and Historical Chronicle, for all the British Plantations in America* (1741), the first of its kind in America. One of Franklin's first jobs as an independent printer was printing Pennsylvania's bills of credit, partly because he had written and published a pamphlet on the need for paper currency in 1729. He later found government printing posts of this kind in Delaware and New Jersey. Franklin's first book, *A Dissertation on Liberty and Necessity, Pleasure and Pain*, was printed when he was working for a printer in London in 1725. It was similar in its rebellious religious opinions to the book that got Shelley expelled from Oxford, though this project did not argue for atheism. It merely argued against the distinction between certain virtues and vices that he was exposed to in London. Franklin decided these radical ideas were too blasphemous to remain in print later in his life, so he burned all existing copies of this pamphlet. Franklin's most successful self-publication was the *Poor Richard, 1739: An Almanack for the Year of Christ 1739*. Franklin started the Poor Richard series in 1732 and ran it continuously for twenty-five years.

The first 1733 issue began with an address to the reader, wherein the narrator confessed that he is "excessive[ly] poor," and that his wife has ordered him to stop gazing at the "Stars," and that she would "burn all" his "Books and Rattling-Traps" if he did not "make some profitable Use of them… The Printer has offer'd me some considerable share of the Profits, and I have thus begun to comply with my Dame's desire."[486] The popular *1739* issue has the same basic components as those that preceded and followed it annually. The address to the reader in this *1739* issue ends by pointing out that after the successes of the *Almanac*, the author ought to be "*Poor Dick* no longer," but alas he still was poor because the "fair Agreement" with his Printer was such that the Printer had retained the "greatest Part of the Profits."[487] Perhaps it was this appeal for the plight of the writer that made readers commiserate with the fictional Poor Richard and sold more copies of this issue. Benjamin was the periodical's author, but putting a poor man's name on the *Almanac* instead was a successful marketing strategy. Impoverished readers who needed an almanac for their farms sympathized with Poor Richard, and wouldn't have sympathized with a business owner like Franklin. Once profits multiplied, Franklin expanded the publication, and included some sub-essays on topics of interest in between the series of wise sayings that he always printed in the latter part of the issues. In these mini-essays, Franklin offers some of the platitudes that he is known for, including those on "How to get RICHES": "It is not only ill Management, but discovers a slothful Disposition, to do that in the Afternoon, which should have been done in the Morning."[488]

Franklin wrote that the *Almanac* made him $10,000 annually, an enormous sum for that century. Only after Franklin retired from the business of printing (though he still continued dabbling in self-publications) in 1748, did he start winning political offices, a trajectory that led him to be one of the contributors to the *Declaration of Independence* (1775), serving as the US Postmaster General after the Revolutionary War, and then as President of Pennsylvania. He was one of the only authors of the Declaration who did not serve as a US President. The terms of Benjamin's retirement instructed that his foreman, David Hall, would maintain the operations of the printing business as his partner, while he would retain "half of the shop's profits for the next eighteen years, which would amount to about £650 annually." This was enough to keep Benjamin comfortable, as he focused his energy and time on scientific experiments, reading, writing, politics and various other ventures that only somebody who is not engaged in the constant pursuit of a paycheck can manage.[489]

---

486   Franklin, *Autobiography*, 445.
487   Ibid., 471.
488   Ibid., 515-6.
489   Isaacson, *Benjamin*, 126-8.

***

The Franklins' influence branched out to various other printers that developed the book trade in the relatively new colonies. Upon migrating to Philadelphia from Holland in 1731, Louis Timothee joined forces with Benjamin Franklin and they jointly started a German-language, biweekly paper, *Philadelphische Zeitung*, which folded shortly thereafter, but left the partners on good terms. So, in 1733 Franklin entrusted Louis with the operation of a business he inherited upon the death of his previous partner in Charleston, South Carolina. There, Louis revived a weekly his predecessor had founded, *The South Carolina Gazette*, simultaneously anglicizing his name to Lewis Timothy, so it would not sound so foreign. Like Ann and James Franklin, Louis also focused on government-contracted printings when he started. When Louis died in 1738, Benjamin transferred the remains of the contract between them to his widow with six small children and another on the way, Elizabeth, who used her minor son's name, Peter Timothy, instead of her own, as the printer.

Franklin explained his partnership with the Timothy family in his *Autobiography*: "In 1733, I sent one of my Journeymen to Charleston South Carolina where a Printer was wanting. I furnish'd him with a Press and Letters, on an Agreement of Partnership, by which I was to receive One Third of the Profits of the Business, paying One Third of the Expense." Franklin explains that Timothy was deficient in his knowledge of accounting, so that no "Account" at all appeared, despite some "Remittances." Matters improved when his wife, Elizabeth, took over the business because "Knowledge of Accompts makes a Part of Female Education" in Holland, so that she made quarterly detailed accounts. She "manag'd the Business with such Success that… at the Expiration of the Term" she "was able to purchase of me the Printing-House and establish her Son in it." Based on similar positive working relationships with female printers, Franklin recommend the creation of "that Branch of Education for our young Females, as likely to be of more Use to them… in Case of Widowhood than either Music or Dancing, by preserving them from Losses by Imposition of crafty Men…"[490] The philosophy that women should be able to take care of themselves in business was behind the successes of other women-

---

490   Franklin, *Autobiography*, 659.

owned presses. Similar widow-printers are much more uncommon in Europe in this period, but in America, they grew out of most major printing and publishing establishments.

In the *Autobiography*, Franklin specifies that his standard contract with the printers that he sponsored by setting them up with a Press & Letters was for a six-year term. This contract also intentionally made it easy for the printers to buy out the tools of the trade at the end of this term to become independent. Franklin's printing business was profitable at its start because his Newspaper was "for a time almost the only one in this and the neighbouring Provinces."[491] While most modern publishers conceal the tricks of their trade and work to keep competitors out of the market, Franklin was knowingly creating competitors for what could have become his printing monopoly in the colonies. Franklin chose the printers he sponsored carefully with an eye for the best workers and those who were the least quarrelsome. He worked to make his contracts as transparent as possible to make sure that all parties walked away on good terms and profits. Thus, this philosophy of deliberately fostering the multiplication of competition and giving workers control over the production process would be termed Marxist today. And yet this communal philosophy built what we assume today to be a "natural" American publishing industry. The foundation of American publishing was nurtured through Franklin's sharing of profits and his active promotion of new printers, who were eager to enter an untapped market.

In an early editorial in the *Gazette*, "Apology for Printers," Benjamin explained that when a customer offered him money to publish "scurrilous and defamatory" accusations, he tested his resolve by going home and committing to drinking only water and eating only bread while sleeping on the floor to make sure that he could subsist without prostituting his press "to the purposes of corruption and abuse."[492]

The contract with Benjamin came to an end a year later, and by that time Elizabeth had the funds to buy out the business and to run it on her own, using her son's name for legal purposes. This meant that Peter was the one named as defendant in a libel suit that resulted from the publication of "some letters about the Whitefield religious controversy, published… on January 8 and 15, 1741."[493] The news articles

---

491   Ibid., 670.
492   Isaacson, *Benjamin*, 67.
493   Hudak, *Early*, 133.

and advertisements Elizabeth ran in the paper were pretty standard, but she did elicit some criticism when she published poems on "the double standard" using the pseudonym "E. R." The first of these was called, "The Ladies Complaint," and it stated:

> …It does not give us equal Measure;
> A pain it is for us to love
> But it is to MEN a Pleasure.
> They freely can their Thoughts disclose,
> Whilst ours must burn within;…
> Then equal Laws Custom Find,
> And neither Sex oppress;
> More Freedom give to Womankind,
> Or to Mankind give less.

She then published a "Reply to Ladies Complaint" by one of her male readers that objected to her derision towards his sex. After this, she printed a follow-up reply:

> How wretched is a *Woman's* Fate,…
> Subject to Man in every State.
> How can she then be free from Woes?
> In Youth a *Father's* stern Command,
> And jealous Eyes controul her Will;
> A lordly *Brother* watchful stands,
> To keep her closer Captive still.

The Gentleman's answer objected that it is a "happy" Fate to be "Free from Care, and free from Woe" under the guardianship of men.[494] There was no other route for a woman to publish pro-equality propaganda at this stage of American history other than in her own press. In 1746, Elizabeth put the control of the printing business into her son Peter's hands. He was twenty-one by this point. She apparently departed for Province to start a general store, and lived in relative obscurity, only announcing that her slave, Flora, had run away in 1756 in print, before her death in 1757. She was relatively wealthy in her last decade because she left eight slaves, "three houses, land, household furniture, money, and wearing apparel" to her three daughters in her will. Peter ran the business until 1781, "when he was taken prisoner by

---
494   Ibid., 138-40.

the British" during the American Revolution, and then his own widow, Ann (Donavan) Timothy took over the operation of the press, so that it survived in their family until 1802.[495]

There might have been many more anti-inoculation and anti-witch (or anti-feminist) campaigns in the colonies if the Franklin family did not spread the free press through their affiliations. Nations of people are defined by the books they print. Benjamin Franklin is a great example of the close relationship between major shifts in political history (America's eventual independence) and the distribution and printing of texts that prompt it. Benjamin's is also a story of the true soul of the American Dream, one where a businessman succeeds by helping others succeed, and uses his winnings to better science, policy, and various other aspects of the flawed humanity.

---

495   Ibid., 146.

CHAPTER 9

The Anti-Plagiarism Campaign and Another Mysterious Death: Edgar Allan Poe's "Voluminous History of the Little Longfellow War" in the Broadway Journal

Edgar Allan Poe's inspiration for starting his own journal might have stemmed from his initial admiration of Charles Dickens' work. Poe must have sympathized with Dickens father's popularly known plight with entering debtors' prison. Poe had spent time there himself at the end of 1831, when his brother Henry died owing $80, and Poe could not repay it as the *de facto* head of household. Poe's foster father, John Allan, received a letter from Poe asking for relief from prison but did not pay the required $20 until five weeks passed.[496] Either because of commiseration or simply because Poe admired Dickens' work, he was very proactive in seeking an interview with Dickens. Mark Twain was similarly enamored with Dickens, so much so that he took his soon-to-be wife, Olivia, to a Dickens reading in 1867 for their third date, during Dickens' second tour of America. As a result of Poe's persistence, he was granted two interviews with Dickens after he sent his books with the hope of receiving some assistance with finding a London publisher. Dickens responded positively and set up the first interview with Poe to talk about the "backwards state of American poetry." They also talked about Dickens' spring 1842 highly popular tour of major American cities. Dickens spent hours shaking hands with his fans in his hotel lobby before sitting down to chat with Poe in Philadelphia. Poe had reviewed *Sketches by*

---

[496] James M. Hutchisson. *Poe*. (Jackson: University Press of Mississippi, 2005), 34.

Boz in the June 1836 *Southern Literary Messenger*, and *Barnaby Rudge* in *Graham's Magazine*. Poe was "hoping to emulate the Englishman in his own career."[497] As Dickens promised, he took Poe's work to his London publisher upon his return to the United Kingdom. This publisher replied that Poe's submission was a "collection of detached pieces by an unknown author" that could not sell in London.[498] Soon after this, Poe's enthusiasm for Dickens waned and he started to see him as another "interior" author with a bloated reputation.

Similarly to his newfound distaste for Dickens, Poe's criticism of Longfellow developed gradually, beginning with his first review of Longfellow's prose romance, *Hyperion*, in October of 1839. Poe was frustrated that his countryman, Longfellow, could make a living from poetry, while he was scraping by despite what he believed was his superior talent. Longfellow held an endowed chair at Harvard, and had married an heiress.

Poe's infamous Longfellow War accused Longfellow of plagiarism. It lasted across countless critical articles and reviews. James M. Hutchisson concludes in his biography of Poe that Poe sacrificed his career when he followed the popularity of "The Raven" with new attacks against Longfellow as a "plagiarist." This is a very dark view of this sequence of events. It presumes that when publishers read that Poe was against plagiarism, they blacklisted him and refused to publish his work despite the success of his most popular, long poem.[499]

Edgar Allan Poe wrote an article for his *Broadway Journal,* when he was working as an editor there, prior to acquiring it, called, "Some Secrets of the Magazine Prison-House," which explains some of the financial and artistic integrity concerns that were on his mind during these years. He reported that American authors are handed out extremely small royalties by publishers and have to turn to writing or editing for journals, where they are also underpaid. His scheme was to attempt to grow "rich" from acquiring the failing *Broadway Journal*. He planned on using the resulting riches to found a brand-new journal he had been dreaming about since 1834, when he was only 25, *The Penn*, named after Pennsylvania, in the hope of starting it in Philadelphia. I suspect I might have seen this name somewhere before I named my

---

497 Ibid., 125-7.
498 Sidney Moss. "Poe's 'Two Long Interviews' with Dickens." *Poe Studies 11, no. 1* (June 1978), 10-2.
499 Hutchisson, *Poe,* 172.

first Anaphora journal the *Pennsylvania Literary Journal*. Poe had spent over a decade working on advertising, fundraising and finding artists and other affiliates to collaborate on *The Penn* with him. Before this plan could materialize, Poe died under mysterious circumstances. The *Broadway Journal* had failed under his ownership only a few months after his acquisition, in January 1846. It is fair to speculate that the parallels between Poe and Shelley's suspicious deaths show the perils of the radical publishing business. There was one set of articles that Poe published in the *Broadway Journal* that received the most critical ridicule from the mainstream, and this seems to be the type of radical work that made it necessary for Poe to seek an independent publishing venue for his unpopular opinions.

Poe's chief radical objection was against plagiarism. He used Longfellow's work as a blatant example of this deep-rooted problem. Longfellow never replied directly to this criticism, but his friends engaged in what Poe termed the "Little Longfellow War" to defend Longfellow against these accusations. Poe's articles were titled: "A Continuation of the voluminous History of the Little Longfellow War" (March 15, 1845), "Imitation—Plagiarism" (March 8 and 29, 1845), "More of the Voluminous History of the Little Longfellow War" (March 22, 1845), and "Plagiarism—Imitation—Postscript" (April 5, 1845). Poe has become one of the most imitated horror and mystery writers of all time. These later imitations might have attracted critics to the study of Poe's War against plagiarism in general. Poe was already heavily imitated even at that early date. In theory, Poe was not upset at specific plagiarisms of his work by Longfellow. But, since Poe publicly acknowledged doing at least some ghostwriting, he might have written something under another name that Longfellow plagiarized. While the plagiarism cause is less socially impactful than Dickens' fight against child labor, or Shelley's fight against the monarchy, it is a cultural illness, which was yet another reason why so many of the best authors were driven towards self-publication.

Poe was particularly critical of Longfellow because of his comparative financial success in literature. One example of Longfellow's opulence was that he even resigned from Harvard when he no longer needed the salary. Longfellow submitted his resignation letter in 1854 when he "finally felt he was financially secure enough to cease teaching at Harvard." His peak earning came in 1857, when he recorded selling a total of over 326,258 copies of his books. *The Song of Hiawatha* had sold 50,000 copies, and the runner-up, *Voices of the Night*, sold 43,500, according to his calculations. He used these profits to finish renovating his house and lands and started living in domestic bliss, by all accounts.[500] He had been frustrated with Harvard since at least 1846, when he published the "Pegasus in Pound" lyric, wherein a "winged steed of Poetry" is put on display in a small village to be "stared at... unfed" until he has the strength to break free and fly to heaven.[501] After the end of the 1854 school year, Longfellow was notified that the Harvard Corporation "had accepted his long-delayed resignation" and this news "brought both sadness and relief ('This separating one's self from one's former life! This breaking away from one's Past')." He was soon using the time he did not have to invest into "college duties" in "'other, little nameless things'" that kept him busy as he steadily worked on his writing.[502] Longfellow even profited from a self-publication investment of $2,600 (taken out of royalties due to Longfellow by Own in 1852) for stereotype plates. He followed this by purchasing the plates to all of his books. Then, he sold the right to re-prints to several different publishers. Charvat calculates the average royalty that Longfellow received from the books he resold in this way at 18.25%, compared with the "traditional ten." Longfellow managed to sell a much higher number of his poetic works than Melville and most of the other writers in this study. He sold 7,000 copies of *Voices of the Night*, 8,968 copies of *The Golden Legend*, and 14,425 copies of *Evangeline*. He made $5,427 for prose and $5,350 for verse, and these sums were only from a select group of reviewed titles. On average, Longfellow's income from teaching and writing between 1840-43 was $1,917, and in the following years it was $3,536. Longfellow profited from selling the same poems to a number of different publications before Graham's acquired a right for exclusive publication of Longfellow between 1843 and 1848.[503] If Longfellow was plagiarizing the works that he was buying plates for and re-selling to multiple buyers, it is easy to imagine why Poe would think of this as a major theft. The same publishers were rejecting Poe's submissions, or paying him a smaller royalty, despite his alleged, comparative, authorial honesty.

500   Charles C. Calhoun. *Longfellow: A Rediscovered Life*. (Boston: Beacon Press, 2004), 198-9.
501   Ibid., 184.
502   Ibid., 208.
503   William Charvat. *The Profession of Authorship: The Papers of William Charvat*. (Columbus: Ohio State University Press, 1968. (Web)), 156-162.

Poe's battles with the literary establishment culminated in his successful libel lawsuit for "defamation of character" after an unfair letter was published in the *Mirror* on July 23, 1846. Poe was awarded $225.06, as well as $101.42 in court costs.[504] This clash began on April 20, 1846 when Poe published his first installment of a series on "The Literati of New York City: Some Honest Opinions at Random Respecting Their Authorial Merits, with Occasional Words of Personality" in the *Godey's Lady's Book*.[505] Poe wrote dozens of sketches, which were occasionally about the editors who published his own work, such as George Colton and N. P. Willis. This series was extremely popular, and sold out the issue in which it was introduced. One of the authors Poe criticized, Briggs, fired back in an unsigned article in the *Evening Mirror*, which had run an advertisement of the series. Briggs exclaimed that Poe should be committed to an insane asylum. A deluge of attacks against Poe followed from countless insulted literati. Poe responded by calling them uneducated, and hitting all the harder in additional sketches. The fire reached an explosive climax in Poe's July 10 reply in the *Spirit of the Times*. The flame was then fanned by English's rejoinder in the July 13 *Mirror* article. English went too far when he challenged Poe to take the debate into a "legal battle." Poe at first attempted to simply post one more reply, but when Godey received the article, "instead of publishing" it "in his own magazine," he paid ten dollars to have it printed in the *Spirit of the Times*, and then "debited Poe's account for the amount." Poe exclaimed that Godey knew how poor he was. He was so outraged that he now accepted Brigg's challenge, agreeing to see them in court. Because Poe presented witnesses that testified to the libel, while the opposition could not recruit any to appear, Poe won this case.[506]

Poe's first editorial job started in August of 1835, when he worked part-time for the *Southern Literary Messenger*, a periodical run by Thomas Willis White in Richmond. It became full-time in November of that year. While Poe was the *de facto* editor-in-chief, the December 1835 issue introduced him thus: "the paper is now under the conduct of the Proprietor, assisted by a gentleman of distinguished literary talents…"

---

504   Sidney Moss. *Poe's Literary Battles: The Critic in the Context of His Literary Milieu*. (Durham: Duke University Press, 1963), 238.
505   Dwight Thomas and David K. Jackson. *The Poe Log: A Documentary Life of Edgar Allan Poe*. (Boston: G. K. Hall, 1987), 641.
506   Hutchisson, *Poe*, 195-200.

This notice sounds like it was written by Poe himself, as the note adds, "we hope to be pardoned for singling out the name of M. EDGAR A. POE," flattering him as possessing "imagination, and… humorous, delicate satire." Then it explains that "decorum" forbids them from "specifying other names," with the hope that "'by their fruits ye shall know them.'"[507] If Poe was writing the bulk of the articles in this paper, there were no "other names" he could have named, but his own, and if this note is written in a satirical light, then he expresses a hope that readers will recognize the extent of his contributions. Thus, Poe did not merely proofread this periodical, but also composed the bulk of it at this early stage of his career. From this point of view, it is a lot easier to see why Poe was so frustrated with the proprietors of these magazines, who paid him a tiny portion of the profits, while he was doing the bulk of the work, and had to disguise his authorship behind unsigned articles. "Having started out as a printer," White "had no training in writing, editing, or marketing and advertising" that was needed to have penned the content himself.[508] Poe left this periodical at the end of 1836, and ran a retirement notice in the January 1837 issue. The January 1838, Vol. IV, No. 1 issue of *Southern* has an introduction called, "The New Year," which, unlike Poe's, while it is verbose, fails to catch the reader's attention and to paint concrete pictures. The prose in 1838 is less dense and includes many repetitions, wherein the author cycles around a point without clearly articulating it. Here is an example from the middle of the second paragraph: "Some useful and elegant talent has been called into exercise, nay, it may be said, has been created; since such is the power of exercise over the faculties, that to afford an attractive field for their exertion is in a great degree to create them."[509] What is this sentence trying to communicate? Why would exertion "create" "talent"? Something is missing from this sentence, and yet something also needs to be deleted. If an editor does so much editing that the linguistic density of a work changes, he might as well have written it. Poe explained his perception of White and his own employment for *Southern* in a letter from Philadelphia, addressed to his cousin William

507   Thomas Willis White. "Publisher's Notice." *Southern Literary Messenger: Devoted to Every Department of Literature and the Fine Arts*. Vol. II, No. 1. (Richmond: December 1835. T. W. White, 1836. Web), 1.
508   Hutchisson, *Poe,* 47.
509   Thomas Willis White. "The New Year." *Southern Literary Messenger: Devoted to Every Department of Literature and the Fine Arts*. Vol. IV, No. 1. (Richmond: January 1838. Making of America Journal Articles. Web), 1.

Poe, on August 14, 1840: "…The drudgery was excessive; the salary was contemptible… my best energies were wasted in the service of an illiterate and vulgar, although well-meaning man, who had neither the capacity to appreciate my labors, nor the will to reward them." Poe began this paragraph by saying that he is attaching the "Prospectus of my contemplated Magazine."[510] The Magazine Poe is soliciting money for from his cousin is *The Penn*. Poe's insistence that White was "illiterate" should be taken at face-value, as Poe seldom exaggerated in his reviews.

Poe titled his letter of solicitation for funding, "Prospectus of *The Penn Magazine*: A Monthly Literary Journal, to be Edited and Published in the City of Philadelphia," and dated it 1840. He began it as an address to the "public." He then announced that after he "resigned" from *The Southern Literary Messenger*, he "always" had it in "view" to establish the proposed *Magazine*. He proposes the venture as an oppositional force not only to his former employer but also to the entire puffing "critical" establishment, and it reads more like a manifesto for honest literary criticism, rather than like a marketing tool to actually obtain funding for a new business. Based on the experiences Melville, Dickens and others had with reviewers, the puffed reviews went hand-in-hand with pricy advertisements, and created the bulk of the profits for periodicals; thus, Poe was setting himself up for failure in this marketplace if he insisted on running honest reviews, as the publishers who needed to market their books would have preferred dishonest, paid-for puffery. Poe then explains that a journal of his own is the only way for a writer or editor to achieve "permanent influence" because it allows for the establishment of "continuous, definite character, and a marked certainty of purpose," a feat that is "only attainable where one mind alone has the general direction of the undertaking… in founding a Magazine of my own lies my sole chance of carrying out to completion whatever peculiar intentions I may have entertained." This echoes Virginia Woolf's hope for a room of her own, and is a clear expression of the yearning all of these author-publishers had for achieving ambitious "intentions." These intentions were political, cultural or literary, and they went beyond the limits of the formulaic establishment they previously attempted to join via the regular routes available to authors and editors. In the following long paragraph, Poe turned more narrowly to

---

510   Edgar Allan Poe. *The Complete Works of Edgar Allan Poe, Volume 17: Poe and His Friends: Letters Relating to Poe*. James Albert Harrison, Ed. (New York: Thomas Y. Crowell & Company, 1902. Web), 55.

his intention to publish "Critical Notices of new books" with the same "trait of severity in so much only as the calmest yet sternest sense of justice will permit." He proceeds to respond to the thought he assumes the readers of his earlier harsh reviews had: "Some years since elapsed may have mellowed down the petulance without interfering with the rigor of the critic. Most surely they have not yet taught him to read through the medium of a publisher's will, nor convinced him that the interests of letters are unallied with the interests of truth." He repeats synonyms of "truth" several times, stressing that he will offer "honest and a fearless opinion." A portion of this tirade has to be offered at length because it expresses many key points that Poe did not stress as eloquently elsewhere. He promised to offer:

> ...absolutely independent criticism... guiding itself only by the purest rules of art... holding itself aloof from all personal bias; acknowledging no fear save that of outraging the right; yielding no point either to the vanity of the author, or to the assumptions of antique prejudice, or to the involute and anonymous cant of the Quarterlies, or to the arrogance of those organized *cliques* which, hanging like nightmares upon American literature, manufacture, at the nod of our principal booksellers, a pseudo-public-opinion by wholesale.[511]

He is clearly referring to Harper's rejection of him as an author because he would not sufficiently puff all of his reviews of their books as the other author-critics did in exchange for publication in Harper or the placement of paid Harper ads in their journals, as I discussed at-length in the Harper section. While the problem was obvious to Poe, apparently, he could not find many readers in his own time who understood what he was implying or cared to change it.

Poe must have hoped that he would find better employment when he "retired" from *Southern*, but he was blacklisted due to his series of negative reviews and could not publish any work or find editorial employment under his own name between his departure in February 1837 and May 1839. When he was most desperate for money, he took on the more profitable job of ghostwriting. In 1838, he ghostwrote "a piece of hackwork for Thomas Wyatt, a British professor and lecturer," called *The Conchologist's First Book*. Hutchisson explains that Poe created this geology textbook by plagiarizing a similar book that was released five

---

511   Ibid., 621-3.

years earlier, with only the introduction and some descriptions being Poe's original work. Poe's response upon being accused of plagiarism was that "all such books were pastiche of common knowledge" and he threatened the accusers with legal action.[512] Previously to sliding into hiring him as a ghost writer, the same Baltimore magazine purchased "Ligeia" for $10. They also purchased some of his poems. He must have been considerably better paid for the ghostwriting, but not well enough to have spent more than a minor amount of time on researching the subject before briskly pulling the materials together. Poe was outraged at all of the plagiarism that was going on around him, which made a request for ghostwriting so commonplace. Given this climate, he was even more outraged that critics were focusing on outing him as a plagiarist. He made it his mission to prove that many financially-successful writers were also relying on plagiarism and ghostwriting. But this proved to be an extremely difficult prospect as most of them were not copying a singular geological book, but rather were mimicking and stealing from poetry that frequently leaned on similar themes and linguistic devices.

In 1839, Poe obtained a part-time editorial position for William Evans Burton's Philadelphia magazine at $10 a week for 10 hours of work. Burton had attained his wealth from acting, and this afforded him the publication of two plays and some sketches, and the acquisition of four theatres, in which he frequently acted himself. These theaters made him an actor-proprietor. He also became an author-publisher when he started his *Burton's Gentleman's Magazine*. In fact, since Burton contributed some of his own pieces to this magazine, he would be a candidate for this study of author-publishers, but his work has not been seriously critically recognized and he never became a popular writer, so his efforts were not influential enough to stand side-by-side with Poe. Poe wrote to the poet, Philip Pendleton Cooke, that he should "not think of subscribing" to *Burton's* because the magazine was full of "twaddle of other people." Poe concluded this note with the hope that he could one day obtain his own periodical, as he frequently did across his career as an editor for other periodicals.[513] Poe increased circulation of *Burton's* in part by promising extraordinary payments to writers of $100 to $1,000. It's possible that Poe was ghostwriting the contents of

---

512   Hutchisson, *Poe*, 73.
513   John Ward Ostrom, Ed. *The Letters of Edgar Allan Poe*. 2 vols. (1948). (New York: Gordian, 1966), Vol I, 118.

the magazine primarily himself, and only made these advertisements of high payments to attract subscribers from among authors who hoped to understand what was required of them to win such large sums for their work. Burton used the profits from Poe's sales successes to begin construction on the National Theatre on Chestnut Street near Ninth in May of 1840, instead of offering Poe a raise for his efforts. This was also the month when Burton fired Poe. In the months leading up to the break, Burton wrote a biting review of Poe's *The Narrative of Arthur Gordon Pym*, which featured some ciphers in maps and hieroglyphs that could be translated with the help of Ethiopian and Arabic letters. Poe had not put his name on this novel, but probably told his boss of his authorship. Burton was also constantly asking Poe to be more positive in his own reviews of other writers. Burton was further suggesting that Poe's negativity reflected his unhealthy state of mind.

Burton was not alone in badgering Poe to write positive reviews, as this was a common propagandistic tactic called "puffing" that unduly praised low-brow literature, initially only by innately American writers (as a kind of nationalist campaign), though it was later applied to all nationalities in a "mutual admiration society."[514] Poe was an oddity for his time because there were few other regular professional review writers, as most reviews were the short, unsigned work of a publication's primary general editor: "laudatory if the publisher advertised or had influence, libelous if someone on the staff, or some favored outsider, disliked the author or the publisher." There were few advertisements being printed in the early 1840s, but this rate grew rapidly after this point, as did inflated, favorable review in exchange for these ads. Bliss Perry called the relationship between advertisements and reviews the "Silent Bargain." Longfellow was at the center of this controversy after the *Boston Daily Evening Traveller* printed a highly negative notice on his *Hiawatha* on November 13, 1855, and then printed an article called, "Attempt to Coerce the Press," with a reproduced letter from Ticknor and Fields asking for them to send a "bill of all charges against us" and threating to withhold future advertising. This debate also stretched into the realm of critics who were being rewarded for positive reviews by the very publishers that were later convinced to release books or articles by the critics themselves. Meanwhile, at the start of the 1840s, publishers started sending out around 150-250 copies for review to the reviewing publications, a number that totaled around 10% of the first

514 Hutchisson, *Poe*, 59.

printings. Many of the receiving, over-worked editors copied reviews from other publications to save time on writing original content.[515] In other words, the odds of a publisher breaking even on a great book that was submitted without parallel advertising or bribery was so slim that it led to the bankruptcy of many of the publishers in this study. Authors like Poe, who insisted on criticizing all books solely based on their merit, and were not afraid to call bad books "trash" were negatively reviewed, even if their work had superior merit.

In part to fund his new theatre, Burton sold *Burton's* to George Rex Graham, the publisher of *The Casket* periodical, for $3,500; this dollar amount matched the number of subscribers. Poe assumed he would be fired by the new owner, and openly circulated a prospectus for his own magazine, *The Penn*. On a side note, a journal called the *Pennsylvanian* had published a positive review of Poe in 1841, so it is a bit odd that he named his own journal *The Penn*, considering his criticism of plagiarism. While at the start of Benjamin Franklin's printing career, there were only one or two major printers per colony, competition had multiplied by Poe's peak of activity. There was also the *Pennsylvania Inquirer*, and at least six papers that started with Philadelphia, including the *Philadelphia Daily Standard*. Burton responded to Poe's pitch for *The Penn Magazine* by immediately firing Poe. He then attempted to collect from Poe a $100 debt he said Poe had previously borrowed, a demand that Poe refused.

Poe failed to secure financing or backings for *The Penn*, though he kept trying until his final days. For example, in 1843, Poe renamed this journal project, *Stylus*. For this new rebirth of the journal, Poe found the editor of the *Saturday Museum*, Thomas C. Clarke, who expressed some interest in becoming Poe's "partner in the enterprise." But, shortly after this success, Poe traveled on his infamous journey to Washington DC to meet with the President, and was so embarrassed or disoriented by what took place there that he put aside his plans for *Stylus*.[516] Then, in 1845, Poe wrote a letter to Charles Anthon, a professor at Columbia University, and early sponsor of *Southern Literary Messenger*, Poe's first place of editorial employment, to solicit a financial contribution to the *Stylus*, and to ask if Anthon could inquirer with his own publisher, Harper's, regarding if they would be interested in tak-

---

515 Chavrat, *Profession*, 172-85.
516 Peter Ackroyd. *Poe: A Life Cut Short: Ackroyd's Brief Lives*. (New York: Nan A. Talese: Doubleday, 2008), 100-4.

ing on his magazine. Harper's replied that they could not work with Poe because they had received "complaints" about him.[517] Thus, Poe winded up back at *Burton's*, which soon merged with Graham's other periodical and became known as *Graham's Magazine*, after the purchase was finalized in October and Graham was now in charge. In less than two years, "by February 1842, when Poe resigned the editorship, the magazine's circulation was forty thousand, making it one of the three or four most successful and important periodicals in American publishing history. Poe made George Graham a very rich man, but he reaped little in return." Poe's young wife, Virginia, was diagnosed with tuberculosis in January of 1842, so his resignation might have coincided with this news. Virginia died five years later on January 30, 1847. Back in 1842, Poe's salary had risen by $300 from what he made at *Burton's* and he now had an assistant editor to take care of some busy work, but this was still a tiny portion of what Graham was reaping and paying authors.[518] Seeing the success he was blooming for the owners wherever he went must have fueled Poe's dreams of making a similar profit if he had a share in the periodical business.

After terminating his employment with *Graham's*, Poe contributed articles to the *New York Evening Mirror* newspaper for a couple of years before he convinced its owner, N. P. Willis, to give him an assistant editor position for $750 per year.

Three years after meeting Dickens, in 1845, Poe started contributing to the *Broadway Journal,* and became its assistant editor under Charles F. Briggs. Only a month later, in February, Poe became a coeditor. Poe was paid a salary and a third of the profits, a three-way split between Briggs, the publisher, and Poe. Poe bought out Briggs' share and became the sole editor in July. He borrowed the money for the purchase "from Horace Greeley, Chivers…, Fitz-Greene Halleck…, and Griswold." Hutchisson and other biographers have argued that thus Poe achieved "his lifelong dream of owning and publishing a literary monthly."[519]

Similarly to Dickens, Poe at one point applied for a political position. But, Poe's application began when he received a letter from Frederick W. Thomas, novelist, poet, and a temporary clerk in the Department of the Treasury. Thomas' letter referred to plenty of open gov-

---
517   Thomas, *Poe,* 476.
518   Hutchisson, *Poe,* 108-9.
519   Ibid., 176.

ernment jobs that pay "$1500 per year." Poe took this as a solicitation, and was ready to take the next train to Washington DC, but Frederick immediately objected that there weren't enough jobs at the moment and that Poe should hold off on this trip. Thomas did encourage Poe that President John Tyler's son, Rob Tyler, liked Poe's poetry. So, Poe was outraged when after applying, he received news that he would not be appointed. Then, Poe insisted on appealing the rejection to the President, and Thomas obliged by setting up an appointment. According to accounts, this trip was a disaster because Poe got drunk and sick, and got into arguments. Hearing of this, Thomas cancelled the appointment with the President, and put Poe on a train back to Philadelphia. The same events could be interpreted as a malicious attack on Poe, if he was accosted by harassing people that pulled him into arguments, and was given tainted drinks or food that kept him ill for days. It is hardly excusable that Thomas asked Poe to spend the money on the trip and hotel in Washington only to be sent back without being allowed to make his appeal.[520] Scathing myths of this sort frequently appear to be true because they are frequently repeated, and the person being accused has failed to make a strong argument for their innocence.

The events that led to Poe's death began in 1849, when Elmira accepted Poe's marriage proposal on September 22. One of the reasons critics have suggested that Poe's death was a suicide is because a letter survived that he sent to his sister Annie on November 16, 1848, when he felt that he would not succeed in winning Helen's hand in marriage, and described how he had taken an ounce of laudanum from despair.[521] Laudanum, the purgative opiate, appeared in this study before as the drug Byron was given by his physicians. Perhaps, Poe also received laudanum from physicians who might have explained that he needed this treatment because of his drinking or irrational behavior. But, his letter to his sister specifies that he used it as a poison with the intention to harm himself.

But, to pick up with the events that led to Poe's death, on September 27, 1849, Poe left Richmond for New York on a Baltimore steamer, with an added stop in Philadelphia, all to edit "poems of a Philadelphia piano manufacturer's wife for one hundred dollars." He supposedly arrived in Baltimore on the 28th, and was found at the Gunner's Hall tavern on October 3 by a "young printer named Joseph W. Walker."

---

520   Ibid., 131-4.
521   Ostrom, *Letters*, Vol. 2, 401-2.

Poe's discovery by a printer seems like an odd coincidence in the context of this study. The printer sent a note to Poe's friend, Joseph Evans Snodgrass, who found Poe in the specified spot. Snodgrass then took Poe to the Washington College hospital.

Also curiously, the Gunner's Hall tavern was being used as a "polling place for the Fourth Ward" on that day.[522] Critics have suggested that Poe had been paid for assisting with election fraud. One proposed payment is the liquor that Poe apparently consumed in a quantity that put him in the stupor in which Snodgrass found him. In contrast to the theory that Poe was assisting electoral corruption, other sources suggest that he attempted to stop such fraud. Hutchisson concludes that Poe must have been the "victim of political violence,"[523] perhaps because he attempted to intervene when he saw corruption, just as he did when he saw plagiarism.

Similarly to Byron's case, the doctor, John J. Moran, and others who were around Poe when he died published accounts of Poe's final days, which all contradict each other, and thereby suggest a conspiracy to hide the truth. Also in parallel with Byron's death, Poe was constantly attended by physicians in his last three days of life at the Washington College hospital. The main difference between Poe and Byron's demise is that Dr. Moran's account disagrees with non- physicians that saw Poe's decline. Dr. Moran is more measured and logical, while Byron's doctors were at the root of his continued illness. Dr. Moral argued that Poe did not die of "any kind of intoxicating drink."[524] On the death certificate, Moran listed the cause of death as "congestion of the brain." The autopsy and diagnosis performed by a staff surgeon and published in the *Baltimore Sun* on October 1849 added that Poe was suffering from "cerebral inflammation, or encephalitis, brought on by exposure."[525]

The Beale Treasure and a Desperate Publisher

The mystery surrounding Poe's death has become part of his persona as a popular classical author. The contradictions and anomalies

---

522   Hutchisson, *Poe,* 244-5.
523   Ibid., 244-6.
524   John J. Moran. *A Defense of Edgar Allan Poe.* (Washington, DC: Boogher, 1885; rpt., New York: AMS, 1966), 18.
525   Hutchisson, *Poe,* 247.

about Poe's end fit Poe's path, as if they are deliberate plot devices in one of Poe's short stories. Unlike most of the other author-publishers in this study, Poe was not always truthful, bending the narrative to fit his ends. More than others, he blurred the line between art and commercial ambition. Poe told lies about himself and others because he believed that fiction was an honorable profession. Fooling and amusing readers was his livelihood. To make sense of him as an author-publisher, we have to return to his work on coded and puzzling messages.

The strange case of the Beale fortune hunters explains the Gold Rush quality of the American publishing marketplace. Unlike early European publishers and printers who viewed this profession as an arduous trade that could sustain a livelihood, but was hardly the path towards extraordinary riches, American publishers saw it as something that could generate a fortune if only the publisher was crafty enough. Publishing gimmicks might have been invented in Britain, but they took on unbelievable dimensions in America. One of the reasons hoaxes and other oddities were more prevalent in America was because, in the first centuries after its founding, the American book market was extremely small, and only printers who worked for state governments made a regular profit; this was the way Benjamin Franklin scraped by in between his other publishing pursuits. In the eighteenth century, there were so few printers that nearly anybody that could purchase a printer and had a brief apprenticeship in the trade was guaranteed a government contract. Then, in the nineteenth century, the population was growing, but the number of people who wanted to be printers and publishers started outgrowing the demand for books. This was the period when some of the best canonical, American writers blossomed, as they thrived in an environment where they had to overcome great odds.

One popularly known literary marketing scheme is, *The Beale Papers: Containing Authentic Statements Regarding the Treasure Buried in 1819 and 1821 near Bufords, in Bedford County, Virginia, and Which Has Never Been Recovered. Price Fifty Cents*. It alleges that a treasure was buried by a man named Thomas J. Beale. The cypher guides to the treasure's location were supposedly left with an innkeeper, named Robert Morriss, who gave them to a friend. Sixty years then went by before this friend, in theory, published the *Papers*. In 2015, Travel Channel's *Expedition Unknown*, Season 1, Episode 7 "Code to Gold," an archeologist, Josh Gates, gave the ciphers from this book to an expert at the NSA, who wrote a computer program to decrypt and evaluate the ciphers. The NSA programmer put the first and the third ciphers through the resulting decryption program. He discovered that there was a section of the text that had a series of repeating letters at the start of the alphabet. The NSA expert concluded that the publisher must have gotten tired and simply repeated those same letters, instead of coming up with random number combinations. Thus, these cyphers were fictional, and could never be cracked. These mistakes meant that if somebody was really trying to solve the cyphers by counting words in a book, they would not have understood the rest of the message after the first mis-numbering. The only way for anybody to have solved this puzzle was if "the person that created the cipher was also" the publisher of the "hoax." In other words, this publication was a marketing ploy for the publishing agency. It was giving hope to readers that if they could track down the first and the second documents used for the cipher; then, they would find a hidden treasure worth millions in gold, silver and jewels. The promise of quick riches is the reason so many people lose money on lotteries and casinos. So, this is hardly a noble way to convince readers to buy your book. The guilty publisher's name was James B. Ward. This is a great example of the length some publishers have gone to for success in this difficult business. And while this myth still lives with us, "unsolved," Ward failed to gain fame and sufficient profits from publishing the pamphlet in question. There is no record of any of Ward's other publications.

One reason critics have concluded that the cipher of the Beale treasure was penned by Poe was because he ran a series of popular cryptographs or ciphers, and word-puzzles as editor of *Graham's*. Earlier in his editing career, back in 1836 at *Southern Literary Messenger*, Poe solicited ciphers from readers, and then successfully solved them, a task that would have been easier if Poe was writing these ciphers himself and attributing them to fictional contributors. One of the reasons it is likely that Poe wrote these ciphers is because they are formulaically similar to each other. Most of them are "simple substitution ciphers, in which a different alphabetical order (called litoreia) or series of numbers corresponded to letters was employed."[526] It is also telling that when Poe ran a contest offering a year's subscription to anybody who could solve his cipher, he withdrew the offer after too many submis-

---

526   Ibid., 112.

sions, probably because one managed to guess correctly.[527] Poe once explained in an article in the July 1841 issue of *Graham's*, "A Few Words on Secret Writing," that the writers of the ciphers frequently broke with the "limits defined in the beginning" as, "Foreign languages were employed. Words and sentences were run together without interval. Several alphabets were used in the same cipher."[528] According to the NSA analyst, who created a computer program to test the substitution ciphers used in the *The Beale Papers*, a cipher that switches codes or makes any mistakes whatsoever in its pattern cannot be solved by anybody other than the cipher maker. Thus, if a writer used a language Poe did not know, did not separate words to make them more palatable, or mixed alphabets, Poe would never have solved these unless he was their originator. *The Beale Papers* were printed by Virginia Book and Job Print, operated by an obscure publisher, James B. Ward, in 1885. This is the only publication that Ward released successfully, and this mystery has led critics to theorize that this was one of Poe's manuscripts released after his death by somebody that retained his cipher. Poe had also succeeded in several mimicry tricks that were later attributed to him, but which he wrote under assumed names. For example, he wrote *The Journal of Julius Rodman: Being an Account of the First Passage across the Rocky Mountains of North American ever Achieved by Civilized Man*, based on close research of Lewis and Clark's journey as well as several other studies. This fictitious work even managed to fool a "United States Senate aide into believing it to be an actual historical document, since a paragraph from the book was quoted in an 1840 report to the Congress on the Oregon Territory."[529]

Poe has managed to convince the US Senate that the name of the first European explorer across the Rocky Mountains was Julius Rodman in 1840, and not Sir Alexander MacKenzie in 1793. Given these types of deceptions, it would not even be a conspiracy theory to propose that Poe might not have died in 1849, but lived on through 1885, long enough to publish the *Beale Papers* to report his continued existence.

---

527   Ibid., 113.
528   Edgar Allan Poe. "A Few Words on Secret Writing." *Graham's Magazine*. (July 1841. 33-38. Edgar Allan Poe Society of Baltimore. Retrieved: 24 April 2016. Web), 34.
529   Hutchisson, *Poe*, 84.

CHAPTER 10

The Catastrophic Bankruptcy of Mark Twain's Charles L. Webster and Co. Venture

The truth is, that when a Library expels a book of mine and leaves an unexpurgated Bible around where unprotected youth and age can get hold of it, the deep unconscious irony of it delights me and doesn't anger me.
—Mark Twain, 1907

I read about Mark Twain's publishing company over a decade in his biography, when I yearned to discover how previous American writers have juggled popular and critical success. Twain's life is a series of quintessential struggles to succeed despite an impoverished background in America. He became a steamboat captain with the same vigor as he applied to venture capitalism and publishing. But he might have been more fiscally successful in the short-run on a steamboat salary or when he married a wealthy woman than when he invested in new technology or in his own innovative writings. Meanwhile, his writings have lived on for over a century past his death, and are only accruing cultural and fiscal value in the long-term.

Half of Mark Twain's siblings died of poverty-related diseases, and only by a miracle of will did he manage to stay alive. With the help of this survival instinct, Twain left school when his father died in 1847, at twelve, and began working as an errand boy and apprentice typesetter for Henry La Cossitt's *Hannibal Gazette*. Twain described what it was like to be an apprentice in dictation on Thursday, March 29, 1906, writing that the position offered "board and clothes, but no money. The clothes consisted of two suits a year, but one of the suits always failed to materialize and the other suit was not purchased as long as Mr. Ament's old clothes held out."[530] From there, Twain, or Samuel L. Clemens, as he was known before he changed his name, worked as an apprentice for a series of publishing enterprises including Joseph P. Ament's *Missouri Courier*, and Orion's *Western Union*. Then he was a typesetter for a string of publications across the map, in New York, Philadelphia, and other places. Twain published his first signed work in the *Western Union*, "A Gallant Fireman," when he was only sixteen.

He worked very hard to establish a newspaper typesetting, editing or reporting career for himself up until 1857. At this point, this path plateaued, as he was struggling to find a way to move ahead in the publishing business. Thus, in 1857, he started training with Horace E. Bixby on the *Paul Jones* steamboat to become a Mississippi River pilot. He was licensed to pilot two years later, and served on the river for two years before he joined the Civil War on the Confederacy side. Military service was not for him, so he started prospecting for silver. Digging for

---

[530] Mark Twain. *Autobiography of Mark Twain: The Complete and Authoritative Edition*. Volume 1. Harriet Elinor Smith, Ed. (Berkeley: University of California Press, 2010), 455

riches did not work either. So, Clemens returned to what worked for him since childhood and became a local reporter for the *Territorial Enterprise* in 1862. He switched around between different papers, including the *Morning Call* in San Francisco. He had escaped to California after being nearly convicted on charges of dueling in Nevada.

Clemens described his one dueling experience in a sarcastic, humorous dictation made on Friday, January 19, 1906, in a segment called, "About Dueling." According to Clemens, after struggling to gain a promotion up from the post of city editor for over two years, he was temporarily promoted to chief editor of Mr. Goodman's Virginia City *Enterprise* during a trip the chief took to San Francisco for a meeting that occupied a number of the region's editors. In addition to editing the paper, the chief's primary job was writing a daily, editorial article. On on April 22, 1864, Clemens decided to write his editorial on Shakespeare's birthday, which fell on the following day. He began this project by copying the encyclopedia, but got bored and inserted a number of insults at a rival editor of the Virginia *Union*, Mr. Laird, calling "him a horse-thief." Then, due to peer-pressure from his colleagues at the paper, Clemens challenged Mr. Laird to a duel. Because this story is written sarcastically, it is difficult to gather from it if Clemens wanted to engage in a duel, or why he felt compelled to send the challenge after he was the one who insulted Mr. Laird, and there was no retaliation in kind back at him. Clemens did not stop at the first challenge, but kept pestering the rival editor. When failing to consent became a matter of honor, Laird accepted. They met at 5am on the following morning in a barn. The only reason they did not exchange shots was because Clemens' friend, Steve, shot the head off a sparrow that flew in just before Mr. Laird arrived, and they insinuated that Clemens was such a great shot that he had managed to shoot the head off himself from a great distance. Laird was supposedly scared off by this and left without fighting. But the news of the attempt spread and was enough for Judge North to decide that the incident could be used as an example to demonstrate a new anti-dueling law that was just enacted. Thus, Clemens and his second, Steve, were advised that they had to leave the Territory or suffer a sentence of two years imprisonment. Curiously, on the day they left, Clemens received a challenge from another person he offended in his writings as editor, Mr. Cutler, but Steve dissuaded him from this new fight.[531] This is a great example of how

---

531   Ibid., 296-8.

Clemens always prided himself in telling the truth about corruption and evil wherever he saw it, even at the risk of losing his life in a duel. He fought for the editor's chair not for money or fame. He wanted the ability to offer radical criticism with his pen and to fight against the censoring forces that edited these comments out. Only the leader or owner of a periodical or a press had the power to say the truth about evil at the highest levels of power. So, Clemens must have wanted to start his own publishing company to be able to have a similar right to write what he felt was moral and just and to criticize the flaws he saw in the society around him. Such radicalism was outside the reach of contracted authors, who were being edited and controlled by the preferences of a publishing company with corrupted interests.

While he was writing for a couple of other papers, he published "Jim Smiley and His Jumping Frog" in the *Saturday Press*. The acceptance of this little story was so encouraging that Twain wrote a full book version of it, *The Celebrated Jumping Frog of Calvareras County, and Other Sketches*, for which he had difficulty finding a publisher until, in 1867, he asked Charles Henry Webb to create a new imprint under the umbrella of the then three-years-old American News Company.

Charles Henry Webb is a full-fledged author-publisher, as he and his partner Bret Harte had founded *The Californian* newspaper in 1864, and he had published a dozen of his own books in different genres. He also wrote numerous newspaper articles before starting the imprint with Twain. The majority of Webb's writings were satires of society morals and popular books, including his parody of Charles Reade's *Griffith Guant* in a book he titled, *Liffith Lank, or Lunacy* (1867), and another parody of Augusta Evans Wilson's *St. Elmo* in his interpretation of the tale, *St. Twelmo, or the Cuneiform Cyclopedist of Chattanooga* (1868). Thus, Webb was radical in his opinions. Perhaps, even more so than Twain, Webb had something to say that would have been censored if he approached a popular publisher.

Webb's partner in *The Californian*, Bret Harte, served as one of Twain's early mentors and solicited Twain's work for *The Californian* in the role as its editor in the fall of 1864. Harte also published satires of works such as Doyle's Sherlock Holmes, "The Stolen Cigar Case" in *Pearson's Magazine*. A section from the middle of this satire sounds a lot like Byron's infamous satire on the King. Harte has Hemlock Jones explain to his physician assistant the various criminal cases he had been laboring over in his absence: "Mere trifles—nothing to speak of. The

Prince Kapoli has been here to get my advice regarding the disappearance of certain rubies from the Kremlin; the Rajah of Pootibad, after vainly beheading his entire bodyguard, has been obliged to seek my assistance to recover a jeweled sword. The Grand Duchess of Pretzel-Brauntswig is desirous of discovering where her husband was on the night of the 14th of February, and last night"—he lowered his voice slightly—"a lodger in this very house, meeting me on the stairs, wanted to know 'Why they don't answer his bell.'" Harte signed this piece as A. C—N D—LE, to stress that Doyle was the real author of this new adventure, and had simply left typos in the characters' names.[532] Twain gave Harte some money before he left the States for an embassy appointment in Europe. Harte never paid him back and abandoned his family back in America. These discourtesies left Twain with many angry words and ended their friendship.

Meanwhile, in 1867, the American News Company was already starting its meteoric growth, and before the end of the century it was the dominant magazine distributor in the country, inspiring an explosion of new periodical publishing ventures and then causing the bulk of these to go bankrupt along with it when it collapsed suddenly a century later in 1957, amidst antitrust lawsuits.

Being among the first to jump on the American News Company train meant that Twain's first release was a success and it helped him climb up in society, where he met the socialite he later married in 1870, Olivia (Livy) Langdon. Proposing to the daughter of a wealthy businessman suddenly opened opportunities for speculation for Twain, and he immediately showed how his passion for publishing overwhelmed his practical business sense. In 1869, with partial funding from Jervis Langdon, Twain bought a third of the interests in Buffalo's *Express* from Mr. Kinney for $25,000, selling it only two years later for $15,000. Twain surrendered this paper because he discovered that all this entity signified was the "privilege" to use stories from the Associated Press' collection.[533] In other words, the paper did not come with the reporters and editors required to create original content. It was an inflated shell and Twain fell for it because he did not have enough experience in business.

In an autobiographical sketch on Wednesday, February 21, 1906,

---

532   Otto Penzler. "The Stolen Cigar-Case." *The Big Book of Sherlock Holmes Stories*. (New York: Pantheon Books, 2015), 23-8.
533   Ibid., 364.

Mark Twain reminisced about the problems he had dealing with his publishers and why he started experimenting in self-publication. Twain describes that he asked for half of profits in royalties for his second book, *Roughing It* (1872). Twain explains that Mr. Langdon, the same man who had convinced him to buy the newspaper a couple of years earlier, now pressured him into signing the contract with the American Publishing Company without alternations. Langdon convinced him to rush through on terms unfavorable to Twain with help from a story from his own business background, wherein he said he lost millions because of delaying a deal that would have made all involved millions. Twain complains: "I followed that advice. It was thirty-five years ago, but it has kept me tired ever since," just as the railroad speculators in Langdon's "inspirational" story felt when they failed to sign.[534] In other words, Langdon told Twain the opposite of what a business adviser with Twain's interests in mind would have said. Twain tried to re-negotiate this contract afterwards with Elisha P. Bliss. Elisha was the secretary of the American Publishing Company between 1867-70 and 1871-73, and also its president in 1870 and 1873-80. Bliss held firm, and refused Twain's request for him to receive half of the profits. Twain explains that Bliss had credited him with saving his publishing house with the profitable release of *The Innocents Abroad* (1869). This single book brought the American Publishing Company from the brink of bankruptcy, so that they cleared their debt and their stocks became highly valuable. Despite these riches, they only paid Twain 5% royalties, or a "fifth of the book's profit."[535] While Bliss did not bend to Twain's demand for half royalties, he did raise Twain's royalties after this negotiation to 7.5% of the retail price for Twain's next two books. Twain's share then went up to 10% for the following two books. Only after returning from a trip to Europe in 1879 was Twain disgruntled enough to insist on "half profits above the cost of manufacture" for *A Tramp Abroad*. Amazingly, Bliss now changed his tactics. Bliss agreed to give Twain the 50% he had been pushing for over the years, but only if Twain left the American Publishing Company for a new publishing venture Bliss proposed starting. Twain agreed. Without discussing it with Twain, Bliss took the new publishing venture contract he thus signed with Twain back to the Company's Board of Directors and proposed selling Twain's rights to them for 75% of profits above manufac-

---

534   Ibid., 370.
535   Ibid., 371.

ture. Thus, Twain ended up back with the Company (without Twain's consent). Shortly thereafter, Bliss died. The process of settling Bliss' accounts finally made it clear to Twain that Bliss had been "robbing" him since 1872.

Twain was so upset at learning that he had been making such a small share compared with what the publisher was pocketing that he left the Company for good, bringing his next book, *The Prince and the Pauper* (1881), to J. R. Osgood. While Twain compliments Osgood for being "loveliest man in the world," he objects that he was an "incapable publisher" because he only made him $17,000 in profits. In an attempt to achieve a higher profit, Twain requested: "I should prefer that he make the book [for *Old Times on the Mississippi* (1876)] at my expense and sell it at a royalty to be paid by me to him. When he had finished making the plates and printing and binding the first edition, these industries of his had cost me fifty-six thousand dollars... my profit on the book was only thirty thousand dollars..."[536]

He paid $56,000 to print a single edition of a small book over a century ago? This amount equals $1.3 million in today's buying power according to the CPI inflation calculator. Why would Twain have been willing to pay over a million to print and bind his book? Did he use golden binding? Even if he printed a million copies in that first run, it would have been a very high price to pay for *Old Times on the Mississippi*. In fact, Twain's dates seem to be off in this chronology. *Old Times on the Mississippi* is an autobiography published in 1876, long before *The Prince and the Pauper* was released, not after it. And why would Twain have expected that sales from an autobiography would be anywhere as high as his pop adventure fiction stories?

As with Poe, some details of Twain's memoirs have questionable truthfulness, as he embellishes the details to create sympathy or to puff up his status. The editor of his autobiography, Harriet Elinor Smith, points out several mistakes (if not lies) that Twain left. One of these is that Twain claims that competing publishers were offering him 50% royalties. But, the correspondences with other publishers from this period show that he was never offered more than 10% in royalties. Smith also confirms that Twain engaged in "slight shuffling" the order of his published books. Oddly enough, Smith argues that it was not the president of the Company, Elisha, who left the Company in 1879 over Twain's book, but rather his son, Francis Bliss, then Treasurer of the

---

536   Ibid., 372.

Company. Francis started his own subscription publishing house to release Twain's *A Tramp Abroad* for 50% of gross profits. With terms like this, it is little wonder that Francis' new firm "did not thrive" and later that same year, while "the book was in production," Clemens consented to transferring the rights to the Company. Elisha, the president, was the winner of this transfer, as half of the Company's "entire profits for 3 years" came from this title, as it took them out of debt.[537] Twain argued that one of his first books with the Company saved it from failure, and yet here is the same argument but made about one of his last books with them. The holes and glitches in the narrative of Twain's struggle with his publishers can be simply the result of his absentmindedness. It is still obvious that the publishers Twain worked with took advantage of him, and benefited from their deals while Twain was constantly manipulated into losing or failing to win a fair share of the profits.

According to Harriet Smith, Osgood initially solicited a book from Twain in 1872, when Twain was under an exclusive contract with the Company. Smith omits the crucial real first publication Twain did with Osgood, *Old Times on the Mississippi* in 1876, this being the fragment of *Life on the Mississippi* he'd release with Osgood seven years later. Only after this initial Twain-sponsored release, was Osgood in a position to release his *A True Story, and the Recent Carnival of Crime* in 1877. They then worked together on *The Prince and the Pauper* in 1881, *The Stolen White Elephant, Etc.* in 1882, and *Life on the Mississippi* in 1883. For the latter book, Twain and Osgood took a trip along the Mississippi River together.[538] Smith points out that in a letter to Osgood in 1883, Twain had direr statistics on the sales of his self-publications with Osgood, wherein *The Prince and the Pauper* and *Mississippi* were "the only books of mine which have ever failed. The first failure was not unbearable—but this second one is so nearly so that it is not a calming subject for me to talk about. I am out $50,000 on this last book—that is to say, the sale which should have been 80,000… is only 30,000."[539] Osgood's accounts calculate that plates, paper and binding for *Life on the Mississippi* cost $39,458.78 in March 1884, and Twain was paying "the cost of renting Osgood's New York office during this period." Smith con-

---

537   Ibid., 596-7.
538   Ibid., 597.
539   Mark Twain. *Mark Twain's Letters to His Publishers, 1867-1894*. Hamlin Hill, Ed. The Mark Twain Papers. (Berkeley and Los Angeles: University of California Press, 1967), "December 21, 1883", 164.

cludes that the $56,000 Twain mentioned in his autobiography might have included the office cost in addition to Osgood's recorded total. Twain makes it sound as if he made a profit after expenses of $30,000, but in the letter to Osgood, he more clearly explains that the book brought in $30,000, leaving him $26,000 in debt for the attempt.

A more factual sequence of events that pertain to Twain's association with Osgood is that in the middle of his dealings with the Company, Twain wrote an autobiography, which the Company probably refused to publish, so he offered to pay for printing it himself with Osgood at a great cost, and managed to see a relatively small profit, which meant that Osgood could use his share to pay for the printing of their second book together, *Prince*, without charging Twain in advance. As Smith explains in the introduction to *Autobiography of Mark Twain*, Clemens spent over a decade on writing his full autobiography at the end of his life, and penned over half a million words, if false starts and sketches that he later partially incorporated in the printed final version are counted. His will specified that researchers could not access the false starts and other drafts until a hundred years after his death. Researchers and teachers alike frequently talk about Twain's time as a steamboat pilot ahead of diving into his literary work, so he succeeded in achieving the notoriety for his life's story that he hoped for when he carefully crafted the narrative. The earlier, self-published autobiography was not simply a matter of vanity in his achievements, but also a brilliant self-marketing campaign, which he was willing to spend a lot of money on.

In the period when Twain was experimenting with alternative publications with Osgood, he allowed his father-in-law, Jervis, to donate funds for the building of a luxurious house for Twain's family in Hartford, Connecticut, which currently serves as a Twain museum. Twain then had the luxury to write full-time at this Hartford estate. And since he was committed to writing, he also wanted to see all of the resulting projects in print.

He might have published many other gems if he worked steadily and focused solely on his writing, but the speculative bug bit him again and he started investing in Paige typesetting machines in 1881, a venture he finally had to abandon during his 1894 bankruptcy. As Harriet Elinor Smith comments, by 1890, "his total investment had reached or exceeded $170,000, despite Paige's failure to produce a successful prototype," but Twain kept negotiating and investing in Paige beyond this point through 1894.[540] Just before Twain was forced to file for bankruptcy in 1894, he was fooled by Paige into believing that Paige had finally "perfected" the typesetter machine, so Twain invested still more into Paige. Twain reports that his total investment was now $150,000, much lower than Smith's estimate, perhaps because naming the actual number would have been too painful on Twain's pride. Twain concludes the section on Paige by adding: "if I had his nuts in a steel-trap I would shut out all human succor and watch that trap till he died."[541] Paige failed to show any progress from the start, but Twain just kept showering him with money until the bitter end. This says a lot about the type of character it takes to start a publishing business and then to run it into bankruptcy after a very long and expensive list of failures. The same obsessive nature is necessary for a great writer, as the best writers keep perfecting the craft across a lifetime of small failures, hoping to write the opus that will immortalize their name.

In 1884, when he was forty-nine, Twain had a midlife crisis and founded the Charles L. Webster and Co. publishing house. It was named after Twain's nephew by marriage, who was also its chief operating officer. Webster was paid $2,500 annually at the start of this employment, as well as a third of the profits up to $20,000. A tenth past this amount was added in 1885, due to the success of the first year. But, Webster could not keep up the same sales levels in the following three years, so that he was forced by Twain into "retirement." Webster also had to step aside due to his ill health in 1888.[542] Twain calls Webster the "clerk and manager" and the publishing house an "experiment outside of my proper line" in his autobiography. Twain was surprised when one of his first self-publications with Webster and Co., *Huckleberry Finn*, made $44,500 in profits in the first three months. This his first author-publisher project "was not altogether a failure."[543] Twain's motivation for founding this subscription publishing business was identical to Dickens' and most of these other ambitious writers: he was dissatisfied with all of his past publishers and hoped he would get a better deal if he self-published. Just as Twain hoped, his first two releases began with steady, high profits. The second of these was *Personal Memoirs of Ulysses S. Grant* (1885).

---

540   Twain, *Autobiography*, 101.
541   Ibid., 106.
542   Ibid., 486.
543   Ibid., 372.

One of the reasons for Webster and Co. later decline was that out of sympathy for other writers like himself, Twain offered extremely kind terms to writers. For example, he paid Grant's widow $200,000 in royalties shortly after Grant's death. In a section of the autobiographical collection, called "The Grant Dictations," with the sub-heading "About General Grant's Memoirs," Twain explains how he came to publish Grant's book as one of his starter projects. Twain explains that Grant's son told him a sob story about General Grant being in debt since he left the White House. Grant had also lost money during the May 5th crash in 1884. Grant was trying to get out of debt by writing articles on the Civil War for the *Century Magazine* for $2,500, which Twain thought was a lowball deal. He had known of Grant's troubles for a while, and had proposed helping him with the publication of his memoir back in 1881. Once Twain finally had a publishing company of his own in 1885, Grant accepted the help and Twain helped him shop the book around to some of the publishers he was familiar with. They offered around 10% in royalties, the same average amount that Twain was receiving. But, Twain convinced Grant that this was an unfair deal for a man of his stature. Knowing full-well that none of these publishers would ever go over 10% from experience, it seems Twain was working his own game by trying to convince Grant that he could do better only if he published with Twain's own new publishing business. They called upon Clarence Seward and another law firm to judge if Twain's or another publishing contract was the best deal, and oddly enough they concluded that a new venture was best simply because of the higher royalty percentage. Twain had offered a $25,000 advance at this point, but says that Grant negotiated him down to a $10,000 advance because he was afraid that Twain might take back some of the money if the book did not end up selling enough copies. They also agreed on 70% of the profits for the book as Grant's royalty.[544] Twain was optimistic about the deal because periodicals and newspapers started running articles like this one: "Over 100,000 Orders for the Set Received by His Publishers." Before the book was finished or advertised, Twain's new publishing business already saw enough orders to make it a success. This and other articles like it in major national newspapers gave a lot of needed press to the budding venture.[545] On the other hand, none of Twain's publishers ever offered him 70% of

---

544 Ibid., 75-81.
545 Ibid., 97.

profits because keeping only 30% of profits is likely to leave little room for salaries and all the other expenses that aren't calculated into basic profits. For example, if Twain gave Grant's widow $200,000 before returns came in, later returns might have cancelled out the bulk of his remaining profits. Taking such an enormous risk with the first venture supposedly was what kept the business going over the following years, but it could have given it a much firmer start if Grant took 50% of the profits or less. A 70% royalty was and remains a very unusual occurrence in publishing. Twain was clearly motivated by the marketing and public relations coup that releasing Grant's memoir would have rather than by how much each sold book would net.

However, the extremely author-sympathetic royalty terms might have been only a minor component in the eventual failure of Clemens' Charles L. Webster & Co. venture. A more sinister element was the extremely hostile articles that were written about it in the press and the direct requests for bribes that Clemens received from major publications in order to clear his name of the spreading libel. Byron and Shelley faced a similar problem when a campaign of negative reviews in rival periodicals drowned their journal in its first issues. One major difference between Clemens' effort and Byron and Shelley's is that he was publishing a general who was an American hero, and this generated enough positive press to drown out the libel. Clemens correctly predicted that there would be a great demand from General Grant's book and by May 25, 1885, he had received 200,000 orders for single volumes, and by September 10, 500,000 were sold. Two months before pre-sales started skyrocketing, a publisher that also bid on Grant's book, Century Co., started an aggressive smear campaign against Charles Co., Clemens and Grant's book in retaliation for losing the contract. A series of articles appeared in major U.S. papers between around March 7 and 9, 1885, which accused Clemens of dishonorably stealing the contract from Century Co. More curiously, the article on March 9 in the *Springfield Republican* referred to Charles L. Webster & Co. as a venture that "publishes his own books," implying that because the only other book Clemens had slated for production other than Grant's was his own, *Adventures of Huckleberry Finn*, the whole enterprise was nothing but a self-publishing project that had no business in dabbling in major releases like Grant's memoir. This article also stressed that it was now the Century's initiative to sever all ties with Clemens and to forbid him from publishing future articles with them in response to his improper behavior towards them in the Grant contract negotiations.[546] This attack is an example of the cutthroat competition in American publishing, wherein businesses attempt to succeed by destroying rivals.

This criticism of Clemens for starting a publishing business to publish himself is the first attack of its kind in this study. Starting a publishing venture in part to publish one's own work was a noble venture in Britain when Scott and Dickens were dabbling in it. The attack on self-publication in 1885 might have coincided by the sudden explosion of new small, independent magazines, the number of which rose from around 700 in 1865 to around 3,000 by that year, 1885, with the help of distribution via the American News Company. This flood of new competitors forced the players that were used to controlling the majority of the publishing market to take extreme measures to overwhelm the other publishers.

The tactic that Clemens was most surprised by was the request for a bribe by the Associated Press in exchange for publishing his paragraph response to the libelous accusations made by the Century. Associated Press is still an agency responsible for distributing articles of general interest to papers across the country. The Press had disseminated the initial objections from the Century. When it came to publishing the response, the representative for Associated Press told Clemens' lawyers, Alexander & Green, that Clemens statement would be "a pretty good advertisement for General Grant's book, and for" Clemens' "publishing firm." The Press further argued that Clemens' response would otherwise be against their preference for articles that were newsworthy rather than pure advertising. Despite these reservations, the rep "said if we would pay $500 he would send it over the wires to every newspaper in the country connected with that institution." Clemens explains that: "This pleasant offer was declined." Meanwhile, Clemens suddenly realized why he had been reading so many "dispatches of prodigious puffs of speculative schemes." One example of an obviously ad-funded scheme was from a "new electric light company of Boston" that frequently had positive coverage in the Associated Press. The publishing of advertising that was presented as news troubled Clemens because he had fallen for many schemes thus advertised, including the Paige typing machine that eventually was one of the major contributors to his bankruptcy. From the request for the bribe, Clemens deduced that the Associated Press was "willing to destroy a man for nothing, but

---

546   Ibid., 95.

required cash for rehabilitating him again," but it is perhaps even more likely that Century Co. had paid $500 to run the negative advertising against Clemens and that the "morals" of his competitors were still loser than he accused them of being. Clemens mentions that there were many similar libels published against him in the mainstream press over the decades and that he infrequently complained because libel law was unfair to the abused.[547] Clemens could joke about the practice of slander and bribery because he had experienced it regularly from his earliest publications; for example, his first magazine story, "Forty-three Days in an Open Boat" (1866), in *Harper's Monthly* misspelled his pseudonym as Mike Swain, instead of Mark Twain, thus preventing him from being able to use this piece to market himself as a "Literary Person" in the northeast.[548] To this day, the technique of slandering and minimizing the significance of small publishers is used regularly to crush the bulk of small publishers to the benefit of the top four giants, which occasionally also manage to knock off one of their top fellow giants, and in these instances increasing their market share not by a fraction but by 10-30%. This unregulated competition can only lead to the victory of a single monopoly publisher that will be free to libel the tiny struggling micro-publishers that would not have the pockets to pay for rebuttals.

Profits from Twain's independent publications trickled down into the negative. Twain tried various strategies to reverse this decline. First, he lowered the number of releases, and then increased their number in the last three years of the press, in the hope of finding a diamond in the rough.

During the life of Webster and Co., up until its bankruptcy in 1894, Twain self-published nearly a dozen of some of his best books with this misnamed company. These included: *Adventures of Huckleberry Finn* (1884), *A Connecticut Yankee in King Arthur's Court* (1889), *The American Claimant* (1892), *Merry Tales* (1892), *The £1,000,000 Bank-note and Other New Stories* (1893) and *Tom Sawyer Abroad* (1894). He also published books by Walt Whitman, Leo Tolstoy and other known and unknown authors, who were probably naturally interested in publishing with a popular writer.

Similarly to Dickens, Twain set out on an enormous world lecture

---

547 Ibid., 92-95.
548 Mark Twain. "My Debut as a Literary Person." *My Début as a Literary Person and Other Essays*. (New York: American Publishing Company, 1903; Google Books, Web), 11-47.

tour to recover from the business' bankruptcy in 1895. The extra work from these shows allowed Twain to finally pay off debts in full by 1898. This was a Herculean effort, as other publishers, like Sir Walter Scott, fell under the challenge of recovering from a bankruptcy, and could not repay the outstanding balance before their deaths. After the debts were cleared, Twain traveled abroad and did not publish any other major works. To sponsor his retirement, Twain sold exclusive rights to all of his work to Harper and Brothers, a mega publishing house that is still thriving to this day in a merged form.

The Harper name has appeared frequently in this study; Edgar Allen Poe, Mark Twain, Queen Victoria, Herman Melville published either short pieces in one of their magazines (*Harper's Bazaar*, *Harper's Monthly*, *Harper's Weekly*), or books with this publisher. Woolf, Luce, Poe and Twain all were also either rejected by them at some point or otherwise insulted or blacklisted. It is amazing how Harper managed to solicit interest from a majority of these writers. They were probably all motivated by the unusually high rates Harper was known to pay the writers its editors admitted. This high rate of payment was an illusion in many cases, as was explained in an earlier chapter. Harper & Brothers had more funds at their disposal because they "owed their initial successes to book piracy." Harper was printing popular British books in the US without paying British authors and publishers a royalty, taking advantage of a lack of international copyright law. They could legally do so up until the 1891 Congressional enactment of reciprocal international publishing agreements, which eventually brought legal sanctions against publishers for piracy. "In retaliation, many English publishers stopped buying American books."[549] Meanwhile, the American reading market had grown large enough for Harper to risk this repercussion to reap enormous rewards. Perhaps because they had a guilty conscience about this piratic start, Harper offered bigger advances and royalties to American authors and sought out the best literary writers it could find.

Colonel George Brinton McClellan Harvey negotiated the contract for nearly exclusive rights to all of Clemens' works (published and unpublished) in 1903 for a sum that made Clemens into "the best-paid writer in the United States."[550] The policy of over-paying the best writers clearly worked out for Harper as it survives in merged-form today.

---

549   Laurie Robertson-Lorant. *Melville: A Biography*. (New York: Clarkson Potter/ Publishers, 1996), 198.
550   Twain, *Autobiography*, 557.

The magazines that the Harper brothers founded now belong to media conglomerates or are out of print. For example, *Harper's Magazine* still operates with a focus on art and politics under the Cowles Media Company and *Harper's Bazaar* is operated by Hearst as one of their mainstream fashion periodicals.

Twain had retained rights to his works during the bankruptcy proceedings with the help of the multimillionaire, Henry Huttleston Rogers, the vice-president of Standard Oil, who guided him in transferring these rights to Olivia Clemens on the grounds that she was owed $60,000 by Samuel's publishers.[551]

One of Clemens' last book publications, *What Is Man?* was printed privately and anonymously in 1906. This self-publication suggests that Clemens stopped writing because he did not want to deal with the sort of outside publisher problems he faced before he started his own publishing venture. If his publishing company had survived, he might have introduced many more Hucks and Toms into the literary canon. Despite its eventual bankruptcy, Clemens' publishing company was a major marketing success that brought into public consciousness his best work. Would Twain be nearly as well-known today if he never started this venture?

Clemens died from developing a severe angina on a trip to Bermuda. A trip to this remote island was hardly the sort of risk a man hoping for a quiet retirement would have taken. Like the other author-publishers, Clemens cared more about learning, teaching, writing and publishing than about his own health. Clemens' publishing venture might have survived him if he was not sabotaged and hoodwinked by unscrupulous competitors. Thus, writers who are similarly inspired to self-publish should read about the obstacles that Clemens faced to avoid these in their own path.

---

551   Ibid., 192.

CHAPTER 11

Herman Melville and the Unpopularity of Highbrow American Literature: The Private Printing of Three Poetry Collections

Herman Melville shared the same publisher with Queen Victoria, John Murray, a member of the publishing house that lasted through numerous generations of Murray Jr. ownerships. Melville did not see the same publishing career path as most other canonical author. Melville was known in his time as a pop adventure fiction writer. But his novels were a bit too literary to attract enough sales for him to retain much of a profit after his publishers took their share. Thus, over the years, as Melville grew richer from other enterprises, his writing grew denser and more complex, as he turned to writing as an intellectual and artistic exercise, rather than as a means to make a living. At the same time, Melville started sponsoring the releases of his literary, un-marketable work, allowing books like *Moby-Dick* to enter the American canon.

His major essay, "Hawthorne and His Mosses," published in *The Literary World* in 1850, and then the 1851 release of *Moby-Dick; or, The Whale* instead of giving him immediate fame were followed by a decade of critical failure. Melville had published his only two popularly successful novels prior to this essay, *Typee* (1845) and *Omoo* (1847) about his travel adventures as a fisherman. *Omoo* was released by Harper in America and John Murray in London. Murray's first four thousand copies printing sold out in a week, so a couple of other printings followed soon afterwards.[552] However, the publishing terms Melville settled for were so skewed toward the interests of his publishers that Melville only made $86.26 via 50% royalties from the sale of 1,286 paperback and 428 hardback copies of *Typee* from Wiley & Putnam in October of 1847. And he spent the bulk of this money on the copies he ordered for himself and Allan. Thus, he was left with a profit of only $7.81 from nearly 2,000 sold books.[553] His 1849 *Mardi, and a Voyage Thither*, released with a London publisher, Richard Bentley, lost money, so Bentley offered Melville only £100 for his next book, *Redburn: His First Voyage* (1849), together with 50% of profits, with Harper & Brothers advancing him $300 for the same, yet to be written book.[554]

Melville realized pretty healthy profits from the sale of his first six novels, totaling $8,069.34 for British and American editions in five years.[555] Then, between 1851 and 1866 he made only $3,430 from "magazine contributions, lectures, and from books published by Harpers" and after this point he started paying for his publications, earning him substantial negative expenses.[556] Even during the period when he

---

552   Robertson, *Melville*, 156.
553   Ibid., 157.
554   Ibid., 198.
555   Charvat, *Profession*, 193.
556   Ibid., 200.

was seeing high royalty profits, Melville was spending more on these publications than was being paid out to him. And across his publishing history, he was only making microscopic amounts from the sale of rights to his novels to Britain, primarily working with Richard Bentley and John Murray. Murray frequently happened to be out when Melville attempted to call on him during his costly visits to London. Murray also refused to sponsor Melville's business trips abroad to negotiate these unprofitable deals. Meanwhile, Bentley lost money on *Mardi* and then offered "£200 for the first 1000 copies of the book," without an advance, so that if 1000 copies did not sell, as they did not, Melville would not get the £200.[557] Charvat does a great job of summarizing the catastrophic fiscal history of Melville's publishing adventures:

> …income seems to have been exceeded by outgo, for in spite of his success Melville owed, in 1851, $695.65 to Harpers and at least $5,000 to Judge Shaw… The Harpers advanced him $500 in February, 1852, and $300 in December, 1853, but from then until 1864 he was in debt to his publishers and drew nothing. Such royalties as accrued were applied to his debt until February 9, 1864, when Melville paid the Harpers $200. From then until 1887, when the records stop, his income from this source was negligible.[558]

With *Moby-Dick*, Melville stepped aside from writing these cheap pop novels into more serious fiction that he hoped would rival Hawthorne's for the title of the great American novel. Clearly, Melville is mulling over his desire to step into highbrow literature in his commentary in "Hawthorne and His Mosses." In this essay, Melville reviews the state of American literature with a bow to Nathaniel Hawthorne, his friend since 1850, as the two visited each other and corresponded. Hawthorne worked for the Boston Custom House 1839-40, and this might have inspired Melville's application for a similar position in New York. In the essay, Melville calms the applause by adding: "There are hardly five critics in America; and several of them are asleep. As for patronage, it is the American author who now patronizes this country, and not his country him." He goes on to philosophize that, "it is better to fail in originality, than to succeed in imitation. He who has never failed somewhere, that man cannot be great. Failure is the true test of

---

557 Robertson, *Melville*, 223.
558 Charvat, *Profession*, 193-4.

greatness. And if it be said, that continual success is a proof that a man wisely knows his powers—it is only to be added, that, in that case, he knows them to be small."[559] If we can trust Melville in that all those who are great fail; then, surely only a great writer who publishes him or herself can succeed. If he trusts society to judge the worth of his work, they will surely reject it. His own publishing story certainly supports this hypothesis.

Melville's relationship with his major publisher, Harper's, was constantly strained by the questionable fiscal agreements, which they kept forcing Melville to accept in exchange for publication. Harper's consistently attempted to charge Melville for their inability to sell his literary fiction. Tellingly, Harper's sent him a bill for $700 for "outstanding charges" when he asked for an advance for *Moby-Dick* (1851). Melville turned to farming corn and potatoes in between writing his grand novel to pay off this debt.[560] The sales from *Moby-Dick* slightly reduced this debt, but then Harper's offered a very discouraging contract for his next novel, *Pierre* (1852). "Melville could not collect royalties until 1,190 copies had been sold to pay for the plates. Of the $500 he was to receive when he signed the contract, only $300 constituted an advance against future royalties, while the balance represented royalties already earned by his previous books. In addition, Harper's offered a flat royalty of 20 cents per copy after expenses, instead of the usual half-profits, and told Melville that he would have to buy review copies and send them out himself."[561] In part because Harper's over-priced *Pierre* for working class readers, who were this radical novel's primary intended audience at $1.50,[562] *Pierre* ended up selling only 1,856 [out of a 2,310 printing] copies in thirty-five years, or an amount that was not too far above the no-royalties minimum set by Harper.[563] Laurie Robertson-Lorant offers slightly different numbers, probably because she only measures initial sales, without accounting for the next thirty years, writing that Melville sold 1,423 copies of both the American and British editions of *Pierre*, received a half-share royalty of $58.25. This left him with around $300 in debt to Harper's.[564]

Aside from the lack of fair royalties, Melville also suffered undue

---

559   Neider, *Essays*, 260-1.
560   Robertson, *Melville*, 271.
561   Ibid., 300.
562   Ibid., 318.
563   Charvat, *Profession*, 249.
564   Robertson, *Melville*, 319.

censorship. The editors of an un-censored version of *Pierre* (in contrast with the initially published censored version that took out radical portions), Harrison Hayford, Hershel Parker and G. Thomas Tanselle, wrote that Melville resented that "the greatest lettered celebrities of the time… full graduates in the University of Fame" were treated as "legal minors forced to go to their mammas for pennies wherewith to keep them in peanuts."[565]

It is curious that one of Melville's lesser known novels, *Israel Potter: His Fifty Years of Exile* (1854-1855), about the American Revolution, falls into the category of rebellion novels, a genre that was popular in this period, and practiced by Scott, Dickens, Stevenson and other radical writers. Rebellion novels were written to subversively support social change by depicting bravery in tragic rebellious events. However, Melville wrote *Israel Potter* very quickly purely for money, and did not insert the pro-revolutionary sympathy that highlights the other novels in this category. Israel's participation in the revolution is only a spark at the start of the work, and the ending is anti-climactic as it depicts an uneventful withering and death of a man who should have been one of the heroes of the depicted Revolution. Melville was probably unenthusiastic about the Revolution because America won this clash and a hundred years later it was hardly radical to support the separation from the United Kingdom.

Back in 1838, in the midst of his sea adventures, Melville was an outspoken supporter of the Hawaii natives' riots and demonstrations in Honolulu, Hawaii, as well as the takeover of the island by the British, rather than the defending Americans. Melville expressed strong anti-colonial opinions. He once insulted a leading missionary on the island, Dr. Gerrit P. Judd, calling Judd a "sanctimonious apothecary-adventurer." These types of public statements made Melville fear that Judd would retaliate by outing him as a deserter from the *Acushnet* and the *Lucy Ann*. Melville had dissolved an indentured contract for $150 in exchange for a year of service to Isaac Montgomery, as a merchant's clerk-bookkeeper.[566] The desire to desert from whaling vessels was common in those days. What was uncommon was the success Melville

---

565 Harrison Hayford, Hershel Parker, and G. Thoomas Tanselle, eds. *Pierre, or The Ambiguities*. Herman Melville. (Evanston and Chicago: Northwestern University Press and the Newberry Library, 1971), 250.
566 Ruth Richardson. *The Making of Mr. Gray's Anatomy: Bodies, Books, Fortune, Fame*. (Oxford: Oxford University Press, 2008), 116.

managed to gain from his liberation. The urge to flee amidst sailors was due to the horrific group living conditions that included some rape of younger shipmates, grotesque food, smells and diseases, and various other indignities. The profits from whaling had a lot in common with book publishing because they also were likely to turn out in the negative after four years of hard labor. Melville received an advance of $84 for equipment and future pay, but because he had to pay for all of his necessities at inflated ship prices, he would have been lucky if he left with $200 in profits at the end of a four-year cruise. And because he deserted, he probably avoided paying money he owed the captain for incurred expenses (if they ended up being negative).[567] He probably managed to tolerate the losses from publishing for all those years and eventually started paying for publication because life on whaling vessels taught him that this was how capitalism worked in America.

Thus, it is more likely that *Potter* was intended as a historically accurate account of a revolutionary participant and only because the biography that Melville used as reference ended in dissolution and obscurity did Melville end his novel in the same way. In other words, Melville probably intended to write a rebellion novel similar to Dickens' *A Tale of Two Cities*, but unlike Dickens he looked at reality rather than at the rosy idealism of liberty and the beauty and attraction of violence. Melville waged a similar "mutiny against injustice" when he defended the authenticity of native cultures, religions and political systems in *Typee: A Peep at Polynesian Life*, his first novel publication. He also showed this type of radicalism in many of his other non-conformist works.[568] Encouraged by *Typee*'s success, Melville attempted a closer-to-home attack on the problems in the US Navy in his *White-Jacket* (1850) novel, but the accusations were so pointed and detailed that the Navy and its defenders violently attacked the book in review publication, leading Harper's to be left with over 5,000 mostly unsold soft and hardcover copies of the novel. While this was a major commercial failure, it mostly likely played a major role in ending flogging in the Navy.[569] Melville's persistence in publishing radical and difficult to read literary works demonstrates that he was fighting for human rights and defending the standing of highbrow American literature, rather than simply striving to profit from his pen.

---

567   Ibid., 91.
568   Robertson, *Melville*, 141.
569   Ibid., 235.

Israel Potter was first serialized in *Putman's Magazine*, and then published in book form by G. P. Putnam and Company. For the latter, Melville received "$421.50 for the 75-cent book, which sold just short of three thousand copies in its first six months at a twelve-and-one-half-percent royalty."[570] These statistics are only for sales from the first six months. Sales stopped there. Putman "was forced to sell the plates of *Israel Potter* during the panic of 1857."[571] Critically and fiscally this was a "commercial failure."

Melville followed *Potter* with a short stories collection, *The Piazza Tales* (1856), and a multi-perspective complex novel *The Confidence-Man: His Masquerade* (1857). The publisher of these two high-brow works, Dix, Edwards & Company, went bankrupt, within a year of being founded in 1857. This failure was a major motivation for Melville's hiatus from commercial publications in the period that followed. Joshua Dix was in his twenties and had been employed by Putnam prior to his partnership in this new venture, which was founded when a group of editors, businessmen and writers bought *Putnam's Monthly Magazine* from Putnam, and then expanded into scholarly books and only a few highbrow novels, including Melville's. One of the other partners was Frederick Law Olmsted, the abolitionist designer of Central Park, who agreed to join and invest the $5,000 that he borrowed from his father (in return for surrendering the farm he had been running to his brother John). Olmsted was eager to join the partnership because Dix and Edwards offered to publish a book of his on the "slave states," *A Journey Through Texas: Or a Saddle-Trip on the Southwestern Frontier* (1857).[572]

In 1860, after a fiscally dry decade when his fiction stopped selling, Melville turned to public lecture tours, and also attempted to publish a collection of his poetry, but it was rejected. In 1866, Melville managed to publish his first poetry collection, *Battle Pieces and Aspects of the War*, with Harper & Bros. Out of the 1,200 copies printing, "more than 300 were given to reviewers, and two years following its publication, only 486 copies had been sold… He lost $300 on the venture." The book also faced negative reviews that indirectly responded to Melville's criticism of Sherman's conduct during the Civil War. Criticism was

---

570   Ibid., 345-6.
571   Charvat, *Profession*, 194.
572   Justin Martin. *Genius of Place: The Life of Frederick Law Olmsted*. (Philadelphia: Da Capo Press, 2011), 109-10.

also sparked because Melville dedicated it to the number of dead on the Union side, without mentioning losses from the Confederacy.[573] Immediately after this failure, Melville attained a post as customs inspector for the City of New York and held this job for nineteen years.

During his decades in customs, Melville experienced a bit of a writer's block, in part because a full-time job limited the free time he had available to write. In the midst of this dry period, Elizabeth Melville describes in her letters that between 1875 and 1876, Melville risked a cut in pay and possible termination from the postal position by writing an 18,000-line epic poem about the Holy Land, *Clarel: A Poem and a Pilgrimage*, during work hours. Melville was concerned because due to rampant corruption in the New York Customhouse, he received a couple of threats of termination before this point. Melville was thus worried about being caught writing a poem, as this would have given the slight provocation needed for them to finally be rid of him. His corrupt co-workers were concerned about keeping him out of their bribing activity. Bribery was so rampant in the Roscoe Conkling machine that it was investigated for "irregularities." The investigation "found a heavily overloaded staff and evidence of bribery." As a result, "20 per cent" of the staff were "reduced" by June 30, 1877. Melville probably had free time to write in the preceding years because jobs were handed out as bribes. Therefore, there was a shortage of work to go around, leaving Melville with a slack duty schedule. The workload was intensified after he survived the firings, so that he went from working "ten-to-three to nine-to-four daily."[574]

Once Melville finished his poem on the Holy Land, it had to be edited. Correcting a complex poem was so tedious that Elizabeth gave up on the task and passed it on to their twenty-year-old daughter, Fanny. Herman was so frantic with worry over the project that Fanny recalled "that her father had roused her out of bed at 2:00 A.M. and thrust printed galleys at her, ordering her to look at them over immediately."[575] Melville signed a contract for this poem with G. P. Putnam & Sons on January 4, 1876. Putnam offered a private printing, which was sponsored in part with funds ($1,200) from Herman's uncle, Peter Gansevoort, who died on this same date. When Melville was charged "an additional $100 for advertising expenses and distri-

---

573   Robertson, *Melville*, 487-97.
574   Charvat, *Profession*, 196-8.
575   Robertson, *Melville*, 534.

bution of review copies" by Harper's, he requested and was granted an addition to the bequest of $100 from his cousin, Kate Lansing, who was supervising Peter's estate at the time. But upon receiving the check from Kate, Herman sent it back, only to receive yet another check from Kate, which he ended up donating to the New York Society for the Relief of the Ruptured and Crippled (mostly veterans of the Civil War). Meanwhile, Harper's sent yet another bill to Melville for $84.12 for galley proofs he "purchased during the writing of *Clarel*."[576] These sums for the printing of 350 copies are substantial at today's book prices. They were astronomical in 1876. Based on a calculation via the In2013Dollars.com website, $1,384 would be worth as much as $29,571.26, or $84.40 per book printed, today. Even for a beautifully bound hardcover two-volume set, "embossed with a gilt Jerusalem cross cradled by palm trees" and other fineries, this sum is extraordinary.[577] In April, the book was "set in type and ready to be plated," and on the urging of his publisher, Melville agreed to put his name on it.[578] 350 copies of this epic were printed in 1876. By 1879, 224 of the unsold copies of this first edition were turned over to a paper mill that pulped the books because Melville was unwilling to buy them from the printer at-cost.

Melville's financial fortunes began to turn after the death of his mother-in-law, Hope Savage Shaw, in 1879, which left "a bequest of $2,000 for each of Lizzie's children and made Lizzie a legatee to their mother's $300,000 estate."[579] This estate was divided between the Melvilles and other family members, including Elizabeth's aunt, Martha Bird Barrett, and her daughter, Ellen Marett, who in turn left the remains to the Melvilles when these relatives also died in the following decades. For example, Ellen Marett Gifford left Melville "$8,000 and a paid share in the New York Society Library…" Lizzie received $10,000, "and each of the children received several thousand dollars."[580] Melville retired with the help of these trickling down funds in 1885. Melville received another $5,000 after Ellen Gifford's death in 1889.

He used some of these retirement funds to privately publish two collections of poetry, printing only 25 copies of each. *John Marr and*

---

576   Ibid., 554.
577   Ibid., 536.
578   Ibid., 535.
579   Ibid., 563.
580   Ibid., 606.

Other Poems was printed by Theodore L. De Vinne & Company in 1888 in a limited edition of 25 copies, and did not include the author's name on the title page because it was "intended for distribution to relatives and friends."[581] He repeated this simple small 25-copy private printing with *Timoleon* in 1891, printing it with the Caxton Press. Robertson explains that Melville was happier with these publications than his earlier tumultuous attempts at publishing via the so-called "traditional" route, as he was "redirecting his energies from dealing with publishers to writing poetry for private publication," thus allowing himself to grow "mellower." The lack of financial pressure generated from attempting to generate pop fiction, allowed Herman's poetry to become a romantic gesture and gift to his wife. They worked on the poems together, without the pressure Melville felt previously to correct them for the sake of higher sales.[582] There were "rumors" that "Melville pushed Lizzie down the back stairs in a fit of anger" in 1856 and hit her on other occasions when he failed to control his anger.[583] So, the mellowing of their relations was a major, positive change. If Herman had mellowed earlier by switching to small private printings, this would have spared them both a lot of grief. But then again, perhaps it was the hundreds of review copies that he paid for in those tumultuous decades that solidified his immortality to this day.

Herman Melville's *Moby-Dick* is one of the most difficult to digest American novels. It has puzzled students for a couple of centuries now. It and Melville's other creations are steeped in painful truthfulness. Narrators, characters and Melville are working to create change in society, culture, and politics. What would be positive change for the majority is frequently an unwelcome loss of profits for a few in power, who manage to suppress the free expression of discontent. Thus, Melville did not only sponsor himself when he released radical books, but also the silent majority without access to such luxurious literary spending. Here is an example of what we would all be missing if *Moby-Dick* was scraped as unmarketable:

> …didn't he call me a dog? blazes! he called me ten times a donkey, and piled a lot of jackasses on top of *that*! He might as well have kicked me, and done with it. Maybe he *did* kick me, and I didn't observe it, I was

---

581 Ibid., 586.
582 Ibid., 607.
583 Ibid., 372-3.

so taken all aback with his brow, somehow. It flashed like a bleached bone. What the devil's the matter with me? I don't stand right on my legs. Coming afoul of that old man has a sort of turned me wrong side out...[584]

Abuses creates a cycle of abuse. One of the best way to civilize abusers is for them to see the error of their ways in fiction. Herman dealt with his own violent past in passages like this one, and it allowed him to improve as a husband. In turn, the same lessons have also positively impacted the novel's millions of readers.

---

584   Herman Melville. *Moby Dick*. (New York: Encyclopedia Britannica, 1892; Google Books, Web), 123.

CHAPTER 12

Henry Luce and Briton Hadden: The Development of Media Moguls and Time Inc.

The twentieth century saw a new breed of lighter newspapers aimed at popular consumption by the larger lower class. Working-class Americans were making enough by the 1920s to afford some luxury purchases, but they were too busy to read detailed news stories. Highly-educated entrepreneurs stepped in to take advantage of this demand. In this climate, Luce and Hadden were disgruntled with the poor working conditions for reporters, so they partnered to give themselves permanent, leadership positions via publishing themselves (and others) in a set of periodicals.

Henry Luce was born in Tengchow, China in 1898 to missionaries and only came to the US to attend the Hotchkiss boarding school in Connecticut, where he worked as the assistant managing editor under Briton Hadden of the *Hotchkiss Literary Monthly*. They both went to Yale after successfully finishing Hotchkiss, and edited *The Yale Daily News* there. After Yale, Luce spent a year studying history at Oxford University, and then worked as a cub reporter for the *Chicago Daily News*. Meanwhile, Hadden wrote for the *New York World*. In 1921, Luce and Hadden deliberately found jobs together with *The Baltimore News*. In 1922, they quit their jobs and formed Time Inc., raising $86,000 to publish the first issue of a magazine that digested the week's news stories, *Time*, in 1923 in New York. When they were working together, they alternated business and editorial roles, though Hadden was usually the editor, and Luce was the business executive.

According to Henry Luce's biographer, Alan Brinkley, Hadden was a heavy drinker and partier towards the end of his life. A memo published in *Time* on May 5, 1965, titled, "Hadden illness & death," was the primary source for Brinkley's description of the tragic events that befell him. Brinkley also used interviews from *Time* with Lilian Rixie, Lila Luce Tyng and others to substantiate these claims about Hadden's behavior prior to his illness. The lack of media or biographical sources outside the *Time* enterprise to support these ideas is troubling. All of these sources argued that Hadden "began to participate in, or provoke, brawls for which he was periodically arrested and spent nights in jail."[585] He also started to play in a youth baseball league in Central Park despite an age limit of eighteen to participate. Hadden wrote a misogynistic speech in 1926 in response to Luce's proposal to appoint a woman to a director position. The idea of a female director threatened Hadden so much that he called all women: "deficient in such fundamentals as sense of humor, fairmindedness, good sportsmanship and sense of responsibility."[586] Aside for these types of backwards insults, Luce was frustrated with Hadden for his social transgressions and business inattentiveness. Hadden was also blocking the creation of a business magazine Luce was working on initiating. Supposedly because of Hadden's partying, he was not sleeping and started complaining in December of 1928 of exhaustion, until he "left the office early" one day "claiming he needed rest" and "never returned."

> Unable to recover from a flu, very likely because of his exhaustion, he also developed a strep infection and was hospitalized in Brooklyn. A few years later he could easily have been cured. But in the absence of sulfa drugs and antibiotics, doctors had a limited range of treatment—which mostly consisted of blood transfusions. Luce and others on the *Time* staff donated blood several times… By mid-January, Hadden had grown so weak that he could no longer even write.[587]

Strep throat usually resolves without treatment, so it is unusual that despite being in a hospital, Hadden's condition worsened. Similarly to

---

585   Alan Brinkley. *The Publisher: Henry Luce and His American Century*. (New York: Alfred A Knopf, 2010), 141.
586   Ibid., 142.
587   Ibid., 144.

Byron's bloodlettings, the blood transfusions only made matters worse for Hadden. Death from sepsis is relatively common in hospitals. But Hadden's symptoms become mysterious when they are considered in parallel with Byron's. Both writers developed mild flu at the start of their fatal illnesses. These flus were somehow aggravated by too much doctoring. The damage done by medical care was similar, despite a hundred-years difference. The results were so final that they had to be due to extreme negligence, if not deliberate assassinations. Luce was frequently visiting Hadden, and reported that Hadden was near-death from "streptococcus." It is interesting that Hadden died on February 27, 1929, "in the middle of the night, six years to the day from the publication of the first issue of *Time*." Instead of a eulogy, Luce published a short notice for Hadden, called, "Bulletin on Mr. Hadden," on March 11, which ended with, "success came steadily, satisfaction never."[588] Then, on March 18, several letters from admirers honoring Hadden were also included in *Time*. These brief notes are hardly fitting for one of the two founders of this enterprise.

"Among Luce's first acts as the solitary leader of the company was to acquire Hadden's stock." Hadden's hastily composed will left his entire estate to his half-brother, Crowell Hadden, with instructions not to sell Time Inc. until "forty-nine years after my death." The will is housed in the Time Inc. Archives. Perhaps because Hadden signed this will with an X due to his weakness during his hospitalization, or perhaps because of purely fiscal reasons, Luce convinced Hadden's estate to sell over 2,800 shares of Hadden's "to a syndicate Luce had created." The shares were valued at $360 in the open market, and Luce, despite already being the majority shareholder, bought 600 additional shares for himself. The Hadden estate was convinced to sell the shares with an offer of "more than a million dollars."[589] Luce thus won control over the bulk of Time Inc. and assigned various roles in the company to himself, while also continuously retaining his preferred title of Editor-in-Chief until 1964. Luce launched a series of magazines after Hadden's death, of which the more intellectual Hadden would have disapproved: *Fortune* (1930), *Life* (1936), *House & Home* (1952), and *Sports Illustrated* (1954), until Time Inc. was the largest magazine publisher internationally. Luce published his own opinion in some of his publications. Luce's best-known story is "The American Century." He

---

588   Ibid.
589   Ibid., 147-8.

also published anti-communist, anti-Cuba and otherwise Republican or ultra-conservative stories.

Luce made public speeches and wrote articles up through his graduation from Yale in 1920, but he refrained from publishing his own work until 1941, when his editors pushed him to make public statements in a time when America was in need of rousing speeches from powerful leaders. A publisher, regardless of if it publishes a magazine read by millions or poetry books for a small circle of friends, only needs motivation to put his or her words into print. After making a few speeches across the United States, Luce published "The American Century" in *Life* on February 17. This essay is a piece of pro-war, nationalist propaganda. In it, Luce uses emotional appeal, saying that, "Americans are unhappy," and that to avoid slipping into "national socialism," America has to use its powers to intervene to help democracies win in this world struggle. Thus, Luce's interests are in stark contrast to the political propaganda that high society radical author-publishers wrote about a century earlier. Byron and Scott certainly did not write about the mighty British Empire and how to become happier the British had to join world-wide wars. Additionally, the Holocaust and mass extermination of millions of minorities across Europe and Asia is not the sort of warfare that Byron and Scott were faced with. *Life* received many negative letters in response to Luce's propaganda. A Pennsylvania woman, Gail Goodin, wrote to the "Editor of LIFE" on February 22, 1941: "You are turning your magazine… into a war monger's tool."[590] The key word here is "your magazine." As the publisher, Luce had the authority to turn *Life* into a purely propagandistic publication in support of anything from the Nazis to wheat bread. Byron received plenty of death threats and letters of disapproval when he published some of his radical works, but he anticipated that the ideas he was propagandizing would be displeasing to the bulk of his aristocratic readers. Luce apparently did not anticipate the backlash and took the criticism as a reason to keep his name off the bylines in his future writings. One of the main challenges self-publishers have always faced is that they can publish pieces, which if they sent them to an editor for screening, might have been kept out if the views expressed are overly extremist in either the liberal or conservative directions. Raw ideas can either be extremely awful or extremely impactful. Thus, Luce's "American Cen-

---

[590] Gail Goodin. "Editor of LIFE." (New York: Time Inc. Archives, 22 February 1941).

tury" article made an impact on American history, while similar articles that preceded it were more tempered by editorial guidance.

Luce announced his retirement from Time Inc. on April 16, 1964, but he maintained "remote" influence over operations, as he traveled abroad. Oddly, after years of his notorious paranoia about the spread of communism, his greatest ambition was vising Mao in China, a goal that proved impossible unlike the honorary degrees and the accompanying grand speeches he was warmly invited to. He even started spending time with his estranged wife, Clare Boothe Luce in Phoenix, and was renovating a new house in Hawaii.

Clare had served as an ambassador to Italy between 1953 and 1956, and then as an ambassador to Brazil in 1959. She was the first U.S. woman to hold an ambassadorial position. She even became a member of the House of Representatives for Connecticut between 1943 and 1947. Clare married Harry in 1935, six years after Hadden's death, and before she started the key roles of her political career. She was Harry's second wife, after Lila Luce Tyng, who he met at Yale in 1919 and married in 1923. Harry divorced Lila after meeting Clare, in the same year as his re-marriage. He cheated on Clare as well, and only occasionally lived with her across their married life.

Briton Hadden never married, nor did he have any long-term relationship with any female partner that the media has reported on. In the years before Luce's death, he socialized, smoke and drank primarily with his male "friends" in New York.

When Harry was with Clare, he spent most of his time writing his memoir. "Although he had been a writer all his life, he had never before tried to write a book and seemed to have trouble deciding how to organize so much material and express so many ideas." Based on my work in spotting plagiarism in student essays, and as a linguist who studied patterns in writing, I believe Luce could not have written his speeches himself, and this was the reason he never managed to finish his memoir. Here is a description that raises my suspicion; Luce was "sometimes borrowing heavily from speeches he had made and articles he had written… What he produced was a series of short and sometimes sketchy essays that reflected many of his lifelong interests and beliefs. (Not much in the manuscript was about himself…)."[591] If a ghostwriter attempted to write a memoir without really knowing much about the personal life of the subject, he or she would compose similar

591   Brinkley, *Publisher*, 450.

bits and pieces if the subject was failing to adequately dictate their life's story. But, why would a Yale graduate have trouble with writing unless the close arrangement he had with Hadden sprung out of Luce's need for somebody to compose his stories for him. This surely would have been a secret worthy of a homicide if its revelation could have jeopardized Luce's control of their media empire. Luce grew up in China, so could he have really acquired enough English there to immediately receive high enough scores in boarding school to be accepted into Yale? If we trace Luce's writing attempts to a time when author-publishers like Byron and Shelley typically published their first self-publications, at the end of their collegiate studies, Luce's attempts were half-hearted failures. During his one-year study-abroad at Oxford, without officially pursuing a degree there, he reported attempting to publish essays in *Harper's* and the *Atlantic* under a pseudonym, "so that rejections— which he consistently received—would not damage his reputation." He was planning on making money from the manufacturing business at this point, and only stumbled back into journalism as a second thought.[592] Going back still further, we come to his first publication in 1908 in a popular children's magazine in China, *St. Nicholas*, where he wrote: "I am a boy born in China. I live in the country near Wi-hsien (Way Shen) city… There are eight dwelling houses, a boys' and girls' school…"[593] There are an awful lot of repetitions here, but he was only ten at the time. Somehow, this early attempt does show a similar extreme ambition to write and publish to the other author-publishers in this study. Additionally, it is amazing that Luce managed to make so many orations across his career as editor-in-chief of Time Inc. because as a child he had a "painful stammer."[594] However, the plagiarism theory seems more unlikely as one considers that Luce started publishing "stories and poems" in boarding school magazines, and put in a tremendous effort to be elected as a member of these publications.[595] But why would somebody who is maniacally obsessed with the publication of his own work, not manage to complete even one full book across decades as the publisher of the world's biggest media company? Thus, the mystery of Luce's potential plagiarism shall remain unsolved.

Luce's death was not all together natural either. After arriving back

---

592 Ibid., 80.
593 Ibid., 18-9.
594 Ibid., 35.
595 Ibid., 35-6.

in Phoenix from California on February 23, 1967, Luce slept in late, "uncharacteristically, and could not hold his food down once he had eaten. He continued to vomit through" the following two days and then was taken to the hospital. "I seem to be unusually sleepy" he said to his doctor, echoing exactly what Hadden said those decades earlier. He went to the restroom in the middle of the night on February 28, yelled "Oh God!" and was unconscious when a nurse reached him. "Fifteen minutes later, he was dead—the victim of a massive heart attack."[596] The timing of this heart attack is the anniversary of Hadden's death in a hospital thirty-eight years earlier. I do not know how the nurse determined that Luce suffered from a heart attack, but surely no autopsy was conducted to check for poisons in his system. There was nobody with him in the restroom, and he could have taken a poison that led to the collapse. He might have started taking something when this mysterious illness started suddenly on February 23. Are there clues of a murder-suicide in the story of Luce and Hadden's deaths? If so, the suicide came after a very lengthy delay, during which the Time Inc. empire was solidified. The *Time* masthead was changed back to naming both founders two decades after Luce's death (after only Luce appeared there after Hadden's demise). If it was a guilt-driven suicide, it is very usual that Luce did not change it back himself. Or did a third-party poison both Luce and Hadden? Or is this all an absurd conspiracy when the evidence points to a shabby medical system that failed to elongate their lives? Either way, the history of Luce and Hadden's publishing careers and Luce's unsuccessful attempts to self-publish are great examples of an alternative outcome for an author-publisher, one that is fiscally much more successful than their nineteenth-century counterparts, but artistically and intellectually an utter failure.

***

For a few years, Hadden and Luce's paths intersected with Harold Ross, when they published *Time* and *The New Yorker* from the same abandoned brewery. Harold Ross had a similar early backgrounding, as he also edited a high school newspaper. Only he did not receive an Ivy League education and instead worked his way up through several different newspapers, writing for *The Denver Post*, *Salt Lake Telegram* and *The Brooklyn Eagle*, before becoming an editor for *The Home Sec-*

---

[596] Ibid., 450-1.

tor. When *The Home Sector* failed in 1920, he tried to work for a new magazine, Judge, but he conceived the notion that he had to break out on his own to really succeed in the publishing game. *The New Yorker*, first released in 1925, was, in part, funded by his first wife, Jane Grant, and then in partnership with a yeast manufacturing heir, Raoul Fleischmann, with whom Ross founded the F-R Publishing Company. Ross edited *The New Yorker* until his death in 1951. Ross's rise is an alternative path an author-publisher has taken in the American publishing landscape. Ross managed to combine intellectual rigor with profitability. This suggests that an Ivy League education might have only harmed Luce and Hadden's writing and editing abilities. Anybody that hopes to start a successful, modern magazine in America, surely has to begin by studying Ross, Luce and Hadden to pick out the parts of their experiences worthy of imitation.

CHAPTER 13

Dudley Randall and Black Power Poetry

The second half of the twentieth century in America was marked by the civil rights struggles of various underprivileged groups. Therefore, it is only natural that some of the best new presses to come out of this climate were those that promoted the free expression of these groups. Just as Dickens fought for the rights of factory workers, and Scott fought for Scottish nationalism, Dudley Randall fought for the access to the press for African Americans. Great author-publishers are created by necessity. If an author cannot find a publisher because his or her opinions are too radical or undesirable by the establishment, it becomes a matter of survival for this author to publish themselves and other writers facing the same blockade. If these author-publishers prove that their radical ideas are also sellable, mainstream publishers inevitably begin accepting similar works and authors. Thus, the most successful niche presses are those that disappear after an extraordinary run, at the end of which they win their struggle. To survive beyond this point, they have to adopt a new struggle, or a new champion to alter the initial motto.

Dudley Randall began Broadside Press when he published two of his radical poems, "The Ballad of Birmingham" (anti-black-church-bombing) and "Dressed All in Pink" (on the Kennedy assassination). They were set to music by folk singer, Jerry Moore, in 1965. Randall printed them on broadsides for $12, a sum that came out of Randall's paycheck. The press launched the careers of many black writers with the releases of their chapbooks. Randall became poet laureate of Detroit, and was active in the civil rights movement. His biography, *Wrestling with the Muse: Dudley Randall and the Broadside Press*, is written by Melba Joyce Boyd, one of Broadside's editors and a professor at Wayne State University. Boyd quotes from a 1974 review of Broadside's *After the Killing* by June Jordan in the *American Poetry Review* that refers to

Randall as "the poet-founding-publisher" and claims that he "rescued the new Black poetry of the sixties from predictable, white rejection." Boyd explains that between 1945 and 1965, "only thirty-five poetry books authored by African Americans were published in the United States, and only nine of these were published by presses with national distribution." Randall's launch of Broadside reflected a need to fill the "dismal publishing terrain for black poets… with an alternative press." Soon after the launch, between 1966 and 1975, Broadside managed to publish "eighty-one books, seventy-four of which were poetry… Each printing was at least 5,000 copies," and if these sold out, 10,000 more were printed. 100,000 of Don L. Lee's books were in print by 1974. Across its history: "Broadside printed more than 500,000 books." Their anthologies and collections introduced many other new, primarily African American authors to a wide reading public.[597]

Randall was driven by the ideas of the Black Power Movement and the Black Arts Movement, and was one of its leading, recognized voices before and during the press' operation. After Randall published himself with Broadside, other African American writers flooded him with requests to do the same for them. When Margaret Walker expressed her desire to publish a book about Malcolm X at the 1966 Writers Conference at Fisk University, Randall jumped in with an offer to help her with the publication.[598]

For the first five years, Broadside was a "one-man operation," so that when Gwendolyn Brooks asked regarding the official title she should use for him, he said: "since I, in my spare time and in my spare bedroom, do all the work, from sweeping floors, washing windows, licking stamps and envelopes, and packing books, to reading manuscripts, writing ads, and planning and designing books," she should "just say that Dudley Randall equals Broadside Press."[599] Randall explains that he started out storing books in his basement. Later, he found bigger and bigger office space, as the stock he was holding continued to grow. He tried to maintain a four-books-per-year limit, but accepted projects without keeping track of the number. As he surpassed his preset limit, he began worrying about his capacity to afford sponsoring all these releases.

To reap higher returns on each release, he specified in his contracts

---

597   Melba Joyce Boyd. *Wrestling with the Muse: Dudley Randall and the Broadside Press*. (New York: Columbia University Press, 2003), 3-4.
598   Ibid., 127.
599   Ibid., 230.

that he was offering a 10 percent royalty.[600] 5-10% royalties became standard in the twentieth century, while as was seen in previous chapters, 25-50% royalties were more common in the nineteenth century. This shift was due in part to the lack of inflation in the cost of books relative to other goods and services. Purchasing a book was a significant expense back then, but became equivalent to the price of a day's food. Even small, start-up publishers like Randall could only offer 10% of profits to writers because at these cheap cover prices, they needed the rest of the profits. Returns, shipping, distribution and various other costs also started to eat into the publisher's share. Additionally, nineteenth century publishers were charging authors if a book's inventory failed to sell. In the twentieth century, such charges were labeled as "subsidies," and any publisher that attempted to openly charge authors was massacred in the media. The extra profits share was needed to provide a safety net for the titles that failed to sell their print runs. Scott, Byron and other canonical writers began their careers by publishing poetry in the nineteenth century, but by the twentieth century this category was stigmatized as a barely marketed niche. Randall was selling similarly sized print runs to Scott or Byron's, but 5,000 copies sold no longer signified a best-seller in comparison with pop romance and mystery novels that now captured the marketplace with millions in sales.

After the successful release of Randall's little broadsides, he transitioned into publishing full, book-length projects. Early releases included Randall and Margaret Danner's, *Poem Counterpoem* (1966). Randall explains that he initially submitted this book to Harcourt Brace, but "they sent it back. I was feeling a little more independent, so I decided since they wouldn't publish it, I'd publish it myself… And that was the first Broadside Press book. As they say in the army, if you work KP and don't get enough to eat, shame on you." Randall is rightfully comparing self-publishing to eating the food cooks in the army produce. It is just as logical for an author-publisher to publish his or her own books, as it is to eat what you are cooking, or to wear what you are sewing.

He initially printed *Poem Counterpoem* with a tiny font, and a size similar to a cheap collection he saw in Russia, but it did not sell until he increased the size to a standard "eight-by-five format." From this Randall concluded: "I guess American people like to buy books like

---

600   Ibid., 231.

cabbages, by the weight or by the size instead of by the content."[601] Randall started releasing up to 55,000 copies of books like Don Lee's (founder of Third World Press, who proposed a merger with Broadside at one point), and all "without book reviews in the mass media. The only reviews of Lee's books have appeared in small black and underground magazines." As was explained in the opening chapters, major American review publications are owned by the Big Four, by US government agencies, or by for-profit, pay-for-review outlets. Thus, a new publisher cannot expect any "major" reviews in this climate. On the other hand, there are plenty of small publications that are only too happy to receive review copies, and do not discriminate based on the size or age of the publisher. For example, *Ebony* only ran an article about Lee in 1969, after he was already popular.[602] Randall explains that for other titles, there might have been a few *Library Journal* reviews, "which prompted considerable library orders."[603] But, there was only one *New York Times* review.

Randall was so frustrated with the lack of reviews that he asked, in a letter to James A. Emanuel, referring to black authors who could also serve as respectable critics: "Why don't we write our own criticism?" The need to review yourself or to create alliances with favorable reviewers to fight against puffery and pay-for-review publications has been a problem for many in this study: anecdotes of self-reviews were related in earlier chapters. Shortly after expressing this desire to Emanuel, Randall wrote a review for *Negro Digest* in praise of Emanuel's book of criticism on Langston Hughes. When this went well, Randall invited him to serve as the chief editor of his new *The Broadside Critics Series* that started in 1970.[604] The series took off slowly because of Randall's attempts to keep the number of releases down, but it eventually proved to be very profitable. The *Critics Series* positively reviewed many of Randall's own authors, including Margaret Walker, Gwendolyn Brooks, and Don Lee.[605]

Aside from fighting to see Broadside's books reviewed, Randall was attempting all of the other standard tricks of the publicity game. Broadside sent out newsletters and press releases on upcoming titles.

---

601 Ibid., 141.
602 Ibid., 233.
603 Ibid., 239.
604 Ibid., 240.
605 Ibid., 241-2.

Further still, "to all viable patrons, periodicals, journals, and critics, and review copies were sent out in considerable number."[606] Despite these marketing campaigns, still only "black journals, such as *Black World*, reviewed many of our books." The lack of market access begs the question: how did Broadside manage to sell so many books? One explanation for Broadside's initial success was the cheap prices that made them attractive to "college courses," especially in Black Studies.[607]

Scott insisted on setting very low prices on his Waverley novels about the Jacobite rebellions so that the poor (a larger portion of the population) could afford buying them. Many of the poorest people in Scotland only had the Bible and a Waverley novel at the peak of their popularity. This campaign to sell pro-rebellion and pro-nationalist ideals successfully incited the Scottish Insurrection. These minimum-prices also eventually led to his own and his publisher's bankruptcy. Thus, it has been a tradition for radical author-publishers to act against their own fiscal or fame-related interests. Many of the twentieth century's author publishers have been radicalized on the left, so it is common among them to adopt socialist principles. Randall's motto when he started Broadside was: "Production for use instead of for profit," a venture "free of aesthetic repression or profit constraints." While Boyd justly calls this an "alternative to a capitalist model," she also understands that "such a noble philosophy of self-determination in the form of cultural activism" was hardly likely to "survive the material realities… that determined institutional longevity."[608]

Since Randall stressed his own socialist ideals, he attracted collaborators that shared these views. Another editor at Broadside was Gwendolyn Brooks, who donated all proceeds of her post-Martin Luther King association book, *Riot* (1969), to Broadside. She had opted to work with Broadside over the great advance that she had been offered by Harper. Brooks ended up hosting "most of the Broadside poets whenever they were in her city," and she advocated for young Broadside writers by "giving book parties and writing generous introductions."[609] This is an example of how non-profit small presses exhibit more longevity in America's competitive market, as they are supported with charitable contributions even if the books are otherwise blocked from

---

606   Ibid., 238.
607   Ibid., 234.
608   Ibid., 134.
609   Ibid., 167.

access to reviews and media coverage.

The press was initially housed in Randall's private home on Old Mill Place, but was moved to a busy street in Detroit at 15200 Livernois Avenue by the time Boyd started there as an editorial assistant for $3 an hour, despite having a master's degree. Broadside's office manager, Bill Whitsitt, was also working as an accountant for the Ford Motor Company. And Randall maintained a full-time job as a reference librarian at the University of Detroit across the peak years of Broadside. Boyd's job was handling all aspects of the editorial department, from acquisitions to proofreading. When she started, she had to work through an enormous backlog that had accumulated by 1972. The press moved into a new office that September and Boyd was promoted to assistant editor. Randall encouraged Boyd to publish her own poetry in the *Broadside Series*, and welcomed her into the readings he was doing at the Highland Park Public Library.[610]

Trouble started brewing for Broadside when debt to the printer started accumulating at an alarming rate as early as in 1972. When finances first became strained, Randall flatly refused to seek "financial or technical help" from white publishers. A group of these Caucasian publishers had held a publishers' organization hearing to offer their help to black publishers via "co-opt publishing initiatives." Randall "insisted on remaining independent," saying that giving up control to white publishers "was like standing upon the slave auction block."[611] These radical sentiments did not help the press escape the red. In 1975, shortly after a lavish tenth anniversary celebration of the press' existence that included fancy dinners, readings, performances and other costly space rentals, Bill Whitsitt announced that the press owed $30,000 to the Harlo Printing Company. The Randalls were funding the press out-of-pocket. Meanwhile, they were owed money by "bookstores and poets alike," so that Boyd argues that "Randall's generosity had become the undoing of the press."[612] Randall and his staff were failing to collect on debts, and were not vigilant when their own debts started to climb. Fiscal responsibility is more important for a small press than for giant one because a $30,000 debt can be a bankrupting event if the total annual revenues of a press is not much higher than this amount. Only small presses that avoid being enslaved by debt are likely to survive dif-

---

610 Ibid., 18-22.
611 Ibid., 239.
612 Ibid., 258.

ficult times.

Another curious conclusion can be drawn from the quote above. In contrast with Boyd's conclusion, the fact that "poets" are included in the list of folks who owed the Randall money suggests that the poets were subsidizing Broadside's publications, at least partially. Here is another clue that Broadside was subsidized: "As a gift for Don L. Lee's thirtieth birthday, Gwendolyn Brooks financed the publication of *Directionscore: Selected and New Poems* in 1972."[613] Randall explained that: "Support for the Press has come from the grassroots, from poets who donated their poems... who steadfastly refused payment... from the many persons who subscribed in advance for *The Broadside Series* and the anthologies, so that they could be printed; and from others who donated sums above their subscriptions. It is the poets and the people who have supported Broadside Press." He further explained that royalties from his own books were always re-invested back into the company and that he never saw profits from the venture.[614] There is a slight contradiction here between Randall's refusal to accept profits, and his failure to repay the printer on outstanding debts. A sharp awareness of profits and losses is not an anti-progressive or an anti-radical stand for a press director, but rather it is an essential ingredient for averting bankruptcy for yourself and for the businesses that depend on your success.

Broadside attempted to collect on outstanding debts with the help of a collections agency, but discovered that the reason for most of the non-payments was the failure of "small bookstores" and the closures of black studies courses in the midst of the recession. In parallel with these problems: "Higher printing costs, as well as the tax on books in storage, had altered the economics of small press publishing." Broadside's account books were suggesting that debts to the printer and others could be repaid if only they collected on the money that was due to them. But a closer analysis showed that the losses were unrecoverable and due to the regular shocks of the publishing business (just like book returns).

Just as Randall was realizing the severity of their fiscal problems, "the Internal Revenue Service audited the press" and they discovered that "books that remained in stock over a specified period of time were considered taxable revenue," so that they started giving books away or trying to sell them at steep discounts to avoid holding onto them and

---
613   Ibid., 238.
614   Ibid., 243.

paying the steep IRS fines.

Amidst this avalanche of problems, instead of holding onto his day job, Randall "took an early retirement from the University of Detroit" in January of 1976 to work full-time to save the press.[615] As Randall made this decision, a new problem appeared: Johnson seized publishing the *Black World Magazine*, "the main source for announcements and… critical space for poets and book reviews" of Broadside's books. This closure eliminating one of the only reviewers that was willing and able to publicize black poetry.[616] In 1976, things were so bad that Whitsitt started a tavern and spent most of his time there. Boyd had been fired from her teaching job at a local college "for union organizing" by this point, but was working towards a PhD at the University of Michigan, managing to continue working at Broadside part-time.

These difficulties aligned until Broadside tipped over. That year, Randall sold the press to the Alexander Crummell Center, "a church-based organization."[617] It is puzzling how Randall managed to find a buyer for the press if it was in the red. It was more of a bailout than a purchase of a business. Boyd concludes on a tragic note: "noble intentions are rarely profitable in business. Dudley Randall was a literary caretaker, not a competitive entrepreneur. So, when the press fell into financial collapse, Randall lost his equilibrium. The world had failed him, which to him meant poetry had failed him." He was depressed for three years before attempting suicide, only to be stopped by his wife. It was at this low point when Boyd started working with him on the biography that the bulk of the information in this chapter is based on.[618]

Boyd's biography gave Randall a new lease on life, and inspired him to return to writing. When Dudley Randall started publishing his poetry again, he also "resumed his affiliation with the press, then renamed Broadside/Crummell Press." He was welcomed back as a consulting editor. After staying in this post for a while, he used a clause in his contract that allowed him to "regain control of Broadside in 1981," thereby once again becoming the leader of the surviving press. When he returned, he launched the Broadside Poets Theater, which played on Sundays for $2, wherein attendees could hear readings by Broadside poets at the Alexander Crummell Center in Michigan.[619] In around

615   Ibid., 258.
616   Ibid., 259.
617   Ibid., 260.
618   Ibid., 3-4.
619   Ibid., 270.

1985, Randall was forced to sell Broadside for the second time, staying on as a "consultant to the new publishers…, Don and Hilda Vest, and retained a 30 percent interest in the business." Taking a 30% share of a business hardly sounds like an anti-profit position. Despite what Boyd and Randall state in the biography, Randall obviously had a profit motif behind the decisions he was making for Broadside. Boyd goes on to state that Randall viewed this latter sale as a "final chapter," wherein he failed in maintaining the independence that he took pride in.[620] After this surrender to dependence, Randall started winning numerous institutional awards, including NEA Life Achievement Award and an honorary Doctor of Letters from the University of Detroit. As the praise was pouring in, Randall reflected about his own writing: "Broadside took time away from my writing, so in that way it may have interfered with my producing poetry. So much bad poetry was submitted; it discouraged me in my writing and in my publishing. Oftentimes I felt I had lost my sense of judgment in poetry. What is good?"[621]

Despite Randall's prediction that re-selling the press was the beginning of the end, it turned out that the new owners managed to gain the fame and recognition for both Randall and his press that he never achieved. Documentaries and other honorary events followed in the 90s. Overall, this is an unusual example of an author-publisher hanging on to a third of his publishing business until his death in 2000. It is always takes a herculean effort for an independent publisher to survive four turbulent decades through the usual hurdles to independent publishing.

Broadside has survived because it has changed hands when a prior holder was too frail to continue the fight. According to the Broadside-LotusPress website: "The Vests sold the Press to a collective of cultural activists in 1998: Richard Donelan, Ed.D., Sondai Lester, Lindiwe Lester, Aombaye Ramsey, Ph.D., Tene Ramsey, and Willie Williams and Gloria House, both of whom had been Broadside Board members during the Vests' direction of the Press, and volunteers during the Crummell Center guardianship years." Assuring a successful succession frequently saves presses from dying or retiring with their founders. And if a press has a social message or a campaign behind it (like feminism or anti-racism), it is more likely that other activists will take over the reins in the modern media climate.

---

620   Ibid., 203.
621   Ibid., 304.

CHAPTER 14

A Quest for Inter-Racial Equality:
Alice Walker's Wild Trees Press

Alice Walker started her Wild Trees Press a few years after the initial failure of Randall's venture. Instead of starting it out of desperation to find a mainstream publisher, she started it when her fame and royalties were starting to flow in. But, the lack of a profit motive and other publishers' invitations for her to make extraordinary sums via her writing alone, set the stage for a short-lived publishing attempt. Few other popular authors have started their own publishing companies in the twentieth century for the same reasons. Dickens was struggling to make a living as a reporter for many years before he started making negligible sums for his fiction. After this struggle, the profits he saw from releasing books with other publishers faded in significance in contrast with the social problems he hoped to fix in his writing. Outside publishers were refusing to publish his novel about the French Revolution, so he started his own periodical with this as his primary aim. Perhaps because modern popular writers lack sympathy or awareness of the plight of the impoverished, there is no similar pushes among them to rebel against the mainstream. Thus, even if Walker's press was short-lived, it is an example of how even very wealthy modern writers can still have the courage to sponsor an independent, free press for their own radical opinions, and for the suppressed voices of other writers.

Long before Alice Walker started Wild Trees Press, she described her encounter with ostracizing and racism towards her Jewish husband Mel Leventhal and herself in the south, her birthplace, in a *New York Times Magazine* article on August 26, 1973: "Choosing to Stay at Home: Ten Years After the March on Washington." She describes Mel as, "a human-rights lawyer who sues a large number of racist institutions a year (and wins) (and who is now thinking of suing the Jackson

Public Library, because a. they refused to issue me a library card in my own name, and b. the librarian snorted like a mule when I asked for a recording of Dr. King's speeches—which the library didn't have)…"[622] Walker then describes several incidents where Mel was "testing" white proprietors by watching how they reacted to Alice entering their whites-only establishments. In another civil rights related story, Walker describes, "we saw a young black man casually strolling down a street near the center of town arm in arm with his high school sweetheart, a tiny brunette. We had been with a friend of ours who was in no mood to witness such 'incorrect' behavior, and who moaned, without a trace of humor: 'Oh, why is it that as soon as you do start seeing signs of freedom they're the wrong ones!'"[623] This was the response of their friend. Imagine how their enemies saw the marriage between a Jew and an African American. Racial tension was a core conflict during Alice and Mel's marriage. As a result, interracial relationships was a topic that Walker wanted to encourage and support in the books she published once she could choose what was worthy of publication in her own press. Mel and Alice divorced in 1976, long before she founded her press. But Mel had a lot of characteristics in common with her lover, Allen, the man she ended up founding the press with. Towards the end of the essay, Walker argues that radical, African American women of times past "would simply ignore the assumption that 'permission to speak' *could be given them*, and would fight on for freedom of all people…" In a sense, when she started Wild Trees Press, she was refusing to wait for permission to publish, and was hoping to help other writers join her in fighting "on for freedom" with radical expression.[624]

Back in 1978, Alice Walker left her husband, Melvyn Leventhal, and moved to San Francisco to live with her lover, Robert Allen. In their first year together, Walker completed *The Color Purple*, which was released in 1982, and was a bestseller by 1984. At the peak of mainstream publishing success, Walker and Allen decided to found a publishing company, Wild Trees Press. In a 2007 *Guardian* article, Walker replied that she received many negative reviews that called her anti-black because of *The Color Purple*'s popularity. Thus, while other best-selling writers typically follow-up a bestseller with a string of simi-

---

622   Jon Meacham, Ed. *Voices in Our Blood: America's Best on the Civil Rights Movement*. (New York: Random House, 2001), 482.
623   Ibid., 483.
624   Ibid., 485.

lar books from the same publisher, Walker was repelled from writing similar works, and instead chose to start an independent publishing company that would allow her to have control over her creative choices.

On the other side of this founding duo, Robert Allen was the Editor of *The Black Scholar*, so he was the one with editorial and publishing experience, and business acumen.

Open Library lists only seven titles as having been released from Wild Trees Press between 1984 and 1988. By 1988, the venture was phased out. Donald Joyce's *Black Book Publishers in the United States* reports that most of Wild Trees Press' early titles sold very well, in the thousands of copies. The publishing venture had ended soon after Walker and Allen separated and started seeing other people. The relationship clearly created an atmosphere that nourished the growth of a publishing house, with the two parties adding something irreplaceable to the equation. Neither started a new press after terminating the partnership.

Evelyn White's Norton biography of Walker's life does a great job of summarizing Walker and Allen's motivations for founding the Wild Trees Press. Walker set up an:

> ...office and living quarters on a forty-acre retreat in Mendocino County that she'd purchased with some of her earnings from *The Color Purple*. Reared in a sharecropping family that had been uprooted at whim, Alice was determined not to suffer the same fate... In launching a publishing company (Robert Allen and friend Belvie Rooks joined her as partners), Alice had in mind Virginia Woolf's success in a similar venture..."[625]

Unlike the other publishers in this study, Walker closed her press because: "'We became too successful and we really didn't want to turn it over to other people because it was our vision.'" As Walker explained, she was concerned that they received too many manuscripts.[626] Alice had to hire Joan Miura just to help her manage the "inquiries" coming in about Wild Trees Press after *The Color Purple* film came out in 1985.[627] While it might seem as if hyper-popularity is no reason to fold a business venture, the assaults from the paparazzi and from hooligans vying for Walker's money and attention might have been much more

625   Evelyn C. White. *Alice Walker: A Life*. (New York: W. W. Norton & Company, 2004), 388.
626   White, *Alice*, 457.
627   Ibid., 434.

serious than she explains in the interviews she gave on this topic.

While it lasted, White states that the Press was "dedicated to the development of marginalized writers." One of Wild Trees Press's titles was *As Wonderful as All That?* This was "a memoir by 1920s-era black musician Henry Crowder about his seven-year affair with white shipping heiress Nancy Cunard…"[628] Because the book dealt with interracial relations, class conflict, and the breaking of cultural norms, it was the most radical of the press's releases. Walker introduced this controversial project by writing about Crowder and Cunard: "The relationship was pivotal for both of them—and it culminated in a remarkable offspring, the publication of the monumental anthology *Negro*, an impressive survey of black achievement, which Nancy edited and dedicated to Henry."[629] Walker was cognizant of the parallels between the affair depicted in this book and her own affair with her co-publisher, Allen. Her passion for the rights of interracial couples inspired her to publish books that highlighted the positive aspects of such unions.

The beginning of the collapse of Wild Trees might be attributed to the backlash against this radical, interracial release, as well as against Walker's other radical engagements. For example, Alice Walker was arrested in June 1987 at the Concord Naval Weapons Station during a demonstration protesting the base's alleged role in the shipment of arms to Central America. It was in this same critical year, 1987, when *Publishers Weekly* reviewed *As Wonderful as All That?* showing how bitter the critics were about this suppressed book's release through Walker's press:

> Shortly after the events described here, Crowder, the black jazz pianist, collaborated with Speck, an American journalist, on a tale about his affair with Cunard, an heiress of the shipping fortune, a poet and a left-wing political activist. The two finished the manuscript but it remained unpublished until now, and there's little wonder as to why: *As Wonderful As All That?* is a mean-spirited, ungracious catalogue of slights that Crowder seems to have suffered during the seven years he was involved with Cunard. Although there must have been much to attract him (Cunard was apparently intelligent, charming and enthusiastic if voluble), he derides everything about her. Their circle of friends (including e. e. cummings and Samuel Beckett and various Parisian expatriates) become props for his bitterness; her Hours Press (which published Ezra Pound and Robert

---

628   Ibid.
629   Ibid., 4.

Graves, among others) is yet another source of spite; and Cunard's book *Negro*, an anthology of work by blacks around the world, occasions the typically nasty remark that Cunard faced "tremendous odds" in putting together the book, "the greatest of which was her own ignorance."

Aside from showing the critic's bitterness, this summary shows the numerous parallels between Crowder's and Walker's lives. As the *Publishers Weekly* critic points out, Nancy Cunard founded and ran a publishing company during the years that she spent with Crowder. The relationship lasted between 1928 and 1935, while the Hours Press was operational between 1928 and 1931. Cunard was independently wealthy, similarly to Walker, and she had also bought a farmhouse and took on the publishing venture to publish experimental and radical writers and to pay them a fairer wage than strictly profit-seeking publishers were able to offer. Cunard published more well-known canonical writers, including Samuel Beckett and Ezra Pound. Meanwhile, Cunard also tossed in lyrics by her own partner, Henry Crowder. Thus, Walker must have wanted to make a statement in support of her own out-of-wedlock affair with a white editor by bringing this notorious affair from the past to the forefront. Editors at Harcourt would never have published *As Wonderful as All That?* and it might have remained unpublished permanently if it was not for Walker's determination to use her publishing company to make politically radical, anti-racist statements.

Similarly to the other radical writers, Walker was forced into attempting an independent publishing house by the boundaries and negative interactions she faced when working with other publishing companies. Alice Walker "felt mismatched, increasingly, with the white male editors she'd been assigned at Harcourt since 1968. She said she'd been rocked when [John] Ferrone, apparently puzzled by her epigraph in *The Color Purple*, one day asked her, 'Who is Stevie Wonder?'" After this and shortly after the publication of *The Temple of My Familiar*, she asked Harcourt for a new editor without notifying Ferrone.[630] At least for a short time, Walker decided that having a boyfriend as her editor was a friendlier and more productive arrangement than clashing with the likes of Ferrone, who simply did not understand her cultural values.

The relationships between Cunard and Crowder, and Walker and Allen were conducive to their publishing ambitions. Working with a lover has been a pattern Woolf, Cunard, Walker and other female pub-

---

630   Ibid., 461.

lishers settled for. While they might not have started publishing companies without these male supporters, when these ties to lovers were broken, all of them were forced to also abandon their publishing ventures. Few, if any, male author-publishers allowed their wives to join into formal publishing partnerships with them. For example, Mary Shelley contributed pieces to Percy Shelley's periodical, but he did not petition for her to become an equal partner in the enterprise (despite her strength as a writer and editor). Given these negative experiences, it seems like a fair advice to encourage author-publishers to avoid tying a publishing business to a lovers' partnership, as the end of love should not spell the end of art. Partnerships are complex enough as they are, and if passions enter this legal agreement, there are too many obstacles for any two creative individuals to overcome. It is difficult enough when authors like Poe and Shelley face assassination schemes for their radical publishing, to have to worry about a lover's quarrel ending a press' run. At the same time, perhaps Walker and Allen, or Cunard and Crowder needed their partner's spark to jump into publishing and to dare to publish outstanding, counter-cultural works. So, it is better that they loved and published, than to never have published at all.

Alice Walker has attained more personal wealth during her lifetime than any other author in this study. Therefore, her radical motivations behind Wild Trees Press have to be questioned. If she truly wanted to create a venue that would promote new African American voices, she could have continued operating Wild Trees as a non-profit. A donation of a few thousand annually could have helped the release of numerous outstanding African American titles. When any of the nineteenth century authors in this study started seeing great profits, they all reinvested the money into promoting their radical agendas. Failing to utilize these funds for this purpose suggests that Walker just wanted to cash in, and to be gloriously famous. This type of apathy has been the downfall of free expression in this past century.

While all of the authors in this study became best-sellers in their genres and eventually became canonized, nobody else attained close to Alice Walker's net worth of $300 million (TheFamousPeople.com) by her current age of 72. In contrast, while Charles Dickens might have sold over 700,000 copies of the *Bleak House* (1852) before his death in 1870 (Economist.com), he made pennies for each of these. If the inflation rate is taken into account, Dickens left a fortune of $10.32 million when he died. While this might be a pretty healthy sum, he had to support dozens of relatives on it. Most of his holdings were also in houses, which he kept selling at a disadvantage whenever he decided on moving. Dickens worked for the sake of a few thousand pounds from readings and other time and energy consuming projects, including his journal, up until his last day. Similarly to Leonard Woolf, he always felt as if he was a step away from bankruptcy, even after he gained riches. It would have been unthinkable for Dickens or the other canonical authors to give up on a press until they were facing a complete break-down, as Virginia Woolf was when she finally agreed to sell her shares of Hogarth. After working for decades to build up a journal of his own, Dickens would never voluntarily have closed its doors. In contrast, Alice Walker might have terminated her press before its time because she did not have something to say that would have otherwise been censored by major publishing houses. By 1984, mainstream publishers were happy to publish pornographically violent scenes, stories with interracial themes, sagas about revolutions, as well as feminist and anti-racist propaganda, as all of these niches were proven to lead to high sales. Thus, radical objectives and financial incentives were dulled for Walker. There were plenty of social problems to rally against, but perhaps the media started overloading, even somebody like Walker, into a sense of powerlessness. Or did she have difficulty breaking the books she published with Wild Trees Press into the mainstream? Her failure to launch Wild Trees titles' popularity probably made these relatively small publications seem unimportant when she could publish works that would be read by millions if released with one of the Big Four publishers. Regardless of the reasons for its brevity, other than Poe's *Penn* journal, which never got off the ground, Walker's press is the most short-lived on the list.

The last thing that Virginia Woolf wrote before her suicide was that Leonard was taking care of the flowers. In contrast, Alice Walker almost viewed her gardening as an equivalent task to cultivating a new publishing company. Her first full-length biographer, Evelyn C. White, explained that as soon as, her name was on the deed, "she began landscaping the property with one hundred fruit trees (pear, persimmon, and peach among them) and several luxuriant gardens."[631] I doubt that Walker was out there planting a hundred trees herself. It seems more likely that she hired somebody for this job, and this was why it was a pleasant endeavor, while Virginia had to worry about maintaining an

---

631   Ibid., 388.

enormous country estate and its gardens with only Leonard's help after Leonard fired her sole housekeeper. It is also unclear why White calls Virginia Woolf's "similar venture" a "success."[632] Virginia and Leonard barely scraped by, and when Virginia committed suicide, she believed that she was destined to live the rest of her life in toil and poverty. In one of her interviews with White, Walker explains her motivation for starting the publishing house: "Of course, I knew about Hogarth… It was part of my thinking. But mostly, Robert and I needed a project we could do in the country having fallen in love with living there. I suddenly had money to do publishing and Belvie was game. We loved doing things together!"[633] It is possible that Walker viewed the number of titles Hogarth released, the high caliber of the writers in the catalog, and Hogarth continued existence under other owners as measures of its success. On the other hand, it is possible that Walker's interviewers and biographers were introducing Hogarth into the conversation and Walker was agreeing that it was an inspiration, without doing any major research into the subject. It is unlikely that Walker read all those biographies, letters and diaries where Virginia Woolf describes how heart-breaking running an independent press was, or Walker would never have started her own. In another section of the biography, White writes: "To be sure, Alice had a room of her own. But unlike Virginia Woolf, Alice wrote with the threat of a firebomb being tossed into her home at any minute, and there was not a Bloomsbury Group with whom she could calmly sip afternoon tea and discuss her fears."[634] This is a warped perception of Virginia Woolf from somebody entirely lacking knowledge on the subject. Virginia heard bombs falling near her homes during both World War I and II, until the second of these conflicts drove her, in theory, to her suicide. And the Bloomsbury Group maintained very tense relationships between its members, and regardless of what they were drinking or wearing when they met, these meetings were anything but "calm." This type of stereotyping of white writers is disturbing, as it is a form of reverse-racism.

 Walker also did not start the press out of a sense that she would never succeed or make money without it, as other author-publishers did. As she says in another interview, she had the money to "do publishing," as opposed to doing publishing to obtain money. The "credo" Walker

---

632 Ibid.
633 Ibid.
634 Ibid., 184.

gave the press is also troubling: "We publish only what we love." I have not seen anything like this with any of the other publishers. How can "love" be measured or evaluated? Virginia Woolf wrote an essay trying to determine the mental acuity needed to properly review a manuscript. Nowhere, in this essay did Virginia propose that "love" was an ingredient in her calculations. It is more likely that Walker was trying to say: "I publish whatever I want." But, this might not have worked for her humanitarian image. It might have been this credo and negative sentiments that kept the best writers of Walker's generation away from Wild Trees, whereas they flocked to the other author-publishers. Walker's isolation on a distant farm might have also kept her out of the best writerly circles. In contrast, Virginia and Leonard suffered through numerous London society meetings and otherwise went out of their way to dig up great writers. Another possibility is a decline in authors worthy of canonization by the second half of the twentieth century. But, why would America's prosperity equal a decline in hyper-literacy?

A close look at Walker's first publication might help answer some of these questions. J. California Cooper released *A Piece of Mine* in November 1984 with Wild Trees Press. This book was later re-printed with Random House in 1991, a few years after Wild Trees closed. In her "Acknowledgment" to the 1991 edition, Cooper thanked Walker, adding that without Robert Allen and Alice Walker's publication, "my stories would still be sitting in a drawer, someday to be thrown out by somebody saying, 'These are useless.'" I doubt Mark Twain ever summarized his stories thusly, or thanked any of his publishers so profusely. The first story in this collection is called, "$100 and Nothing!" and begins with: "Where we lie is not a big town like some and not a little town like some, but somewhere in the middle, like a big little town." Is this description useful, or does it fail to communicate something vital and worthy of being in the handful of books that Alice Walker thought merited her financial investment? Walker certainly had great hopes for Cooper, describing *A Piece of Mine* thus in the Foreword: "In its strong folk flavor, Cooper's work reminds us of Langston Hughes and Zora Neale Hurston… Like theirs, her style is deceptively simple and direct, and the vale of tears in which some of her characters reside is never so deep that a rich chuckle at a foolish person's foolishness cannot be heard." There is a fine line between simplicity and low-brow pop. Hughes and Hurston both inserted layers of metaphor, symbolism, and linguistic tricks behind what looks like "simple" poetry. Meanwhile, tragi-comedy is also difficult to achieve. If a work had chuckles in the middle of tears, the reader might be startled out of their suspension of disbelief or sympathy with the teary characters as they are feeling an urge to chuckle. So, with compliments like this, why did Walker choose Cooper from millions of living writers as her first author? "Cooper could not believe her good fortune when she was asked directly by Alice to submit a manuscript for review. At the time, she was known primarily as a dramatist and had never been published in any other genre." In an interview with White on February 3, 1998, Cooper described the solicitation thus: "Alice attended one of my plays and afterward asked if I could recast the text as short stories… You better believe I went home and started writing." Cooper was named Black Playwright of the Year in 1978 for *Strangers*, and this might have been why Walker was particularly excited about working with her a few years later. Cooper knew that the giant publishers would be interested in just about anything she produced in the future if she released a book with Walker's press, and as White specifies, her "subsequent" books did find major publishers.

The next short stories collection Cooper released, in 1986, was with St. Martin's Griffin imprint, *Homemade Love*, which won the 1989 American Book Award, and she released books regularly after this point. The Author's Note in *Homemade Love* begins with: "I choose the name 'Homemade Love' because it is love that is not bought, not wrapped in fancy packaging with glib lines that often lie… Many more things, the best things, were all made at home, first. The Stradivarius, the first beds, even toilet paper…" Then the first paragraph of the first story, "Swimming to the Top of the Rain," includes this line: "Most mothers be your friend and love you…" And then a couple of paragraphs down the narrator says that she always prayed: "'Lord, please don't let me be no big fool in this life!' Cause you got to be thinking, and think hard…"[635]

Cooper also published a novel about a slave family that featured rape, baby-switching, and racism, *Family* (1991), with Random House, and several other books. Most were bestsellers and highly profitable. However, what competing books were rejected for *Homemade Love* to win an award? Did it win primarily because of Cooper's association with Walker? Minimalism has worked for many authors, but this con-

---

635   J. California Cooper. *Homemade Love*. (1986). (New York: St. Martin's Griffin, 1998), 1.

tent is repetitive, trite, cliché, and just a boring read. J. M. Coetzee, a Nobel laureate who pulls off minimalism classically, described Walker's *The Temple* as: "…enough… cliché-ridden prose… to give one pause…"[636] It just reads like hack work made for a living, and certainly not like work deserving of a major award.

Cooper never published another book with Walker. When describing the process of releasing a book with Walker, Cooper said: "I was consulted on the design of the book, its distribution, everything… People were riding Alice pretty rough because of *The Color Purple*. But from what I could see, she just concentrated on Wild Trees and her own writing."[637] There are serious moral problems with portraying rape, abuse and other problems in a graphic manner and then allowing it to be produced into a movie. The other author-publishers reviewed in this book were facing criticism and censorship because their views were pro-atheist, pro-democratic, anti-monarchical, and otherwise supported causes that have since been recognized as essential human rights. In contrast, why should Walker be excused for commercializing the brutalization of women in a style closer to *Fifty Shades of Grey* than to Dickens' *Bleak House*? Are some of these reservations behind Cooper's comments about *The Color Purple*? If not, why didn't Cooper submit a new book? One explanation is that unlike Dickens and Scott, Cooper was a somewhat unwilling writer. She gave only a few other interviews to newspapers where she explained her craft. One of these was with *The Dallas Morning News* on July 24, 1994,[638] in which Cooper said that she "writes her stories in bed, in longhand, usually in the early-morning hours. She says she is 'a bed-crazy person,' and that writing by hand 'is the only way I can get these people (the characters' voices to come.' Later, she will 'fill out the skeleton' of narrative as she transfers her work to a computer, to be printed out in manuscript form." Then she adds: "I don't know how to write… I just do it." She also repeats her own saying from *Homemade Love*: "Don't let me be a fool." Apparently, this is one of her favorite sayings… She also said that she worked "as a manicurist, a waitress, a secretary, a loan officer," and <u>even as a truck</u> and bus driver for the Teamsters in Alaska. In a later

636   J. M. Coetzee. "The Beginning of (Wo)man in Africa." *New York Times*. (30 April 1989), 7.
637   White, *Alice*, 388-9.
638   Michael Merschel. "Rare Interviews with J. California Cooper, Who Died Saturday." 26 September 2014. *The Dallas Morning News*. (Retrieved: 4 April 2016. Web).

interview with the same paper, she said that she bought her house in Marshall, Texas for $4,000 and put in $30,000 into fixing it up over the years. She also bought a new house in California in the year this interview took place, November 2, 1994. Thus, clearly her literary efforts finally allowed her to retire from all of the hard work she was doing previously. A decade later, on December 6, 2004, in another interview, Cooper said: "I'm not a real writer. I write because these people tell me these things." She adds: "It's important that this book sells because I've been gone so long [17 years]. The next contract is coming up, and also, I love this book…" Curiously, she also responded to "someone" "recently" comparing her work to Zora Neale Hurston. Walker had made this same parallel, but a good while earlier. To the comparison with Hurston, Cooper replied: "It was irksome, and it told me this person doesn't read. Sure, it's a compliment to be described as the 'new Zora Neale Hurston,' but it's not quite accurate… I know I'm nowhere near Tolstoy…" The last half of a century has seen comparatively few canonized writers, and those who win awards and gain popularity frequently talk about voices that are telling them what to write or writing in a dreamy stream of consciousness. At least, Cooper is self-reflective and aware that her fame and fortune stem more from luck than from the quality of her work.

If Poe was alive today, he would have written a very different review of Cooper's books than the glorifying ones that have appeared in *Publishers Weekly*. Puffery has become the norm. Cooper might have been onto something when she stated that anybody who compares her to Hurston must not have read neither her nor Hurston. Reviewers' main job is to be able to discern between a Hurston-caliber writer and a Cooper-caliber writer. Without a proper hierarchy of writerly achievement, students of modern literature are starting to believe that previously set literary quality rules have been turned on their heads. But, I have digressed into a study of Cooper because understanding her work is central to explaining why Walker closed her press four years after starting it…

Even more oddly, why didn't Walker choose to release even one of her own books with her own publishing company? Releasing radical works nobody else was willing to publish was the primary motivation for starting their own publishing companies for the other authors examined, and this might have been another reason why, lacking this motivation, Walker could more easily walk away from her press. In the first year of Wild Trees' operation, she had released a poetry collection, *Horses Make a Landscape Look More Beautiful*, with another major press. There were no boundaries to entry into the mainstream for Walker because horses and beautiful landscapes are not exactly the sort of thing that has the power to revolutionize society.

Before she started Wild Trees, she was facing some censorship, such as the attempted suppression of her story "Coming Apart" by the "antiporn faction." Walker was fighting for pornography… While it seems like this must be an exaggeration, it is not. I previously quoted from D. H. Lawrence on this point, and it needs to be repeated here: "But even I would censor genuine pornography. It would not be very difficult. In the first place, genuine pornography is almost always underworld, it doesn't come into the open. In the second place, you can recognize it by the insult it offers, invariably, to sex, and to the human spirit."[639] The term "porn" signifies that something depicts sex without artistic merit. Nude forms have been present in art since before the first Venus figurines from 35,000 years ago. There are plenty of fornicating couples in outstanding Greek and Roman art. So, for a writer to support "porn" or the dehumanizing sex act on film is troubling for any serious art critic. Yet, Walker encouraged her friends to watch *Deep Throat* with her when it first came out. Walker said that she was inspired by this porno about a woman that had a clitoris in her throat. While the promotion of the clitoris might be somewhat feminist, no viewer of this film can ignore that the lead actress, Linda Lovelace, was raped during the filming. Instead of being appalled, this inspired Walker to write an essay called, "Coming Apart" in 1980. This essay shows a husband who enjoys looking at pornographic magazines from the woman's perspective. Here are segments from it: "He studies the young woman—blond, perhaps (the national raze), with elastic wastes and inviting eyes—and strokes his penis. At the same time, his bowels stir with the desire to defecate…" Then the wife discovers this magazine and she is upset that her husband is looking at white women, and so he gets a magazine with black women and the wife observes, "a woman… twisted and contorted in such a way that her head is not even visible. Only her glistening body—her back and derriere-so that she looks like a human turd at the man's feet." Then they go to 42nd Street and the husband is "elated to see the blonde, spaced-out hookers, with their black pimps…" Then they get to a motel room, and watch two black

---

[639] Ibid., 74.

women, with one of them wearing "a chain around her ankle," singing: "'Free me from my freedom, chain me to a tree!'"[640] Walker apparently succeeded in placing this story into many school districts in the United States. It is clear that she was running a campaign to have it placed into the curriculum because some of the schools she queried "banned" it "temporarily."[641] Why and how did a story that advertises pornos enter any school curriculum? Is the current epidemic of children watching pornography online at all connected to Walker's placement of this very adult content into school districts? In contrast, Dickens burned a good deal of materials to keep his affair with an actress secret. There might have been sexual content in Virginia Woolf's novels, but she definitely never fought for sex and nudity for their own sake. Alice Walker certainly thought it was a worth-while effort, as she said in another interview with White: "Certain forms of censorship of a writer's work can be seen as honoring the writer… I have come to understand that it is 'the glimpse of life beyond the words' that those who censor writers are seeking to blot out."[642] Walker believed that the censorships she was a victim of for *The Color Purple* were racially motivated. Did she really have a case in this regard?

The Color Purple was released in 1982, received the Pulitzer Prize in 1983, and this led it to be popularly assigned in high schools across the United States. Meanwhile, Walker refused to attend the "lavish luncheon" and award ceremony that were standard Pulitzer activities saying about this decision: "I didn't have to show up and the check arrived in the mail."[643] What kind of a writer would willingly miss making their Pulitzer or Nobel Prize speech? These are anthologized and re-quoted by literary critics for decades to come. Take for example, Arthur Miller's acceptance speech for Distinguished Contribution to American Letters Award, made recently in 2001, where he talks about the difference between common and literary playwriting: "This stuff did not just happen nor had it been overheard. It was a highly composed, often sumptuous language…" Miller also talks about the role highbrow and common-folk linguistics have in writing: "For the English, consciousness of linguistic style springs from an unshakable fascination

640 Alice Walker. "Coming Apart." *The Other Woman: Stories of Two Women and a Man*. Susan Koppelman, Ed. (New York: Feminist Press at CUNY, 1984. 323-34), 324-6.
641 White, *Alice*, 328.
642 Ibid., 387.
643 Ibid., 363.

with class, which governs speech from the top of the social ladder down to the Cockneys who make a daunting point of artificiality by refusing to speak like other Englishmen. They are free to invent outrageous new usages that generally mock the proprieties of their betters." Miller and other canonical writers have used these types of speeches to support their stylistic or content choices. If Walker believed that writing just happens, and that African Americans are committing linguistic rebellion when they use dialects and slang, this was her chance to express these literary theories and to be heard by some of the brightest minds in America. But she refused to attend because she did not have to? She has made at least one speech on this topic, "The Black Writer and the Southern Experience," at her *alma mater* Sarah Lawrence college in 1984, a year after she could have given the Pulitzer speech. This speech was naturally anthologized inside *In Search of Our Mothers' Gardens, American Culture: An Anthology*, and several other sources. In it, she states: "…One wants to write poetry that is understood by one's people, not by the Queen of England. Of course, should she be able to profit by it too, so much the better, but since that is not likely, catering to her tastes would be a waste of time." Walker makes this argument in response to a white, middle-aged Northerner, supposedly one of her professors at college, telling her that she could not become a poet because she was a '"farmer's daughter.'"[644] The rest of this essay is spent on criticizing racism in other writers, and their lack of authenticity, while she does not return to the explanation for why her people would not understand the poetry of Keats. She uses Keats to explain that she had been educated in the classics, but she presumes that other farmers and poor blacks were never exposed to the same texts. Walker must have read Keats in school because Keats has long been on the standard curriculum. Thus, regardless of her contemporaries' race or class, they were exposed to Keats and the other classics Walker read. It is a very pessimistic and racist view of the American education system to suggest that the lower class and members of certain races are incapable of retaining British classics. These types of stereotypes perpetuate the education gap, so it is troubling that the wealthiest African American female writer expressed these stereotypes on anthologized rhetoric. She might have done much more for the betterment of African Americans if she

---

644   Alice Walker. "The Black Writer and the Southern Experience." (1984). *American Culture: An Anthology*. Anders Breidlid, Ed. (New York: Routledge, 2013), 214.

wrote books for the vibrant audience of highly educated blacks, like herself, in a style that rivaled Keats and appeased the Queen. Walker's point is that she is writing for the popular market, knowing the low literacy rates that it represents. She is selling to this poorly educated majority because only a small percentage of world readers could understand denser linguistic prose. Perhaps she did not give this speech at the Pulitzer because she thought she would not get another one if she confessed this. The Pulitzer, after all, is meant for "literature" and not for pop fiction.

White explained that Walker felt mistreated when *The Color Purple* was nominated for only eleven Oscars. These Oscars included a best supporting actress nomination for Oprah Winfrey, and a best actress nomination for Whoopi Goldberg, for both of whom this was a "debut screen performance."[645] Walker was offended because her film did not win in any of these categories. But, who nominated her for so many Oscars? And can somebody thus exalted honestly complain that she is being discriminated against because she did not win the top prize? This film was even rated PG-13, once again disregarding its incestuous sex, violence, language and drug content. In an interview on October 9, 1997 with White, Whoopi Goldberg said: "The Hollywood NAACP cost us every one of the Academy Awards… They killed the chances for me… I truly believe that. And blacks in Hollywood paid a price for years to come. But after all the hell that was raised, the studios didn't want to do any more black movies for fear of the picket lines and boycotts." In other words, the sexual and otherwise explicit content in this film was so offensive that the entire African American film establishment suffered for it. Meanwhile, "Walker viewed the loss as beneficial because it highlighted her 'purity' and avoided the corruption that prizes often bring." During the Academy Awards, there were protests in front of the theater with signs like "*The Color Purple* Destroys The Color Black!" Walker had to cross a picket line for the first time in her life to get in to view the awards.[646] Why was she this eager to attend these pop awards (stepping over the bodies of her protesting black peers), and skipped the Pulitzer? Walker and the others involved with this film all stress that the criticism was faulty, but statistics about the impact of this film and others like it certainly point to the factuality of the sign that Walker refused to acknowledge as she crossed it to

---

645 White, *Alice*, 430-1.
646 Ibid., 433.

attend a glitzy party.

Long before Steven Spielberg knocked on Walker's door to solicit the rights to make the movie, at the end of the 1983-1984 school year, in May, an African American mother of a student at the Far West High School in Oakland, California, a predominantly African American district, filed a complaint with her local Board of Education, asking for *The Color Purple* to be removed from the curriculum.[647] White summarizes that this mother, Donna Green, complained that the novel "was sexually explicit, sacrilegious, exceedingly violent, biased toward lesbianism, and degrading to black people through its use of an 'embarrassing' folk dialect." While free speech is a commendable fight, of which I am usually a full supporter, perhaps the abuse of readers with this barrage of linguistic violence is something deserving of the typically villainized pro-censorship position. A panel of literary experts supported Walker in Oakland, but several other campaigns to ban the book sprung up in West Virginia and Oregon. White argues that *The Color Purple* has thus "joined an illustrious list of books by American authors that had been challenged in the past," but can it really be equivalent in literary value with Mark Twain's *Huckleberry Finn*, John Steinbeck's *The Grapes of Wrath*, or Langston Hughes "Ballad of the Landlord" as White suggests? Did Walker deliberately push the censorship boundaries to join this list, as White suggests she started Wild Trees to imitate Woolf's example? Rape and brutality certainly should be present in novels if they are true to the author's experience, but is there a line where rape becomes pornographic and thereby truly obscene? And are linguistically folksy novels spreading this semi-literate dialect to students? If students adopt the illiterate slang into their daily conversations, they are more likely to fail at the standardized tests that test their knowledge of the standard dialect? The real test of radicalism for a book is a refusal to publish from the mainstream publishers. And there are plenty of mainstream publishers willing to publish stories about rape and murder. All of the literature that White compares Walker's to is fighting for social justice on behalf of the poor, migrants, tenants, and other disenfranchised groups. In contrast, *The Color Purple* is more like the 1986 film about fetishism and abuse, *Blue Velvet*, which seems to be mimicking Walker's title. Can it even be compared with Nabokov's *Lolita*, which was banned as obscene in France (1956-

---

647   Richard Colvin. "Mom Objects to Prize Novel for High School Reading List." *Oakland Tribune*. (3 May 1984).

9), England (1955-9), Argentina (1959) and New Zealand (1960)? While it has been outlawed around the world, it was only challenged once in the United States by the Mario-Levy Public Library System in Ocala, Florida in 2006 on the grounds that it was "unsuitable for minors." Naturally, considering the central topic of child sexual abuse, *Lolita* is never taught in American middle or high school classes, so it has no history of bans by school boards. So, how did Walker find critics anywhere who were willing to overlook similar problems in *The Color Purple*? It features more brutal, graphic, and continuous child non-consensual sexual abuse, beatings and incest, in contrast with the more gradual introduction of consensual molestation in *Lolita*. The fights against prohibitions of outstanding canonical works are for the social well-being of all. Schools would lose some of their best teaching materials if the following books had been successfully banned: Aldous Huxley's *Brave New World*, George Orwell's *Animal Farm*, Kate Chopin's *The Awakening*, and Jack London's *The Call of the Wild*. On the other hand, why did John Updike's *Rabbit, Run* ever enter Aroostock County, ME community high school libraries in 1976, and why was it taught in English classes at the Medicine Bow, WY Junior High School in 1986, so that it had to be removed from the required reading list for sex and profanity?

I "met" John Updike once shortly before he died at a signing he held in Cambridge, Massachusetts. The line of people who wanted to purchase his books was longer than for any other author signing I have ever seen: it stretched across an auditorium and out of the door. I stood at the front and watched him interact with the buyers. He would smile to them, but only said a few words as he focused on processing the ordered books with signature. I had never read his books before, but the line inspired me to glance at what it was all about. I scanned one of the *Rabbit* books, and they were all just bad-mouthed pop novels. Having gone to a lot of signings, exhibits and the like, I think these books are read simply because of the hype around them. But, why would this fan-mania justify putting a hollow, insulting, anti-feminist, or otherwise inappropriate and inartistic book on a school curriculum? Meanwhile, school districts are only too happy to ban great works to object to social ills in a beautiful and literary way; perhaps, these literary masterpieces are likely to change the world for the better, while pop-mania continues a cycle of violence, rape, and the general devolution of American culture.

Did the popularity of *The Color Purple* and similar novels in the eighties cause the African American culture to spin toward hip-hop, slang and insult-driven linguistics? Hip-hop only had one popular hit before 1983. But, in this same year as Walker's release, a wave of hip-hop began the process of establishing it as the top best-selling music genre that it is today. According to the National Association for the Advancement of Colored People, the overall number of incarcerated people in American rose from 500,000 in 1980 to 2.3 million in 2008. "African Americans are incarcerated at nearly six times the rate of whites," making up nearly half of the total prison population, or around 1 million. Further still, "One in six black men had been incarcerated as of 2001." According to an article titled, "Chart of the Week: The black-white gap in incarceration rates," published on the PewResearch.org website: "While institutionalization rates rose for both blacks and whites from 1980 to 2000, it was especially sharp among the less educated black men—rising from 10% in 1980 for those ages 20 to 24 to 30% in 2000." The sharpest incline was among the least educated men. Perhaps, reading and listening to literature and music with the sort of messages that Donna Green objected to in 1984 is what is driving this downward trend.

Why would it be empowering to read stories that are written in the "simple," colloquial style? Walker has clarified that she believes that adopting this vernacular shows one's allegiance with other African Americans. Arguing that linguistics is racially-determined is racist. The standards of the English language are set by dictionaries and by accepted pronunciation norms. To say that any race should have unified linguistic rules is absurd. Linguists have found regional variations in American usage, grammar, pronunciation and other patterns, but linguistic similarities in a racial group spread out across the country indicates that these elements are picked up from shared music, books and other pop content.

Between Brown vs. Board of Education (1954) that ended segregation in schools and the Voting Rights Act of 1965 that guaranteed no discrimination at the polls for blacks and on through 1984, African American activists kept pushing for equality in the education system. Walker was born in 1944, before segregation ended, but she was still at the start of her education in 1954 when it did, so that she graduated as a valedictorian from the Butler-Baker High School and successfully enrolled in Spelman College in 1961. Later, she worked on voter registration in Georgia in 1965, so she saw the changes brought about by the Voting Rights Act first-hand. In the following three years, she graduated from a school that she transferred to, Sarah Lawrence, worked for the welfare office in New York City, married an attorney, Mel Leventhal, published her first book, *Once*, and became a writer-in-residence at Jackson State College. Walker won a contract with Harcourt Brace Jovanovich, one of the biggest publishers of the day. This deal was struck with the help of her agent, Monica McCall, who convinced the publisher to run a poetry collection first before they could get a novel deal with Walker. At first the editor declined, but when McCall said everybody else had said "no" too, he accepted it, and it sold 3,000 copies, a high number for poetry.[648] Harcourt later paid $30,000 for the paperback rights to *The Color Purple*, despite the fact that an earlier Walker novel, *Meridian* "had sold very few copies." The high advance for *The Color Purple* was achieved with the convincing help of her editor, Susan Ginsburg, who said in an interview with White on November 1, 1995, that she convinced them to gamble on a novel "in dialect and written in letter form…" *The Color Purple* ended up staying on the bestseller list for a year, so Harcourt was more than happy to work with Walker on future projects.[649]

Back in 1971, Walker was accepted for a writing fellowship at the Radcliffe Institute in Cambridge with an application essay that stated: "…although I have recently published my first one, I am sometimes not sure I know what a novel is…" She added that she wanted to be among writers and scholars because: "Mississippi has been anything but inspiring."[650] She was accepted into Harvard because she said she did not understand what a novel was? Another component of her application was a recommendation letter from Walker's college professor, Jane Cooper, who also applied, but was not awarded the fellowship, unlike her incredibly "lucky" student.

Publicity stories that attempt to portray Walker as a victim stress that her eye was injured in a BB gun accident by one of her brothers and that she was molested, and then later became suicidal as a result of these traumas. But, these are isolated incidents, while Virginia Woolf's entire biography is made up of countless strings of similar traumas. 20% of women are raped during some part of their life, and 25% of

---

648   White, *Alice*, 163.
649   Ibid., 362.
650   Ibid., 208.

girls are sexually abused before they turn 18 according to the National Sexual Violence Resource Center. There is a similarity in this regard between Woolf and Walker because of this frequency, but Virginia became rigid and had very negative sexual experiences after the molestation, while Walker had a healthy sexual life with multiple partners, including women, who clearly made her very happy. There is no sign of the trauma impacting Walker's later life, so why do biographies and stories about Walker stress these isolated moments? When she got a job as a contributing editor for *Ms.* For $11,500 in 1974, she negotiated on never attending meetings, insisted on a private office, and avoided talking with the rest of the staff because she argued: "It was hard to be among the first wave of black people to integrate white institutions, even feminist ones, like *Ms.*"[651] If she segregated herself, how was she fighting for integration? This is a fairytale first book sale story: a writer with her first little poetry collection miraculously scores an agent, and then a top publisher. This rise was immediate and meteoric, and unlike all the other writers that started their own presses, there were no apparent obstacles to this climb towards a successful academic career and publication. Why didn't Walker choose to write about these honest triumphs in her life, instead focusing on painful childhood memories that made up a small fraction of it? Is *The Color Purple* really authentic in its linguistics and narrative to a valedictorian who married a lawyer and became a professor? Walker is a member of the first post-segregation generation, so the following generations looked up to her for examples about what black people should sound and act like, and she had a responsibility to show that it was her intellectual work that won her acclaim.

Should Some Books Be Banned?

The point of equality in school funding after desegregation should have been a right to become equally literate with white students. The adoption of mainstream "white" linguistics should have made America a linguistically race-less society. The African American dialect and slang should have been submerged when they started attending the same schools and being offered the same rigorous level of education to whites. Of course, some slang and linguistic regional diversity has been a natural component of world culture and sometimes linguistic

---
651   Ibid., 266.

uniqueness identifies a culture even if their dress or customs have been assimilated into mainstream culture. Just as the first integrated African American generation was coming of age, having completed their education in de-segregated schools, the hip-hop epidemic emerged in parallel with the rise of gangs and a pro-criminal culture. This epidemic has been spreading without any serious attempts by the most successful African Americans to overturn this trend. Can Alice Walker really argue that popularizing a culture of violence, abuse, slang and illiteracy is a cause that she should not have been censored for? If this was her crusade, why didn't she publish a novel still more violent and sexually explicit when she could do whatever she wanted with her own publishing company?

Dickens, Poe, Byron and Shelley were writing during the first push towards a free public education system, which has allowed for the education of all willing students in modern societies across the world. However, too many Americans are not willing to put in an effort despite the free admission. According to the 2013 article, "The U.S. Illiteracy Rate Hasn't Changed in 10 Years," in the *Huffington Post*, 14% of Americans can't read. How is this possible with a universal education system that allows for every child to receive 12 years of free education? If these students enter the school system, and leave it after 12 years, still illiterate... it seems that it has to be pressure from American culture or from their peers that is convincing them that despite opportunities, they can refrain from taking advantage of them. *The Huffington Post* article concluded that there is a correlation between illiteracy and imprisonment, "85 percent of all juveniles who interface with the juvenile court system are functionally illiterate, and over 70 percent of inmates in America's prisons cannot read above a fourth grade level."[652] It is little wonder that with stats like this, a novel that uses simple vocabulary, slang and minimalist linguistics can attain far more popularity than a structurally and linguistically complex novel that would be above the vast majority's reading level. So, is Walker fighting for a right to illiteracy with her fiction? Perhaps, such a fight should be censored?

Because I found myself asking these dangerous questions regarding if there is room for censorship, I looked up an article called, "Banned and/or Challenged Books from the Radcliffe Publishing Course Top 100 Novels of the 20th Century" on the ALA website. This lengthy

---

652 "The U.S. Illiteracy Rate Hasn't Changed In 10 Years." *Huffington Post.* Posted: 6 September 2013. Web. Retrieved: 14 June 2017.

summary, derived from Robert P. Doyle's 2010 ALA release, *Banned Books: Challenging our Freedom to Read*, is helpful for remembering instances where censorship has been unfair because it stemmed in fears of radicalism or of social movements. In this list, there are (naturally) may objections from Baptist and other religious colleges, schools and churches on the grounds of religious morality. One of these is a solitary objection to F. Scott Fitzgerald's, *The Great Gatsby*, by the Baptist College in Charleston, SC in 1987. Some of the books with the longest lists of censorship objections include *The Catcher in the Rye* by JD Salinger. One early 1963 objection in a Columbus, Ohio high school to *Catcher* argues that the book is "anti-white"; later appeals added that it had too much sex, violence and the occult. Many of these objections are prudish or absurd. On the other hand, as in some cases of censorship of publishers of radical literature reviewed in other sections of this study, some authors on this banned list have faced jail terms for publishing politically radical content.

For example, John Steinbeck's eleven, Turkish, *Grapes of Wrath* publishers were put on trial in a martial law tribunal and were accused of "spreading propaganda unfavorable to the state." The threat of up to six months in prison is certainly too harsh a sentence for publishing a novel about western migration. Green's complaint to the Oakland Board of Education was not alone in voicing outrage about the negative image blacks had in literature. The battle over *Grapes of Wrath* started in Bakersfield, one of the poorest California counties, which was dealing with a significant portion of the western migration by impoverished Americans who were all desperately seeking employment with their giant farming manufacturers, and were accepting horrible working and living conditions in exchange for these desperately needed jobs. *Grapes* challenged these mega-farmers and threatened their ability to see extraordinary profits on the backs of these migrants. So, these farmers and the associations that represented them brought a complaint against the book to the Kern County Board of Supervisors. They took advantage of the Red Scare to cloud their fight against deregulation and fair wages with the notion that the book was socialist propaganda. With the help of Supervisor Stanley Abel, they passed a resolution to ban the book on the grounds that it "has offended our citizenry by falsely implying that many of our fine people are a low, ignorant, profane and blasphemous type living in a vicious and filthy manner." Further still, it accused Steinbeck of presenting "public officials, law enforcement officers and civil administrators, businessmen, farmers… as inhumane vigilantes, breathing class hatred and divested of sympathy or human decency…" The criticism continued that it was "filled with profanity, lewd, foul and obscene language…" The Board of Supervisors resolved, "in defense of our free enterprise," that the planned production of the motion picture version of the novel be stopped by Fox, and a ban on it be executed in "libraries and schools." This resolution passed four to one without any discussion, but it led to many similar bans and much more lively discussions on the matter in other regions. This ban eventually hit hardest in Turkey, despite the fact that the big farmer-administrators attacked in this book were specifically tied to Bakersfield. This wave of banning of *Grapes* in other regions was paddled, in part, by the Associated Farmers of California, and especially their Kern County chapter, who aided bans in as far away as Turkey and Kansas City.[653]

Harper Lee's *To Kill a Mockingbird* was challenged in Warren, IN schools in 1981 on the grounds that it was doing "psychological damage to the positive integration process" and represented "institutionalized racism under the guise of good literature." When they failed to ban the novel, "three black parents resigned from the township human relations advisory council." The resignation speaks to the commitment of these parents and their moral fortitude; if they were not sincerely concerned, they would not have gone this far to protest this book. Green had complained about similar social issues. The bulk of the following requests for bans were regarding the appropriateness of the work for young readers due to sex and violence. There was one complaint in a New Burn, North Carolina High School in 1992 regarding the main character being raped by her stepfather. This storyline has been one of the more direct explanation for the violence and sex objections. More recently, in 2002, it was challenged by the Parents Against Bad Books in Schools in Fairfax County, Virginia's elementary and secondary libraries because it was said to "contain profanity and descriptions of drug abuse, sexually explicit conduct, and torture."

A high percentage of Walker's books have been sold to "elementary and secondary" school districts for class use and to libraries. The movie ranking system insists that to see an R-rated movie, anybody under 17 has to be accompanied by an adult. The minimum age went

---

[653] Rick Wartzman. *Obscene in the Extreme: The Burning and Banning of John Steinbeck's* The Grapes of Wrath. (New York: PublicAffairs: Persues Book Group, 2008), 7-10.

up from 16 to 17 in 1970, but book rankings have been moving in the opposite direction. A typical R rating comes with warnings about: violence, language, substance abuse, nudity, and sexual content. If Walker's *The Color Purple* includes every one of these categories, how did it get in any high, middle, or elementary schools? The bulk of the students reading it are under 17. According to "American Teens' Sexual and Reproductive Health," an article published by the *Guttmacher Institute* in 2014: 48% of American adolescents have had sex by 17. If they were not accessing pornography and sexually explicit materials before this age, would this number be this high? The vast majority of these kids will not marry until their mid-twenties, a decade later. And at least 11% of 18-year-olds describe their first sexual experience as being "unwanted." Before age 15, a majority of girls report that their first experience was non-voluntary. The biggest change between 1988 and 1998 was that the rate of adolescent females, 14 and under, having intercourse went up from 11% to 19%. If these youths were not exposed to *The Color Purple* and other similarly objectionable novels, would more of them have refrained from having intercourse at such a young age? Has anybody seriously suggested teaching in the middle school curriculum Marquis de Sade's *Nouvelle Justine* (1791) about a virtuous woman who is abused and raped, or the novel about her sister, *Juliette* (1799), an amoral nymphomaniac murderer? These are works for which de Sade was imprisoned and classified as a pornographer. The linguistic style of these books is highly dense and sophisticating and presents a more valuable artistic achievement than Walker's. Thus, de Sade is surely more deserving to have his work purchased by all major libraries. Still, there is no sane high school teacher who would put either of de Sade's novels on the syllabus. Is there any chance that a majority of teens who became sexually active did so after reading *The Color Purple*, considering how popular it is in school curriculums? The book's popularity has only grown because of the few objects that have been raised against it. Toni Morrison's *Beloved*, the 1987 Pulitzer Prize winner, was challenged by the Coeur d' Alene School district in Idaho in 2007 by parents saying that "parental permission" should be required for students to read it. The more I study ALA's banned books summary, the more I realize that it includes the vast majority of the books I was assigned at the Framingham High School in Massachusetts. Why are these books so popular in high schools? Of course, many of these works are central to understanding the world we live in, but why does the curriculum include so few books without bannable content? What would an un-censorable, non-R-rated book look like?

***

But, to return to Walker's interviews with Evelyn C. White, published in her biography. Walker hired an assistant, Joan Miura, "a former arts administrator," who helped "with the deluge of fan mail, speaking invitations fund-raising pitches, and inquiries about Wild Trees Press." Miura explains that this barrage was problematic: "What we'd envisioned as a one-day-a-week job quickly expanded into a full-time enterprise. Alice received cartons of gifts and bouquets of flowers. You name it, it came through the door."[654] It is unclear why gaining a full-time job was "staggering" for Miura, and why she did not quit if it was overwhelming, as a good deal of Virginia Woolf's early assistants did, unless Miura was well enough paid to have stuck with it regardless of the workload. Of course, if Miura started making a full-time salary that was sufficient to entice a "former arts administrator," perhaps this expense became so high over the four years of the press' operation that by the end, closing the press meant saving a great deal of money. Each book would have had to become an extraordinary best-seller to employ even a single administrator of this caliber. Walker probably quickly learned that without a publicity and marketing budget that matched those provided by the giant publishers that sold millions of her own books, she could not create equivalent bestsellers. The only other alternative she had was producing an enormous quantity of books, but apparently Miura failed at being dedicated enough to spend extremely long days on bringing this to fruition, or perhaps Walker did not let her have a go at it. "We became too successful and we really didn't want to turn it over to other people because it was our vision." In a similar situation, Woolf got her assistant to pay her to purchase her share of the company, so why didn't Walker attempt this or its variant with Miura? White summarizes that Wild Trees Press was "dedicated to the development of marginalized writers,"[655] but the term "development" usually implies working with a writer as their career progresses, rather than publishing solitary works without any prior or consecutive oversight or assistance. The term "marginalized" means "insignificant

---

654   White, *Alice*, 434.
655   Ibid., 457.

or peripheral." This word started gaining popularity in the seventies. While it is frequently used, it sounds to me like an insult that has been applied to minority writers. Does anybody want to be called "insignificant"? Why would any publisher set out to publish insignificant writers? And if Walker was going after those who are truly ostracized and discriminated against, why pick somebody like Cooper, who had just won a major award for her play? Virginia and Leonard Woolf certainly did not set out to publish insignificant writers, and a big part of finding great writers is looking for them.

One of the two biographical books Wild Trees Press released was *Ready from Within: Septima Clark and the Civil Rights Movement* (1986). It was narrated by Septima Clark in a mixture of English and an African-American, South Carolinian dialect to the editor, Cynthia Stokes Brown. In the forward of this book, Brown thanked Walker, Robert Allen, Belvie Rooks and "their production staff," implying that they had more than one employee, for their "enthusiasm" in soliciting the book from her.[656] Septima describes that male African American Civil Rights leaders, "just thought that women were sex symbols and had no contribution to make. That's why Rev. Abernathy would say continuously, 'Why is Mrs. Clark on this staff?'/ Dr. King would say, 'Well she has expanded our program…'"[657] While this seems uplifting, she later explains that, "like other black ministers, Dr. King didn't think too much of the way women could contribute. But working in a movement he changed the lives of so many people that it was getting to the place where he would have to see that women are more than sex symbols."[658] These quotes are repeating the term "sex symbol," but they are contradicting each other in meaning. One says that King is known for supporting women, while another stresses that he viewed them as objects. These types of contradictions create distrust for the author's exactitude, and show a lack of editing, a step essential for a work to attain academic status deserving of a major civil rights activist like Septima Clark.

Another notable publication from Wild Trees Press was the 1987, *As Wonderful as All That?: Henry Crowder's Memoir of His Affair with Nancy Cunard 1928-1935,* by Henry Crowder. He put his own name

---

656 Septima Clark. *Ready from Within: Septima Clark and the Civil Rights Movement.* (Navarro (CA): Wild Trees Press, 1986), ix.
657 Ibid., 77.
658 Ibid., 79.

into the title of his autobiography in the third person... Oddly, for a story about a love affair, there are only a couple of references to sex. In one of these, Crowder writes, for some reason, again in third person: "Neither she nor Henry had much to say about their sex life. Its importance faded with time; each found other lovers. Like some women who have been sexually abused in childhood, Nancy was promiscuous while also experiencing difficulty in being sexually satisfied..."[659] "Negro" appears in this book 52 times, according to Google Books. This term was part of Henry's seduction strategy over Nancy: "But she was interested and eager to learn. I told her of Negro writers; told her where she could get books on and by them. Gradually, she began to build up her library with Negro books..."[660] "White woman" appears 32 times, in references such as, "...publicly on intimate terms with a wealthy white woman, even if it was in Europe, adopted an inoffensive amiability as a kind of defensive covering..."[661] The frequency of these terms is natural to the central topic of the book, the love affair between a black man and a "wealthy white woman." She is also referred to as Nancy 83 times, a count that is only twice larger than the general "white woman" reference. Then again, neither of them are glorified: "If Nancy was flawed, Henry was no gem. What was it, finally, that they saw in each other, that each apparently found so irresistible? Did they love each other, or was their relationship simply an instance of mutual use and abuse?"[662] Well, this is an honest question from the editor. This book is an exploration of an interracial relationship with all its flaws, and Walker was interested in it because her own marriage to a white, Jewish man did not end happily either. It offers a glimpse at the racial tensions during segregation, when interracial couples were putting themselves at risk of not only being deported,[663] but also potentially lynched back in the States.

Good intentions shine through the releases Walker solicited for *Wild Trees*. They promised to be biographies and works of fiction by the most famous, award-winning and politically active African American writers she could easily access. But, despite its triumphs, it is clear

---

659   Henry Crowder. *As Wonderful as All That?: Henry Crowder's Memoir of His Affair with Nancy Cunard, 1928-1935*. (Mendocino County: Wild Trees Press, 1987), 198.
660   Ibid., 83.
661   Ibid., 196.
662   Ibid., 198.
663   Ibid., 12, 102.

that this was not a sustainable business venture. There was a lack of editorial passion that might have kept it afloat for a longer duration.

There are similarities between the other radical author-publishers and Walker in her direct accusations of injustice against the government, and groups like the "white" people. She also funded rebels, and participated in demonstrations. However, there is also something strangely different about the types of problems she was fighting for in this modern age. For example, in early 1990s she helped to raise funds to defend "Mumia Abu-Jamal, a black journalist serving a death sentence for alleged murder of a white police officer in Philadelphia."[664] Mumia was found with a wound and an empty gun right near the shot officer, who was there because he was conducting a traffic stop of Mumia's brother, William Cook. There were no other potential shooters, and Mumia had no business coming across the street with a gun, unless he intended to shoot the officer to stop him from questioning his brother. Is this really the sort of case that liberals in American have been defending from the time of this incident, in 1981, to the present day, 2017, when Mumia is still alive and well, though still incarcerated? After visiting Mumia, Alice complimented him on his "gentle, masculine beauty"… So she gathered money for his defense because he was pretty (even if he might have been guilty)? Walker also commented in 1991 that the accused, African American sexual harasser, Supreme Court Justice Clarence Thomas, should spend five days with a cappella singer, Bernice Johnson Reagon, so she "could bring Clarence around." It is highly disrespectful to Anita Hill, the victim who filed the complaint, to suggest that all Clarence needed was to find a real woman to make him behave like a good boy. As a victim of violence and harassment herself, it is very strange that Walker consistently takes these strange positions.

While Dickens was less than polite with Queen Victoria during the interview he had with her shortly before his death, Alice Walker outright refused to meet President Bill Clinton, writing to him a letter saying that she disliked his Cuban embargo policy: "Would you want Chelsea to have no milk?… You are a large man, how would yourself survive?"[665] Can the last bit count as a death threat? Did Clinton go on his vegan diet after this suggestion? Was this really a serious po-

---

664   White, *Alice*, 460.
665   Alice Walker. "A Letter to President Clinton." *Anything We Love Can Be Saved*. (New York: Random House, 1997), 215.

litical argument that she used for refusing to meet the President? Such a meeting would have allowed her to make this or a string of similar arguments in person. Walker's story is ongoing, so there can be no conclusion here.

CONCLUSIONS

Several patterns and discrepancies apparent from the experiences of previous major author-publishers have been discussed across this study. To understand how they fit in the history of publishing and to draw conclusions a comparative study is needed. Thus, this section will compare the focal authors in a series of parameters, and will explain the results statistically and theoretically.

Political Causes of Author-Publishers

All of the central author-publishers had a political cause they championed that made it difficult for them to publish their books with publishers that conformed to mainstream, government and church-approved policies. Some of their causes were actual revolutions. Others were aimed at problems within the publishing industry. A majority of these causes were on behalf of the contested social reforms of their time.

Sir Walter Scott spent most of his career as a judge, or a representative of the United Kingdom's government. As such, publicly, he was against reforms. But, anonymously, he funded a relatively radical publishing company with which he published a string of Waverley novels about the Jacobite rebellions, and other topics related to Scottish cultural and political independence. His novels and his lobbying convinced George IV to visit Scotland (the first such visit in hundreds of years) and to wear a kilt that represented Scottish national pride. Scott's Waverley series also contributed to inspiring the Scottish Insurrection of 1820, which failed, but stirred up the dormant rebellious desire to separate that the Scottish and Irish "kingdoms" have continued to display.

Lord Byron tried to argue for reforms as a member of the House of Lords in his youth. But, by the end of his life, he decided that poetry and political rhetoric could not solve the problems the world was facing. So, he sponsored militarily and financially the Greek War of Independence, which eventually succeeded in 1832. This war is the reason Greece is currently an independent country.

Author	Political Cause	Outcome of the Struggle
Sir Walter Scott	Scottish nationalism and independence, as well as preservation of the Scottish cultural heritage	George IV visited Scotland and wore a kilt; Scottish Insurrection of 1820 failed
Lord Byron/ Percy Shelley	Greek War of Independence/ atheism	Succeeded, 1832/ criminal blasphemy outlawed, 2008
Charles Dickens	US copyrights and fair royalties rights for authors	US joined UCC (1955) and Berne Convention (1989)
Virginia Woolf	Feminism and women's rights to independence	Women won the full right to vote in the UK in 1928, after *To the Lighthouse*
Benjamin Franklin	American independence	Won the American Revolution in 1783
Edgar Allan Poe	Anti-plagiarism campaign	No confessions/ charges
Mark Twain	Fair author profit sharing	Went bankrupt offering Grant and others 50%
Herman Melville	Fight for highbrow American literature	Spent a fortune on privately printing poetry
Henry Luce (and Briton Haddon)	Acquisition of stock control and American imperialism	Luce controlled Time, and influenced perspective on America as a world power
Dudley Randall	Black Power/ Art Movement	Published/ popularized numerous black writers
Alice Walker	Inter-racial relationships rights and black rights	Civil Rights Movement led to desegregation and other civil rights laws

Fig. 2. Authors and Their Political Causes

Charles Dickens traveled to the United States twice to discuss the pirated editions of his books with the publishers who were pirating them and to lobby for international copyrights laws. This legislation would make it illegal for American printers to reproduce his work without his permission, or without paying him royalties. Dickens sacrificed his health on the second trip, as it was an arduous sea voyage back then, but did manage to reach agreements with some of these publishers. International copyright is still a contested issue. But, the US did join the Universal Copyright Convention (UCC) in 1955, and the Berne Convention in 1989. These agreements mean that the signed countries promise to honor copyrights made in the other signed countries. Dickens started his own journal rightfully thinking that he would make a bigger share of the profits if he published, wrote and edited it himself. This step was an extension of his fight for international royalties, and, in general, higher royalty shares for authors.

Virginia Woolf started publishing novels with her own independent press before the United Kingdom gave women the right to vote. Her feminist books, such as *To the Lighthouse*, might have contributed to the British women's struggle, as they advocated for it to a relatively large audience. She also wrote *A Room of One's Own* and other non-fiction women's rights books after the full vote was granted in 1928. Virginia was faced with pressure from her physician, Dr. Savage, and others, who instructed her that women who read and write are likely to go crazy because they think too much. Thus, it was a radical struggle for her to stand up for women's rights to independence in employment and habitation in this critical period.

Benjamin Franklin's cause is more obvious as he was one of the Founding Fathers and played a central role in the American Revolution, which ended in 1783. Up to this point, American printer-publishers were frequently imprisoned on sedition, libel and other charges that also plagued printer-publishers in the United Kingdom. As one of the leading practitioners of this trade in the States, Benjamin was actively helping new printers to become established. Thus, he had to support the Revolution to prevent this ongoing harassment of publishers who released books that were critical of the monarch or the Church. Not only the Revolution, but the growth of American publishing succeeded once American publishers had the freedom to express their sincere political views. The press was instrumental in spreading the message of the revolutionary movement. If the King had succeeded in suppressing the American free press, the Revolution would not have been possible.

Edgar Allan Poe had more difficulty breaking into full-time employment as an editor, author, or even as a freelancer than the other writers in this group. When he found editorial work, he frequently clashed with the publisher and ended up leaving months, or, in the best cases, a bit over a year later. At least at one low point, he ghostwrote a book for another author, and he might have made up for his fiscal deficiencies by ghostwriting across his turbulent career. Because he dabbled in this area, Poe was particularly concerned about plagiarism among the top-earning authors of his day, who were also comfortably employed as academics, such as Longfellow. Because he had ghostwritten for some of them, he suspected others of taking advantage of ghostwriters, or, even worse, stealing their content without paying for the other writer's work. There was plenty of evidence pointing to mimicry of poetic style, topics, and even outright theft of lines that Poe detailed in his criticism. Poe also attempted to publish a pop novel, which was similar to Melville's early travel fiction, with Harper. But, Poe hardly made anything from it despite sacrificing his artistic standards to write a formulaic book. In the process of publishing a pop novel, he also learned about puffed reviews that are written in exchange for ads in a journal, or in exchanges for positive reviews from competing writers. He resented that others were getting ahead using these unethical practices and he wrote about it. Poe's radical opinions frequently cost him jobs, but he kept at it until the end. The same problems with plagiarism and puffing still persist, but Poe's openness about it has helped provide backing for modern research into this field.

While all of these writers were struggling for fair profit shares from publishers, Mark Twain took this idea to the extreme. He used his wife's money and his own extensive profits from publishing popular novels to start his own publishing company. He then offered the sort of 50% of profits royalties to authors that included General Grant that he had always wanted when he was selling his works to other publishers. This experiment proved that the other publishers were prudent to offer smaller royalties because of the uncertainties in the publishing market. Instability meant that some of Twain's releases sold very few copies out of those printed, and thus resulted in major losses. The negatives from the unpopular titles could have been recuperated if his best-sellers made more through a larger royalty share. Twain did not grow rich by his fair profit-sharing with the authors he published. But he published many of his best books himself, and he retired on the profits he made from selling copyrights to these to a giant publisher.

Herman Melville began his life as a whaler. This working-class background made him very self-conscious about the literary quality of his published works. At first, he wanted to publish books that would see a profit from Harper, but sufficient profits never materialized, so he took a position in the postal office, and was only able to write in his free time on the job. Meanwhile, he spent a large part of his mounting inheritance on releasing books such as an epic poem about the Holy Land. While these works were hardly fiscally logical, Melville's *Moby-Dick* is one of the most literary American novels written to-date.

Another outstanding author-publisher, Briton Hadden pulled Henry Luce ahead with him through the start of their career as they founded Time Inc. But, after Hadden's early death, it was up to Luce to keep the brand alive. Luce's goal was different from the other authors on this list, and yet he was just as passionate about it. Luce was driven to acquire capital and to expand his corporation exponentially. He bought up stock from Hadden's family after Hadden's death, despite their conflicting interests, and fought to have majority control of the company. Luce did not write much, unlike Hadden. But, his best-known article, "American Century," has been credited with being a major contributor to the development of the image of America as the leading world power. It inspired American politicians and businessmen to strive for empirical and fiscal global dominance, rather than settling for being one in a group of super-powers. Luce's goals were globalization and corporatocratic control. Similar goals among the Big Four have contributed to the hyper-merging and takeover-mentality that created the media corporations that we are left with today. I do not agree with Luce's goals. Still, Luce formed this ambition to conquer at a time when this type of greed was a radical outlier.

Dudley Randall became a librarian in a segregated world, where only a handful of African American poets had ever been published with any big or small publisher. His goal was to assist his fellow black writers with being published and recognized as artists. He succeeded in helping numerous writers enter the mainstream. Randall also popularizing the unique qualities of African American writing as quintessentially American. The Black Arts and Black Power Movement that Randall championed in turn helped Alice Walker and numerous other black writers to become internationally recognized bestsellers. Randall himself is not as well known today for his own poetry as these other writers because he played a role behind the curtain and invested his savings into the mostly unprofitable business of creating genre-breaking art.

Alice Walker started her publishing business, Wild Trees Press, a couple of decades after Randall began his, so she was in a significantly less hostile publishing environment. Unlike Randall, Walker was able to secure a top publisher for her own series of novels by the time she started Wild Trees. Alice Walker had fought alongside her lawyer husband in the midst of the Civil Rights Movement that came before this high point, and contributed in various ways to breaking assumptions about race in the books she published independently, as well as in her radical political activities.

All of these authors were fighting for causes that were contrary to the majority's will. They wanted change, and they started publishing ventures that allowed their agendas to be heard. Few of their publishing businesses succeeded fiscally, but most of their causes were eventually successful. The radical ideas they fought for have had a major impact on the world we live in today.

Patterns in the Lives and Businesses of Central Author-Publishers

Aside from all of the central author-publishers being champions for radical causes, there are many other similarities in the path their lives took toward independent publishing. Oddly enough, their businesses and lives also mostly ended in tragedy. Individually, these stories are compelling, but when seen in contrast, they point to engrained problems in the publishing industry. The table above compares most of the central author-publishers, except for Alice Walker because she is still alive, and thus her story is still ongoing.

The first element most of these writers have in common is that they began their professional lives with a grueling and strenuous employment or apprenticeship. Sir Walker Scott copied hundreds of pages daily for his father's law firm, so that he was not tempted to stay in this firm when his apprenticeship ended and took the more competitive route of becoming a judge. Lord Byron took his family's seat in the House of Lords at a very young age, and then unlike the vast majority of the other Lords there, he took a position on issues that became increasingly radicalized before he outwardly supported the Greek Revolution. Charles Dickens famously worked in a shoe blacking factory, so that when he started working as a congressional reporter, he was only too happy to work faster and harder than his co-workers to avoid returning to factory work. Virginia Woolf took advantage of her family connections to start profiting from writing freelance articles for The

Life Plot Movement	Sir Walter Scott	Byron/ Percy Shelley	Charles Dickens	Virginia Woolf	Benjamin Franklin
Apprenticeship, first employment, or source of financing	Copying clerk, father's Chalmers & Scott law firm (1786)	House of Lords member/ traveling poet with an allowances	Boot and shoe blacking factory, then as a congress reporter	Freelanced articles for *The Times Literary Supplement*	Apprenticed to his brother James' printing business in Boston
First major publication	*Marmion* (1809), poetry	*Various Occasions/ Necessity of Atheism*	*Sketches by Boz* (1836), stories	*The Voyage Out* (1915), novel	*Liberty & Necessity, Pleasure & Pain*
Motive for starting a publishing business	Started a Tory quarterly with Murray, *Quarterly Review*, to rival Constable (Whig)	Repeated attempts to start a radical paper/ literary ambition	Low royalties, disregard for his editorial preferences, rejections of radical work	Only her abusive half-brother published her first two novels, need for freedom	Desire to break the indenture to brother and to profit from printing trade
Source of funding	£1,600 annually judge's salary and inheritance	Primarily Byron's inheritance, but also Shelley's	Dickens' profits from previous publications	Virginia's inheritance, £9,000, and book profits	Meredith's (partner) father supplied £200
Top success in publishing	*The Lady of the Lake*: £10,000 in profits	£377.16.0 in profits from the first issue of the *Liberal*	700,000 copies sold of *Bleak House* (1852-70)	Sold half of Hogarth to Lehmann for £3,000, 1938	$10,000 annually from *Poor Richard's Almanac*
Bankruptcy or the worst fiscal problem	Trade bankruptcy: £121K; Ballantyne £90K; Constable £250K	Leight Hunt accumulated £1,790.19.10 in debt by 1824 during editorship	His reporter father and Charley Jr. went bankrupt, so he was frugal	When in 1946 Lehmann asked to exit, Leonard had to sell Hogarth	Remained profitable, but could have grown if he focused on it
Likely cause of death	Malpractice: blistering, bleeding, seton, travel	Malpractice: poisoned/ "Drowned" in a schooner	Georgina, sister-in-law/ lover(?) poisoned dinner	Malpractice by psychiatrists and/or suicide	Old age
Future of the publishing venture after the author's death	Bankrupted before his death	It was closed due to low subscriptions before Byron's death	Son inherited it, and ran it for a couple of decades before closing	Leonard sold it to Chatto and became one of its directors	It did not survive under his name, but offshoots of partners did

Fig. 3. Life Plot Movements of Central Authors

Times Literary Supplement at a time when few other women were engaged in strenuous "brain" activity. Benjamin Franklin apprenticed to his brother's printing business as a teen and worked there on a hand press, learning the patience needed for a lifetime of rigorous mental

Life Plot Movement	Edgar Allan Poe	Mark Twain	Herman Melville	Henry Luce/ B. Haddon	Dudley Randall
Apprenticeship, first employment, or source of financing	Part-time editor for the *Southern Literary Messenger*, 1835	Apprentice typesetter for La Cossitt's *Hannibal Gazette*, 1847	Indentured whaling contract deserted to work as a clerk, Hawaii	Cub reporter, *Chicago Daily News*/ reporter, *New York World*	Worked in the foundry of the Ford Motor Company
First publication	*Pym* (1838), Harper, whale novel	*Celebrated Jumping Frog* (1867)	*Typee* (1845), Harper, cannibals novel	"The American Century" / *Time*	*Cities Burning* (1968), poetry
Motive for starting a publishing business	Inspired by Dickens' after meeting, extreme difficulty finding steady work in publishing	Desire to make 50%+ royalties, publisher's rejection of his more literary works	Desire to establish himself as a literary writer inspired him to privately print books	Desire for independence vs. working as reporters for somebody else's paper or publisher	Small quantity of black writers that were published before it was started
Source of funding	Borrowed for partnership, failed to launch *Penn*	Wife's inheritance, profits from earlier publications	Inheritances from relatives, profits from books	Raised $86,000 from various parties	Savings from librarian job at University of Detroit
Top success in publishing	100 copies sold of *Pym* in London, paid for loss	*Huckleberry Finn* made $44,500 in 3 months	First six novels made $8,069.34 in profits	Luce worth $100 million in Time Inc. stock at end	100,000 of Don L. Lee's books printed by 1974
Bankruptcy or the worst fiscal problem	Poe served in debtors' prison in 1831 after brother Henry died owing $80	Bankruptcy in 1895, sold rights to Harper to repay debts by 1898	Inheritance paid Harper to print epic poem, *Clarel*, for $1,384, in 1876	Haddon's family sold their shares for around a million in 1929 to Luce	$30,000 debt to Harlo Printing Comp; sold press twice, retained third
Likely cause of death	Malpractice and poisoning during elections	Developed a severe angina on a trip to Bermuda	Old age/ "cardiac dilation"	Old age, heart/ flu > strep infection: hospital	Old age
Future of the publishing venture after the author's death	He sold a share in his partnership, and never started sole venture	He closed it before his death, and Harper printed his books afterwards	His privately printed books are not as well known as *Moby-Dick*	Time Inc. merged with Hachette Livre pred. in 1968, after Luce' death	Still operates under a collective of cultural activists

Fig. 3. Life Plot Movements of Central Authors

and physical activity. Later in life, he made it a point to carry a load of paper and other equipment to his print shop himself to show that he took pride in the trade of performing most of the printing himself. Edgar Allan Poe's career started when he worked as a part-time editor for the *Southern Literary Messenger*, a job that paid little considering that he wrote, edited and otherwise pulled together most of the paper. Mark Twain apprenticed as a typesetter for La Cossitt's *Hannibal Gazette* long before he set out to become a steamboat captain on the Mississippi. Herman Melville indentured on a whaling ship and then deserted to work as a clerk in Hawaii, in parallel with Dickens' abandonment of factory work for a desk job. Both Henry Luce and Briton Hadden served as reporters before realizing that even with an Ivy League education, their only chance for advancement above low-paying reporting was independently publishing a magazine or newspaper of their own. Also echoing Dickens and Melville, Dudley Randall worked in the foundry of the Ford Motor Company long before he became a librarian with a graduate degree and could invest in his own press. The only exception to this work ethic philosophy was Percy Shelley, who relied on his parents' money to travel around and fall in love, after he was kicked out of Oxford for writing about atheism. But then again, Shelley started writing complex political pamphlets and poetry earlier than many of these other author-publishers, so he was really employed in writing across these early years, similarly to Virginia Woolf.

When these author-publishers were married or romantically involved with other writers, including the Shelleys and the Woolfs, they typically started publishing ventures with these ambitious spouses. However, these businesses partnerships ended in some type of a disaster each time, as relationship and business interests clashed.

All of these author-publishers stand out from the writers who never started their own publishing companies because they are workaholics from the start and took on risky, labor-intensive, and low-paying jobs in order to survive independently, while they were learning the skills they would need in business. They also stand out from publishers who never published their own writing because they started submitting their short works while they were still employed on whalers or in factories. For the author-publishers, promoting themselves as writers motivated them to start their own ventures. Also, most of these writers worked in printing early in their careers, so that they knew enough about the trade for it not to appear overly exotic. The writers who had printing backgrounds were able to help with the printing process themselves before business took off.

The first publications from these writers fell into two categories, either they were their most radical work (a youthful rebellion), or their most popular or light projects (due to a youthful lack of linguistic sophistication). Walter Scott's *Marmion* was light for him as a judge because even publishing poetry publicly was controversial, as this was a mode that was barely socially acceptable at the time. Byron's *Poems on Various Occasions* served a similar purpose to *Marmion*, allowing him to show his educational achievements and to raise his public image. And Randall's *Cities Burning*, while it was certainly radical, having to do with police brutality and the Civil Rights Movement, was also, in a way, an attempt to display his poetic artistry, rather than being intended for mainstream consumption. On the other hand, Shelley's *Necessity of Atheism* was certainly radical, considering that he distributed it in a strict, religious school, and it led to his expulsion, thus blocking him from becoming an advocate like Scott, or a politician like Byron. Franklin's *A Dissertation on Liberty and Necessity, Pleasure and Pain* echoes some of Shelley's frustrations, as Franklin argues that there are contradictions in religious doctrines, and particularly that humans are not superior to other animals in God's eyes. Franklin did not distribute it to clergy, so the consequences were not as harsh for him as they were for Shelley. Both Shelley's and Franklin's first published book was privately printed. On the other hand, Charles Dickens' *Sketches by Boz* stories are similar to Mark Twain's collection, *Celebrated Jumping Frog*, as both resulted from a few popular publications in magazines or newspapers, which were then admired by a publisher that solicited a book-length collection. Other writers, like Woolf, published highbrow books as their first publications (without needing to go the pop route) by working with relatives, as she did by printing *The Voyage Out* with her half-brother, despite his earlier sexual abuse of her. Both Poe and Melville published their first novels with Harper: *Pym* and *Typee*. These were very formulaic travel adventures, a popular genre among Harper's bestsellers. Melville's novel sold a lot better than Poe's. As a result of this mainstream failure, Poe never wrote another novel. In contrast, Melville wrote several more before he started spending more money on these publications than he was making, so he also switched to highbrow literature, as Poe did after his first attempt. Luce and Hadden are the outliers in this comparison, as Hadden primarily wrote articles for papers, and Luce did not even write any outstanding articles until his later "The American Century" piece, which might have been hyper-publicized because having anything in print with Luce's name on it was so rare. These first publications appear to be very different in purpose and outcome, but they are similar in that they all show extreme ambition for literary acclaim, as the authors attempt to join the mainstream publishing establishment.

Dissatisfaction with the publishers that released their earlier works is the primary reason these author-publishers started their own publishing ventures. Walter Scott explained that he sponsored the founding of Murray's Tory *Quarterly Review* to rival Constable's *Whig Periodical*. Scott was not only concerned that he could not express his party's opinions in the existing paper, but more importantly, the political rivalry was bringing about negative reviews of his books. Once Scott was in control of a paper, he positively reviewed his own books, and encouraged his "friends" to do so as well. Many of the other authors that started their own periodicals were also aware of puffed review exchanges and anonymous self-reviews. A journal review was better than a simple catalog or flier in convincing booksellers to stock and promote a new title. The same problems persist today, leading to the concentration of a few hyper-reviewed titles at the top, with most of these coming from the Big Four publishers, which also contribute most of the advertising funding that has historically contributed to puffing. Byron attempted to convince Murray and others to start a new *Liberal* journal with him long before he found willing partners in the Hunts and Shelley. From the start, Byron was motivated by negative reviews of his books in rival publications, as well as by his drive to publicize himself as a respected author. Authors who were employed as editors for other periodicals, such as Dickens and Poe, expressed frustration over their literary opinions being overruled by poorly educated publishers, who were primarily interested in running a profitable business rather than in the literary art. Authors who went a step beyond a periodical to start a full publishing venture were frequently dissatisfied with the perceived low royalties they were receiving. Dickens, Poe, Twain, and Melville all mentioned, in their journals or letters, a desire to receive a 50/50 profits split, and how their outside publishers typically fell short of this royalty goal. Many of these writers also cited other author-publishers as having inspired them to enter publishing, Poe cited Dickens, and Walker cited Woolf. While some of them had previously become bestsellers with other publishers, many of these writers rightfully knew that without a publishing house of their own, they would never enter the mainstream or manage to attract a significant readership to their writing. In general, these authors wanted more liberty to publish whatever radical concepts they could imagine, and they wanted to pocket the majority of the profits, instead of seeing this money go to a silent party that is doing nothing but investing the initial capital.

Most of the writers used their inheritance, employment income and profits from previous publications to launch a publishing business. Based on their experiences, attempts to raise capital from outside investors typically leads to bankruptcy or failure to make enough to return the investments. On the other hand, obtaining outside capital also leads to bigger peak profits, as the infusion of capital allows a publisher to print enormous review copy runs, advertisements and larger print runs than they would be able to afford, if they were only using their own funds. Luce and Hadden raised $86,000 in New York City to launch *Time*, an amount that was necessary to purchase the printing equipment, space and other components in that region. This was a lot of money to find, but it meant that Time Inc. could print its own work without relying on a third-party printer. As a result of this start-up foundation, Time Inc. stayed afloat across the lives of both of its founders. Randall could not have raised enough money to buy his own press as the price of a printing press rose exponentially in half-a-century. So, Randall had to rely on an outside printer. The resulting debts to this printer led to his publishing business' first collapse and sale. Even though Poe did not need too much capital to buy a hand press in the nineteenth century, he could not find even small-scale backers for his *Penn* because he blatantly insisted in his proposal that the purpose of the periodical would be art, rather than profit. Thus, this journal never materialized.

Scott needed more funds than his judge salary could afford to upgrade his Abbotsford mansion. His publishing collaborators, Constable and Ballantyne, also had luxurious abodes that were beyond their means. So, they applied for financing from banks and took on so much debt that by the time they were forced to declare bankruptcy, Scott owed £121,000, Ballantyne owed £90,000 and Constable owed £250,000. These amounts are enormous when they are adjusted for inflation. The banking crisis that struck England right before their collapse was brought about by other businesses taking on similar risky loans.

Journals were less risky because they could not justifiably accumulate this much debt before their founders saw fit to close them. For example, Leigh Hunt accumulated £1,790.19.10 in debt during his editorship to his brother, the printer, and much of this was because he was traveling across Europe and had expected that Byron would pick up the check. *The Liberal* did not show a significant profit after the first issue. It became obvious to all parties that the negative press their competitors were throwing at it would not let it bloom via accumulating subscribers. John Hunt would go on printing and publishing other books in London, while Byron saved himself indebtedness by exiting this investment opportunity. In contrast, Dickens' journal built on the fame of the earlier successful periodicals that he ran but did not own. As a result of Dickens' prior education, *All the Year Round* remained profitable for decades after his death, allowing his son, Charley, to make an independent living before he finally closed it for a job with Macmillan. Unlike Shelley and Byron, Dickens has worked as a professional writer, editor and had helped to keep previous periodicals profitable, so he understood that great art could not survive without a readership willing to buy it.

As was mentioned earlier in this section, one of the problems that plagued some of these ventures was disagreement between partners. When more than one partner funds a venture, it can break apart into independent units or collapse under pressure. For example, Franklin broke away from his brother's print shop. And across Benjamin's career dozens of printers apprenticed and worked under him before breaking off and founding their own publishing businesses in the colonial landscape. In contrast, when Virginia Woolf sold her half of Hogarth to their assistant, Lehmann, in 1938, they saw what seemed to be a better profit than their earnings from the previous releases of Virginia's books, £3,000. The Woolf's left an exit option open for Lehmann, so that he could quit and ask for a refund of his £3,000 investment. Not surprisingly, when Lehmann grew tired of working with the domineering Leonard and asked for a payout, Leonard had to sell the company to Chatto to honor this agreement. Luce, on the other hand, had to be pretty crafty to convince Hadden's family to sell all of their shares to him and his affiliates, and if he had not performed this trick, Time Inc. might have fallen apart at that point without unified leadership. Luce's net worth at his death was second only to Alice Walker out of the author-publishers I researched, at $100 million. The acquisition of wealth and the growth of his corporation was the American "century" Luce had always hoped for. Mark Twain is the only writer of these who managed to pay off his debts after filing for bankruptcy. He achieved this recovery by selling the rights to all of his writings to Harper. Bankruptcies are very common for author-publishers because the risk-taking that is likely to lead to catastrophe is necessary to start a publishing company. Any author that wants to become an author-publisher has to study these examples to avoid falling for the illusion of posthumous fame. Building a following for a canonical, literary author typically only materializes after they are not around to reap the rewards.

The end is seldom natural, even when the coroner's report states so, for radical and ambitious author-publishers. The sagas of how these authors died is a string of unsolved mysteries, with many potential culprits and several clues that suggest nefarious actions. Only Franklin, Melville and Randall are likely to have died simply of old age, and perhaps Hadden, though even his case is a bit suspect. Malpractice played a role in all of the other deaths. Scott, Byron, Woolf, Poe, Twain and Luce all died under very similar circumstances. They took a trip just before they died: Scott toured Europe to "recover" from strokes; Byron was staying in Greece for the Revolution; Woolf had gone to London on a business trip for Hogarth during WWII; Poe traveled to Baltimore during elections; and Twain developed severe angina on a trip to Bermuda. Some of these deaths were surrounded by several other deaths of their friends, relations, or coworkers. In Twain's case, he died shortly after the suspect death of his daughter (who had just returned from a mental institution) in a bathtub. The trips created various minor health issues, like the flu for Byron, or exhaustion for Scott. Typically, two or more physicians were solicited, or the patients were taken to a public hospital (Poe). Each of the physicians prescribed a dangerous drug that was known to have negative interactions with the drugs prescribed by other physicians on the case. These mixtures of drugs created a cocktail that made the author-publisher worse. The new symptoms were used to suggest even more harmful procedures. Scott, Byron, Woolf and others all suffered from blistering, bleeding, and seton creation, which sapped their energy and stopped them from being able to protest against the continuation of these tortures that eventually ended in their slow and painful deaths. Some of the deaths were a bit more unusual, such as Shelley's drowning in a schooner right near the coastline in a minor storm. Dickens' loss of consciousness after eating his sister-in-law's (and potential lover's) dinner is also strange because it suggests the use of a quick poison with the goal of gaining an inheritance immediately. Hadden's death demonstrates the malpractice pattern as he was merely complaining of being tired before he signed into a hospital. Once he had checked into the hospital, he was diagnosed with the flu, which became strep throat as he remained there immobilized for weeks without improvement. The hospital profited from his decline because he kept paying for each day of the hospital stay. During this illness, Luce gained control over the company, and made $100 million before his own death decades later from having the controlling share over Time Inc. Big corporate publishers ended up buying many of these author-publisher founded businesses, including Twain's and Woolf's rights. Did any of these giant, acquiring publishers play a role in these repetitively suspicious deaths? None of these deaths were officially recognized as homicides or assassinations on the death certificates. Did a majority of non-author-publishers die under similar malpractice scenarios across this period? This is a question for another study.

Hopefully, my readers will have learned about what they should do as authors or publishers, and what they should avoid from the examples of these canonical author-publishers. The point of reading about history is to avoid repeating what has led to failures, and to mimic the parts that brought about success. The modern publishing climate is in need of such guidance as there are too many entities barely surviving at the bottom, while the Big Four feast on the world's desire to consume books. Meanwhile, illiteracy and anti-literacy are growing, so it is pivotal now for publishers to find ways to release books that will persuade people around the world to become better readers.

BIBLIOGRAPHY

Ackroyd, Peter. *Poe: A Life Cut Short: Ackroyd's Brief Lives*. New York: Nan A. Talese: Doubleday, 2008.

Adrian, Arthur A. *Georgina Hogarth and the Dickens Circle*. Oxford: Oxford University Press, 1957.

Argenti, Philip P., Ed. *The Massacres of Chios Described in Contemporary Diplomatic Reports*. "9 July 1822." 1822 London: Bodley Head, 1932.

Ashley, Mike. *A Brief History of British Kings & Queens: British Royal History from Alfred the Great to the Present*. New York: Carroll & Graf Publishers, 2002.

Ballantyne and Co. *The History of the Ballantyne Press and Its Connection with Sir Walter Scott*. Edinburgh: Ballantyne and Co., 1871. Google Books. 23 March 2011. Web.

Bass, Gary J. *Freedom's Battle: The Origins of Humanitarian Intervention*. New York: Alfred A. Knopf, 2008.

Beale, Thomas J. *The Beale Papers: Containing Authentic Statements Regarding the Treasure Buried in 1819 and 1821 near Bufords, in Bedford County, Virginia, and Which Has Never Been Recovered. Price Fifty Cents*. Lunchburg: Virginia Book and Job Print, 1885.

Bell, Quentin. *Virginia Woolf: A Biography*. New York: Houghton Mifflin Harcourt, 1972.

Bellaigue, Eric de. *British Book Publishing as a Business since the 1960s: Selected Essays by Eric de Bellaigue*. The British Library Studies in the History of the Book. London: The British Library, 2004.

Blum, Deborah. *The Poisoner's Handbook: Murder and the Birth of Forensic Medicine in Jazz Age New York*. New York: Penguin Press, 2010.

Boyd, Melba Joyce. *Wrestling with the Muse: Dudley Randall and the Broadside Press*. New York: Columbia University Press, 2003.

Brando, Marlon and Donald Cammel. *Fan-Tan*. New York: Vintage Books: Random House Inc., 2006.

Brando, Marlon and Robert Lindsey. *Brando: Songs My Mother Taught Me*. New York: Random House Inc., 1994.

Brinkley, Alan. *The Publisher: Henry Luce and His American Century*. New York: Alfred A Knopf, 2010.

Brokaw, Cynthia J. and Kai-wing Chow, eds. *Printing and Book Culture in Late Imperial China*. Berkley: University of California Press, 2005.

Brozen, Reed. "Gyromitra Mushroom Toxicity." MedScape: WebMD Health Professional network. 14 April 2015. Web.

Bryan, Frederick VanPelt, Judge. "Opinion by Judge Bryan on *Lady Chatterley's Lover*." (1959). *Versions of Censorship*. John McCormick and Mairi MacInnes, eds. Garden City (NY): Anchor Books, 1962. 232-50.

Burke, Edmund. *Reflections on the Revolution in France*. (1790). Frank M. Turner, ed.

Oxford: Oxford University Press, 2009. Print.

Byron, Lord George Gordon. *Byron's Letters and Journals, Volume I-XII*. Leslie A. Marchand, Ed. Cambridge: Harvard University Press & Belknap Press, 1973-1982.

Byron, Lord George Gordon. *Lord Byron: Selected Letters and Journals: The liveliest and most revealing letters from the acclaimed 12-volume edition—together in one volume*. Leslie A. Marchand, Ed. Cambridge: Harvard University Press & Belknap Press, 1982.

Byron, Lord George Gordon. "The Vision of Judgment: By 'Quevedo Redivivus.'" Jack Lynch, Ed. Newark: Rutgers University. Retrieved: 27 July 2016. Web.

Byron, Lord George Gordon. *The Works of Lord Byron: Letters and Journals*. Rowland E. Prothero, Ed. 6 Vol. London: 1898-1901.

Calhoun, Charles C. *Longfellow: A Rediscovered Life*. Boston: Beacon Press, 2004.

Campbell, Gordon and Thomas N. Corns. *John Milton: Life, Work, and Thought*. Oxford: Oxford University Press, 2008.

Carlyle, Thomas. *Chartism*, Second Edition. London: Chapman and Hall, Strand, 1842. Google Books. 31 Mar. 2011. Web.

Carlyle, Thomas. *The French Revolution: A History*. (1837). New York: Modern Library, 2002. Print.

Cash, Arthur H. *John Wilkes: The Scandalous Father of Civil Liberty*. New Haven: Yale University Press, 2006.

Charvat, William. *The Profession of Authorship: The Papers of William Charvat*. Columbus: Ohio State University Press, 1968. (Web).

Clark, Septima. *Ready from Within: Septima Clark and the Civil Rights Movement*. Navarro (CA): Wild Trees Press, 1986.

Coates, Irene. *Who's Afraid of Leonard Woolf: A Case for the Sanity of Virginia Woolf?* New York: Soho Press Inc., 2000.

Coetzee, J. M. "The Beginning of (Wo)man in Africa." *New York Times*. 30 April 1989.

Colvin, Richard. "Mom Objects to Prize Novel for High School Reading List." *Oakland Tribune*. 3 May 1984.

Cooper, J. California. *Homemade Love*. (1986). New York: St. Martin's Griffin, 1998.

Cooper, J. California. *A Piece of Mine: Stories*. (1984). New York: Anchor Books, 1991.

Crews, Ed. "The Poisoning of King George III." *Colonial Williamsburg Journal*. Spring 2010. Retrieved: 29 May 2016. Web.

D'Arcy, Julian M. *Subversive Scott: The Waverley Novels and Scottish Nationalism*. Hagatorgi, Iceland: University of Iceland Press, 2005. Print.

Dickens, Charles. *Barnaby Rudge*. (1841). Oxford: Oxford University Press, 2008. Print.

Dickens, Charles. *The Pilgrim Edition of the Letters of Charles Dickens*, 12 vols. Madeline House, Graham Storey, Kathleen Tillotson and others, eds. Oxford: Oxford University Press, 1965-2002.

Dickens, Charles. *The Selected Letters of Charles Dickens: The Great Letters Series*. Frederick W. Dupee, Ed. New York: Farrar, Straus and Cudahy, Inc., 1960.

Dickens, Charles. *A Tale of Two Cities*. (1859). New York: Signet, 2007. Print.

Dooley, Allan C. *Author and Printer in Victorian England*. Charlottesville: University Press of Virginia, 1992. Print.

Dore, Mary, Director. *She's Beautiful When She's Angry*. Salt Lake City: Mary Dore Productions, 2014.

Duke, Alan. "'Perfect storm' of drugs killed Michael Jackson, sleep expert says." 14 October 2011. CNN. Retrieved: 19 July 2016. Web.

Elwin, Malcolm. *Lord Byron's Wife*. New York: Harcourt, Brace & World, Inc., 1963.

Emerich, John, Ed. *The Cambridge Modern History, Volume 10*. New York: University Press, 1907.

Emsley, John. *The Elements of Murder: A History of Poison*. Oxford: Oxford University Press, 2005.

Erickson, Lee. *The Economy of Literary Form: English Literature and the Industrialization of Publishing, 1800-1850*. Baltimore: Johns Hopkins University Press, 1996. Print.

Evans, Harold. *My Paper Chase: True Stories of Vanished Times*. New York: Little, Brown and Company: Hachette Book Group, 2009.

Exman, Eugene. *The Brothers Harper: A unique publishing partnership and its impact upon the cultural life of America from 1817 to 1853*. New York: Harper & Row, Publishers, 1965.

Feather, John. *A History of English Publishing*, Second Edition. New York: Routledge, 2004. Print.

Forrester, Viviane. *Virginia Woolf: A Portrait*. New York: Columbia University Press, 2015.

Fowell, Frank and Frank Palmer. *Censorship in England*. (1913). London: Benjamin Blom, 1969. Print.

Franklin, Benjamin. *Autobiography, Poor Richard, and Later Writings*. New York: The Library of America, 1997.

Gamba, Count Pietro. *A Narrative of Lord Byron's Last Journey to Greece*. London, 1825.

Gilmour, Ian. *Byron & Shelley in Their Time: The Making of the Poets*. New York: Carroll & Graf Publishers, 2003.

Goldstein, Robert J. *Political Censorship of the Arts and the Press in Nineteenth-Century Europe*. New York: St. Martin's Press, 1989. Print.

Griffiths, Ralph. *The Monthly Review, Or, Literary Journal, Volume LVI*. London: R. Griffiths, 1823.

Hamilton, John Maxwell. *Casanova Was a Book Lover: And Other Naked Truths and Provocative Curiosities about the Writing, Selling, and Reading of Books*. Baton Rouge: Louisiana State University Press, 2000.

Hansard, Thomas Carson. *Parliamentary Debates from the Year 1803 to the Present Time*. London: Hansard, 1824.

Hartley, Jenny, Ed. *The Selected Letters of Charles Dickens*. Oxford: Oxford University Press, 2012.

Hayford, Harrison, Hershel Parker, and G. Thoomas Tanselle, eds. *Pierre, or The Ambiguities*. Herman Melville. Evanston and Chicago: Northwestern University Press and the Newberry Library, 1971.

Hobhouse, John Cam, Lord Broughton. "Lord Byron in Greece." *Westminster Re-*

view, II (July 1824). 225-62.
Hudak, Leona M. *Early American Women Printers and Publishers, 1639-1820.* Metuchen (NJ): The Scarecrow Press, Inc., 1978.
Hutchisson, James M. *Poe.* Jackson: University Press of Mississippi, 2005.
Inquisitors-General. "The Condemnation and Recantation of Galileo." (1633). *Versions of Censorship.* John McCormick and Mairi MacInnes, eds. Garden City (NY): Anchor Books, 1962. 56-62.
Isaacson, Walter. *Benjamin Franklin: An American Life.* New York: Simon & Schuster, 2003.
Jackson, T. A. *Charles Dickens: The Progress of a Radical.* (1937). New York: Haskell, 1971. Print.
Johnson, Edgar. *Charles Dickens: His Tragedy and Triumph: A Biography.* Boston: Little, Brown and Company, 1952.
Johnson, Edgar. *Sir Walter Scott: The Great Unknown, 2 vols.* Boston: Little, Brown and Company, 1970.
Jones, Colin, Josephine McDonagh and Jon Mee. *Charles Dickens, A Tale of Two Cities and the French Revolution.* New York: Palgrave Macmillan, 2009. Print.
Jouve, Nicole Ward. "Virginia Woolf and Psychoanalysis." *The Cambridge Companion to Virginia Woolf.* Sue Roe and Susan Sellers, eds. Cambridge: Cambridge University Press, 2000.
Lehmann, John. *Thrown to the Woolfs.* London: Weidenfield and Nicolson, 1978.
"Literature: Catalogue of the Smithfield Club Cattle Show." *The Athenaeum.* N. 1728. Saturday, December 8, 1800. London: British Periodical Limited, 1860. Web.
Lockhart, John Gibson. *Memoirs of the Life of Sir Walter Scott,* 5 vols. Boston: Houghton, Mifflin and Company, 1902.
Lovell, Ernest J. Jr. *His Very Self and Voice.* New York: The Macmillan Company, 1954.
Luce, Henry R. *The American Century.* New York: Farrar & Rinehart, 1941.
Lupton, Ellen, Ed. *Indie Publishing: How to Design and Produce Your Own Book.* New York: Princeton Architectural Press, 2008.
Macinnis, Peter. *Poisons: From Hemlock to Botox and the Killer Bean of Calabar.* New York: Arcade Publishing, 2005.
Malin, Patrick Murphy. "Smut, Corruption, and the Law." *Versions of Censorship.* John McCormick and Mairi MacInnes, eds. Garden City (NY): Anchor Books, 1962. 203-17.
Marchand, Leslie A., Ed. *Selected Poetry of Lord Byron, Vol. II.* New York: Modern Library, 2001.
Marks, Andreas. *Japanese Woodblock Prints: Artists, Publishers and Masterworks, 1680-1900.* Tokyo: Tuttle Publishing, 2010.
Marshall, William H. *Byron, Shelley, Hunt, and* The Liberal. Philadelphia: University of Pennsylvania Press, 1960.
Martin, Justin. *Genius of Place: The Life of Frederick Law Olmsted.* Philadelphia: Da Capo Press, 2011.
Marx, Karl. "The Manifesto of the Communist Party" (1848), "Capital" (1867), "The German Ideology" (1845), and "Results of the Immediate Process of Production" (1867). *Karl Marx: Selected Writings,* Second Edition. McLellan, Da-

vid, ed. Oxford: Oxford University Press, 2005. Print.

Maurois, Andre. *Ariel: The Life of Shelley*. (1924). New York: Frederick Ungar Publishing Co., 1968.

McCormick, John and Mairi MacInnes, eds. *Versions of Censorship*. Garden City (NY): Anchor Books, 1962.

Meacham, Jon, Ed. *Voices in Our Blood: America's Best on the Civil Rights Movement*. New York: Random House, 2001.

Merschel, Michael. "Rare Interviews with J. California Cooper, Who Died Saturday." 26 September 2014. *The Dallas Morning News*. Retrieved: 4 April 2016. Web.

Miller, Henry. "'Defense of the Freedom to Read,' a letter to the Supreme Court of Nortway in connection with the *Sexus* case." (1959). *Versions of Censorship*. John McCormick and Mairi MacInnes, eds. Garden City (NY): Anchor Books, 1962. 223-30.

Millingen, Julius. *Memoirs of the Affairs of Greece*. London, 1831.

Milton, John. *Areopagitica*. (1644). *Versions of Censorship*. John McCormick and Mairi MacInnes, eds. Garden City (NY): Anchor Books, 1962. 8-34.

Moore, Doris Langley. *Lord Byron: Accounts Rendered*. New York: Harper & Row, 1974.

Moore, Thomas. *Letters and Journals of Lord Byron, With Notices of His Life*. London, 1830.

Moran, John J. *A Defense of Edgar Allan Poe*. Washington, DC: Boogher, 1885; rpt., New York: AMS, 1966.

Moss, Sidney. *Poe's Literary Battles: The Critic in the Context of His Literary Milieu*. Durham: Duke University Press, 1963.

Moss, Sidney. "Poe's 'Two Long Interviews' with Dickens." *Poe Studies 11, no. 1* (June 1978).

Murray, John. *A Publisher and His Friends: Memoir and Correspondences of John Murray*. 2 vols. Edinburgh: John Murray/ Samuel Smiles, 1891.

Nasaw, David. *The Chief: The Life of William Randolph Hearst*. Boston: Houghton Mifflin, 2000.

Negev, Eilat and Yehuda Koren. *The First Lady of Fleet Street: The Life of Rachel Beer: Crusading Heiress and Newspaper Pioneer*. New York: Random House Publishing Group, 2012.

Neider, Charles, Ed. *Essays of the Masters*. New York: First Cooper Square Press, 2000.

Orwell, George. *All Art Is Propaganda: Critical Essays*. Orlando: Harcourt, 2008. Print.

Orwell, George. "The Prevention of Literature." (1946). *Versions of Censorship*. John McCormick and Mairi MacInnes, eds. Garden City (NY): Anchor Books, 1962. 285-99.

Ostrom, John Ward, Ed. *The Letters of Edgar Allan Poe*. 2 vols. (1948). New York: Gordian, 1966.

Panken, Shirley. *Virginia Woolf and the Lust of Creation: A Psychoanalytic Exploration*. Albany: SUNY Press, 1987.

Parker, Elizabeth. *Popular Poems selected by 'EP'*. London, JW Parker, 1837.

Parker, John W. *Words by a Working Man about Education, in a letter to Lord John Russell*. London: J. W. Parker, 1852. Web.

Parker, John W. and Son. *The Opinions of Certain Authors on the Bookselling Question.* 2nd ed. London, J.W. Parker and Son, 1852. Web.

Parker, Samuel Dunn. "Corruption of the Poor and Unlearned by Certain Opinions." Excerpt from *Report of the arguments of the attorney of the Commonwealth, at the trials of Abner Kneeland, for blasphemy: in the Municipal and Supreme Courts, in Boston, January and May, 1834. Versions of Censorship.* John McCormick and Mairi MacInnes, eds. Garden City (NY): Anchor Books, 1962. 167-70.

Parry, William. *The Last Days of Lord Byron.* London, 1825.

Perrin, Noel. *Dr. Bowdler's Legacy: A History of Expurgated Books in England and America.* New York: Atheneum, 1969.

Picken, Elanor Emma. "Reminiscences of Charles Dickens from a Young Lady's Diary." London: *Englishwoman's Domestic Magazine*, 10 (1871).

Poe, Edgar Allan. *The Complete Works of Edgar Allan Poe, Volume 17: Poe and His Friends: Letters Relating to Poe.* James Albert Harrison, Ed. New York: Thomas Y. Crowell & Company, 1902. Web.

Poe, Edgar Allan. "A Continuation of the voluminous History of the Little Longfellow War." *Broadway Journal.* March 15, 1845. Edgar Allan Poe Society of Baltimore. Web.

Poe, Edgar Allan. "A Few Words on Secret Writing." *Graham's Magazine.* July 1841. 33-38. Edgar Allan Poe Society of Baltimore. Retrieved: 24 April 2016. Web.

Poe, Edgar Allan. "Imitation—Plagiarism." *Broadway Journal.* March 8, 1845. Edgar Allan Poe Society of Baltimore. Web.

Poe, Edgar Allan. "Imitation—Plagiarism." *Broadway Journal.* March 29, 1845. Edgar Allan Poe Society of Baltimore. Web.

Poe, Edgar Allan. "More of the Voluminous History of the Little Longfellow War." *Broadway Journal.* March 22, 1845. Edgar Allan Poe Society of Baltimore. Web.

Poe, Edgar Allan. "Plagiarisim—Imitation—Postscript." *Broadway Journal.* April 5, 1845. Edgar Allan Poe Society of Baltimore. Web.

Poe, Edgar Allan. "Prospectus of *The Penn Magazine*: A Monthly Literary Journal, to be Edited and Published in the City of Philadelphia." (1840). *The Selected Writings of Edgar Allan Poe: A Norton Critical Edition.* G. R. Thompson, Ed. New York: W. W. Norton & Company, 2004. 621-3.

Poe, Edgar Allan. "Some Secrets of the Magazine Prison-House." [Text-02], *Broadway Journal.* February 15, 1845, 1:103-104. Edgar Allan Poe Society of Baltimore. Web.

Poynter, Dan. *Self-Publishing Manual: How to Write, Print and Sell Your Own Book.* Santa Barbara: Para Publishing, 2007.

Prothero, Rowland E. *The Works of Lord Byron, Letters and Journals,* 6 vols., 1898-1901. London: John Murray, 1922.

Robertson-Lorant, Laurie. *Melville: A Biography.* New York: Clarkson Potter/ Publishers, 1996.

Robinson, Charles E. "Chapter Two: Hazlitt and Byron: With a New Look at *The Liberal.*" *Publishing, Editing, and Reception: Essays in Honor of Donald H. Reiman.* Michael Edson, Ed. New York: Rowman & Littlefield, 2015.

Rosen, Fred. *Murdering the President: Alexander Graham Bell and the Race to Save James Garfield.* Lincoln: Potomac Books: University of Nebraska Press, 2016.

Savage, George H. Sir. *Insanity and Allied Neuroses: Practical and Clinical.* Philadelphia: Henry C. Lea's Son & Co., 1884.

Schiffrin, Andre. *The Business of Books: How International Conglomerates Took Over Publishing and Changed the Way We Read.* London: Verso, 2000.

Scott, Sir Walter. *Letters of Sir Walter Scott, Volume I.* H. J. C. Grierson, Ed. London: 1932-7.

Scott, Sir Walter. *Rob Roy.* (1817). New York: Penguin, 2007. Print.

Scott, Sir Walter. *Waverley.* (1814). New York: Penguin, 1994. Print.

Scott, Sir Walter. *Waverley: or, 'Tis Sixty Years Since, in Two Volumes.* (1814). Volume I. Boston: Wells and Lilly, 1815. Google Books. 15 Nov. 2010. Web.

Scott, Walter. *Waverley.* (1814). Harmondsworth: Penguin, 1972. Print.

Shaw, George Bernard. "The Necessity of Immoral Plays." *The Shewing-Up of Blanco Posnet.* (1909). *Versions of Censorship.* John McCormick and Mairi MacInnes, eds. Garden City (NY): Anchor Books, 1962.

Shelley, Percy Byssh. *The Complete Poetical Works of Percy Bysshe Shelley.* Volume I. Thomas Hutchinson, Ed. Oxford Edition: 1914. Project Gutenberg. Retrieved: 27 July 2016. Web.

Smith, Adam. *The Inquiry into the Nature and Causes of The Wealth of Nations.* R. H. Campbell, A. S. Skinner, and W. B. Todd, eds. Oxford: Clarendon Press, 1976.

Smith, Adam. *The Theory of Moral Sentiments.* Raphael D. D. and A. L. Macfie, eds. Indianapolis: Liberty Fund, 1982.

Spater, George and Ian Parsons. *A Marriage of True Minds: An Intimate Portrait of Leonard and Virginia Woolf.* New York: Harcourt Brace Jovanovich, 1977.

Spinoza, Benedict de. *Tractatus Theologico-Politicus.* (1670). *Versions of Censorship.* John McCormick and Mairi MacInnes, eds. Garden City (NY): Anchor Books, 1962. 75-84.

Stanhope, Leicester F. C. *Greece in 1823 and 1824, to which are added, Reminiscences of Lord Byron.* London: Sherwood, Gilbert and Piper, 1825.

Staman, Louise A. *With the Stroke of a Pen: A Story of Ambition, Greed, Infidelity, and the Murder of French Publisher Robert Denoel.* New York: Thomas Dunne Books: St. Martin's Press, 2002.

"State of Facts: Wilkes against the Earl of Halifax." Public Record Office, TS.II/1027/4317. ff, 4-25, 131.

Sultana, Donald. *The Siege of Malta Rediscovered: An account of Sir Walter Scott's Mediterranean journey and his last novel.* Edinburgh: Scottish Academic Press, 1977.

Sutherland, John. *The Life of Walter Scott.* Oxford: Blackwell Publishers Ltd., 1998.

Sutherland, John. *Victorian Fiction: Writers, Publishers, Readers.* New York: MacMillan, 2006. Print.

Temple, Earl. *A Dissection of the North Briton, Number XLV. [by John Wilkes], paragraph by paragraph, inscribed to... Earl Temple. [The preface signed, Philanthropos.].* London: G. Burnet, 1764. Google Book. Retrieved 14 July 2016. Web.

Thomas, Donald S. *A Long Time Burning: The History of Literary Censorship in England.* New York: Praeger, 1969. Print.

Thomas, Dwight and David K. Jackson. *The Poe Log: A Documentary Life of Edgar Allan Poe.* Boston: G. K. Hall, 1987.

Tomalin, Claire. *Charles Dickens: A Life.* New York: The Penguin Press, 2011.

Twain, Mark. *Autobiography of Mark Twain: The Complete and Authoritative Edition.* Volume 1. Harriet Elinor Smith, Ed. Berkeley: University of California Press, 2010.

Twain, Mark. *Mark Twain's Letters to His Publishers, 1867-1894.* Hamlin Hill, Ed. The Mark Twain Papers. Berkeley and Los Angeles: University of California Press, 1967.

Victoria, Queen and A. Helps. *Leaves from the Journal of Our Life in the Highlands, from 1848 to 1861. To Which Are Prefixed and Added Extracts from the Same Journal Giving an Account of Earlier Visits to Scotland, and Tours in England and Ireland, and Yachting Excursions.* New York: Harper & Brothers Publishers, 1868.

Victoria, Queen. *Queen Victoria's Highland Journals.* David Duff, Ed. Exeter (UK): Webb & Bower, 1980.

Walker, Alice. "The Black Writer and the Southern Experience." (1984). *American Culture: An Anthology.* Anders Breidlid, Ed. New York: Routledge, 2013.

Walker, Alice. "Coming Apart." *The Other Woman: Stories of Two Women and a Man.* Susan Koppelman, Ed. New York: Feminist Press at CUNY, 1984. 323-34.

Walker, Alice. "Introduction." *As Wonderful as All That?: Henry Crowder's Memoir of His Affair with Nancy Cunard, 1928-1935.* Mendocino County: Wild Trees Press, 1987.

Walker, Alice. "A Letter to President Clinton." *Anything We Love Can Be Saved.* New York: Random House, 1997.

Walpole, Horace. *A Letter from Xo Ho: A Chinese Philosopher at London, to His Friend Lien Chi at Peking.* London: J. Graham, 1757. Internet Archive. Retrieved 5 June 2016. Web.

Walpole, Horace. "'The Wilkes Affair' from *Memoirs of the Reign of George III.*" *Versions of Censorship.* John McCormick and Mairi MacInnes, eds. Garden City (NY): Anchor Books, 1962. 152-65.

Wartzman, Rick. *Obscene in the Extreme: The Burning and Banning of John Steinbeck's* The Grapes of Wrath. New York: PublicAffairs: Persues Book Group, 2008.

Watkins, John. *Memoirs, Historical and Critical, of the Life and Writings of the Right Honourable Lord Byron, with Anecdotes of Some of His Contemporaries.* London: 1822.

Wellesley, Arthur, Duke of Wellington. "Castlereagh to Wellington, 14 September 1822." (delivered posthumously). *Despatches, Correspondence, and Memoranda of Field Marshal Arthur, Duke of Wellington, Vol. I.* London: John Murray, 1867.

White, Evelyn C. *Alice Walker: A Life.* New York: W. W. Norton & Company, 2004.

White, Thomas Willis. "The New Year." *Southern Literary Messenger: Devoted to Every Department of Literature and the Fine Arts.* Vol. IV, No. 1. Richmond: January 1838. Making of America Journal Articles. Web.

White, Thomas Willis. "Publisher's Notice." *Southern Literary Messenger: Devoted to Every Department of Literature and the Fine Arts.* Vol. II, No. 1. Richmond: December 1835. T. W. White, 1836. Web.

Whyte, Kenneth. *The Uncrowned King: The Sensational Rise of William Randolph Hearst.* Berkeley: Counterpoint, Random House, 2009.

Woolf, Leonard. *Beginning Again: An Autobiography of the Years 1911 to 1918.* New York: Harcourt, Brace & World, Inc., 1964.

Woolf, Leonard. *The Journey Not the Arrival Matters*. London: The Hogarth Press Ltd., 1969.
Woolf, Virginia. *The Diary of Virginia Woolf, 5 Vols*. Ed. Anne Olivier Bell, Ass. Andrew McNeillie. New York: Penguin Books, 1977-84.
Woolf, Virginia. *The Letters of Virginia Woolf, 6 Vols*. Nigel Nicolson, Ed. London: The Hogarth Press Ltd / Chatto & Windus, 1976-80.
Woolf, Virginia. *A Room of One's Own*. (1929). Orlando: A Harcourt Brace Modern Classic: Harcourt, Inc., 1991.
Woolf, Virginia. *Moments of Being: Unpublished Autobiographical Writings*. Jeanne Schulkind, Ed. New York: Harcourt Brace Jovanovich, 1976.
Woolf, Virginia. *A Writer's Diary: Being Extracts from the Diary of Virginia Woolf*. Leonard Woolf, Ed. London: Berg Collection, 1953.
Wootton, David. *Galileo: Watcher of the Skies*. New Haven: Yale University Press, 2010.
Young, Mary De. *Encyclopedia of Asylum Therapeutics, 1750-1950s*. Jefferson: McFarland, 2015.

Book Image Citations

Beard, Daniel Carter, Artist. *Knight in Armor Tilting at Man in Modern Dress in Tree onto Which a Man in Modern Dress Has Climbed for Refuge*. 1889. Photograph. Retrieved from the Library of Congress. (Accessed July 30, 2017.)
Bush, Charles Green, Artist. *Mr. Charles Dickens and his former American acquaintances—"not at home"* / drawn by C.G. Bush. Boston Massachusetts, 1867. Photograph. Retrieved from the Library of Congress. (Accessed July 30, 2017.)
Edwin, David, Engraver. *Lord Byron* / Edwin, sc., 1814. (Published by M. Thomas) Photograph. Retrieved from the Library of Congress. (Accessed July 30, 2017.)
Harris & Ewing, photographer. *Censorship Board*. (Between 1910 and 1920) Photograph. Retrieved from the Library of Congress. (Accessed July 30, 2017.)
Herman Melville. ca. 1860. Photograph. Retrieved from the Library of Congress. (Accessed July 30, 2017.)
Keppler, Joseph Ferdinand, Artist, and Merkel & Ottmann Mayer. *"Mark Twain," America's best humorist* / J. Keppler; Mayer, Merkel & Ottman, Lith. 21-25 Warren St. N.Y., ca. 1885. New York: Published by Keppler & Schwarzmann, Dec. 16. Photograph. Retrieved from the Library of Congress. (Accessed July 30, 2017.)
Mark Twain, three-quarter length portrait, seated, facing slightly right, with cigar in hand. ca. 1907. Photograph. Retrieved from the Library of Congress. (Accessed July 30, 2017.)
Sadd, Henry S., Engraver, and William Allan. *Sir Walter Scott, Bart. in his study at Abbotsford* / Painted by W. Allan, R.A.; engraved by H.S. Sadd, N.Y. Abbotsford Scotland, 1846. New York: printed by J. Neale at the Albion Office. Photograph. Retrieved from the Library of Congress. (Accessed July 30, 2017.)
Sadd, Henry S., Engraver, Tompkins Harrison Matteson, and John Neale. *Benja-*

min Franklin—born in Boston, Jany. 17th 1706—died in Philadelphia, April 17th 1790 / painted by T.H. Matteson, Esqr.; engraved by Heny. S. Sadd., ca. 1846. (New York City: Printed by J. Neale, 1847) Photograph. Retrieved from the Library of Congress. (Accessed July 30, 2017.)

Stanziola, Phil, photographer. *Clare Boothe Luce, U.S. ambassador to Italy, and husband, publisher Henry Luce, arriving at Idlewild Airport, New York, New York / World Telegram & Sun* photo by Phil Stanziola. 1954. Photograph. Retrieved from the Library of Congress. (Accessed July 30, 2017.)

U.S. Lithograph Co, George Cochrane Hazelton, Edgar Allan Poe, and Hazelton & North. *Mr. Henry Ludlowe in The Raven the love story of Edgar Allan Poe* by George Hazelton., ca. 1908. (Cincinnati; New York: U.S. Lithograph Co) Photograph. Retrieved from the Library of Congress. (Accessed July 30, 2017.)

INDEX

A

All the Year Round, 9, 27, 45, 164, 171, 174-6, 353
assassination/ assassin, 10-1, 13, 15, 58, 61-2, 74, 80, 82-4, 93, 97-102, 115-6, 119, 122, 131, 134, 136, 141-3, 150, 152, 180, 182, 189, 197, 233, 236, 296, 302, 316, 355
Austen, Jane, 138, 199

B

Ballantyne Publishing Company, 9, 28, 105-7, 109-12, 116-9, 121, 352, 356
bankrupt, 8, 14, 22, 27-9, 46, 109-10, 112, 116-7, 121, 165, 171, 174, 176, 193, 195, 233, 260, 267, 271-2, 275-6, 279-82, 289, 306-8, 317, 352-4
Beale treasure, 263-6, 356
Brando, Marlon, 28, 235-7, 356
Broadway Journal, 250-2, 261, 361
Burke, Edmund, 189, 356
Byron, Lord Gordon, 9, 11, 13, 15, 19, 27, 34, 59, 62, 72-3, 77, 80, 84, 95, 113-6, 120, 122-63, 177, 181, 196, 262-3, 270, 278, 296-9, 304, 332, 341, 346, 350-1, 353-4, 357-64
    Vision of Judgment, The, 9, 122-3, 144, 146-7, 149, 357

C

Carlyle, Thomas, 50, 175, 357
censor, 8-9, 11-3, 15, 17, 21, 24-5, 55-104, 106, 133, 139, 146-7, 162-3, 186, 209, 225, 234-5, 237, 240-1, 270, 287, 317, 321, 323-4, 327, 332-3, 336, 356, 358-64
Coetzee, J. M., 321, 357
Constable, Archibald/ & Co., 27-8, 32-3, 107, 109-12, 117-8, 121, 137, 140, 206, 351-2

D

Dickens, Charles, 9, 15, 27, 31, 36, 42, 44-5, 50, 71, 137, 164-82, 189, 232, 250-2, 256, 261, 276, 279-80, 287-8, 302, 311, 316-7, 321, 324, 332, 339, 342-3, 346, 349-54, 356-62, 364
    Tale of Two Cities, 9-10, 36, 71, 164, 175, 179

F

Franklin, Benjamin, 8, 11, 14, 16, 22, 27, 31, 73, 217, 220, 223, 226, 232, 239-49, 260, 264, 343, 347, 350, 353-4, 358-9, 365
    Poor Richard, 240, 244-5, 358
French Revolution, 9, 71, 83, 146, 175, 189

G

Galileo, Galilei, 8-9, 16, 22, 62-70, 85, 91, 359, 364
Gamba family/ Count Pietro, 134-5, 153, 155, 162, 358
George III, 56-61, 72-4, 79-80, 97, 114, 131, 140, 146-7, 149, 155, 357, 363
George IV, 58-61, 114-7, 122, 126-8, 133, 135-7, 140, 144, 158-61, 341

H

Hachette Book Group/ Hachette Livre, 25, 27-9, 139, 234-7, 358
Hadden, Briton, 10, 16, 28-9, 294-301, 345, 349-50, 352-4
Harpers/ HarperCollins, 10, 27-36, 38-45, 144, 178, 211, 257, 260-1, 280-91, 299, 306, 344, 350, 354, 358, 360, 363
Hogarth Press, 10, 27, 46-7, 165, 171, 173, 177, 183-215, 317-8, 353-4, 356, 364

J

Jackson, Michael, 102-3, 108, 258

K
Khrushchev, Nikita, 88-9

L
Lawrence, D. H., 47, 55, 92-3, 323
Lehmann, John, 46, 183, 204-9, 353, 359
Liberal, The, 9, 122-63, 353, 359, 361
Lockhart, John Gibson, 118, 121, 359
Longfellow, Henry Wadsworth, 250-3, 259, 344, 357, 361
Luce, Henry R., 10, 16, 27-9, 31, 235, 281, 294-301, 345, 349-56, 359, 365

M
Macmillan, 27-8, 44-5, 176, 353, 359, 362
malpractice, 10-1, 93, 98-103, 150, 156, 354-5
Marx, Karl, 247, 359
Melville, Herman, 10, 16, 27, 30, 34-44, 117, 139, 253, 256, 281, 283-93, 344-5, 349-51, 354, 358, 361, 364
Miller, Henry, 87-8, 360
  Sexus, 87-8, 360
Milton, John, 66-71

O
Orwell, George, 86-7, 205, 328, 360

P
Penguin/ Penguin-Random House, 12, 28, 45-7, 93, 164, 186, 202, 356, 362, 364
plagiarism, 10, 113, 120, 361
Poe, Edgar Allan, 10, 13, 16, 27, 30-1, 37, 40-3, 120, 250-66, 281, 316, 322, 343-4, 350-4, 360-2, 365
poison, 10-1, 60, 84, 93-8, 101, 103, 116, 130, 142, 151-61, 177-8, 188, 198, 203, 214-5, 227, 262

Q
Queen Victoria's Highland Journals, 179, 363

R
Randall, Dudley, 10, 14, 16, 27, 233, 302-11, 345, 349-54, 356

S
Savage, Sir George, 98-100, 157, 178, 197-203, 291, 343, 362
Scott, Sir Walter, 9, 11, 27-9, 31-2, 61, 71, 74, 91, 98-9, 105-21, 137, 139, 165, 173, 179, 196, 232, 279, 281, 287, 297, 302, 304, 306, 321, 341, 346, 350-2, 354, 356-7, 359, 362, 364
  Rob Roy, 362
  Waverley, 9, 33, 71, 105, 108-9, 114, 118, 173, 306, 341, 357, 362
seton, 98-9, 119, 354
Shaw, George Bernard, 85, 362
Shelley, Percy, 9, 15, 27, 34, 113, 114, 118, 122-63, 244, 252, 278, 299, 316, 332, 349-54, 358-60, 362
Simon & Schuster, 28, 51-3, 241, 359
Spinoza, Benedict de, 71, 362

T
Twain, Mark/ Samuel Clemens, 10, 15-6, 27, 30, 111, 118, 250, 267-83, 319, 327, 344, 349-51, 353-5, 363-4
  Charles L. Webster and Co., 10, 27, 267-83

W
Walker, Alice, 10, 16, 27, 47, 233-4, 311-40, 345-6, 351, 353, 363
Walpole, Horace, 79-81, 84, 363
Wilkes, John, 57, 71-85, 88, 357, 362-3
Woolf, Leonard, 10, 14, 27, 30, 46-7, 118, 183-215, 317-9, 337, 353, 357, 362-4
Woolf, Virginia, 9, 14-6, 27, 30, 46, 94, 98, 118, 178, 183-215, 233, 256, 313, 317-9, 324, 330-1, 336-7, 343, 346, 349, 353, 358-60, 362, 364
  Room of One's Own, A, 195, 343, 364

OTHER ANAPHORA LITERARY PRESS TITLES

PLJ: Interviews with Gene Ambaum and Corban Addison: VII:3, Fall 2015
Editor: Anna Faktorovich

Architecture of Being
By: Bruce Colbert

The Encyclopedic Philosophy of Michel Serres
By: Keith Moser

Forever Gentleman
By: Roland Colton

Janet Yellen
By: Marie Bussing-Burks

Diseases, Disorders, and Diagnoses of Historical Individuals
By: William J. Maloney

Armageddon at Maidan
By: Vasyl Baziv

Vovochka
By: Alexander J. Motyl